(photograph)

Reverend Sun Myung Moon speaking before the
United States Senate Judiciary Subcommittee
on the Constitution, June 26, 1984.

Constitutional Issues
in the Case of Rev. Moon

Amicus Briefs Presented to the United States Supreme Court

*   *

Edited by
Herbert Richardson

Studies in Religion and Society
Volume 10

The Edwin Mellen Press
New York and Toronto

Constitutional Issues in the Case of Reverend Moon: Amicus
Briefs Presented to the United States Supreme Court.

Edited by Herbert Richardson

Studies in Religion and Society; vol. 10
ISBN 0-88946-873-7

Studies in Religion and Society
ISBN 0-88946-863-X

Printed in the United States of America

"I joined with the more than 40 *amici curiae* to ask the Court to grant certiorari because this case involves important considerations of substance on First Amendment protection for freedom of religion, one of the high-risk provisions of the Constitution.

"The *Moon* case also involves important matters of due process; if it is not reversed by the Supreme Court, it would create a crime to fit the accused, a practice long held unacceptable in American jurisprudence."

Senator Eugene J. McCarthy

STUDIES IN RELIGION AND SOCIETY

PREFACE

This volume contains the *amicus curiae* briefs presented to the United States Supreme Court in conjunction with the case of the Reverend Sun Myung Moon.

A summary of the facts of the case is given in the brief presented by Laurence Tribe to the United States Court of Appeals. (See pages 2-16.) Tribe's argument, at this stage, concerned the form of the trial, evidences admitted, and the judge's instructions to the jury. Though the appeal was lost by a 2-1 vote, the dissenting opinion noted that the case raised troubling questions relating to religion.

These troubling questions became, once the petition for *certiorari* was filed, a matter of special concern to a large number of religious and political groups. Forty groups submitted *amicus* briefs to the Supreme Court. Although the majority of the *amici* represented religious groups--Catholic, Protestant, Jewish, Mormon, and others--a smaller number expressed the concern of the states, of civil liberties groups, and of political organizations. Though the *amici* represent over 160,000,000 Americans, the government dismissed their submissions as "ill-informed."

The purpose of this volume is to gather, in an easily accessible form, both the briefs of the *amici* and the submissions to the appeals court so that the full record can be easily studied. The *amici,* as is always the case, were not animated by a special concern for Reverend Moon. Rather, they saw in the form of government's action against him a fundamental attack on the Constitution itself. In this sense, then, the case of Reverend Moon has exposed tendencies in America which threaten the rights of us all.

Herbert Richardson
Lewiston, New York

TABLE
OF
CONTENTS

CONSTITUTIONAL ISSUES IN THE CASE OF REV. MOON

PART I:
BACKGROUND:
THE COURT OF APPEALS

Brief for Appellant Sun Myung Moon

TABLE OF CONTENTS

ii

iii

iv

v

TABLE OF AUTHORITIES

vi

vii

viii

ix

x

xi

Constitutional Provisions

xii

xiii

United States Court of Appeals

FOR THE SECOND CIRCUIT

No. 82-1275

◆

UNITED STATES OF AMERICA,

Plaintiff-Appellee,

—v.—

SUN MYUNG MOON

and

TAKERU KAMIYAMA,

Defendants-Appellants.

ON APPEAL FROM THE UNITED STATES DISTRICT COURT
FOR THE SOUTHERN DISTRICT OF NEW YORK

◆

BRIEF FOR APPELLANT SUN MYUNG MOON

Preliminary Statement

Reverend Sun Myung Moon appeals from a judgment of conviction entered July 16, 1982, after jury trial, in the United States District Court for the Southern District of New York, Hon. Gerard L. Goettel, District Judge, and from post-trial rulings issued by that court on July 14, October 13, and November 5, 1982.

1

STATEMENT OF THE ISSUES

1. Whether the government's veto of bench trial in response to Reverend Moon's public criticism of its motives abridged his freedom of speech.

2. Whether, on this record, the judge's denial of bench trial violated Reverend Moon's right to a fair trial.

3. Whether the judge's refusal to give Reverend Moon the option of testifying through an interpreter of his own choice violated the Court Interpreters Act of 1978 or unduly fettered his right to decide whether to testify.

4. Whether the trial court's charge to the jury: (a) misstated the law of trusts; (b) impermissibly shifted the burden of proof to defendant; (c) violated the Religion Clauses; or (d) misdirected the jury on the element of wilfulness.

5. Whether the evidence was insufficient as a matter of law to establish: (a) that Reverend Moon's tax returns contained false statements; (b) that such falsity, if any, was wilful; (c) that Reverend Moon engaged in a conspiracy to file false statements on his returns; or (d) that he took part in a cover-up conspiracy.

6. Whether the trial court erred in admitting certain immigration documents as "similar acts" evidence.

7. Whether, on this record, Reverend Moon's claim of selective prosecution was improperly dismissed without discovery or an evidentiary hearing.

8. Whether the post-trial inquiry into extraneous influences on the jury in this case was prematurely terminated and its results improperly disregarded in denying a new trial.

9. Whether the trial court abridged freedom of speech and press by issuing a broad prior restraint barring any communication that might reach former jurors—even through the news media—on the subject of prejudicial influences on the jury in this case.

2

STATEMENT OF THE CASE [1]

A. Nature of the Case.

Reverend Sun Myung Moon appeals (No. 82-1275) from a judgment of conviction entered on July 16, 1982, after jury trial, for filing false income tax returns and for conspiracy, and from denial of post-trial motions on July 14, 1982, by the Honorable Gerard L. Goettel, United States District Judge for the Southern District of New York. Reverend Moon also appeals (No. 82-1357) from the denial by Judge Goettel on October 13, 1982, of post-trial motions for further investigation into extraneous influences on the jury and for new trial based on such influences, and appeals (No. 82-1387) from the issuance on November 5, 1982, of a gag order relating to the jury inquiry.

The indictment—returned while Reverend Moon was traveling abroad (*see* S161)—charged him in Count I, along with senior Unification Church member Takeru Kamiyama,[2] with conspiracy (18 U.S.C. § 371) to file false federal income tax returns (26 U.S.C. § 7206(1)), to obstruct justice (18 U.S.C. § 1503), and to make false statements to government agencies (18 U.S.C. § 1001) and to a federal grand jury (18 U.S.C. § 1623). Counts II, III, and IV charged Reverend Moon alone with filing false tax returns for 1973, 1974, and 1975, in violation of 26 U.S.C. § 7206(1). Reverend Moon voluntarily

---

1   The docket entries and relevant pleadings, papers filed by the parties, and rulings issued by the court are reproduced in a three-volume Joint Appendix, citations to which will be to "A__," and an index to which appears at the beginning of its first volume. The transcripts of the pre- and post-trial hearings, and the trial transcript—as well as the government's and defendants' trial exhibits and the post-trial exhibits—are reproduced in 15 volumes entitled "Exhibits," an index to which appears in a separate, unnumbered volume entitled "Exhibits Index." Citations to pre-trial hearing transcripts will be to "P__," citations to trial transcripts will be to "T__," citations to post-trial hearing transcripts will be to "S__," citations to government trial exhibits will be to "GX__," citations to defense exhibits will be to "DX__," and citations to post-trial exhibits will be to "PX__."

2   Mr. Kamiyama alone was charged in Counts V-XIII, as well as in a separate one-count indictment, with substantive offenses of aiding and abetting, filing false statements, obstruction of justice, and perjury.

3

returned from Korea to the United States to stand trial on these charges. *See* S161.

The government's case on the three substantive counts against Reverend Moon (Counts II, III, and IV) focused on the omission of interest income from Chase Manhattan Bank accounts in Reverend Moon's name that the government claimed were beneficially owned by him. Count II also charged that the 1973 return stated a false source for the taxable income it did report, and failed to report as income the receipt of Tong Il Enterprises stock that the government claimed was beneficially owned by Reverend Moon.[3]

The jury returned its verdict against Reverend Moon on all four counts on May 18, 1982. T6723-24. On July 16, 1982, the court sentenced Reverend Moon to 18 months in prison and a $25,000 fine plus costs. A1936.[4] Sentence was stayed pending appeal.[5]

B. Proceedings Below.

Pre-trial, Reverend Moon filed various procedural and substantive motions. A150-345. On January 15, 1982, the judge denied several of these, including Reverend Moon's motion for dismissal based on selective prosecution (P166), his motion for severance (P165), and his motion for use of his own translator if he should testify (P108-11). On March 1, 1982, the court issued a written opinion denying other motions, including Reverend Moon's motion to dismiss the substantive counts and

---

3   The initial indictment, returned October 15, 1981 (A26), failed to charge that Reverend Moon beneficially owned the Chase accounts or the Tong Il stock. *See* A28-29. On December 15, 1981—after Reverend Moon moved to dismiss Counts II, III, IV, and part of I on this ground (A150, 265-73)—a superseding indictment adding allegations of ownership was returned. A45; *see* A47-48.

4   Mr. Kamiyama. who was also convicted on all counts, was sentenced to six months in prison and a $5,000 fine. His arguments on appeal, which Reverend Moon adopts by reference insofar as they are relevant to his case, Fed.R.App.P. 28(i), are presented in a separate brief.

5   On August 10, 1982, over government opposition, Judge Goettel made a binding recommendation to the Attorney General, pursuant to 8 U.S.C. § 1251(b), disqualifying Reverend Moon's conviction as a basis for deportation. S190-91.

4

part of the conspiracy count against him. *United States v. Moon*, 532 F.Supp. 1360 (S.D.N.Y. 1982) (A719).

On March 10, 1982, pursuant to Fed.R.Crim.P. 23(a), Reverend Moon moved, with Mr. Kamiyama, for a bench trial on the ground that pervasive public hostility precluded the selection of a fair and impartial jury. P330; *see* A798. Faced with the government's refusal to consent (A811, 1022; P370), the judge denied this motion (P381-82), and on March 22, 1982, proceeded with voir dire. T59. After seven days of juror interviews, the defendants renewed the request for a bench trial (A1038, T1701), but the government persisted in its opposition and the judge refused the request (T1751-52).

Trial began April 1, 1982, and lasted approximately six weeks. During the course of the trial, the defense moved unsuccessfully for a mistrial based on the admission of prejudicial evidence abridging free exercise rights (*see, e.g.*, T2544-51, 3314, 4009-10, 4287, 5719) and on the admission of certain "similar acts" evidence (T6040). At the close of the government's case in chief (T5491-5523, 5562, 5580; A1161, 1173), and again at the close of the evidence (T6138), Reverend Moon moved unsuccessfully for dismissal of each false-statement specification and for judgment of acquittal on all counts.

Post-trial, Reverend Moon again moved for a judgment of acquittal (A1774) and moved in the alternative for a new trial to be held before a judge and severed from the trial of any co-defendant (A1474). Additionally, he moved for discovery and an evidentiary hearing on his selective prosecution claim. A1809. All of these motions were denied in open court on July 14, 1982. S92. Judgment was entered on July 16, 1982. A1936. Notice of appeal was timely filed. A1938.

On September 1, 1982, the defendants returned to the trial court to request an inquiry into whether the jury had been exposed to prejudicial extraneous information. A1954. Based on defendants' factual showing, the trial court ruled that such an inquiry was required under *United States v. Moten*, 582 F.2d 654 (2d Cir. 1978). A2055. On October 13, 1982, after hearing testimony from three of the jurors, the judge terminated the entire inquiry and denied defendants' motion for a new trial brought on the basis of testimony already given (S665), as well as their motion to conduct further inquiry

5

(S659). On November 5, 1982, on the government's motion
(A2068) and over defense objection on First Amendment
grounds (A2130), the judge issued a prior restraint against the
parties and any of their "agents," prohibiting them from
communicating "in any manner whatsoever" (A2142)—including through the press (*see* A2146)—with anyone who had
served as a juror or prospective juror in this case. Defendants'
notices of appeal from these rulings were timely filed (A2066,
2148), and all of the appeals were consolidated.

C. Facts.

Reverend Moon is the "founder and prophet," *Holy Spirit
Association for the Unification of World Christianity v. Tax
Commission*, 55 N.Y. 2d 512, 519 (1982), of the international
Unification Church movement, which arose in Korea a quarter
of a century ago as one of a host of revivalist Christian
religions flourishing in the aftermath of the 40-year Japanese
occupation, and which now involves "more than 120 national
Unification Churches throughout the world propagating a
common religious message under [Reverend Moon's] spiritual
guidance," *id. See* A720. Reverend Moon is regarded by his
several million worldwide followers as the very embodiment of
the Unification faith[6]—a faith that, "by any historical analogy,
philosophical analysis, or judicial precedent . . . must be
regarded as a bona fide religion." *Unification Church v.
Immigration and Naturalization Service*, 547 F. Supp. 623, 628
(D.D.C. 1982).[7] In late 1971, Reverend Moon came to the
United States to embark upon an ambitious evangelical ministry, on behalf of the international Unification Church move-

---

6   As an affidavit submitted by 40 Unification Church presidents from
around the world explained, "Just as the disciples of Jesus viewed him as the
head of the Church (Eph. 1:22) and themselves as the body (1 Cor. 12:27), so
the Unificationists view Reverend Moon. [He] is considered to be the third
Adam, the embodiment of God's ideal of heart and love. . . . The churches
which he founded in America, Korea, Japan and elsewhere, are extensions of
his faith, give life by the transfusion of his religious fervor, in continuing and
holy collaboration with a Circle of Elders." A1509; *see* A1509-10, 1512-13.

7   *See also Ward v. Connor*, 657 F.2d 45 (4th Cir. 1981), *cert. denied*,
102 S. Ct. 1253 (1982); *Troyer v. Town of Babylon*, 483 F. Supp. 1135, 1137
(E.D.N.Y.), *aff'd*, 628 F.2d 1346 (2d Cir.), *aff'd mem.*, 449 U.S. 988 (1980).

6

ment, in the land he and his disciples viewed as central to the fulfillment of God's providence. *See* A625, T3418-19, 5712.[8] He became a permanent resident of the United States in early 1973. By the mid-1970's, the international movement had grown and several corporate arms had been organized in America.[9]

The trial focused on two sets of assets openly held in Reverend Moon's name: (1) accounts at the Chase Manhattan Bank, to which the bulk of the evidence was related; and (2) $50,000 worth of stock in Tong Il Enterprises, Inc., an importer of products from Korea run by members of the Unification Church. The central issue at trial was whether, as the government claimed, Reverend Moon beneficially owned these assets and therefore owed taxes on the bank interest and the stock value, or rather held these assets as trustee for the followers of the Unification faith and therefore owed no such taxes.

1. The Chase Manhattan Bank accounts.

At a March 1972 meeting to plan the American evangelical campaign, Unification Church leaders proposed the opening of a bank account specifically in Reverend Moon's name in order to facilitate contributions from Japanese members who would

---

8   As part of his first major evangelical campaign in the United States, Reverend Moon conducted a seven-city tour in 1972 seeking converts to the Unification Church. T2747. Aided by missionaries from the Japanese and European branches of the Church, he continued his international One World Crusade with a 21-city tour in late 1973 and a 32-city tour in early 1974. T2786. As part of this crusade, United States Church members, assisted by many members from the Japanese and other overseas branches of the Church, traveled in teams to preach and to gather funds with which to support themselves and advance the religious mission of the Church. T2770, 3374-75, 4294-95.

9   These corporate arms included the Holy Spirit Association for the Unification of World Christianity ("HSA"), incorporated in 1961 and granted tax-exempt status in 1963 (T2757, 4273); the Unification Church of New York ("UCNY"), incorporated in early 1974 (T3929); and the Unification Church International, Inc. ("UCI"), incorporated in 1975 as a not-for-profit corporation (*see* T3523) to represent formally the international Unification Church movement that Reverend Moon already led (*see* GX230, 231A, T3671; DX AA1-5, T5780).

7

be wary of making religious donations directly to newly formed and unfamiliar American branches of the Church. T5713-14; *see also* T3125. In March 1973, such an account was opened and thereafter maintained in Reverend Moon's name at the Chase Manhattan Bank in New York.[10]

Although Church members described the Chase funds as "coming from [the] movement overseas . . . to be used for the work of [the] International Church" (T4090; *see also* T4086, 4088, 4094, 4144, 4738-39), it was unclear to what extent those funds were *raised* overseas and to what extent they were raised *by* overseas members seeking cash contributions within the United States. *See, e.g.,* T4513, 4528, 4563, 4749.[11] But nothing in the government's charge turned on *where* the funds were raised (*see* T5518-19, 5520-21, 6113), and there is no question that, in either event, all of the funds derived from *Church* fundraising.[12] Indeed, there was no evidence of any *other* source of the Chase funds. Moreover, all of the evidence bearing on the *intent* of fund donors showed that they sought by their contributions to advance the Unification faith and its evangelical movement. *See, e.g.,* GX591A (loan agreement reflecting transfer of $200,000 to Reverend Moon "to help finance various projects for the salvation of the United States of America"); *see also* T2751-52, 2774-77, 3402, 3405, 3415, 3418, 3124-25.

---

10   Originally, two accounts—a checking and a savings account—were opened with three checks totaling $82,400. T2255, 2262-67; GX4A, 4B, 4C. Later deposits were made mostly in cash. T2268-78, 3543-48, 3557-65. Some of the funds in the original accounts were later transferred to time deposit accounts with higher yields. T2389, 3650-55. Beginning in December 1975, transfers of the Chase funds were made to a UCI account (GX870, 870A; T3864, 5788-90)—and the Chase accounts were closed. T5868-73, 5939-41. No evidence or testimony was introduced to explain why, if Reverend Moon had wished to conceal income from the Internal Revenue Service, he would have chosen so visible and indeed conspicuous a form of "concealment" as the deposit of large sums of cash into readily documentable bank accounts.

11   It was not disputed that international Church teams—including Japanese members, T2432-34, and German members, T3386-87, 3405-06—engaged in fundraising in the United States. *See* T2164, 2770, 4280-84.

12   In addition to engaging in public solicitation, foreign members of the Unification faith entrusted funds directly to Reverend Moon. *See, e.g.,* T3117-20, 3124-25, 4605-08.

8

The government introduced a mass of evidence to show what was never disputed—namely, that the Chase accounts were openly held and administered in Reverend Moon's own name,[13] and that the funds in those accounts were sometimes referred to within the Church solely by reference to Reverend Moon, either by name or as "Father" of the faith in Unification theology (see A1513).[14] *Nothing* in this "evidence," however, established that Reverend Moon held the accounts *as beneficial owner* rather than as trustee or nominee for Church members—the only matter in dispute. Moreover, Church officials often referred to the Chase funds as "the Church's money" and so described those funds to their accountants and attorneys. *See* T3864, 3866, 4182-83, 4185-86, 4189-90, 4333-34, 4579. Indeed, in the minds of those who dealt with the Chase funds, "the name of the church and of Reverend Moon became synonymous." T3670; *see* T3489, 3662-63, 3668-69, 4333.

The government also introduced a mass of data regarding the *uses* made of the Chase funds—uses the government characterized as "non-religious" and therefore as signifying beneficial ownership by Reverend Moon personally. *See, e.g.,* T2160, 2168, 2171, 6462, 6465, 6471, 6484-87. But none of this data showed that the uses in question were anything other than those of a trustee holding funds for the advancement of a

---

13   This evidence included numerous bank records, memoranda and letters showing that the accounts were designated "personal" by the bank (T2242; GX1, 2, 2A, 2B) and referred to by Reverend Moon as "his"(GX89, 100, 110, 111, 113, 116, 118, 123, 146 (letters); T3654-55), and that Reverend Moon used his own name in signing various account documents (GX42-88 (checks)). In addition, the government introduced a number of documents that referred to transfers from the Chase accounts as loans from Reverend Moon (GX468, 478, 500, 501, 528; *see* T2863, 3292-93), and an agreement showing a loan of $200,000 to Reverend Moon, corresponding to a Chase deposit (GX591A, GX31).

14   Thus there was testimony that Mr. Kamiyama referred to the Chase funds as "Father's money." T5186. And in connection with a proposed transfer of property purchased in part with Chase funds, there was evidence—admitted over strenuous defense objection as "authorized agent admissions" (T3219-20, 3224, 5484, 5559-61; *see* A1153, 1677)—that Church officials and attorneys had discussed changing title "into Father's name." GX452, 461A; *see* GX434, T2869-70.

9

religion and acting in full accord with the intent of the assets' donors. Indeed, the evidence showed that a major use of the Chase accounts was to transfer funds directly to various branches of the Unification Church,[15] and that *all* of the other uses of the Chase funds were either personal disbursements of the sort a church leader would commonly have discretion to make on his own behalf and which Reverend Moon segregated as such, or were investments on behalf of and for the benefit of the Unification Church itself.

a. Personal disbursements.

In 1973, various disbursements were made from the Chase checking account to pay for clothing, medical services, travel, school tuition for Reverend Moon's children, and the like, which were reported as taxable income on Reverend Moon's 1973 return. *See* GX590, 591, 597, 800; T3729-30, 3735, 3812-13, 4094, 4982-98; *see also* DX H. Beginning in May 1974, all such personal disbursements were made from a separate "household account." GX597; T3581-82, 3630-31.[16]

Chase funds were used for a personal purpose on only one other occasion: in late 1975, Reverend Moon borrowed $80,000 in order to buy stock in the Diplomat National Bank, a bank then being organized to provide financial services to the Asian community in Washington, D.C. *See* T3498A, 3501.[17]

---

15   Transfers were made from the Chase accounts to HSA in the amount of $285,000 (GX83; T3645-46), to UCNY in the amount of $146,000 (GX85, T3646), and to UCI in the amount of $87,000 (GX87, 88; T3521, 3603-04). *See* DX N; T5009-11.

16   On one occasion, in August 1974, the sum of $5505.72 was transferred from the Chase checking account, where it had been erroneously deposited by the bank, into the household account to cover an overdraft. *See* T3629-31.

17   Reflecting his personal purpose, Reverend Moon transferred this $80,000 from the Chase accounts into the household account and then paid for the stock with a "household" check. *See* GX82, 82A, 556; T3501, 3642-45, 4771-72, 4776-77. In December 1976, Reverend Moon sold this stock and in March 1977, he repaid the $80,000 to the UCI account, with interest. *See* T3507-11, 4811-15, 5873; GX210B, 210C, 210D, 561, 661.

10

b. Investments.

i. Holy Spirit Association property purchases:
East Garden and Belvedere.

On several occasions, Chase funds were supplied to HSA, the main American branch of the Unification Church, to help finance property acquisitions. Thus in late 1973, $361,000 of Chase funds were used to help purchase East Garden (T2863-64), an estate that became the spiritual headquarters of the worldwide Unification Church and provided lodging to Reverend Moon, his family, Church staff, and frequent Church guests (T2991, 3017). This amount, which had been requested by HSA after it was unable to obtain outside financing (T2863, 3275-76), was originally denominated a loan on HSA books, but was later reclassified as a contribution to HSA (T5845, 5905-06).[18]

Similarly in November 1975—again at HSA's request after its efforts to obtain outside financing had failed—$175,000 was advanced from the Chase account to cover mortgage payments and avert foreclosure on Belvedere, another estate owned by HSA. GX86; *see* GX514-20. A week later, HSA repaid $70,000 of this amount to the Chase checking account (T5922-23, 4333-34, 4815-17), and the remaining $105,000 was reclassified on HSA books as a contribution (T5922-23).

ii. KCFF investment guaranty.

In 1974, $250,000 of the Chase funds were pledged as collateral for a loan from the Bank of America to the Korean Cultural & Freedom Foundation ("KCFF")—an organization which, although separate from the Unification Church, was

---

18   After Reverend Moon moved into East Garden, a decision was made to explore the possibility of transferring title into his name. *See* GX434, 452, 461A; T2869-70, 2948-50, 3292-96. HSA's attorneys advised that such a title transfer would require Reverend Moon to furnish full consideration in order to avoid adverse tax consequences for HSA or himself or both. *See* T2891, GX456A. Pursuant to this advice, a Release and Cancellation of Indebtedness in the amount of $700,000—which included the East Garden loan of $361,000 along with other sums listed on HSA books as loans from Reverend Moon—was executed by him in July 1974. GX472. The proposed transfer, however, was abandoned in August 1974 (*see* GX437, T2993), again on legal advice. *See* T3307.

11

regarded by Church members as fulfilling a Church-related educational mission (T5584-96)—to finance the construction of a children's performing arts center. *See, e.g.,* GX230-233A; T2669-71, 2700-03, 4963-67. When the collateral was forfeited upon KCFF's default in July 1974, KCFF borrowed $250,000 from Chase, upon similar guaranty, to replace the forfeited collateral. T5864. This collateralization, according to the information known to Reverend Moon's tax attorney, was "not done for Reverend Moon personally," but rather was "done for the Church." T4551.

iii. Investment ventures: Microparticles and Stradco.

In April 1973, at the suggestion of the president of the Unification Church's English branch that it "would be a good investment for our movement" (T5694-95), $125,000 was transferred from Chase to the Sun Myung Moon Foundation in England for investment in Microparticles, Ltd., an English paint company. *See* DX X; GX590; T4547, 5766-68, 5770-71, 5818-19.

Similarly, in February 1975, at the suggestion of Church elder Sang Ik Choi, Reverend Moon drew a check on the Chase account for $200,000 payable to Frank Broes, the president of Stradco Iron Company, and signed a contract to form a joint venture with Stradco for the purpose of mining and shipping iron ore. T3422-92, 4083-84. Testifying for the defense, Mr. Choi said that he had recommended this investment to help "the international movement of Christianity." T5613-19.

*   *   *   *   *

There was *no* evidence that these or indeed any investments made with Chase funds were ever undertaken for purposes other than to benefit the international Unification Church, or that any such transactions conflicted in any degree with the religious aims of those who entrusted the funds to Reverend Moon.

2. The Tong Il stock.

In 1973, Reverend Moon signed a subscription agreement for $50,000 worth of stock in Tong Il Enterprises that was issued in his name. T2456-60. Other Church members sub-scribed for the remaining authorized stock. T2460-66. Rever-

12

end Moon's obligation to pay for the stock was cancelled in exchange for merchandise, worth more than the subscription price of the stock, that UCNY had purchased from two Korean companies[19] and then contributed to Tong Il "in honor of Reverend Moon" (T4683). *See* GX325, 401D & E; T2402-20, 2436-38, 2456-66, 3814-17, 4111, 4118-20, 4194-96.

Nothing in the government's evidence showed that Reverend Moon held this stock as beneficial owner rather than as trustee. Indeed, even Michael Warder, a disaffected former Church member who was the government's chief witness, conceded that he did not know whether Reverend Moon owned the stock for himself or for the Church. T5285. Moreover, Warder also admitted that he did not regard the Tong Il stock issued in *his* name as his own, but rather felt that he held it on behalf of either the Church or Reverend Moon. T5284-85. And when Reverend Moon divested himself of Tong Il stock in August 1977, he transferred it to One-Up Enterprises, a wholly-owned subsidiary of UCI. T4659-62.[20]

3. Reverend Moon's tax returns.

Reverend Moon's 1973 tax return was prepared at Mr. Kamiyama's request by UCNY president Joe Tully, who was inexperienced in the preparation of income tax returns. *See* T4092-93. The return reported $14,458.41 as gross income (GX800) which, according to Tully, represented interest on the Chase savings account as well as personal disbursements. DX H; T4104-05. Tully testified that he had obtained these figures by reviewing financial records and that he had no contact or communication with Reverend Moon about the tax return. T4031. There was no evidence to the contrary. The return was filed on October 15, 1974,[21] but without Reverend

---

19   These two companies were Il Shin, a stone works (T2417-18; GX326), and Il Hwa, a pharmaceutical company that Reverend Moon had founded (T2435-43, 5132-35).

20   The absence of any evidence establishing Reverend Moon's beneficial ownership of Tong Il *stock* sharply contrasts with the evidence regarding the *salary* he received as a Tong Il employee (T2470-72)—salary which he treated as his own from the outset and on which, accordingly, he paid taxes. *See* GX801, 802.

21   An attachment to the 1973 return, in which Tully attributed the

13

Moon's signature. GX800. On December 18, 1974, Form RSC-12 was submitted, signed by Reverend Moon, acknowledging the unsigned return as his own. GX800A; T4085-86.

Reverend Moon's 1974 and 1975 tax returns were prepared by the firm of Peat, Marwick, Mitchell & Co. ("PMM"). T3773, 4172-73. The 1974 return reported $20,774 in gross income, comprised of $20,520 in Tong Il salary and $254 in interest on the Chase savings account. GX801; T3780-84. The 1975 return reported $37,344 in gross income, comprised of $37,080 in Tong Il salary and $264 in Chase savings interest. GX802; T3832. There was no evidence to show that, in preparing the returns, PMM or any Church members from whom PMM received information ever consulted Reverend Moon. T4178-79, 4807-08. The returns, filed on August 15, 1975, and June 9, 1976, bore Reverend Moon's signature. *See* GX801, 802.[22]

4. Alleged "cover-up" activities.

The government attempted to prove a "cover-up" by introducing evidence which it claimed showed that Mr. Kamiyama had lied to the grand jury and that various documents prepared by Church members after the Internal Revenue Service ("IRS") had begun to investigate Reverend Moon's tax returns were "phoney." These documents included:

(1) Loan agreements reflecting transfers of funds from foreign Church members to Mr. Kamiyama. *See, e.g.,* GX760-64. Although the government made much of the undisputed fact that these agreements were "backdated" (T3398, 5372-87, 5402-04; *see* T6507, 6215), there was *no* evidence that the agreements failed to memorialize *actual prior transactions* in which Church obligations were *in fact* incurred to those who had transferred the funds, as the defense contended. *See, e.g.,* T3394-95, 3414-15; *see also* T4528-29, 4563.

---

unavailability of W-2 forms to the recentness of UCNY's incorporation, formed the basis of the false source allegation in Count II.

22   In an effort to prove that Reverend Moon wilfully intended to make false statements on these tax returns, the government introduced, under the rubric of "similar acts," evidence showing that Reverend Moon had obtained his permanent resident status in the United States on the basis of statements by others regarding his wife's employment prospects—statements the government claimed were false. *See* T6009-12, 6062-63; GX825, 840.

14

(2) The Japanese Family Fund Ledger, which listed dates and amounts of contributions from Japanese Church members between June 1972 and March 1976. GX861A. A Church member testified that she had prepared this ledger in late 1976 or early 1977, but from contemporaneous memos (T4593-97, 4639-40); the government, however, claimed that she did so by reconstruction from bank statements (T4609-15, 6209-12, 6506).

(3) Amended minutes of the first meeting of the Tong Il board of directors, which had been held in 1973. GX421. It was undisputed that the changes in the minutes, which were made in 1978, added a statement that merchandise had been exchanged for the stock issued to Reverend Moon. *See* T2637-41; GX401C, 421. But there was no evidence that the changes were inaccurate.[23]

The record is barren of any evidence whatsoever that Reverend Moon was involved in or consulted about the preparation of *any* of these three sets of documents. Indeed, the government introduced, in its "cover-up" case, only one document actually involving Reverend Moon—an agreement reflecting a $200,000 loan from Mr. Kamiyama to Reverend Moon dated November 14, 1973. GX591A; T4741, 4533. But, again, there was no evidence even suggesting that this loan was *not* made at that time; on the contrary, the amount of the loan corresponded to a contemporaneous Chase deposit. GX31.

Nor did the record otherwise show that Reverend Moon was involved in any of the alleged "cover-up" activities supposedly undertaken by others. Although the government's case stressed Reverend Moon's day-to-day involvement in many of the Church's business affairs (*see* T5086-97, 5114-15, 5121, 5128, 5133-34, 5137-38, 5161-87), *none* of that evidence showed *any* involvement by Reverend Moon *in the response to the IRS investigation.* To the contrary, Warder admitted that Reverend Moon was *not* a party to *any* discussions about what, if any, "tactics to adopt" with regard to the IRS. T5213; *see also*

---

23   Indeed, a letter dated 1973 supported the amendment to the minutes. GX424. And, although the government contended that this letter had been written in 1974 and backdated (*see* T5377-78, 5381-83), any such "backdating" would have *preceded* the Internal Revenue Service investigation by two years.

15

T5217, 5085-5106. Moreover, Church members testified that important decisions were often made by Church leaders other than Reverend Moon (*see* T2432-33, 3919-21, 4763, 5059-62, 5104-05), and that Reverend Moon consulted other Church leaders regularly—for example at daily breakfast meetings at East Garden (T5057, 5097, 5100, 5127, 5254, 5267)—in connection with decision-making about the Church's financial as well as spiritual affairs.

*   *   *   *   *

Thus, when the case was submitted—to the jury that Reverend Moon had sought to avoid—the evidence showed neither Reverend Moon's involvement in any "cover-up" nor any conduct by Reverend Moon that he might have wished to "cover." From the time the assets at issue were placed in his name as founder and spiritual leader of the Unification Church, to the present, he and his followers openly treated those assets as belonging to the Church that was all but universally identified with his name.

SUMMARY OF ARGUMENT

Reverend Moon, a much-maligned religious leader who voluntarily returned to the United States from Korea to face trial on charges he thought baseless and politically motivated, encountered a prosecution insistent that he be tried before a jury—the one body he feared would share the prosecutor's bias rather than a judge's neutrality. Because the government demanded a jury trial in response to Reverend Moon's public criticism of its motives, Reverend Moon's freedom of speech was abridged. § I. And the judge's denial of Reverend Moon's request for bench trial violated his right to a fair trial—before the voir dire, when the risk a fair jury could not be found was already unacceptably high (§ II.A); after the voir dire, which yielded an unfair jury (§ II.B); and at trial, where that jury's known preconceptions and weaknesses were exploited by the government but at the same time prevented defendants from presenting an exposition of Unification theology and of Reverend Moon's place within that theology that would have been helpful to his defense (§ II.C).

16

At the trial, Reverend Moon was denied the right to use an interpreter of his own choice should he decide to testify—a denial that impermissibly fettered his right to choose *whether* to testify. § III. Nor was Reverend Moon accorded a properly instructed jury. Indeed, the charge to the jury obscured the burden of proof (§ IV.B) and the element of wilfulness (§ IV.D), and, moreover, distorted the law of trusts (§ IV.A) and the principles of the Religion Clauses (§ IV.C) so as to invite the jury improperly to find the assets to be Reverend Moon's rather than his Church's no matter *who* entrusted them to him or *why*.

Wholly lacking in evidence that would have supported a verdict against Reverend Moon consistent with the law of trusts and the Religion Clauses, this case should not have gone to the jury at all but should have resulted in a *directed acquittal* on the substantive counts (§ V.A) as well as on the conspiracy count (§ V.B). Moreover, when the case went to the jury, it did so infected with inadmissible "similar acts" evidence regarding Reverend Moon's entry into the United States (§ VI)—evidence the government hoped to leverage into Reverend Moon's expulsion from America. But neither that motive—nor other improper motives suggested by congressional communication to the IRS in this case as well as by other evidence offered by Reverend Moon—were explored, for Reverend Moon's plea for discovery and a hearing on selective prosecution was summarily and improperly rejected. § VII. And, although he was permitted to call three jurors to the stand post-trial to pursue unsolicited leads indicating improper extraneous influences on the jury, that inquiry was abruptly and erroneously ended even after it had generated uncontradicted evidence of just such influences § VIII.

Finally, a Unification Church press release critical of this truncated inquiry was met, much as Reverend Moon's pre-trial public speech had been, by official punishment for the exercise of First Amendment rights—this time, in the form of a gag order so sweeping as to chill even remarks to the media, by Reverend Moon or any of his followers, critical of the jury that found him guilty or of the judge for refusing to explore improper influence on that jury. § IX.

17

ARGUMENT

I. THE GOVERNMENT'S VETO OF BENCH TRIAL ABRIDGED REVEREND MOON'S FREEDOM OF SPEECH.

The government persistently refused to consent to defendants' request for a bench trial. It gave as its reason a post-arraignment public speech by Reverend Moon, later published in *The New York Times,* which had criticized the government's motives for prosecuting him, and had suggested that the prosecution was impelled by racial and religious prejudice. *See* A811-12, 1028-29. The government asserted that a *jury* trial was thus necessary lest Reverend Moon "blame any adverse result in this case on religious or racial bigotry" (A1029)—even though it was fear of that very bigotry that had motivated Reverend Moon's request for a *bench* trial (*see* § II *infra*). By withholding its consent—and thus compelling Reverend Moon to face a jury trial—in response to his public criticism, the government in substance and effect *punished* him for exercising his rights to freedom of expression.

As has long been recognized, even if an individual is not independently entitled to a particular benefit, the government may not withhold that benefit on a basis that infringes his freedom of speech. *Perry v. Sindermann,* 408 U.S. 593, 597 (1972); *Pickering v. Board of Education,* 391 U.S. 563, 574 (1968); *accord, Russo v. Central School District No. 1,* 469 F.2d 623, 631 (2d Cir. 1972), *cert. denied,* 411 U.S. 932 (1973). And even where the government may deny a benefit without giving *any* reason, it cannot predicate such a denial on an *impermissible* reason—such as retaliation against an individual for the exercise of First Amendment freedoms. *See Perry v. Sindermann, supra.*[24] But that is precisely what occurred here: the government denied consent to a bench trial—the one benefit Reverend Moon sought in order to ensure a fair trial—in order to punish and thus still his criticism of the prosecution, even though "[c]riticism of government is at the

---

24 *Cf. United States v. Vasquez,* 638 F.2d 507, 534 (2d Cir. 1980) (although judge need not give reasons for sentencing decisions, if he does so, they must be proper), *cert. denied,* 450 U.S. 970 (1981).

18

very center of the constitutionally protected area of free discussion." *Rosenblatt v. Baer,* 383 U.S. 75, 85 (1966). *See also Wood v. Georgia,* 370 U.S. 375 (1962); *Craig v. Harney,* 331 U.S. 367 (1947); *Pennekamp v. Florida,* 328 U.S. 331 (1946); *Bridges v. California,* 314 U.S. 252 (1941).

Nor can the government claim any legitimate interest in protecting its reputation—or that of the judiciary—against such criticism. As the Supreme Court recognized in *New York Times Co. v. Sullivan,* 376 U.S. 254, 272-73 (1964), "[i]njury to official reputation affords no . . . warrant for repressing speech that would otherwise be free." Indeed, in *Rosenblatt v. Baer,* 383 U.S. at 83, the Court held vindication of the government's good reputation *per se* invalid as a ground for suppressing or punishing speech.[25] In short, the government's reason for opposing the defendant's bench trial request was flatly unconstitutional; accordingly, the judge's failure to reject that opposition was constitutional error requiring reversal.

II. THE JUDGE'S DENIAL OF BENCH TRIAL VIOLATED REVEREND MOON'S RIGHT TO A FAIR TRIAL.

It is beyond cavil that a defendant is entitled to "a fair trial by a panel of impartial, 'indifferent' jurors," *Irvin v. Dowd,* 366 U.S. 717, 722 (1961), "drawn from a pool broadly representative of the community . . . assur[ing] . . . a diffused impartiality," *Taylor v. Louisiana,* 419 U.S. 522, 530 (1975), and "free from outside influences," *Sheppard v. Maxwell,* 384 U.S. 333, 362 (1966). But, just as a *jury* ordinarily serves to protect the accused from oppression *by officialdom,* so a *judge* may in exceptional circumstances be needed to protect the accused from oppression *by a hostile public.* Accordingly, in

---

25   Moreover, the government's claim that a jury trial was necessary to protect the *judge* from anticipated criticism (*see* P371) was not only baseless—for Reverend Moon had expressed "respect and confidence in the United States *judicial system*" (emphasis added) in the same speech that criticized the motives for his *prosecution* (A813)—but was also illegitimate. The First Amendment shields criticism of judges as well as prosecutors (see the *Bridges* line of cases cited *supra*); and, in any event, as Judge Goettel recognized, the government need not "worry" about "blame" being placed on a federal judge, since "the framers . . . took that into account 200 years ago" when they gave federal judges life tenure (P371).

19

Singer v. United States, 380 U.S. 24 (1965), which upheld the constitutionality of Fed. R. Crim. P. 23(a),[26] the Court recognized that, when the "Government's insistence on trial by jury" would result in an *unfair* trial, 380 U.S. at 37, the rule's government-consent requirement cannot be read so broadly as to eliminate a court's power—and indeed duty—to ensure a fair trial by overriding the government's choice. Judge Weinfeld expressed a similar view to a Judicial Conference of this Circuit shortly before *Singer. See* "The Problems of Long Criminal Trials," 34 F.R.D. 155, 205 (1963).[27]

Here, however, despite his stated belief that a nonjury trial would have been "fairer" (T1760; *see* T1752, 1759, 1761), the trial judge concluded both before and after the voir dire that

---

26   Rule 23(a) provides:

> Cases required to be tried by jury shall be so tried unless the defendant waives a jury trial in writing with the approval of the court and the consent of the government.

27   To read Rule 23(a) as vesting in the prosecutor veto power over a defendant's access to a trial without a jury would be impermissibly to abdicate to the Executive Branch the *judicial* power to safeguard the constitutional rights of the defendant. *Cf. United States v. Nixon,* 418 U.S. 683, 704 (1974) ("The judicial power of the United States, vested in the federal courts by Art. III, § 1 of the Constitution, can no more be shared with the Executive Branch, than the Chief Executive, for example, can share with the Judiciary the veto power."); *Irvin v. Dowd, supra* (statute could not properly be read to "condition" upon the consent of the prosecutor the "duty of the judiciary" to take steps to ensure fair trial). *See also Commonwealth v. Wharton,* 435 A.2d 158, 168 (Pa. 1981) (opinion in support of affirmance) (prosecutor's absolute veto over defendant's request for nonjury trial unconstitutionally "restricts the exercise by trial court judges of their constitutional authority to conduct a fair trial").

At least three federal district courts have granted defense motions for bench trials over government opposition. *United States v. Braunstein,* 474 F.Supp. 1, 14 (D.N.J. 1979); *United States v. Panteleakis,* 422 F. Supp. 247 (D.R.I 1976); *United States v. Schipani,* 44 F.R.D. 461 (E.D.N.Y. 1968). And courts of appeals have recognized a trial judge's power to do so. *See, e.g., United States v. Morlang,* 531 F.2d 183, 187 (4th Cir. 1975); *United States v. Farries,* 459 F.2d 1057, 1061 (3d Cir. 1972), *cert. denied,* 410 U.S. 912 (1973); *United States v. Ceja,* 451 F.2d 399, 401 (1st Cir. 1971). Furthermore, the ABA Standards on Trial by Jury note that a defendant should have an absolute right to waive a jury when "there is reason to believe that, as a result of the dissemination of potentially prejudicial material, the waiver is required to increase the likelihood of a fair trial." Commentary to Standard 15-1.2.

20

he was powerless under the circumstances to "overrule the government's choice to have a jury trial" (*see* S26). This conclusion was gravely erroneous.

A. Before Voir Dire, There was an Unacceptable Risk that a Fair Jury Could Not be Selected.

As the evidence submitted in support of defendant's request for a bench trial overwhelmingly demonstrated—and the trial court recognized—Reverend Moon suffers "substantial unpopularity . . . in the public eye." S132. Indeed, that evidence leaves no doubt that Reverend Moon was, pre-trial, the subject of profound public hostility, reflected in—and inflamed by—extensive, dramatic publicity depicting him as a charlatan who supposedly "brainwashes" young people, breaks up families, and exploits his followers for personal financial gain.[28] This public hostility, the trial court itself recognized, was "such as to imperil [Reverend Moon's] opportunity of getting a fair jury trial." P372, 381.

Yet despite this stark recognition, and despite his expressed "reservations about the ability of even a searching voir dire to pick out those who may have what are to them known biases [toward a "distinctly unpopular" defendant] that they do not

---

28   That evidence featured an opinion survey by Stephen Roth, a noted public opinion researcher, which, although initially designed to help select a jury, led Roth to conclude that the unique level of hostility to Reverend Moon precluded selection of any fair jury at all. A818. The overwhelming majority of the 1,000 persons surveyed knew of and were negatively predisposed toward Reverend Moon (76.4% responding unfavorably to the name "Reverend Moon," 70.4% unfavorably to the name "Sun Myung Moon," 67.3% unfavorably to the term "Moonies" (*see* A822) and almost all using such pejorative terms as "crook," "hoax," "racketeer," who "brainwashes" and "exploits the young" to describe Reverend Moon (*see* A801-03, 916-1002)). Indeed, as many as 42.9% acknowledged that "[i]f [they] had the chance, [they'd] throw Reverend Sun Myung Moon *in jail*" (A819-20, emphasis added). The results of the survey were supplemented by two large boxes of newspaper clippings, all of which attacked Reverend Moon and the Unification faith (P353); two books similarly hostile to the Church (P354); reviews of a film then playing in Manhattan—"Ticket to Heaven"—which the *New York Daily News* described as "an indictment of the Unification Church" (P355); and information concerning two separate instances where business concerns, linked only by rumor to Reverend Moon, were practically driven out of business by negative public reaction (P358-59).

21

choose to reveal" (P381), the judge, believing he had no choice under the circumstances, proceeded to conduct a voir dire, stating that "we have to go ahead and try to select a jury, as the government requests" (P382). He did so despite the fact that a search for a jury indifferent to defendants would necessarily be a search for a jury atypically ignorant of current events and thus *not* representative of the community. *See* T1766. And he did so despite the fact that the government not only had "put[] nothing in the balance . . . to weigh against the overwhelming showing of sound reasons [for a bench trial] presented by defendants," *see United States v. Braunstein,* 474 F. Supp. 1, 14 (D.N.J. 1979),[29] but had put in *worse* than nothing by having withheld its consent for an "ignoble," *see Singer v. United States,* 380 U.S. at 37, and indeed unconstitutional reason (*see* § I *supra*).

In short, because this was a case of "compelling" circumstances, *Singer,* 380 U.S. at 37, in which there was *in advance* a "reasonable likelihood," *Sheppard,* 384 U.S. at 363, that " 'passion, prejudice . . . and public feeling' " against Reverend Moon and his religion, *see Singer,* 380 U.S. at 37, would "prevent a fair trial," *Sheppard,* 384 U.S. at 363, it was error to proceed to conduct a voir dire.

B. The Voir Dire Failed to Produce a Fair Jury.

Even the briefest review of the extensive voir dire[30] reveals that the jury was saturated with negative information about Reverend Moon and the Unification religion.[31] As the judge

---

29   Indeed, the government conceded that it was "well aware of the factors which [would] make selection of an impartial jury more difficult [here] than in many other cases" (*see* A1027); nor did it ever suggest that the trial court might be biased or might try the case less fairly than would a jury (*see* P372).

30   The voir dire lasted seven days and was recorded in over 2,000 pages of transcript. Of the 200 veniremen empaneled (*see* T6-7), 63 were interviewed to select the regular panel (*see* T300-1698), and 17 to select the six alternate jurors (*see* T1699-1700, 1773-1900, 1933-2121).

31   Only six out of the 63 veniremen interviewed for the regular panel reported that they had never heard of Reverend Moon, the Unification Church, or "Moonies." *See* T609-12, 623-29, 769-76, 817-21, 1266-77, 1586-94. And only one out of that 63 reported hearing anything positive

22

acknowledged at the conclusion of the voir dire, "to the extent
people know about [Reverend Moon] and his religion it is true
that their attitudes are negative." T1758.

Nor was the jury that was ultimately selected cleansed of
such prejudiced attitudes.[32] Indeed, the record demonstrates
quite the contrary. Almost all of the jurors selected had heard
criticism of Reverend Moon, or thought they knew enough
about him to tag him as the leader of a "cult" that makes
money on the street and "brainwashes" young recruits.[33]

—*i.e.,* that the "Moonies" had been "cleaning the street in Times Square"
(T1195). Virtually everyone else had heard something negative—most typically something about Reverend Moon "brainwashing" and/or "exploiting"
young people. See n.33 *infra* for examples of hostile accounts heard by the
jurors ultimately selected.

Moreover, during the course of the voir dire, discussions occurred in the
halls and at lunch that created a danger that prejudicial information might
spread through the jury pool. *See, e.g.,* T851, 1392, 1521-22, 1530-32,
1536-37, 1755-56. The trial judge's concern (*see* T1743) that jurors would
exchange prejudicial information and that outsiders would attempt to communicate with the jurors prompted him to comment that this problem alone
"is a very good reason why the Government should have agreed to waive a
jury here . . . ." T1756.

32   The total number of challenges afforded defendants was insufficient
to permit them to eliminate from the panel all jurors admitting to knowledge
of information prejudicial to Reverend Moon. Of its total challenges for
cause, the defense was allowed seven (six to regulars, T717, 719, 730, 991,
1556, 1622, and one to an alternate, T1992), but was denied eleven (ten to
regulars, T716, 724, 730, 913, 1074, 1076, 1230, 1502, 1583, 1655, and one to
an alternate, T1903). The judge, *sua sponte,* excused 13 regulars (T388, 799,
886, 933, 1072, 1108, 1143, 1150, 1307, 1334-35, 1475, 1482, 1509) and two
alternates (T1903, 1963). Although the judge gave the defense 20 peremptory
challenges to the regulars (T734), and four to the alternates (T1764-65), the
defense used almost half of them to eliminate prospective jurors against
whom challenges for cause had been denied, exhausted all the rest in
eliminating those jurors manifesting the clearest bias (T1087-89, 1384-85,
1698, 2124), and was denied any additional peremptories (*see* T734, 1697; *see
also* T1752, 1764-65).

Nor can the absence of a challenge for cause to one or another juror who
ultimately sat be deemed a waiver of objection. More challenges for cause
would have been pressed but for the judge's warning that, if he "knock[ed]
off all the close ones [pursuant to challenges for cause] [he would] not . . .
be so generous with the extra peremptories" (T542)—a warning given *before*
he had determined how many peremptories he would grant.

33   Among the negative preconceptions articulated during voir dire by
jurors who sat at trial were these:

23

In the face of such extensive negative preconceptions, defendants were forced to compromise between juror bias and juror ignorance. Seeking to avoid those jurors who had "heard the worst things about the Moonies and had the strongest feelings," the defense had to use its challenges against jurors that "read the most and [were] the most affluent" (T1776)—precisely the kinds of jurors that, under normal circumstances, the defense would have preferred in a tax case. See T1765-1766. As the judge frankly recognized,

> in attempting to get an unbiased jury, the leaning has been heavily towards people who don't read much, don't talk much and don't know much because they are obviously the persons who start off with the least bias. Conversely,

---

—*Mary K. Nimmo,* forelady, had heard that the Unification Church was a "cult," "making money on young people," and "wouldn't have wanted [her] children to have been a part of it." T473; see also 449, 477-80.

—*Esperanza Torres* knew of a "deprogramming" controversy involving a Unification Church member and concluded "that the parents [of the member] are right . . .," doubted Reverend Moon was a genuine spiritual leader (T847-48), and considered the Unification Church a "cult" involving "mostly young people" (T857). See T849, 852, 858, 862-63, 871, 873-75.

—*Rosa Spencer* did not "think" that it was proper for religious groups to invest in businesses, and felt that it was improper for religious groups to solicit funds publicly. T1349-50; see also 1358.

—*Doris Torres* had heard that "some people think [Moon] is a god" (T1391) and that the Unification Church "brainwashes" people. T1394.

—*Claudette Ange* had heard that Moon "was brainwashing some teenagers" and "has children selling . . . things . . . to get the money to buy property." T1514-15.

—*Maria Abramson* had not heard of Moon, but thought that religious cults brainwash young people (T1588), and believed religious groups "should collect their money in the church," not in public (T1587-88).

—*Paul Shanley* had heard about deprogramming and young people being "brainwashed" and "used for selling things." T1650; see T1631-32, 1636.

—*Freddie Bryant* thought that churches should raise funds by donations from their own members and not by "go[ing] into a complete business." T1683-85.

—*Amerria Vasquez* had heard that the "Moonies" "indoctrinate the young people in the church," and "are taking over New York City." T2052.

—*Ernest Fetchko* had heard that the "Moonies" get members "by brainwashing them." T2106.

24

> they would . . . tend to be the less educated and less
> intelligent people. T1759-60.

See also T1593-94, 1923; S26. The upshot was a jury which,
the judge acknowledged, might have difficulty comprehending
a "complicated" case. T1760.

Thus, despite the extensive voir dire, the jury selected had
two strikes against it: it was rife with prejudicial information
about Reverend Moon and his religion, and its educational
level and ability to comprehend complex facts were unrepre-
sentatively low. Faced with this jury, the judge expressed
serious reservations about the fairness of proceeding with a
jury at all, saying: "I would have thought it fairer to have this
case tried without a jury." T1760; *see* T1761, S26. Nonetheless,
since the voir dire had not persuaded the government to alter
its position, defendants' renewed request for bench trial
(A1038, T1701) met with no success. The judge, constrained by
his view that "the rule [Fed.R.Crim.P. 23(a)] and the judicial
interpretations of it seem to put no restrictions upon the
prosecution being able to insist upon a jury" (T1752), once
again deferred to the government's demand for a jury trial.
Such deference, in the teeth of this pre-trial record, was clearly
reversible error.

C. The Nature of the Evidence Exacerbated the Unfairness of Trial Before This Jury.

The government's case belied the two fundamental assumptions on which the judge had based his decision to go forward
with this jury: first, that religious issues would not enter the
case; and second, that the government's case would be a simple
one. Because both of these assumptions proved wrong, the
jury's deficiencies compounded one another: faced with confu-
singly complex evidence, the jury was by necessity thrown back
on its preconceptions. Unable to understand clearly what the
government's great fuss was about, the jury was all the more
likely to rely on what it had heard—that Reverend Moon was a
"cult" leader who "brainwashed" and "exploited" the young
for his own gain—however remote that "knowledge" was from
the alleged offenses for which he faced trial.

25

1. Trial by religious innuendo.

The judge's conclusion that the jury would be "capable of putting aside [its] bias . . . and deciding the case on the merits of the charges" (T1759), was based upon his supposition that this trial would *not* be about religion:

> If this criminal case were being tried on the issues of whether or not the Unification Church is a true religion or a cult, or whether or not it has been beneficial to America, the situation would be pretty critical . . . .
>
> I don't mean to suggest that general attitudes toward the church and to the Moonies don't impact on juror attitudes. But they won't impact as directly . . . as [they would if] those were the issues to be tried. T1758-59.

As it turned out, however, the government's presentation of its case put precisely such issues on trial. Indeed, despite repeated defense objection (*see* T2484-88, 2544-57, 4008-10, 5117, 5645-47, 5676-78, 5718-23, 5784-85), the jury was exposed to a flood of government testimony touching upon the very Unification Church beliefs and practices about which the jurors harbored negative impressions.[34]

Thus, reinforcing the myth that Reverend Moon lures young people away from their natural families, the jury heard that Reverend Moon's "sect" (T5675) was comprised of young people unrelated by blood who considered Reverend Moon their "True Parent" (T5676) or "Father" (T2870, 2903, 3009, 3013, 3946, 5014, 5049, 5784-85, 6267); call each other "brothers" and "sisters" (T2429, 2508-10, 2653, 3400, 4278); live and support each other communally (T2499-2500, 2659-61, 4012, 4049-50, 5811, 5813); and accept marriage partners chosen by Reverend Moon (T5718-23).

Reinforcing the myth that Reverend Moon commands obedience by "brainwashing" his young followers into carrying out his will, the jury heard that Reverend Moon was referred to as "Master" (T4008-10, 4377-79, 5723-24, 5784-85) and "Leader" (T3408-13, 4298, 5723-36, 5784-85); that his "fol-

---

34   The judge allowed in such testimony notwithstanding his express recognition that "matters that go to theology . . . might prejudice the jury." T5721; *see also* T5117, S24.

26

lowers" paid him strict devotion, loyalty and obedience (T2192, 2652-53, 3371, 3400, 4008-10, 4645-46, 4690-91, 5677-78); and that they might do anything they thought would help Reverend Moon (T5302; *see* T5262, 5623, 5677, 5724, 6443).[35]

And, reinforcing the myth that Reverend Moon "exploits" others for his own personal gain, the jury heard how Reverend Moon organizes young recruits into armies of fundraisers (T2751-52, 2762, 4014-15, 4278-91) who devote themselves to helping build what the government insinuated was a vast international economic empire for Reverend Moon's benefit, while they gladly do without (T2164-65, 2432-33, 2435, 2508-10, 2544-46, 2763-66, 2769-71, 4015-16, 4022-24, 4278-81, 4377-79, 4645-46, 4690-91, 5129-32, 5138-43).

Finally, in its closing argument to the jury, the government conjured up all the worst fears associated with the "Moonies"—fears of mind control and mindless obedience—by blaming the government's difficulty in "reconstruct[ing] what really happened" on the fact that, among Unification Church members, there were simply "too many . . . *closed minds* and . . . closed mouths." T6184 (emphasis added).

By this steady infusion into the trial of Unification Church beliefs and practices—distorted and presented out of context—the jury was invited to try a case the judge had assumed would *not* be tried—a case directly implicating collateral religious issues. Worse yet, confronted by the jury in this case, the defense was not free to meet these issues head on; it was not free to present a full and accurate picture of the special role Reverend Moon plays in the Unification faith or of the special relationship between church and "business" in that theology— for, as even the judge acknowledged, such a presentation would have inflamed the jury. *See* T1758-59, 5117, 5721. Indeed, the judge recognized post-trial that a defense built on an exposition of Unification theology and of Reverend Moon's place within that theology—*i.e.*, in the judge's words, a "messiah defense" (S60)—"would have been disastrous to try before

---

35   The government used this "brainwashing" theme most perniciously, suggesting that, because of Reverend Moon's "special relationship" with his followers (T5676-77), Church members could not be believed as witnesses on the stand. *See* T5719-21, 5725-6, 6443, 6498.

27

a jury" (*id*).[36] But such an exposition, placed in proper context before a fact-finder free from bias against his religion, would have been helpful, if not indispensable, in explaining the *innocence* of Reverend Moon's conduct and state of mind. Thus fettered in advancing a full defense,[37] Reverend Moon was plainly denied a fair trial. *See Chambers v. Mississippi*, 410 U.S. 284, 294 (1973); *Webb v. Texas*, 409 U.S. 95, 98 (1972); *United States v. Corr*, 543 F.2d 1042, 1051 (2d Cir. 1976) ("a defendant's right to present a full defense is a fundamental element of due process . . ."). *See also Brooks v. Tennessee*, 406 U.S. 605, 609-13 (1972) (defendant's right to determine defense *strategy*—including "important tactical decisions" and "planning" under the "guiding hand of counsel"— is a right that must remain wholly "unfettered").

2. Trial by mesmerizing complexity.

While acknowledging the limited educational and intellectual background of this jury, the judge nonetheless concluded that it would "probably" be "quite capable" of reaching a sound verdict provided this turned out to be "a simple criminal case" raising issues of "credibility," and did not become "complicated" or "get into complicated bookkeeping and accounting procedures and things of that nature." T1760.

---

36   The record makes clear that it was indeed fear of jury bias that prevented defendants from presenting such a defense. As defense counsel explained to the judge on the third day of trial, "we are put in a position where we think that we will have to introduce evidence that relates and goes to the doctrines of this Church, to the practices of this church" (T2554-55), but cannot do so *before the jury* "because we try this case in the atmosphere [of] . . . the hostile views of the community, views which these jurors say they don't have but nevertheless many of them have read about" (T2555-56). In contrast, defense counsel did not hesitate to present explanations of Unification theology *to the judge*. Thus, prior to the opening of the evidence, the defense proffered to the judge several submissions explaining Unification faith practices and beliefs (A620, 1106; T1905)—some, but not all, of which the judge took into account (*see* A720, 1115). And at trial, defense counsel cited points of Unification religious doctrine in arguments presented only to the judge. *See, e.g.*, T2545-46, 5512, 5524-25; A1167-68.

37   Compounding the constraint created by the presence of the jury, the judge made a series of rulings curtailing those efforts the defense *was* willing to risk in order to place Reverend Moon's actions in their proper church context. *See, e.g.*, T3044, 4818-20, 5102, 5254-57, 5681. *See also* § IV.C(3) *infra*.

28

As it turned out, however, the government's case proved to be anything but simple. Not only did it focus exhaustively on "complicated bookkeeping and accounting" procedures,[38] but it also required determination of an issue that was in itself exceedingly complex—namely, whether a religious leader administering assets from church sources in his own name is a beneficial owner or merely a "nominee" or "trustee" with dominion and control. Moreover, the government's case involved over 2,000 documentary exhibits, many of which were redundant,[39] and large numbers of which would have been confusing and arcane even to highly educated jurors.[40] To *this* jury, the government's tedious parade of documents and multicolored charts[41] could only have been so mesmerizing as to create the sense that something in real dispute had been demonstrated.

So great was the complexity of the evidence that the judge repeatedly expressed concern with the difficulty the jury was having comprehending the case, and more than once admonished the government that it was making its case "a lot more complicated than it needs to be." T2811. *See also* T3032

---

38   Among these complex procedures were time-deposit account procedures including roll-overs and reinvestment (T2322-24, 4974-76), and "double accounting" (T2363-66, 2370); commercial letters of credit (T2409-21, 2674-83, 2701-03, 3616-20); property title guarantees and delivery (T2706-08, 3304-06, 3351-57); corporate inventory transfers (T3814-16); and accounting procedures including balance sheets (T5836-37, 5842-43, 5848-50).

39   For example, as the judge noted regarding certain letter-of-credit evidence, the government could have made the relevant showing with "one single document," instead of the many it introduced in over 60 pages of trial transcript. T2474.

40   These documents included accountants' workpapers (T3773-75, 3860-73, 4172, 4215-19, 5839-69, 5881-5931); stock subscriptions (T2455-58, 2524-25, 3984-87, 4575, 5821); loan agreements (T2610-26, 3391-3407, 3839-40, 3950-51, 4044-45, 4325, 4525-35, 4574-78, 4696-4701, 4738-59, 4773-92, 5371-77, 5968-71, 5977-79); and corporate records including payroll sheets, budgets, financial statements, and stock purchase certificates (T2453-62, 2483-84, 3498-3501, 3912-17, 3936, 3962-68, 4275-78, 4289-99, 5150).

41   *See* T2474 (judge notes that the government was "putting the jury to sleep by throwing all these scads of documents at them").

29

("the jury will not be able to sort [the evidence] out in . . . two months of Sundays").[42]

Thus, just as the problem of jury prejudice increased the risk of jury incomprehension—by requiring the selection of an unusually uneducated and uninformed jury—so the problem of evidentiary complexity increased the risk that the jury would substitute prejudice for reasoned judgement, denying a fair trial.

III. THE TRIAL COURT'S MISCONSTRUCTIÓN OF THE COURT INTERPRETERS ACT OF 1978 IMPERMISSIBLY BURDENED DEFENDANT'S RIGHT TO DECIDE WHETHER TO TESTIFY.

Long before trial, Reverend Moon recognized the special problem he faced as a criminal defendant whose ability to speak English was extremely limited (*see* T3346, 5051)—a problem that would be especially acute were he to choose to testify. Accordingly, he moved for permission to use an interpreter of his own choice in lieu of any interpreter the court might otherwise appoint for him pursuant to the Court Interpreters Act of 1978, 28 U.S.C. § 1827(d). A152. The judge, construing the waiver provision of that Act, § 1827(f), narrowly and artificially in response to the government's request (*see* A416-17), ruled that Reverend Moon could use an interpreter of his choice only for the purpose of *listening* to the court proceedings, *not* for the purpose of *speaking* on the stand. P108-11. In other words, the court ruled that Reverend Moon could take the stand *only* by agreeing to speak through a court-selected voice.

This ruling burdened Reverend Moon's Fifth and Sixth Amendment rights to present a full defense and to choose—unfettered—whether, when, and how to take the stand. *See Brooks v. Tennessee*, 406 U.S. at 609-11; *United States v. Corr*, 543 F.2d at 1051. For just as a defendant's opportunity to decide whether or not to testify cannot constitutionally be confined to one *phase* of the trial, *Brooks v. Tennessee, supra*,

---

42   For other comments by the judge about the confusing complexity of the trial, see T2337-38, 2487, 2811-13, 2841, 2885-86, 3032, 3530-32, 4427, 5504, 5509, 5580, 5917, 5935, 6099-6116. *See also* S62.

30

so his choice whether or not to testify cannot constitutionally be inhibited by confining him to one *form* of testifying that he expressly does not wish to use. It is on the stand, after all, that the defendant has the greatest need for an interpreter through whom he can most comfortably and reliably comprehend and communicate. Compelling a defendant to testify, if at all, only through a voice he mistrusts unconstitutionally limits his freedom to decide, in planning and presenting his defense, *whether* to take the stand or to remain mute. *See Brooks,* 406 U.S. at 610-12.

Such a debilitating constraint on a defendant's trial rights is *not* mandated by the statute. On its face, § 1827 does not, as the judge read it (*see* P108-09), deny to criminal defendants the option to testify through interpreters of their choice rather than the court's. To be sure, § 1827(f)(1) provides that only "an individual *other than a witness* who is entitled to interpretation" (emphasis added)[43] may waive a court-selected interpreter in favor of his own. But the statute itself *distinguishes between* the interpretation rights of a "party (including a defendant in a criminal case)," and those of a "witness," in extending separately to *each* a right to a court-appointed interpreter. § 1827(d). And § 1827 nowhere states that a criminal defendant suddenly sheds his status as a "party" and assumes the status of a "witness"—thus losing the waiver option that § 1827(f)(1) otherwise gives him—the minute he takes the stand.

Nor does the legislative history contain a word of support for the judge's construction. Indeed, the Act was passed with the rights of the criminal *defendant* to participate meaningfully at his trial squarely in mind. *See* H.Rep.No. 95-1687 (Oct. 4, 1978), *reprinted in* [1978] U.S. Code Cong. & Ad. News 4652, 4653-54. And the House Judiciary Committee expressly noted that the waiver provision "was included so as to not penalize an individual who, because of special circumstances, could communicate more effectively in the proceedings with a non-

---

43   There is no doubt that Reverend Moon was "entitled to interpretation" for purposes of § 1827(f)(1), as he plainly satisfied the prerequisite under § 1827(d) that he "speaks only or primarily a language other than . . . English."

31

certified interpreter of such individual's own choice," *id.* at 4658, and nowhere ruled out that such "special circumstances" might be those of the accused who takes the stand.

If the court's construction of the statute were put into practice, moreover, the result would be unworkable: the defendant would *speak* through one interpreter—the court's—and *listen* through another interpreter—his own.[44] This procedure would unfairly bifurcate the foreign-language criminal defendant's participation in his trial.[45]

Because the judge's construction of the statute was thus misconstruction that unconstitutionally fettered the defense, it requires reversal.

IV. THE TRIAL COURT'S INSTRUCTIONS TO THE JURY WERE FATALLY DEFECTIVE.

A. The Court's Instructions Misstated the Law of Trusts.

At the heart of the government's claim that Reverend Moon filed false statements on his 1973, 1974, and 1975 tax returns was the issue of beneficial ownership.[46] Only if the funds in the Chase accounts and the Tong Il stock *belonged to Reverend*

---

44   The judge's suggestion that Reverend Moon's rights could be protected in some way by having his own interpreter "monitor the official court interpreter" (P110) would only compound this impracticality, for it could constitutionally mean nothing less than that the defendant would be entitled to have his *own* interpreter translate for him, *as he testified,* the *court* interpreter's *version* of his testimony. *See United States ex rel. Negron v. New York,* 434 F.2d 386, 389-90 (2d Cir. 1970) (pre-Act case, cited in legislative history as part of the Act's "impetus," *see* H. Rep. No. 95-1687, *supra,* [1978] U.S. Code Cong. & Ad. News at 4653) (translation of testimony is constitutionally inadequate unless given to defendant along with the testimony rather than later).

45   As the First Circuit has recognized, it is fundamental that a criminal defendant receive meaningful translation during his trial lest he "face the Kafkaesque spectre of an incomprehensible ritual which may terminate in punishment." *United States v. Carrion,* 488 F.2d 12, 14 (1st Cir. 1973), *cert. denied,* 416 U.S. 907 (1974). *Cf. F.* Kafka, *The Trial* (1925).

46   The law is clear that dominion and control over funds does not, by itself, establish taxability where funds are beneficially owned by another. *See, e.g., Brittingham v. Commissioner,* 57 T.C. 91 (1971) (money deposited in taxpayer's account with informal understanding that it was to be spent for his mother is not income, since there is no accrual of gain or benefit to taxpayer); *Seven-Up Co. v. Commissioner,* 14 T.C. 965 (1950) (amounts

32

Moon beneficially could the omission from Reverend Moon's tax returns of the interest on the Chase accounts and of the receipt of the stock be found to constitute falsehoods.[47]

Although the judge recognized that the issue of beneficial ownership was "key" (T6583), he failed to recognize that this case placed that issue in a very specialized context. For this case did *not* deal with a claim that an ordinary, lay taxpayer simply held certain assets in a private trust for the benefit of another. Rather the claim was, and the undisputed evidence showed, (a) that this taxpayer was the founder and leader of a worldwide religious movement, the members of which regarded him as the embodiment of their faith; (b) that the assets in question had been entrusted to him by members of his faith; and (c) that the donors intended their contributions to be used by him for religious purposes. *See* pp. 5-7 *supra*. On such a record, New York law[48] establishes a presumption that the religious leader holds the assets in charitable trust.[49]

---

received by taxpayer to be held and used for advertising campaign are not income to taxpayer who received funds as an agent, despite lack of formal agency agreement). *See also Poonian v. United States,* 294 F.2d 74 (9th Cir. 1961); *Broussard v. Commissioner,* 16 T.C. 23 (1951).

47   Two cases involving the question at issue here—whether amounts placed in the account of a religious leader will be treated as given in trust for his religion for purposes of federal income taxes—have answered this question affirmatively. Thus, *Winn v. Commissioner,* 595 F.2d 1060, 1065 (5th Cir. 1979), held that, where money was given to a church officer in response to a church-sponsored solicitation, and was used, as intended, to support the work of the church, it was sufficiently established that the funds were donated "for the use of" the church to permit the contributing taxpayers to claim deductions for contributions. And *Morey v. Riddell,* 205 F. Supp. 918, 921 (S.D. Cal. 1962), held that, where money contributed to a religious association was used to meet expenses of the church, including a minister's living expenses, in implementing its purposes, deductions for religious contributions would be permitted.

48   Since state law controls in the determination of ownership, *see United States v. Mitchell,* 403 U.S. 190, 197 (1971); *see also* Treas. Reg. 301.7701-9; *United States v. Manny,* 645 F.2d 163, 166 (2d Cir. 1981), New York trust decisions must govern here. However, the principles at issue are universally accepted, and, as discussed in § IV.C *infra,* may be constitutionally compelled.

49   This presumption derives from several principles:

First, the law favors charitable trusts and will draw any reasonable

33

Under this presumption, when a member of a religion makes
a contribution to an official of that religion, the donor is

inference, resort to any available legal rule, resolve any ambiguity, to find
and uphold them. *In re Price's Will*, 264 App. Div. 29, 35 N.Y.S.2d 111,
114-115, *aff'd*, 289 N.Y. 751, 46 N.E.2d 354 (1942); *In re Estate of Nurse*, 35
N.Y.2d 381, 362 N.Y.S.2d 441, 446 (1974); *In re Estate of Carper*, 67 App.
Div. 2d 333, 415 N.Y.S.2d 550 (1979); *In re Pattberg's Will*, 282 App. Div.
770, 123 N.Y.S.2d 564, 566 (1953). *See* New York EPTL § 8-1.1; 18 N.Y. Jur.
2d *Charities* § 6.

Second, when a gift appears to have been made for charitable (including
religious) *purposes,* it is presumed that the gift has been made *in trust* even if
no trust language has been used and even if the gift was "in form absolute."
In re Durbrow's Estate, 245 N.Y. 469, 157 N.E. 747, 749 (1927) ("A trust is
almost inseparably involved with a gift for charitable uses"(citation omitted)); *New York City Mission Society v. Board of Pensions*, 261 App. Div.
823, 24 N.Y.S.2d 395, 397 (2d Dept. 1941); *In re Hendrick's Will*, 1 Misc. 2d
904, 148 N.Y.S.2d 245, 256 (1955); *In re Walter's Estate*, 150 Misc. 512, 269
N.Y.S. 402, 405 (1934).

Third, where the *donee* of a gift is a religious institution or official, the gift
is typically *construed* as a gift in trust for religious purposes, even where the
donor did not *expressly manifest* an intent that the gift be for such purposes.
IV A. W. Scott, *The Law of Trusts* § 371.3 at 2885 & n.4, § 351 at 2797-98
(3d ed. 1967). The cases holding that a minister or other church official who
held title to property in his own name did so as trustee for members of his
religion are, in fact, legion. A few of the scores of these cases are: *Biscoe v.
Thweatt*, 74 Ark. 545, 86 S.W. 432 (1905); *In re Geppert's Estate*, 75 S.D.
96, 59 N.W.2d 727 (1953); *In re Estate of Fitzgerald*, 62 Cal. App. 744, 217
P. 773 (1923); *In re Creighton's Estate*, 60 Neb. 796, 84 N.W. 273 (1900);
Sears v. Parker, 193 Mass. 551, 79 N.E. 772 (1907); and *Jones v. Habersham*, 107 U.S. 174 (1883). *See also* 50 N.Y. Jur. *Religious Societies* § 111
at 11, ("*In some . . . churches, title to all or much of the church property
. . . is taken and held by . . . certain of [the church's] authorities.* Under
the Roman Catholic church system, title to church property ordinarily is
vested in the bishop of the diocese, and is by him transmitted to his
successor" (footnotes omitted, emphasis added)).

Fourth, the presumption of a trust is deemed to be reinforced where, in
addition to the fact that the donee is a religious official, the *source* of the
assets is a *church source.* Thus, in *Fink v. Umscheid*, 40 Kan. 271, 19 P. 623
(1888), a Catholic bishop had used money supplied by his congregation to
purchase land, in his own name, to be used for maintaining a church and
school. When the bishop later attempted to sell the property, representatives
of the local unincorporated congregation successfully overturned the conveyance on the ground that the bishop held the land in trust for the congregation
and thus did not have absolute discretion in disposing of it. *See also Hill v.
Hill*, 34 Tenn. App. 617, 241 S.W.2d 865 (1951); *Archbishop v. Shipman*, 79
Cal. 288, 21 P. 830 (1889).

34

assumed *not* to intend to make a personal gift to the official and his heirs—even if the contribution is made in the official's own name—but rather is assumed to intend the funds to be used solely for purposes of the religion. Indeed, making contributions in a religious leader's own name has, historically, been one way religious donors have *signalled* their intent that contributions be used solely to advance the leader's religious calling. Thus, John Wesley, the founder and leader of the Methodist Church in eighteenth-century England, explained in a May 9, 1739, entry in his famed *Journal*, that his followers in London had insisted on contributing to his ministry not through trustees or "feoffees," but solely "in [Wesley's] own name," lest the trustees, or indeed anyone, "turn [him] out of the [meeting house he] had built" if he "preached not as they like." Even if unexpressed, such intent is *assumed* by the law (a) because, as a matter of experience, this is the intent that religious donors ordinarily *have*, and it is recognized as being of the utmost importance to give effect to the donors' *actual intent*; and (b) because, as a matter of *public policy,* it is deemed *preferable*, especially in a close case, to err on the side of construing a gift to be for a charitable purpose, rather than on the side of construing it to be for the personal enrichment of an individual.[50]

The trial judge was plainly required to instruct the jury on the critical issue of beneficial ownership in accordance with the foregoing principles. Instead, the judge's instructions misstated and distorted the law of trusts in at least four ways.

First, the court erred when it instructed the jury:

> Whether a trust is created depends on the intent of the
> person giving the property at the time of transfer, and that

---

50   The rationale for the presumption of a charitable trust may be underscored by imagining that Reverend Moon died in 1974, and the issue of beneficial ownership arose in the context of a property dispute between the international Unification Church movement and Reverend Moon's heirs. There can be no question that a court in that circumstance would presume that the assets in dispute had been given to Reverend Moon in a charitable trust. The court would recognize such a presumption as being essential to protect the rights of the donors, and to vindicate the demands of public policy. The issue here was precisely the same as the issue in this hypothetical case. Thus, the trial judge here was required to apply the same presumption, and for the same reasons.

35

intent must be *clear and unambiguous*. T6586 (emphasis added).

While New York law may require that the intent to create a *private* trust be manifested by clear and unambiguous evidence,[51] New York law applies very different rules of construction to a *charitable* trust. Indeed, far from requiring that the intent to create such a trust be "clear and unambiguous," New York law actually provides that there is a *presumption* of such intent, which can only be *overcome* by clear and convincing evidence to the contrary. The instruction given here was therefore the *opposite* of what it should have been.

Second, although the trial judge explicitly recognized that it was necessary to inform the jury that, if those who gave the assets to Reverend Moon "intended [them] to be for the [i]nternational Unification Church movement," the assets could "be viewed as not . . . his but . . . the [m]ovement's" (T6122-23), he unaccountably failed to so instruct. Indeed, the trial judge refused (T6107, 6114) to grant defendant's request to charge (*see* A1371-72) that the existence of a trust is supported by evidence that (a) the parties who donated the funds to the religious leader "intended" that the funds be used "for Church purposes," (b) the funds "came from . . . church sources," or (c) the funds were used primarily for "church purposes"—evidence that would in fact be sufficient to create a *presumption* of a charitable trust.[52]

---

51   The case cited by the government in support of its request to charge on this issue (A1308), *Gagliardi v. Gagliardi*, 55 N.Y.2d 109, 432 N.E.2d 774, 447 N.Y.S.2d 902 (1982), was indeed a *private* trust case.

52   Instead of granting defendant's proposed instruction, the trial court buried the key issues of source and intent—without any guidance that these were the *critical* factors—in the middle of a laundry list of eight factors. *See* T6584-85. Moreover, this list—to which the defendant expressly objected (T6157-59, 6660-61)—omitted other factors critical to the defense: *e.g.*, that Reverend Moon was the founder and spiritual leader of the Unification Church (*see* A1365); that no particular formalities are required to create a religious movement (*id.*); and that the Unification Church in fact operated internationally (*see* T6120). The upshot of this prejudicially skewed list was to invite the jury to find no trust relationship *despite* factors that, as a matter of law, bring such a relationship into being.

36

Third, the judge instructed the jury that, in determining whether Reverend Moon held the assets in trust for the international Unification Church movement, it "should consider":

> whether the [m]ovement had a specific organizational structure, written charter or constitution [and] the existence of other Unification Church corporate entities . . . . T6584.

But one of the cardinal rules of the law of charitable trusts—a rule codified in New York by statute (New York EPTL § 8-1.1)—is that a charitable trust cannot fail by reason of the indefiniteness or uncertainty of the beneficiaries, who, in fact, need not be designated at all. IV A. W. Scott, *The Law of Trusts* § 364 at 2838-39 (3d ed. 1967); 18 N.Y. Jur. 2d *Charities* § 5. Thus, by suggesting that if "the *[m]ovement*," unlike "*other*. . . Church . . . entities," had not been incorporated, then its members could not be beneficiaries, the judge conveyed a wholly erroneous view of trust law.[53]

Fourth, the trial court gave a series of erroneous instructions regarding the misuse of trust funds, and what the jury could conclude if it found that Reverend Moon had used a portion of the assets at issue for "personal" or non-Church purposes.

(a) Thus, the trial court instructed, over defense objection (T6661-63), that "[t]here is no trust if the person who receives the money is free to use it for his own benefit." T6586. Contrary to this instruction, it is quite common—and entirely consistent with principles of trust law—that a trust may exist even though the trustee is endowed with the freedom to use for his own personal benefit a portion of funds he holds in trust, and that such use will *not* nullify the existence of trust.[54] This

---

53   Nor did the judge cure this error by subsequently instructing that "the lack of a *formal corporation* does not prevent a religious movement from being the beneficial owner of property held in the name of another" (T6585, emphasis added), and that it was "legal for an unincorporated *church* or religious *association*" to be a beneficial owner (T6588, emphasis added). For these instructions still left the jury with the impression that a movement lacking an organizational structure as definitive as that of a "corporation," an "association," or a "church," could *not* be a beneficiary.

54   Indeed, the law is clear that when a trustee disburses money out of a trust for personal purposes, such disbursement does *not* make the corpus his

37

is, of course, particularly common in situations involving monies held in trust by *religious leaders*, since use of entrusted funds to pay a leader's living expenses in such situations has traditionally been regarded as well within the scope of a church's religious purposes, even though such expenses might obviously be regarded as "personal" in other contexts. *See, e.g., Morey v. Riddell*, 205 F. Supp. 918, 921 (S.D.Cal. 1962).

(b) In a similar vein, the trial court instructed the jury that, to find the interest on the Chase accounts "not . . . taxable income to Moon," the jury must "find that the funds in [those] accounts were . . . held in trust by Moon . . . *and used for church purposes* and that the interest on those funds also . . . were [*sic*] used for [the church] . . . ." T6584 (emphasis added). The fatal vice of this instruction is that it invited the jury to find that use of *any portion* of the funds (or indeed use of any portion of the interest on the funds) for non-Church purposes would destroy the trust as a whole. That is plainly not the law. *See* n.54 *supra*.

(c) Finally, the judge instructed over defense objection (T6662-63):

> If a trust does exist and the trustee diverts trust property to his own use, the funds diverted become taxable to him at the time and to the extent so diverted. T6586-87.

This instruction was at fatal variance with the theory on which Reverend Moon was indicted and on which this entire case was tried.[55] For the theory of the government's case was *not* that

personally—and hence does not affect the taxability of interest earned on the funds not so disbursed. *See Herbert v. Commissioner*, 377 F.2d 65 (9th Cir. 1967). *Accord, United States v. Scott*, 660 F.2d 1145 (7th Cir. 1981), *cert. denied*, 102 S.Ct. 1252 (1982) (only those campaign funds diverted to personal use are taxable to candidate as income; diversion of some monies does not make entire fund taxable to candidate); Rev. Ruling 71-499, 1971-2 C.B. 77.

55   Moreover, even assuming that it was not error *per se* for the judge to charge on diversion, the particular diversion instruction which the judge gave was clearly inadequate.

First, the instruction failed to explain that, even if Reverend Moon had improperly diverted *some* of the Chase funds to a non-trust use, such partial diversion could *not* make the entire corpus, and thus the interest thereon,

38

Reverend Moon had "diverted" to his own use funds originally given in trust, *but rather that the funds were never in trust to begin with.* See P99-100; T6662. Thus, the trial court's decision to inject the issue of diversion into the case was wholly gratuitous and could only have confused, and invited error by, a jury already severely taxed by the complexity of the issues presented and contaminated with negative notions about Church investments.

B. The Instructions Unconstitutionally Shifted to the Defendant the Burden of Proof on the Issue of Beneficial Ownership.

A jury instruction that indicates, even indirectly, that the *defendant* bears any burden of proof on an element of the offense is constitutionally improper. *Mullaney v. Wilbur,* 421 U.S. 684 (1975); *In re Winship,* 397 U.S. 358, 364 (1970). But here, the instructions on beneficial ownership did just that.

First, the jury was charged that "*if*" it found the Chase funds "were the property of . . . or were held in trust by Moon for the [i]nternational Unification Church [m]ovement," "*then*" the interest "would *not* be taxable income to Moon." T6584 (emphasis added). The plain implication of this "if-then" formulation was that, *unless* Reverend Moon affirmatively convinced the jury that the property belonged to the international Unification Church movement, the jury was required to find for the prosecution. In *Notaro v. United*

---

taxable to him (*see* T6662-63). Contrary to the judge's suggestion (T6662), the bare inclusion of the phrase "to the extent so diverted" could not possibly have conveyed this concept adequately to this jury.

Second, the instruction failed to explain what it would *mean* to engage in diversion on the facts of this case. It left the jury free to conclude—quite incorrectly—that Reverend Moon's use of Chase funds for personal expenses automatically constituted diversion, even though such use by a religious leader is traditionally considered within the scope of a church's purpose and even though disbursements from the Chase checking account for such expenses were reported as personal income to Reverend Moon. It also left the jury free to reach the plainly erroneous conclusion that any use of Chase funds for business investment constituted diversion, *per se*, even though religious groups commonly and necessarily seek the highest possible return on their money, and even though there was direct evidence in this case that the business investments made with Chase funds were made for the benefit of the Church (*see* pp. 10-11 *supra*).

39

States, 363 F.2d 169, 175-76 (9th Cir. 1966), the court condemned just such an "if-then" formulation on the ground that
a direction to the jury that *if* it finds a particular fact, *then* it
should acquit, inevitably obscures the locus of the burden of
proof.[56]

Second, the instruction that to create a trust, the donor's
"intent must be *clear and unambiguous*" (T6586, emphasis
added), not only misstated the law of charitable trusts (*see*
§ IV.A *supra*), but also placed the burden of proof squarely on
the defendant. Worse yet, it made discharge of that burden
contingent upon the submission of "clear and unambiguous"
proof of intent to create a trust. Under this instruction, even if
the evidence proved such intent by a *preponderance* of the
evidence—proof that should have more than *defeated* the
government's position—the jury could well have found *for* the
government.[57]

---

56   Reversal is required here *a fortiori* because the shift in burden of
proof implicit in the judge's "if-then" instruction was reinforced by other
aspects of the charge. Thus, the judge listed "the *essentials* of a trust" that
must be found "[i]n order for a trust to exist" (T6585-86)—again suggesting
to the jury that, unless affirmatively convinced of a pro-defense fact, it was
required to find for the prosecution. Further, by identifying the "key issue"
as "whether *or not*" Reverend Moon personally owned the property (T6583,
emphasis added; *see* T6584, 6586, 6589), and by juxtaposing the defendant's
"contention" that the assets were held in trust with the government's
"contention" that the assets "belong[ed]" to Reverend Moon (T6583; *see*
T6585), the judge presented the issue of beneficial ownership as if it were a
disputed issue in a civil case, about which the jury was to decide which side
was more nearly right.

57   Although defendant excepted to the instructions on beneficial
ownership on burden-of-proof grounds (T6664-66), the trial court, relying on
the fact that the discussion of beneficial ownership included a reference (at
T6589) to "beyond reasonable doubt," refused to supplement its charge.
T6665. But when the instructions on beneficial ownership are read as a
whole, *see Cupp v. Naughten*, 414 U.S. 141, 146-47 (1973), it is apparent that
the solitary mention of reasonable doubt—which came at the tail end of a
six-page discussion and contained no reference to burden of proof—was
completely insufficient to counteract the overall message communicated by
the instructions—namely, that the burden of proof on this issue was on the
defendant. Moreover, any curative benefit from this tail-end reference to
reasonable doubt was further eroded by the prejudicially skewed way (*see*
n.52 *supra*) in which the judge marshalled the factors to be considered on the

40

C. The Instructions Violated the Religion Clauses of the First Amendment.

There can be no question that the issue of beneficial ownership in this case was, in essence, an issue of who owned church property—the flock or its religious leader. Thus the trial court was duty-bound to approach the issue with a scrupulous regard not only for the charitable trust principles discussed above, but also for the limitations imposed on secular tribunals in such matters by the First Amendment. These limitations include the following.

First, a secular court is required to respect the integrity of a religion's doctrines and precepts. *Presbyterian Church v. Hull Church*, 393 U.S. 440, 449 (1969). Although a court may consider evidence that those doctrines and precepts are not held in good faith—evidence the government did not, and could not, offer here—a court *cannot* judge, or permit a jury to judge, their reasonableness or validity. *United States v. Ballard*, 322 U.S. 78 (1944). *See also Thomas v. Review Board, Indiana Employment Security Division*, 450 U.S. 707, 714 (1981).

Second, secular institutions are required to respect activities undertaken by churches to obtain financial support as fully as other religious undertakings. *Murdock v. Pennsylvania*, 319 U.S. 105, 111 (1943). Although taxes may sometimes be assessed on profits earned by churches on their investments, such assessment does not render the *investments* non-religious. Thus the Christian Brothers engage in *religious* activity when they invest in wines and brandies, the Trappists when they sell fruit jams—even if the profits on these investments are taxable. Moreover, the fact that a business in which an investment is made may have no inherent religious significance cannot render the *act of investing* non-religious. Thus a church need not *worship* iron for its investment in an iron works to be a *church* investment.

Third, as the New York Court of Appeals held in *Holy Spirit Association for the Unification of World Christianity v. Tax*

---

trust issue. Indeed, the way the judge marshalled these factors virtually directed a verdict for the government.

41

Commission, supra,[58] a secular court is required to accept the distinction between "the religious," on the one hand, and "the economic," "the political," or "the personal," on the other, as *itself* a religious distinction. "[W]hen . . . particular purposes and activities of a religious organization are claimed to be other than religious"—as the New York City Tax Commission had claimed in *Holy Spirit Association* or as the prosecution claimed here—"the civil authorities may engage in but two inquiries":

> Does the religious organization assert that the challenged purposes and activities are religious, and is that assertion bona fide?

55 N.Y.2d at 521. Civil authorities may *not* "go behind the declared content of religious beliefs any more than they may examine into their validity." *Id.* Thus, in *Heritage Village Church v. State*, 299 N.C. 399, 263 S.E.2d 726, 735-36 (1980), the North Carolina Supreme Court—in holding that a religious organization could not be denied a license to solicit charitable contributions on the ground that it devoted an "'unreasonable percentage' of the contributions solicited" to non-charitable purposes—stated:

> Absent narrow circumstances of outright fraud or collusion or other specific illegality, the propriety of a religious organization's expenditures can be evaluated only by reference to the organization's own doctrinal goals and procedures. The question of proper purpose is an ecclesiastical one, and its resolution necessarily entails an interpretive inquiry into possible deviations from religious policy. "But this is exactly the inquiry that the First Amendment prohibits . . . ." *Serbian Orthodox Diocese v. Milivojevich*, 426 U.S. 696, 713 [1976].

Fourth, a secular court is required to recognize that a religion's organizational structure and its approaches to internal governance, no less than its ecclesiastical doctrines, are distinctively religious matters. *Serbian Eastern Orthodox*

---

58   This decision, issued during the course of the trial in this case, was brought to the court's attention during the charging conference. T6132-34.

42

Diocese v. Milivojevich, 426 U.S. at 713, 721-22; *Maryland and Virginia Churches v. Sharpsburg Church*, 396 U.S. 367, 369 (1970) (Brennan, J., concurring); *Kedroff v. St. Nicholas Cathedral*, 344 U.S. 94, 116 (1952). It follows that these matters cannot be probed by a secular court, and that any action that penalizes a religion by virtue of its particular organizational structures or governmental practices violates the First Amendment. *Id.; see also Larson v. Valente*, 102 S.Ct. 1673 (1982); *Heritage Village Church v. State, supra.*

Fifth, a secular court can resolve the type of property issue presented by this case in only one of two ways. The court can adopt the approach of *Watson v. Jones*, 80 U.S. (13 Wall.) 679 (1871), and simply enforce the property decision made within the church's own governing structure. *See Maryland and Virginia Churches v. Sharpsburg Church*, 396 U.S. at 368-69. Or the court can follow a "neutral principles" approach that (a) is "completely secular in operation" and does "not . . . rely on religious precepts"; (b) "accommodate[s] all forms of religious organization and policy" and is not biased against any religious sect; and (c) is flexible enough to allow parties to express their intent with confidence that it will be given effect, and "to ensure that a dispute over the ownership of church property will be resolved in accord with the desires of the members." *Jones v. Wolf*, 443 U.S. 595, 603-04 (1979).

Under these Religion Clause principles, it is clear that the trial court's instructions here were fatally defective.

1. The jury was empowered to decide, on whatever basis it wished, whether various expenditures were "religious."

The government's case against Reverend Moon relied heavily on the notion that he had freely expended certain of the funds at issue for "personal" or "business" purposes,[59] as *opposed to* "religious" purposes, and that the jury could use this "fact" as proof that the funds were not being held by Reverend Moon

---

59   The trial judge incorrectly characterized Reverend Moon's position as one of freedom to use the monies turned over to him "without restrictions." S71; *see* S69-70. In fact, defendant contends that his use of the money *was* subject to restriction—namely, the intent of the donors that it be used only to advance the religion.

43

for the international Unification Church movement. *See, e.g.,*
T2160, 2168, 2171, 6179, 6269-70, 6461-62, 6473-77. But,
because the Religion Clauses require a secular court to view the
distinction between "the religious," on the one hand, and "the
economic" or "the personal," on the other hand, as itself a
constitutionally protected religious distinction, the jury was
bound to accept the Unification faith's *own* definition of what
was religious—unless the government had proved that this
definition was put forth by the Unification Church movement
in bad faith. *See United States v. Ballard, supra; Watson v.
Jones, supra.* Here, since the government never claimed that
the religious doctrine of the Unification Church was *not* held
in good faith, the Religion Clauses required that, in deciding
what was or was not religious, the jury not substitute its own
views—or, for that matter, *any* set of external, secular views—
for those of the Church.

But the instructions contained no such guidance.[60] Having
wrongly charged that, for a trust to exist, the assets had to be
used "for church purposes" (T6584), the judge never advised
the jury that it had to apply the Unification Church's *own* view
of what its purposes were. Accordingly, the trial judge left the
jury free to draw the line between the religious and the

---

60   The trial judge failed to give such guidance despite his acknowledgement that, "although the government seems to want to get away from it," the
fundamental question raised by the case was "whether Moon can simultaneously be a business and a religion" (T5520), and that Church members, in
their own view,

> . . . thought they were working for a higher cause. They thought
> they were advancing the Unification Church's movement interna-
> tionally.
>
> But when you say in effect it doesn't matter what they thought
> they were accomplishing, if he took these monies and spent them on
> his own businesses and on his own goals he was not doing so as a
> religious leader and you come back to the same question, can he
> simultaneously be a businessman and a religion. T5521.

While this was the right *question*, the judge failed to inform the jury that the
answer to that question must be guided solely by the Church's own definition
of what purposes are "religious." *See Holy Spirit Association for the
Unification of World Christianity v. Tax Commission,* discussed at pp. 40-41
supra.

44

non-religious *wherever* and *on whatever basis* it wished—in clear violation of the Religion Clauses.[61]

2. The jury was invited to draw adverse inferences from the Unification Church's organizational structure.

One of the government's principal arguments was that Reverend Moon could not have held the Chase funds and Tong Il stock in trust for the international Unification Church movement because that movement simply did not exist as an "entity." *See, e.g.*, T5516-17, 6488-92. Thus, the prosecution stressed that this movement was neither incorporated nor even an "organization" (T6490), in contrast to other entities within the international Unification Church movement that *were* formally organized. T5516-17, 6489; *see also* T3410-11, 3416, 3760. The government claimed that the jury could infer from this contrast that there *was* no international Unification Church movement at all. But this remarkable argument—according to which the worldwide Catholic, Episcopal, or Methodist Churches, for example, would not "exist"—violated the basic constitutional rule that prohibits a secular tribunal from using secular standards to assess a religion's organizational structure. Indeed, the Religion Clauses required an affirmative instruction to the jury that the structure of the Unification Church or of any of its branches or entities could play *no* role in their deliberations.

But the court not only failed to give such an instruction; it compounded the problem by charging the jury that, in determining whether the movement "existed and whether the [m]ovement owned the [assets]," the jury "should consider . . . such factors" as

> whether the [m]ovement had a specific organizational structure, written charter or constitution, [and] the exist-

_____

61   Even assuming there was a *possibility* that the jury *may* have evaluated the evidence on the basis of suitably neutral principles that respected the integrity of the Unification religion's theological precepts, this would *not* be enough to sustain the jury's verdict. For under the rule of cases such as *Stromberg v. California*, 283 U.S. 359, 368-70 (1931), and *Street v. New York*, 394 U.S. 576, 585-88 (1969), the presumption is entirely the other way. So long as it is possible that the jury *may* have rested its verdict on an *un*constitutional basis, the conviction cannot stand.

45

ence of other Unification Church corporate entities
. . . . T6584.[62]

This instruction was an express invitation to the jury to conduct a flatly unconstitutional inquiry, and to impose a forbidden penalty on the church's organizational structures and practices.[63]

3. The jury was not instructed to consider the religious identity and intentions of the donors nor Reverend Moon's religious position and role.

The trial judge's refusal to charge that a religious trust may be found on the basis of evidence that the assets "came from . . . church sources" and were "intended" by the donors to be used for "Church purposes" (*see* p. 35 & n.52 *supra*) not only flew in the face of trust law (*see* § IV.A *supra*); it also violated the Religion Clauses. As *Jones v. Wolf, supra,* makes clear, those clauses require "neutral principles" flexible enough to allow the parties to express their intent with confidence that it will be given effect, and calculated to "ensure that a dispute over the ownership of church property will be resolved *in accord with the desire of the members.*" 443 U.S. at 603-04 (emphasis added). The instructions here, however, failed to focus the jury's attention on just that issue—"the desire of the members" as reflected in their donative intent.

Moreover, this failure was compounded by the judge's refusal to instruct the jury on Reverend Moon's role in the Unification Church and on the unique place he occupies in its theology. Reverend Moon specifically asked the court to instruct the jury that:

> There is evidence in the case tending to prove that the international Unification Church movement existed as an unincorporated association which was personified by Rev-

---

62   As discussed in § IV.A *supra*, this instruction was also invalid as a matter of trust law because the indefiniteness of a beneficiary cannot defeat a charitable trust.

63   The instruction actually exposed Reverend Moon and his followers to a *double* penalty—a penalty both *for* incorporating some religious entities and for *not* incorporating the global movement as a whole.

46

erend Moon, founder and spiritual leader of the world-wide Unification Church movement, and which supported and directed the activities of the various national church entities in the United States and elsewhere. A1365.[64]

By this refusal, the judge deprived the jury of the basis to understand *why* a reference to Reverend Moon was indeed interchangeable, for those who believe in him, with a reference to the international Unification Church movement itself.

Moreover, this refusal, coupled with the judge's refusal to instruct the jury regarding the significance of the *source* of the assets and of the *intent* with which they were donated, put Reverend Moon in the worst of all possible worlds. For it left the jury free to view the facts totally divorced from their religious context, and indeed to view the facts darkly—through the distorting glass of secularization[65]—as portraying Reverend Moon to be running, in the court's words, a "Fagin-like operation" with "hundreds of people collecting money and turning it over to him." (T4878). The jury was thereby encouraged to see and to declare the assets as belonging not to the Church but to the defendant and his heirs. This was a flat breach of what the donors intended, directly contravening the Religion Clauses, and in effect redistributing those assets in indirect contravention of the Fifth Amendment, *see Terrett v. Taylor*, 13 U.S. (9 Cranch) 43, 51-52 (1815).

---

64   Notwithstanding the limited nature of this request—which does not even refer to the fact that Reverend Moon is regarded as potentially the new Messiah (*see* A1508)—the judge rejected it out of hand, stating:

> . . . I am sure not going to say what Mr. Stillman wants me to say, that the Unification Church International is embodied in its spiritual leader Reverend Sun Myung Moon that makes him a walking unincorporated association. T6119.

65   The Court sounded this theme of secularization at the outset of the charge by stating:

> I have told you before and I repeat it again, that the . . . religion . . . of the defendants is of no consequence whatever . . . . T6538.

While this instruction, taken from the government's requests (A1187), might be appropriate in an ordinary case, it was erroneous here, for Reverend Moon's defense *required* that the jury give consideration to his religious beliefs and those of his followers.

47

D. The Instructions On the Element of Wilfulness Were Clearly Erroneous.

The court's charge on wilfulness (T6590-97) had two fatal defects. *First,* it stated:

> If you find that Moon provided the person who prepared the tax return with full and honest information as to his income and that Moon then adopted, signed and filed the tax returns as prepared in the belief that the return contained the full and honest information he had provided to the preparers regarding income, then you must find defendant Moon not guilty. T6595.

This instruction not only shifted to Reverend Moon a burden of proving certain matters; the particular proof called for by this instruction—proof that he had provided and affirmed *"full and honest information"*—required nothing less than an affirmative showing of his *innocence.* Thus, the instruction imposed on Reverend Moon precisely that burden which the Constitution forbids. *See Mullaney v. Wilbur, supra.*[66]

Second, the judge instructed that "dealing in cash"—a common practice in the Orient—could be considered an act of concealment from which wilfulness could be inferred. T6592. In this context, the court indicated to the jury that it could treat the "deposit by Reverend Moon of some $1.6 million in cash into his Chase accounts" as circumstantial proof of wilfulness. T6593. This instruction, given over defense objection (T6655, 6667), gave to the use of cash a sinister connotation totally unsupported by the record of this case: there was simply no evidence that the deposit of cash in the Chase Manhattan Bank, by Reverend Moon or his followers, was for the purpose of concealment. Nor can the placement of cash into a readily documentable bank account support an inference that concealment was intended. On the contrary, as the Tax Court once observed, one "trying to secretly channel a large sum of foreign income to himself . . . would find a more discreet way of doing so than to openly deposit $241,000 into

---

66   This shift in burden was reinforced by the parallel shift in burden effected by the judge's instructions on beneficial ownership. *See* IV.B *supra.*

48

his own bank account." *Brittingham v. Commissioner,* 57 T.C. 91,101 (1971).

Moreover, this instruction contravened the Religion Clauses by inviting the jury to treat as suspect in itself the Church's practice of soliciting cash contributions from the public—a practice that some jurors had said on voir dire they disapproved, *see* n.33 *supra*—when it should have cautioned the jury *not* to draw any adverse inference on the basis of the Church's fund-raising preferences. *See Larson v. Valente, supra* (church fund-raising cannot be treated less favorably by law simply because over half involves donations by non-members); *Murdock v. Pennsylvania, supra* (church's fund-raising activities cannot be treated as any less protected than its worship and preaching).

V. A DIRECTED ACQUITTAL WAS REQUIRED AS A MATTER OF LAW.

A. The Substantive Tax Offenses.

In order to convict on the substantive tax counts, the jury was required to find beyond a reasonable doubt: (1) that the statements alleged by the government to be untrue were in fact false; and (2) that Reverend Moon filed those false statements "wilfully." The evidence was insufficient to establish either of these elements.

1. The evidence was insufficient as a matter of law to establish that the allegedly false statements on Reverend Moon's tax returns were, in fact, false.

Given the law of charitable trusts and the precepts of the Religion Clauses, none of the evidence, even when viewed most favorably to the government, provided a legally sufficient basis for finding that the Chase funds and the Tong Il stock were beneficially owned by Reverend Moon.

a. Evidence of the use of Reverend Moon's name.

The government's mountain of testimony and documents "showing" the undisputed fact that the assets were held in Reverend Moon's name, without a formal designation of

49

"trustee" or "nominee," and were often referred to as "his" (*see* p. 8 & n.13 *supra*), cannot overcome either the *presumption* or the *evidence* that Reverend Moon held the assets *in trust*. Indeed, such a showing does nothing to undermine the conclusion that the donors intended their contributions to be for religious purposes, or to suggest that the public policy in favor of charitable trusts should be disregarded in this case. This is especially true given (a) the fact that it has long been common practice for religious officials to hold in their own name assets owned beneficially by their churches, and (b) the uncontradicted evidence that Reverend Moon was regarded as the *embodiment* of the international Unification Church movement, so that a reference to "Reverend Moon" was, understandably, interchangeable with a reference to that movement.[67]

Further, in light of these two factors, a finding that the presumption of a trust could be overcome by the undisputed fact that Reverend Moon held the assets in his own name would doubly run afoul of the Constitution. *First*, by effectively denying to the Unification Church the use of a practice recognized and accepted when used by other religions— namely, a religious leader's holding of assets in his own name[68]—such a finding would unconstitutionally discriminate against the Unification Church.[69] *Second*, such a finding would

[67]   Contrary to the government's post-trial suggestion (A1913-14), there is no logical or legal inconsistency between the fact that Reverend Moon is regarded as the *spiritual* embodiment of the international Unification Church movement and the conclusion that he holds property in trust *for* that movement. The government's suggestion not only confuses *spiritual* identity with *legal* identity; it also flies in the face of the extensive precedent cited above (*see* n.49 *supra*) treating church leaders—who are, to varying degrees, considered to embody their faith—as holding assets in trust for their followers.

[68]   *See, e.g.*, N.Y. Relig. Corp. Law § 91 (statutory presumption of trust impressed upon property held by certain designated officials of the Roman Catholic Church "by virtue of their offices").

[69]   *See Larson v. Valente*, 102 S.Ct. at 1683 ("[t]he clearest command of the Establishment Clause is that one religious denomination cannot be officially preferred over another"). And, given the fact that political contri-

50

necessarily rest on an assumption that the belief of the international Unification Church movement that Reverend Moon is its very embodiment is a sham. For only by rejecting this belief—a belief that makes use of Reverend Moon's name the most natural way to speak of the religion itself—can the use of that name be viewed as tending to overcome the trust presumption. But such a rejection, on this record—where there is no proof or even any allegation that this tenet of the Unification faith is insincere—would clearly violate the Religion Clauses. *See United States v. Ballard, supra.*[70]

b. Evidence of Reverend Moon's use of the assets.

The government's extensive evidence, including a plethora of documents and charts drawn to show that Reverend Moon *used* the funds in the Chase accounts for personal disbursements and for investments, simply cannot rebut the existence of a charitable trust, for two major reasons.

First, notwithstanding the government's conclusory *characterization* of these uses as "non-religious," the government introduced absolutely no *evidence* showing that these uses were in fact non-religious from the perspective of the Unification Church—the only constitutionally appropriate perspective (*see* § IV.C *supra*). Without such evidence, the bare—and again undisputed—fact that some cf the Chase funds were used for such items as clothing, medical services, travel and children's school tuition is *not* proof rebutting a religious trust—especially given the tradition of religious leaders using entrusted

---

butions are presumed *not* to be personal income even when they are placed in the candidate's personal bank account (*see* n.54 *supra*), such a finding would also amount to improper discrimination between religious and *non*-religious activity. *See Widmar v. Vincent,* 102 S.Ct. 269, 273-78 (1981).

70   As an adjunct to its emphasis on the use of Reverend Moon's *name,* the government repeatedly "demonstrated" the fact—also undisputed—that Reverend Moon maintained personal administrative control over disposition of the assets. *See* p. 8 & n.13 *supra.* But the *raison d'etre* of a trust is to permit the trustee to exercise administrative control over the trust property; that is indeed *why* legal title is vested in him. Thus, the fact that Reverend Moon exercised such control can hardly count *against* the presumption of a trust.

51

funds for living expenses.[71] Nor, without such evidence, could the bare fact that some of the Chase funds were invested in what might be regarded as conventional business enterprises rebut a religious trust,[72] since just such investments are made by religions of all stripes to help support their work.[73]

Second, even assuming the government had shown that the uses were inconsistent with the donors' intent, such a showing *still* could not rebut the existence of a trust. For the issue of whether a trust has been created depends, as a matter of law, on the donor's intent at the time the trust property is donated; evidence of how a donee later uses the funds cannot be relied upon to support a finding that the assets were *not* impressed with a trust *ab initio*. Indeed the law is clear (*see* § IV.A *supra*) that where a trustee uses a portion of the trust for purposes that exceed its scope, such use does *not* nullify the existence of the trust; *at worst*, such use—*if* contrary to the intent of the donors—would constitute *diversion*, making only those funds that were diverted taxable as income to the trustee, while leaving the trust itself intact.[74]

---

71   The fact that Reverend Moon reported such disbursements from the Chase checking account as income on his 1973 tax return further shows that he treated the Chase funds as the Church's, not as his own.

72   Even if, in a given case, the return on a given investment would have been taxable, that does *not* prove in the slightest that the investment itself was made in a personal rather than a church capacity, but only that taxes would have been payable by the beneficial owner of the investment. On this record, however, there is absolutely no evidence to overcome the presumption that the beneficial owner was the international Unification Church movement, and *not* Reverend Moon in his personal capacity.

73   Moreover, to the extent that there is evidence on the record concerning the purpose with which Reverend Moon expended Chase funds, that evidence shows that virtually all of the Chase expenditures in connection with investment transactions were expressly undertaken for the benefit of, or on behalf of, specific Church-related entities. *See* pp. 10-11 *supra*.

74   Here, the government did *not* proceed on a diversion theory (P99-100; T6662). Nor could it have done so, since there was absolutely no evidence that Reverend Moon's uses of the funds were in fact contrary to the religious intent of the donors.

52

c. Evidence that the international Unification Church movement did not exist as an entity.

Based on the fact that the international Unification Church movement, in contrast to other groupings or associations within the religion, lacked formal corporate status, the government argued that the movement *did not exist* as an "entity" (T5517, T6444, T6475-76, 6489), and hence could not be the beneficiary of a trust. But the underlying premise of this argument—that a charitable trust cannot exist unless the beneficiary is a specific entity—is plainly wrong, for a charitable trust cannot fail by reason of the indefiniteness or uncertainty of the beneficiaries. *See* § IV.A *supra.* Accordingly, the government's argument that the movement simply did not "exist" as an "entity"—an argument that might shock the movement's millions of adherents—was powerless to rebut the trust claim. Moreover, this argument contravened the Religion Clauses by calling upon the jury to draw adverse inference from its lay perception of the organizational structure and practices of the Unification Church. *See* § IV.C(2) *supra.*

d. Evidence of a "cover-up."

The government's evidence of a purported "cover-up" (*see* pp. 13-15 *supra*) was surely the most dramatic part of its case: as the trial judge observed, it was *only* this evidence that transformed a civil tax investigation into a criminal prosecution. T5533. But notwithstanding its dramatic nature and the government's assertion to the contrary (T6112), this evidence could not support a finding that a trust did not exist. For the existence of a charitable trust is an objective matter, established here by evidence of the source of the assets, the intent with which they were entrusted to Reverend Moon, and his position in the Unification Church. Thus, evidence that some members of the Church may have been motivated to conceal certain facts[75] could give rise, at most, to an inference that those members *felt* there was something to conceal—perhaps reflecting their lack of understanding that the assets were held

---

75   As discussed in § V.A(2) and § V.B *infra,* there is absolutely *no* evidence that Reverend Moon participated in, knew of, or connived at *any* of the alleged acts of concealment.

53

in trust as a legal matter despite the absence of formal documents so specifying. Whatever the *subjective* reason for *any* such concealment—assuming *arguendo* that there *was* concealment—it is totally irrelevant to the *objective* issue of whether or not a trust existed *in fact*.

2. The evidence was insufficient as a matter of law to establish that the allegedly false statements on Reverend Moon's tax returns were wilfully made.

"Wilfully," as defined within the context of the substantive offenses here, means that the filing of the statements at issue was done knowing that they were false and with the "evil purpose" of voluntarily and intentionally violating a "known legal duty." *United States v. Pomponio*, 429 U.S. 10, 11-13 (1976); *see United States v. Winston*, 558 F.2d 105, 107-08 (2d Cir. 1977).

The government's proof was insufficient to establish this element with respect to any of the specifications charged.

a. The specifications regarding false income.

To show that Reverend Moon wilfully filed false statements underreporting his income, the government had to prove that he *knew* that he was under a legal duty to report the interest on the Chase funds and receipt of the Tong Il stock as taxable income on his returns.

The government, however, presented *no* evidence that Reverend Moon knew, *subjectively,* that the income stated on his tax returns was false, and the record precludes any *inference* of such knowledge. *First*, Reverend Moon's knowledge of any falsity in his *tax* returns could not be inferred from evidence of his detailed and careful supervision of *business* affairs—supervision the government tried to dramatize as "fanatical" (*see* T5506, 6243, 6295). Indeed the evidence showed, to the contrary, that Reverend Moon was wholly uninvolved in the preparation of his tax returns—which he delegated to others (T3722, 3939, 3958, 4091, 4821, 6508) with whom he had no direct communication on the matter (T4031). *Second*, the fact that Reverend Moon *signed* his tax returns, while perhaps a basis to infer that he knew their *contents,* is *not* a basis to infer

54

that he knew that the contents were *false*. As this Court recognized in *United States v. Ruffin,* 575 F.2d 346, 355 (2d Cir. 1978), there must be, in addition to a taxpayer's signature, *"some additional affirmative act* . . . in furtherance of [the defendant's] intent to defraud the government of taxes before [the jury] could conclude that he knew that the contents of the returns were false."[76] *Third,* even if any proof of later acts of concealment by others were to support an inference of *their* consciousness of falsity, such consciousness could *not* be imputed to Reverend Moon, who was in no way personally implicated in any such concealment (*see* § V.B *infra*).[77]

Nor did the government show that as an *objective* matter, any court was so unlikely to view the assets as held *in trust* by Reverend Moon that Reverend Moon's wilfulness could be *inferred*.[78] Because the matter of Reverend Moon's beneficial ownership—understood in light of the law of charitable trusts and the Religion Clauses (*see* §§ IV.A & IV.C *supra*)—posed

---

76   *See also United States v. Brooksby,* 668 F.2d 1102, 1104 (9th Cir. 1982) (approving jury instruction requiring government to "prove wilfulness by evidence independent of the understatement of income").

77   The government could not fill this vacuum of proof of subjective knowledge with its "similar acts" evidence, which it claimed showed that Reverend Moon's application for permanent resident status was supported by false statements by others regarding his wife's employment prospects. *First,* the evidence does *not* establish that those statements by others were false. The fact that *subsequent* records of the listed employer did not show payment of salary to Mrs. Moon (*see* T6063) does *not* mean that, at the time the statements were made, they did not reflect genuine expectations. *See* A1660-62. *Second,* there was no basis in the evidence—or in the law—to impute "knowledge" of any such false statements to Reverend Moon. *See United States v. Tavoularis,* 515 F.2d 1070 (2d Cir. 1975) (cannot impute knowledge from one conspirator to another); *United States v. Forrest,* 620 F.2d 446 (5th Cir. 1980) (marriage does not support inference of sharing of guilty knowledge). Moreover, the admission of this "similar acts" evidence was itself reversible error. *See* § VI *infra.*

78   As the judge explicitly recognized at the charging conference, "it comes down to . . . whether or not [Reverend Moon's] position that the monies were not his but were the [i]nternational [m]ovement's is *so clearly wrong* that his *wilfulness* in failing to do it constitutes a criminal offense." T5509 (emphasis added).

55

at worst a close issue, the taxability of Reverend Moon's unreported income was *at worst* "uncertain" or "problematical" rather than settled by clear precedent. *United States v. Garber*, 607 F.2d 92, 98-100 (5th Cir. 1979) (en banc).[79] In such circumstances, it is settled that wilfulness *cannot* be found, nor even reached, regardless of the defendant's subjective intent. *Id. See also James v. United States*, 366 U.S. 213, 221-22 (1961); *United States v. Critzer*, 498 F.2d 1160, 1162-64 (4th Cir. 1974); *Kahr v. Commissioner*, 414 F.2d 621 (2d Cir. 1969).[80]

b. The false source specification.

The government's proof also fails on the issue of wilfulness with respect to the false source allegation. There is simply *no* evidence that Reverend Moon—or his tax preparer—ever *intended* to submit *any* false statement about the "source" of the income reported on Reverend Moon's 1973 tax return.

First, the statement the government charged as falsely representing that UCNY was the "source" of that income (*see* A115, T6581-82) does not even *contain* such a representation. The statement—which was attached to the return pursuant to

---

79   Thus even if Reverend Moon's tax returns had contained false statements—which Reverend Moon vigorously disputes (*see* § V.A(1) *supra*)—the most he could be charged with would be an *error of law*. But, as the government conceded at trial (A1227), and as the judge correctly instructed the jury,

> wilfully does not mean inadvertence, carelessness or honest misunderstanding of what the law requires. There is no wilfulness in errors of law, mistakes in fact, or bad judgment. T6602.

Likewise, Reverend Moon's failure to file a tax form 1087 indicating fiduciary status (T4191; *see* T6588-89) could at most signify mere inadvertence or error of law. There was *no* proof that this omission was criminally motivated. Nor may any such motivation be inferred on this record, for the fact that the assets were held openly in bank accounts militates against any finding that this omission was intended to hide income.

80   It would be especially improper to penalize Reverend Moon for failing to guess that a court might forge a "pioneering interpretation" of the law, *see Garber*, 607 F.2d at 100, in deciding the issue of a church leader's beneficial ownership of assets. For this is an issue strongly implicating First Amendment rights (*see* § IV.C *supra*)—an area in which the greatest precision is required to avoid the chill the Constitution forbids. *See Village of Hoffman Estates v. Flipside, Hoffman Estates, Inc.,* 102 S.Ct. 1186, 1193 & n.15 (1982).

56

the direction on line 9 to "[a]ttach Form W-2; if unavailable, attach explanation"—said merely:

> Because the Unification Church was incorporated in New York only in March of 1974 the books were not clearly established and matters such as W-2's were not yet organized. This happened because in general no one in the Unification Church receives any compensation whatsoever, wages and salaries, and the corresponding forms (W-2's) have never been needed. GX800.

This statement, *on its face,* pertains only to *why* no W-2s were attached to the tax return; it makes no reference to "source of income" at all; and it certainly does not identify *UCNY* as the "source."

Second, there is absolutely no evidence that either Reverend Moon—or Tully, who prepared the 1973 tax return—understood that the attachment of this "explanation" as to the "unavailab[ility] of W-2s" could be viewed by anyone as a representation of any sort as to the source of Reverend Moon's income. Indeed, Tully testified—without contradiction—that he was not "trying to fool" the Internal Revenue Service or to "hold back on what [he] was reporting as [Reverend Moon's] income for that year." T4107; *see* T4108. And, although the record does not explain *why* Tully referred to the incorporation of the Unification Church in New York, the answer may well lie in the simple fact that it was the *New York branch* of the Church to which Tully *belonged.*

Third, the record is barren of any suggestion that Reverend Moon was even *aware* of the existence of this "explanation." Tully testified that he did not discuss it with Reverend Moon. T4106. And although a taxpayer's signature is usually an adequate basis to infer knowledge of the contents of a tax return, *see United States v. Ruffin, supra,* in this case all that Reverend Moon *signed* was a *separate form* (RSC-12) in which he adopted the return but which did *not* repeat any of its substantive statements. GX800A; T4085-86.

*   *   *

A finding of insufficiency of evidence on the false source allegation requires at least a new trial on the false amount

57

allegation of Count II—and vice versa—since, under the judge's instructions on this count (*see* T6579-81), it is impossible to say that the jury did not base its finding of guilt on the legally *in*sufficient specification. *United States v. Natelli,* 527 F.2d 311, 325 (2d Cir. 1975), *cert. denied,* 425 U.S. 934 (1976); *see Yates v. United States,* 354 U.S. 298, 311-12 (1957), *Stromberg v. California,* 283 U.S. 359, 367-68 (1931).[81]

B. The Conspiracy Count.

It is settled that a conviction for conspiracy cannot be sustained unless the government establishes, beyond a reasonable doubt, that the defendant knowingly "entered, participated in, or furthered" the conspiracy, *United States v. Cianchetti,* 315 F.2d 584, 587 (2d Cir. 1963), with the "specific intent" to commit the offense or fraud which constitutes its object, *United States v. Cangiano,* 491 F.2d 906, 909 (2d Cir.), *cert. denied,* 419 U.S. 904 (1974).

Here the government charged, in essence, a dual-object conspiracy: a conspiracy, first, to file false statements on Reverend Moon's tax returns; and, second, to cover up that falsity by subsequently submitting additional false statements to the government.[82] But notwithstanding the sheer *quantity* of materials the government introduced against Reverend Moon on the conspiracy charge, much of it through co-conspirator hearsay, the government wholly failed to prove that Reverend Moon "entered, participated in or furthered" a conspiracy with the "specific intent" to commit either object.

---

81   Reverend Moon fully preserved his right to such relief on appeal under *Natelli* (*see* 527 F.2d at 327, 329) by challenging the sufficiency and moving to dismiss each specification separately. T5576-80; *see* T5495-96, 5498; *see also* A1173.

82   Although, as set forth in the indictment, the objects of the conspiracy are described in five separate phases, and although the judge at one point counted three objects (*see* T6557-59), the conspiracy case presented by the government actually collapsed into two phases—a "cheating" phase and a "cover-up" phase. *See, e.g.,* T6297; *see also* T6179, 6181.

58

1. The evidence was insufficient as a matter of law to establish that Reverend Moon engaged in a conspiracy to file false statements on his income tax returns.

As demonstrated above, § V.A(2), the government failed to establish beyond a reasonable doubt that Reverend Moon acted wilfully in filing the statements at issue—and without wilfulness there can be no finding of the intent necessary to establish a conspiracy in this case. *See United States v. Winston,* 558 F.2d at 107-08.

Furthermore, even if one could discern on this record a sufficient basis to permit the substantive tax counts to stand— which defendant submits is legally impermissible—the record is barren of any evidence of an *agreement* with Reverend Moon whereby *anyone* would act unlawfully to file false statements on his tax returns.[83] Indeed, there is *no* evidence that there was even any *contact,* much less conspiratorial conversation, between Reverend Moon and those who prepared his tax returns during the relevant years. *See* pp. 12-13 *supra.* And although the government asked the jury to infer that Mr. Kamiyama had consulted with Reverend Moon about what the returns should contain (T6257, 6272; *see* T5531-32), there is absolutely no *evidence* of such consultations.[84]

2. The evidence was insufficient as a matter of law to establish that Reverend Moon participated in a cover-up conspiracy, especially in light of the principle of *strictissimi juris.*

The only direct evidence of any conspiracy to "cover up" was that provided by former church member Warder, who testified that he, along with Mr. Kamiyama, Runyon and Tully,

---

83   In fact, as the judge specifically recognized, "[a]lmost all the conspiratorial evidence here concerns the cover-up. *There is almost none going toward [the omissions from Reverend Moon's] . . . return[s]."* T5531 (emphasis added).

84   Nor is there a reasonable basis to infer such consultations. Whatever "control" Reverend Moon may have had over financial details in business area, there is no evidence that he had *any* "control" over the contents of his tax returns, and certainly no evidence that he must have consulted with Mr. Kamiyama about those returns.

59

had discussed the "possible" ways that the investigations into Reverend Moon's financial affairs by various government agencies could go, possible "tactics to adopt" toward the IRS investigation, and possible means of concealing information from the government. T5212-15. But Warder did not once implicate Reverend Moon in *any* of these alleged discussions, or in *any* supposed plan to cover up.[85] Indeed, as the trial judge noted, there was no direct evidence that *anyone* conferred with Reverend Moon about how to respond to the investigations. *See* T5531-32.

Nor did the government introduce any circumstantial evidence sufficient to connect Reverend Moon to any cover-up. Most critically, there is *no* evidence suggesting that Reverend Moon knowingly participated in or authorized, or indeed even *knew* about, the activities that were at the heart of the government's charge of a cover-up—namely, the preparation and presentation, first to the accountants, and later to the government, of documents representing the existence of transactions which the government insinuated, but did not prove, had not occurred.[86]

Thus, notwithstanding all the material introduced by the government to suggest that the Japanese "family fund" ledger was fabricated, after the fact, to throw the IRS investigation "off track" (T6208) as to the source of the Chase funds (*see* T2188-89, 6208-12, 6294-96, 6506), *no evidence* linked Reverend Moon to that ledger in any way.

Nor, with one exception, was Reverend Moon linked to any of the loan agreements which the government asserted were

---

85   To the contrary, Warder testified on direct that he had "no" conversations with Reverend Moon relating to the ongoing investigations (T5217; *see* T5213); and he admitted on cross-examination that Reverend Moon had never instructed him to misrepresent the latter's affairs in official inquiries (T5261, 5262, 5266).

86   Although the government tried to suggest that certain activities—in particular Reverend Moon's transfer (after the IRS had commenced its investigation) of Tong Il stock to One-Up Enterprises, Inc., and of Diplomat National Bank stock to Unification Church International, Inc.—also evidenced a cover-up (T5536-39), those transfers did not and could not have concealed Reverend Moon's original ownership of these stocks, and hence obviously could not have furthered an object of "covering up."

60

fabricated for the same purpose. The exception was a loan agreement between Mr. Kamiyama and Reverend Moon, dated November 14, 1973 (GX591A), that was found in the PMM work papers, attached to two loan agreements between Mr. Kamiyama and representatives of overseas branches of the Church. *See* T3773, 4046. Relying on the undisputed—and not necessarily incriminating—fact that *other* loan agreements, including one of the two attached, were backdated (*see* T5372-87, T5403-04, GX760-64), the government asked the jury simply to *infer* that *this* agreement was in fact "phoney" (*see* T6214-16). But the government introduced no evidence about how or why this agreement was created, or when or why Reverend Moon signed it. More importantly, the government introduced no evidence whatsoever that the November 14, 1973, agreement was *false* in any respect. Indeed the amount of the loan corresponded to a contemporaneous Chase deposit. GX31. And no direct evidence relating to the loan agreements established that these agreements did not in fact reflect the actual transactions they purported to memorialize.[87]

Moreover, even if the government's evidence could permit the inference that others had engaged in a "cover-up" conspiracy for the purpose of protecting Reverend Moon from investigation and/or prosecution,[88] there is absolutely no evidence that they did so at *Reverend Moon's behest* or even with his *knowledge*. In an attempt to bridge this gap in its case, the government asked the jury to infer from evidence of Reverend Moon's leadership and supervisory role in Church affairs that no "cover-up" activities *could* have occurred without his personal approval, if not his direct input. *See, e.g.,* T5166-70,

---

87   As the judge instructed the jury, if

the loan documents were simply drawn up and signed at a later time in order to memorialize [earlier] transactions, then [the jury could] draw no adverse inference from the later creation of the documents because this in and of itself would not have been improper. T6642.

88   Thus, Warder testified that he had previously lied under oath because he somehow thought this would "help" Reverend Moon (T5225), and the government, of course, argued that a similar motive prompted all of the alleged cover-up activities. *See, e.g.,* T5192, 5195, 5213, 5539, 6244, 6443.

61

6272, 6295, 6243-45. But to permit Reverend Moon's conviction to rest on any such inference is not only to permit an
improper finding of guilt by association, *see Healy v. James,*
408 U.S. 169, 185-86 (1972); *De Jonge v. Oregon,* 299 U.S.
353, 365 (1937); it is also to violate the doctrine of *strictissimi
juris.* Under that doctrine, which holds that whenever a charge
of criminal conspiracy arises out of group activity protected by
the First Amendment, the sufficiency of the evidence regarding
each defendant's specific intent must be scrutinized "according
to the strictest law," *N.A.A.C.P. v. Claiborne Hardware Co.,*
102 S.Ct. 3409, 3429 (1982) (*citing Noto v. United States,* 367
U.S. 290, 299 (1961)),[89] evidence of Reverend Moon's spiritual
hegemony in the Unification Church could *not* substitute for
evidence of his actual involvement in illegal activity. But
evidence of such involvement is entirely missing from the
record in this case.

**3. Insufficient evidence on either object of the conspiracy
requires reversal and new trial on the other.**

Under the judge's instruction, the jury was required to find
Reverend Moon guilty of only *one* of the objects of the
conspiracy in order to return a guilty verdict on the *entire*
conspiracy. T6559. But since a general verdict was returned on
the conspiracy count, it is impossible to determine whether the
jury found Reverend Moon guilty of a conspiracy to file false
returns or of a conspiracy to cover up that conduct, or both.
Accordingly, if the evidence as to either is insufficient, a new
trial is required on the other. *United States v. Kavazanjian,* 623
F.2d 730 (1st Cir. 1980); *United States v. Dansker,* 537 F.2d 40,
51 (3d Cir. 1976), *cert. denied,* 429 U.S. 1038 (1977). *Cf.
United States v. Natelli, supra.*

---

89   *See also Scales v. United States,* 367 U.S. 203, 232 (1961); *United
States v. Dellinger,* 474 F.2d 340, 392-93 (7th Cir. 1972), *cert. denied,* 410
U.S. 970 (1973); *United States v. Spock,* 416 F.2d 165 (1st Cir. 1969). These
cases make clear that the doctrine of *strictissimi juris* seeks to avoid the
unacceptable risk of imputing criminal intent to a defendant on the basis of
constitutionally protected associational activity rather than for actual
criminal involvement.

62

C. Insufficient Evidence Either on the Substantive Counts or the Conspiracy Count Requires Reversal on the Sufficient Count(s).

1. Effect of dismissal of conspiracy count against Reverend Moon.

As this Court has recognized,

> [A] defendant in a trial in which the conspiracy count has been dismissed is likely to be prejudiced in defending the charges in the substantive counts by evidence, particularly hearsay testimony, which was admissible on the conspiracy count but which could not have been used against him in a separate trial on the substantive counts.

United States v. Branker, 395 F.2d 881, 888 (2d Cir. 1968), *cert. denied*, 393 U.S. 1029 (1969); *see also United States v. Bentvena*, 319 F.2d 916, 955 (2d Cir.), *cert. denied*, 375 U.S. 940 (1963).

Here, not only was Reverend Moon subjected to the admission against him of a mass of evidence, particularly hearsay evidence, pursuant to the conspiracy count, but that evidence was disproportionate to the evidence against Reverend Moon on the substantive counts.[90] It must be assumed, therefore, that the jury's deliberation on the substantive counts against Reverend Moon was substantially affected—if not totally dominated—by its consideration of the conspiracy count. Accordingly, if the conspiracy count against Reverend Moon is dismissed on appeal, then under the law of this Circuit, the substantive counts against him should be reversed as well.[91]

---

90   As the judge observed at the close of the government's case:

There is almost [no evidence] going toward why [Reverend Moon] decided to leave the time deposits out of the income tax return.

*   *   *   *

It is the attempt to cover up and all the shifting around that made this into a criminal tax case. It is subsequent obstruction, if proved, that makes a wilful tax fraud out of an initial failure to declare the time deposits. T5531, 5533.

91   See *United States v. Kelly*, 349 F.2d 720, 758 (2d Cir. 1965), *cert. denied*, 384 U.S. 947 (1966), for the necessity of granting Reverend Moon severance on any retrial of the substantive counts.

63

2. Effect of dismissal of substantive counts against Reverend Moon.

On the record of this case, it must be assumed that, just as the jury's consideration of the substantive counts was affected by its consideration of the conspiracy count, so too the reverse occurred. For the court instructed the jury that proof of the substantive counts constituted "some evidence as to the existence of the conspiracy," and that the jury might

> find it easier to consider the substantive counts first, since they are simpler and your verdict on those counts may but need not necessarily affect your decision as to each defendant on the conspiracy charge. T6553-54.[92]

In light of this instruction, it must be assumed that the jury's determination that Reverend Moon was guilty on the conspiracy count was directly *predicated*, at least in part, on its verdict against Reverend Moon on the substantive counts.

Accordingly, dismissal of any of the substantive counts against Reverend Moon requires reversal on the conspiracy count as well.[93]

VI. THE TRIAL COURT ERRED IN ADMITTING CERTAIN IMMIGRATION DOCUMENTS AS "SIMILAR ACTS" EVIDENCE.

At the close of the defense case, the trial judge decided (T6040), over emphatic defense objection (*see, e.g.*, T6022, 6028-33, 6037, 6040, 6674; *see also* A757), to permit the

---

92 Further, the court observed during the charging conference, "If they [*i.e.*, the jurors] have the sense God gave a goat they will leave the conspiracy count until last." T6113.

93 Additionally, in the event that Mr. Kamiyama's conviction is reversed, either on the conspiracy count or any of the substantive counts against him, Reverend Moon's conviction must also be reversed. This is so particularly given the prejudicial nature of each of the obstruction and the perjury charges against Mr. Kamiyama—that he supposedly submitted false documents and lied to cover up wrongdoing by Reverend Moon—which necessarily spilled over into the jury's deliberations against Reverend Moon himself, and any count of which could well have been indispensable to the jury's conspiracy verdict against Reverend Moon.

64

government to introduce, in its rebuttal case, Reverend and Mrs. Moon's applications for permanent resident status and related documents (GX825, 840; T6062-63) which the government claimed would show that Reverend Moon entered this country on the basis of false statements. The government's theory was that Mrs. Moon's application for permanent resident status fraudulently misrepresented her employment prospects; that Reverend Moon knew of that alleged fraud when he based his application for permanent resident status on his wife's status and on statements by others regarding her employment prospects; and that the evidence therefore demonstrated Reverend Moon's "capability of forming the intent to file false documents with the United States." T6009-12. The government offered and the court agreed to admit the immigration documents as evidence of "similar acts" relevant to Reverend Moon's intent. T6017, 6018, 6060. But the government satisfied neither of the two independent requirements for the admission of similar acts evidence.

First, the government failed to show, as required by Fed. R. Evid. 404(b), that the supposed falsity of immigration statements—which Reverend Moon vigorously disputes were false (*see* n.77 *supra*)—was *relevant* to the issue of Reverend Moon's intent to submit false information regarding his taxes. *See United States v. Figueroa*, 618 F.2d 934, 939 (2d Cir. 1980); *United States v. O'Connor*, 580 F.2d 38, 40 (2d Cir. 1978). The mere fact that both a claimed prior act and the crime charged allegedly involved the submission of false statements is not in itself sufficient to constitute the "close parallel" required to establish the relevance of the prior act to the issue of intent to commit the crime charged. *United States v. Corey*, 566 F.2d 429, 431 (2d Cir. 1977). In *Corey*, where the prior act involved submission of falsified overtime slips to an employer and the crime charged involved submission of falsified purchase receipts also to an employer, the court noted that "the fact that [the defendant] may have deliberately [committed the prior act] hardly proves that he had the knowledge or intent [to commit the crime charged]." *Id.* at 432. And in *United States v. Halper*, 590 F.2d 422, 432 (2d Cir. 1978), the court refused to find evidence of a defendant's submission of false Medicaid

65

invoices "relevant to the question whether [he] knowingly intended to submit a false personal income tax return"—or vice versa. Significantly, in *Halper* the court found lack of relevance even though both situations involved defrauding the government in connection with *financial* matters; here—where one situation involved immigration, the other taxes—the lack of relevance follows *a fortiori*.

Second, apart from the relevance requirement, the government failed to show, as independently required by Fed. R. Evid. 403, that the probative value of the evidence was "*not* . . . substantially outweighed" by its unfair prejudice to the defendant. *See United States v. Figueroa*, 618 F.2d at 939; *United States v. Williams*, 577 F.2d 188, 191 (2d Cir.), *cert. denied*, 439 U.S. 868 (1978). The probative value of the evidence was, at best, extremely low. As in *Corey*, 566 F.2d at 432, the "attenuated similarity" between the claimed prior act and the crime charged—each involving different substantive matters (immigration vs. taxes) and occurring at different times (the signing of the immigration application, in February 1973; the signing of the first tax return close to two years later, in December 1974)—"demonstrates the low probative value of [the claimed prior act] as circumstantial evidence of intent to commit the crime charged." Moreover, the evidence did not establish that the alleged prior act had even *occurred*: not only is the claim of falsity in the immigration statements based on spurious reasoning (*see* n.77 *supra*); there is also no factual or legal basis to find that Reverend Moon *personally knew* of any falsity in those statements and thus did anything *wrong*.

On the other side of the balance, the risk of unfair prejudice from the introduction of the evidence was extremely high. The very subject matter of the alleged prior act—submission of false immigration statements—created a serious risk of spillover from the evidence introduced to show that Reverend Moon's co-defendant, Mr. Kamiyama, had obtained a favorable immigration status for himself and then allegedly misrepresented his actions before the grand jury (*see* T4909-10, 6513). Even more insidiously, the introduction of the alleged prior act diverted the jury's attention away from the tax charges and toward an implicit charge that Reverend Moon had obtained

66

his permanent resident status in this country under false pretenses.[94] Such a diversion was unfairly prejudicial especially because it invited the jury to find what no immigration official or court had ever found, and indeed to find what the government conceded post-trial would be difficult to prove in an immigration proceeding (*see* S184)—namely, that Reverend Moon's entry into this country had been founded on fraud.[95]

In short, the unfair prejudice to Reverend Moon from the immigration evidence so clearly outweighed any arguable probative value that its admission as "similar acts" evidence was reversible error. *United States v. Figueroa, supra.*

VII. REVEREND MOON'S CLAIM OF SELECTIVE PROSECUTION REQUIRED JUDICIAL INQUIRY.

Reverend Moon contended both pre- and post-trial that his prosecution had been motivated by hostility to his religion. A151; 1809. But the trial judge, notwithstanding his explicit recognition that the investigation of Reverend Moon's taxes

---

94   The government played upon this implicit charge in its summation when it invited the jurors, in considering "those INS documents," to ask themselves,

> "Rev. Moon was coming back *for what*? There are a number of stories, that is, versions of why he was coming back." T6226 (emphasis added).

By so arguing, the government directly invited the jury to find that Reverend Moon was "coming back" for some illicit purpose.

95   The "similar acts" evidence was thus used at trial in effect to bootstrap one insufficient case—for fraudulent entry—into another—for tax avoidance. Just as the government tried to use the immigration evidence unfairly to help obtain Reverend Moon's conviction, so it sought to use Reverend Moon's conviction as a basis for his expulsion from the country, either through deportation or exclusion. The government's attempt to bootstrap the conviction into deportation halted when the trial court issued its binding recommendation to the Attorney General disqualifying Reverend Moon's conviction as a basis for his deportation (S190-91), and, shortly thereafter, when the government terminated efforts to exclude Reverend Moon from the United States on the basis of how he had entered. So too, the attempt to bootstrap the alleged immigration fraud into a tax conviction under the rubric of "similar acts" evidence should not have been allowed.

67

would have been less likely if he had been the leader of a less controversial religion (*see* S36-37), denied Reverend Moon's motions for discovery and a hearing on his claim of selective prosecution. *See* P166; S92. This denial was error. For Reverend Moon presented ample grounds for suspecting that the government had indeed singled him out for investigation and/or prosecution on the basis of "such impermissible considerations as race, religion, or the desire to prevent his exercise of Constitutional rights." *See United States v. Berrios*, 501 F.2d 1207, 1211 (2d Cir. 1974).

First, Reverend Moon's post-trial motion set forth a clear basis for suspecting that the original impetus for the prosecution against him was congressional animosity towards his religion. Specifically, Reverend Moon showed that, shortly before the IRS began to investigate him, Senator Robert Dole, then a ranking member of the Senate Finance Committee, had written to the Commissioner of Internal Revenue urging that a tax investigation be targeted at the Unification Church because the Senator suspected the Church of involvement in "mind control and indoctrination" rather than the pursuit of "religious faith,"[96] viewed the Church's faith as involving "political purposes," and regarded the Church's founder as leading a "far more affluent life" than he thought appropriate for a "clergyman." A1816.[97] Such motives, if in fact the basis for the tax prosecution, plainly violated not only Reverend Moon's right to equal treatment under the law, *see Yick Wo v. Hopkins*, 118 U.S. 356 (1886); *see also Oyler v. Boles*, 368

---

96   Even though many mainstream religions demand extreme discipline, austerity, and obedience as manifestations of faith, *see* Ahlstrom, *A Religious History of the American People* 491-509 (1972), similar or even milder demands on the followers of less familiar religions are often condemned as instances of "coercive persuasion" or "mind control." *Cf. Van Schaick v. Church of Scientology of California*, 535 F. Supp. 1125, 1139 (D. Mass. 1982).

97   Reverend Moon similarly showed (A1826) that a congressional subcommittee had investigated the Unification Church—out of motives similar to Senator Dole's but without success—for evidence of wrongdoing. *See Investigation of Korean-American Relations: Report of the Subcommittee on International Organizations of the House Committee on International Relations*, 95th Cong., 2d Sess. 311-90 (Oct. 31, 1978).

68

U.S. 448 (1962), but also his rights to freedom of religion and expression. *See United States v. Berrios*, 501 F.2d at 1209 ("selective prosecution [must not] become a weapon used to discipline [the] political foe and the dissident").[98]

Second, the very fact that the government decided to return the indictment against Reverend Moon at a time when it knew he was traveling abroad (*see* S162)—and knew therefore that he might be tempted to *remain* abroad rather than to return to this country to face trial—provides a basis to suspect that the motive for the prosecution was, from the outset, to rid the country of an unpopular religious leader. *Cf. Unification Church v. Immigration and Naturalization Service, supra* (reversing government decision to refuse entry to Unification Church missionaries). Moreover, this suspicion was reinforced by the government's inclusion in its case of a claim that Reverend Moon's immigration into this country had been founded on fraud (*see* § VI *supra*), and by its attempt to use the conviction obtained in part on that evidence as a basis for expelling Reverend Moon from the country even while acknowledging that its fraud claim would not be easy to sustain in an immigration proceeding. Surely it is impermissible for the government to use a criminal tax prosecution to circumvent obstacles to some otherwise unobtainable end, such as exclusion or deportation. *See* n.95 *supra*.

Third, the way the government chose to try its case in itself provides grounds for suspecting *pre*-trial prosecutorial bias. Specifically, as Reverend Moon pointed out to the court in his post-trial motion (A1828-29), the government evinced sharp hostility to Reverend Moon and his religion when it denied consent to his request for a bench trial in retaliation for his speech criticizing the prosecution (*see* § I *supra*), and when it injected religious innuendo into the trial to play upon any juror willingness to mistrust unorthodoxy (*see* § II.C *supra*).

Fourth, Reverend Moon's post-trial motion sets forth a clear showing that *others* have engaged in comparable conduct

---

98   *See also United States v. Falk*, 479 F.2d 616, 620 (7th Cir. 1973) (en banc); *United States v. Steele,* 461 F.2d 1148, 1152 (9th Cir. 1972); *United States v. Crowthers,* 456 F.2d 1074, 1079 (4th Cir. 1972); *United States v. Wayte,* Cr. No. 82-630, slip. op. (C.D. Cal. Nov. 15, 1982).

69

without being prosecuted. *See United States v. Berrios,* 501 F.2d at 1211. Specifically, Reverend Moon submitted evidence that officials and ministers of other churches hold church funds in accounts in their own names, and have discretion to spend such funds on some of their personal needs on as well as the needs of their churches, but have never been required to pay income taxes on the interest accrued on the corpus of such accounts nor been prosecuted for not doing so. *See* A1813-15, 1817-18b.[99]

Yet despite this showing of more than "some evidence," *Berrios,* 501 F.2d at 1211, to furnish grounds to suspect that his prosecution was in fact persecution, Reverend Moon was flatly denied even the most minimal discovery on his claim. Plainly Reverend Moon should, at the very least, have been granted disclosure of government documents or other information that could have permitted him to explore the link between Senator Dole's exhortations and the ensuing tax prosecution, and otherwise to probe the prosecution's motives in a full adversary hearing.

VIII. THE POST-TRIAL INQUIRY INTO IMPROPER INFLUENCES ON THE JURY WAS ERRONEOUSLY CUT OFF.

The judge's decision to conduct a post-trial jury inquiry was based on his recognition that, under *United States v. Moten,* 582 F.2d 654, 664 (2d Cir. 1978), "jury inquiry is necessary whenever 'reasonable grounds exist' to believe that the jury may [have] be[en] exposed to 'extraneous influence.' " A2055. Such grounds, the judge found (*id.*), were provided by information the defendants had brought to his attention—information suggesting that inflammatory, extra-record charges and

---

99   Such a showing of *objective* evidence that one was singled out from comparable others for prosecution should not even be necessary where, as here, one has shown evidence of *subjective* intent on the part of the government to single one out. *Cf. Arlington Heights v. Metropolitan Housing Corp.,* 429 U.S. 252, 265-66 & n.14 (1977) ("a single invidiously discriminating governmental act . . . [is] not immunized by the absence [of proof] of such discrimination in the making of other comparable decisions").

70

suspicions concerning Reverend Moon and his Church may have been injected into the jury room. *See* A1962.[100]

After hearing testimony from only three of the jurors—Virginia Steward (S463), forelady Mary Nimmo (S572), and John McGrath (S626)[101]—the judge abruptly terminated the inquiry, denying defense requests to ask further questions, to call additional jurors to testify, and to grant a new trial based on the testimony already given. S659, 665. Stating that he found Steward "not . . . particularly credible," that he found Nimmo, who had in certain respects contradicted Steward, "credible," and that he found McGrath neither to have corroborated Steward nor to have impeached Nimmo "in any material respect," the judge declared, "I think these proceedings have gone far enough, and I do not propose to call any further witnesses." S659. In a memorandum accompanying a subsequently issued order (*see* § IX *infra*), the judge attempted to discount even "the credible evidence" as having "established . . . no basis for the proceedings." A2145.

But the judge's decision to cut off the inquiry and to deny defendants all relief was error. For the testimony of the three jurors did not *eliminate* "reasonable grounds" to believe that the jury may have been exposed to "extraneous influence." On the contrary, *undisputed facts* which emerged from that testimony *confirmed* that the jury had indeed been exposed to just such influence.

---

100   This information had been presented, unsolicited, to a Unification Church member by one Bruce Romanoff, who had obtained tape recordings of two post-trial telephone conversations between an associate of his, John Curry, and a member of the jury with whom Curry was personally acquainted, Virginia Steward. In these taped conversations, Steward told Curry: (a) that the forelady, Mary Nimmo, had stated to other jurors that Reverend Moon "brainwashes" young people and "twists their minds" (A2078-79), and that one of Reverend Moon's children was a "troublemaker" at school (A2082); (b) that another juror, Esperanza Torres, had been "scared" during the trial after "somebody shot a B.B. through her window" and "somebody hit her car from behind," and had stated that she thought these incidents might have been messages from "somebody" who wanted to influence her verdict (A2080); and (c) that newspapers had openly been brought into the jury room (A2081).

101   Prior to hearing the three jurors, the judge called to the stand both Bruce Romanoff and John Curry. S270, 352.

71

First, the undisputed testimony of all three jurors revealed jury exposure to press coverage of the case—press coverage the judge had specifically instructed the jury to avoid (*see, e.g.,* T68-70, 261, 1386, 2154-55).[102] Moreover, all three jurors admitted hearing about and *discussing* with other jurors *in the jury room* one particular newspaper article about the case that was especially prejudicial to the defendants (S512-13, 525-26, 582-84, 628)—a *New York Daily News* article entitled "MOON JUDGE HOPES JURORS SEE THE LIGHT." That article, published on April 1, 1982—the opening day of trial—reported that the judge doubted whether the jury was "smart enough to understand the case," and that he therefore "would have preferred to try the case *without a jury, as Moon had requested*" (emphasis added).[103] The jurors testified not only that they thought that this article had tagged them "dummies," "not a very bright bunch" (*see* S513, 582); but also that forelady Nimmo had been quite indignant about the article, and had reported her daughter's desire to write a letter telling the judge that *her* mother was no "dummy" (*see id; see also* S513-14, 583, 643).

In the face of this evidence, it was error to block defense efforts to find out to what extent the jurors had discussed Reverend Moon's request not to be tried by a jury, as reported in the "dummies" article. *See* S645; A2034-35. Moreover, it was error to refuse to call any other jurors to explore "the entire picture" surrounding newspapers in the jury room. *United States v. Moten,* 582 F.2d at 667; *see Remmer v. United States,* 350 U.S. 377, 379-80 (1956).

Second, the undisputed fact emerged from the testimony that one of the jurors had reported believing that she had been

---

102   All three jurors testified that there were newspapers *in the jury room* (*see* S512-13, 582-83, 646-47). McGrath testified uncontradictedly that these newspapers contained articles "*about the case*" (S646) (emphasis added); and when asked, none of the three could rule out the possibility that other jurors had read and/or discussed the contents of these articles (*see* S512-13, 582-83, 646-47).

103   That same morning, a defense request for a poll of the jurors to determine if any had read or heard about the article was flatly denied. T2050-52.

72

the target of intimidation efforts by the defense. Specifically, both Steward *and* Nimmo testified, uncontradicted by Mc-Grath, that juror Esperanza Torres had reported to her fellow jurors that during the trial she had been *shot at* through a window of her home. S517-20, 586-88; *see* T629-30. Moreover, Steward, uncontradicted by Nimmo or McGrath, testified that Torres had announced to the other jurors that she suspected that the source of the shots "might be one of *Reverend Moon's people* trying to get to the jury." S520 (emphasis added).

Faced with this evidence, the judge surely was required to explore "the entire picture" surrounding the shooting incident. Few extra-record "facts" could be so prejudicial, *see United States ex rel. Owen v. McMann,* 435 F.2d 813, 818 n.5 (2d Cir. 1970), *cert. denied,* 402 U.S. 906 (1971), as the supposed "fact" that a defendant's "people" had tried to intimidate a juror. *See United States v. Gersh,* 328 F.2d 460 (2d Cir.), *cert. denied,* 377 U.S. 992 (1964) (post-verdict jury inquiry is required, absent specific defense waiver, when a juror reports receipt of anonymous telephone calls during trial). The risk of prejudice is especially great when the alleged means of intimidation are violent and, in contrast to what occurred in *Gersh,* the threatened juror overtly "connect[s] [the threatening incidents] with the defendants." *See* 328 F.2d at 463. Because a defendant is entitled to a trial at which *not even one juror* is prejudiced by extraneous information, *see United States v. Rattenni,* 480 F.2d 195, 198 (2d Cir. 1973), it was clearly necessary at the very least to call *Torres* to the stand. But the judge "flatly and unequivocally" refused to do even that. S597-99.

In short, even though these two lines of undisputed evidence plainly laid the basis for further inquiry, if not for a new trial, they were utterly ignored by the judge in his ruling. Faced with such a stark sketch of extraneous influences—upon jurors with the preconceptions known to exist here (*see* n.33 *supra*)—the court was manifestly obligated, at the very least, to explore "the entire picture."

73

IX. THE TRIAL COURT'S SWEEPINGLY BROAD GAG ORDER ABRIDGED THE FREEDOMS OF SPEECH AND PRESS.

After the court cut off the jury inquiry, the government proposed a sweeping gag order restraining the parties and their attorneys and agents, on pain of contempt, from *"communicating with*, or contacting *in any manner whatsoever*," any actual, alternate, or prospective juror involved in the case without the prior consent of the court. A2142 (emphasis added). In opposing that order, defendants objected particularly to the *breadth* of its restraint, arguing that it could chill even the release to the press of information and opinion bearing on the questions of bias by, or improper influences on, the jury that sat on this case. *See* A2133. The trial court, however, issued the gag order precisely as the government had proposed it, without in any way narrowing it to limit its chill. *Compare* A2142 *with* A2068.

The trial court's memorandum accompanying the order removed any uncertainty that the order was indeed intended to chill communications to the news media—even if issued by those related to Reverend Moon simply as members of the worldwide Unification Church. For the judge based his order in part on a Unification Church press release—submitted to him by the government (A2115-16)—which he called a "distorted and incomplete" account of the jury inquiry. A2146. Although the press release was issued not by Reverend Moon but by HSA, was issued only after the proceedings had officially been ended and unsealed, and was transmitted only through ordinary media channels, the judge opined that the release "virtually invited other jurors to respond with any information that might help impeach the jury's verdict" (A2146 n.3), and so helped to support a "finding of clear and present danger to the administration of justice" (A2145).

Given this gloss on its meaning, the gag order (a) must be read as directed to all members of the Unification Churches around the world and of any organization deemed by the government to bear some connection with Reverend Moon, and (b) must be understood as imposing not simply a narrow bar on juror interviews without court permission, but rather a

74

prior restraint even against use of the press or other media on any subject related to jury prejudice in this case.

The order thus plainly violates the First Amendment. For whatever power a court might have to restrain the participants in a judicial proceeding from direct post-trial contact with jurors (see A2144-45), there can be no doubt that a gag imposed upon so many,[104] and covering virtually all discussion that might be construed as in any way encouraging former jurors to come forward, contravenes the "heavy presumption" the First Amendment imposes against prior restraint. *New York Times Co. v. United States,* 403 U.S. 713, 714 (1971) (per curiam); *Near v. Minnesota,* 283 U.S. 697 (1931); *see Nebraska Press Association v. Stuart,* 427 U.S. 539 (1976).[105]

The prior restraint here is particularly improper because triggered in part by a constitutionally protected communication. Just as Reverend Moon was penalized on the eve of his trial by being compelled to face *jury* trial because he had publicly criticized the government's conduct (see § 1 *supra*), so Reverend Moon, and all who are affiliated with him in his religious mission or otherwise, have been penalized *after* the trial by a gag order issued in part because they had dared to inform the public about a jury inquiry they thought inade-

---

104　The government claim that the very virtue of the order is its vast reach, embracing a cast of "thousands of agents" (see A2124), is hardly consistent with the well-established requirement that "[a]n order issued in the area of First Amendment rights must be couched in the narrowest terms." *Carroll v. President & Commissioners of Princess Anne,* 393 U.S. 175, 183 (1968). *See also Shelton v. Tucker,* 364 U.S. 479, 488 (1960).

105　A prior restraint creates a higher risk for would-be speakers than does a threat of subsequent punishment. For while one about to be penalized for having made some out-of-court communication may successfully assert as a defense that his speech was in fact protected by the First Amendment, *see, e.g., Landmark Communications, Inc. v. Virginia,* 435 U.S. 829 (1978); *Wood v. Georgia, supra; Craig v. Harney, supra; Pennekamp v. Florida, supra; Bridges v. California, supra,* one bound in advance by a restraining order not to make certain communications cannot assert the order's substantive invalidity as a defense to his disobeying it, *see Walker v. City of Birmingham,* 388 U.S. 307 (1967). So long as the gag order at issue here stands, Reverend Moon and his followers must, on pain of civil and criminal contempt, avoid—or at least severely censor—all further exercises of their freedoms of speech and press on the broad subject of jury prejudice in this case.

75

quate. An order in such clear contravention of the First Amendment must be dissolved.

CONCLUSION

Reverend Moon is entitled to reversal of his conviction and entry of a directed judgment of acquittal because the evidence against him was constitutionally insufficient (§ V).

Failing that, Reverend Moon is entitled to a new trial on the basis of any and all of the grounds advanced in §§ I, II, III, IV, and VI. In addition, Reverend Moon is entitled to dismissal of the indictment, or at least to discovery and a hearing, on his claim of selective prosecution (§ VII); to a new trial or, at least to further inquiry, on his claim of improper influence on the jury (§ VIII); and to dissolution of the gag order insofar as it bars public discussion of juror prejudice in this case (§ IX). Finally, Reverend Moon is entitled to reversal or a new trial if on any of the grounds raised by Mr. Kamiyama—all of which Reverend Moon incorporates by reference, Fed. R. App. P. 28(i)—Mr. Kamiyama's conviction is reversed.

Respectfully submitted,

LAURENCE H. TRIBE
1525 Massachusetts Avenue
Cambridge, Mass. 02138
(617) 495-1767

CHARLES A. STILLMAN
STILLMAN, FRIEDMAN &
  SHAW, P.C.
521 Fifth Avenue
New York, New York 10175

JEANNE BAKER
DAVID J. FINE
BAKER & FINE
133 Mt. Auburn Street
Cambridge, Mass. 02138

BERNARD S. BAILOR
CAPLIN & DRYSDALE, Chartered
1101 Seventeenth Street, N.W.
Washington, D.C. 20036

Counsel for Appellant Sun Myung Moon

November 30, 1982

Petition for Rehearing and Suggestion for Rehearing En Banc of Appellant Sun Myung Moon

TABLE OF CONTENTS

ii

iii

TABLE OF AUTHORITIES

iv

v

INTRODUCTION

Even the majority of the split panel that affirmed Reverend Moon's conviction recognized that the defense has raised "troubling issues of religious persecution and abridgment of free speech." Op.[1]6373-74.[2] Because the panel's resolution of these issues is no less troubling, plenary reconsideration is required.

I. THE MAJORITY GRAVELY MISREADS CONTROLLING STATE LAW ON WHO OWNS, FOR FEDERAL TAX PURPOSES, PROPERTY ENTRUSTED TO A RELIGIOUS LEADER BY HIS FOLLOWERS.

The majority rejects defendant's challenge to the trust law instructions, reasoning that the trial court erred in deeming the evidence sufficient to require it to charge on the trust issues at all, and that the instructions given were correct. Op.6392. Judge Oakes' dissenting opinion cogently refutes the majority on both points, and is a compelling argument in itself for rehearing this important case *en banc. See also* MB 31-39; MRB 35-41. Only the following need be stated here.

First, the majority concedes that there was indeed evidence that several donors "gave money to Moon, intending it as a donation to their church." Op.6393; *see also* Op.6395 (conceding testimonial evidence "establishing that a charitable *gift* had been made *to the Church*" (emphasis added)). But, under New York law, evidence that funds were given to a religious leader as a *gift for his church* is in itself evidence that the funds were given *in trust for that church.* For, if *no* trust restrictions were

---

1   "Op." refers to the panel's slip opinion, filed September 13, 1983. Reverend Moon's opening brief will be referred to as "MB," the government's brief as "GB," and Reverend Moon's reply brief as "MRB." For form of Appendix cites, *see* MB 2 n.1.

2   Those issues prompted the filing in this Court of amicus briefs on behalf of the New York and American Civil Liberties Unions, the Christian Legal Society, and a group of churches with an aggregate membership of over forty million.

2

implied in such a gift, the leader would be free to use the funds for non-church purposes, defeating the intent of the donors.[3] Accordingly, the presence of *any* evidence of such a gift sufficed to require that trust instructions be given—especially since, as the majority also concedes, Op.6392-93, the burden of proof on beneficial ownership rests on the government.[4]

Second, the need to give such instructions in the form recognized in Judge Oakes' dissent, *see* Op.6439-44, likewise follows from the basic proposition that, regardless of formalities,[5] New York law seeks to prevent the intent of charitable donors from being defeated by faithless recipients. No one who has ever made a charitable donation would have it otherwise.[6]

---

3   *See, e.g., In re Durbrow's Estate*, 245 N.Y. 469, 477, 157 N.E. 747, 749 (1927) ("A trust is almost inseparably involved with a gift for charitable uses"); *In re Brundett's Estate*, 87 N.Y.S.2d 851, 852 (1940) ("Every gift to a charitable organization for a charitable purpose involves a trust in the real sense of the word"), and discussion at MB 32-33 n.49, MRB 40 n.64.

4   The majority further concedes that, since beneficial ownership was an "element of the crime charged," Op.6393, Reverend Moon's trusteeship of the assets would not be an affirmative defense on which *he* could have been required to bear a burden of persuasion, *id.* Therefore, apart from the errors of state trust law in the instructions, it was federal constitutional error to impose any such burden on Reverend Moon. *Mullaney v. Wilbur*, 421 U.S. 684 (1975); *In re Winship*, 397 U.S. 358 (1970). But as Reverend Moon demonstrated, *see* MB 31-39; MRB 41-42, the instructions on beneficial ownership did just that, leaving the jury free to convict Reverend Moon unless he convinced them that the "essentials of a trust," *see* MB 39 n.56, were present. Thus "the burden of proof improperly placed upon the defendants was made heavy indeed." Op.6443-44 (Oakes, J., dissenting).

5   As Scott put it, "[c]ertainly, *in New York* a charitable trust may be created although the gift is not expressly stated to be in trust." IV A.W. Scott, *The Law of Trusts*, § 397.2 at 3042 (3d ed. 1967) (emphasis added). Thus the majority is wrong to place dispositive weight on the fact that the donors "never mentioned the word 'trust' or, more importantly, gave any indication that they intended to create a trust relationship." *See* Op.6393. In fact, neither the use of the word "trust" (*see* dissent, Op.6441 n.4), nor contemplation of a formal, ongoing trust relationship, is necessary to the creation of a charitable trust.

6   The panel never addresses defendant's argument, *see* MRB 20 n.31, that, even absent direct evidence of intent, the law imposes a *resulting trust* if

3

Third, the panel's very division on the principles of New York trust law that all concede lie at the heart of this case underscores the compelling need for rehearing *en banc*. As Justice Frankfurter observed long ago, "no matter how seasoned the judgment of [a federal judge] may be [on state law], it cannot escape being a forecast rather than a determination." *Railroad Commission of Texas v. Pullman Co.*, 312 U.S. 496, 499 (1941). The defendant who is sued *civilly* in federal court at least has the choice of seeking abstention under *Pullman* on state-law questions. But since the state-law question here is wrapped in a federal criminal prosecution, the defendant here has no such choice—unless the Second Circuit should conclude that, despite the absence of a statutory certification procedure expressly open to federal courts, the views of New York's highest state court may be sought by the circuit court in aid of its jurisdiction.[7] Given that absence of choice, the accused should *at least* be entitled to more than a mere forecast by a closely divided federal panel on a state-law matter that could mean his imprisonment. Fairness to the defendant, and fair respect for values of federalism, require that the panel's decision be reconsidered *en banc*,[8] especially since

---

the "circumstances . . . raise an inference that [the donors did] not intend that the person taking or holding the property should have the beneficial interest therein. . . ." II Restatement (Second) of Trusts § 404 at 322.

7   It is by no means clear that a state appellate court that may decide a question of law on certification from a lower *state* appellate court, N.Y. Const., Art VI, § 3(b)(4), could properly disregard an analogous question put to it by a *federal* appellate court that found itself unable authoritatively to answer that question. *Cf. Testa v. Katt*, 330 U.S. 386 (1947) (the Supremacy Clause requires a state court to assume jurisdiction of federal claims analogous to state claims that the court would willingly entertain). Nor is there any reason why *Pullman* abstention should be limited to *civil* litigation.

8   The inherent difficulty of the state law question at issue here also calls into question the sufficiency of the evidence of willfulness. If, as the split decision of the panel confirms, the state-law standards regarding beneficial ownership are difficult and unsettled, then the taxability of the assets is inherently problematic. In such circumstances, the Fifth Circuit in *United States v. Garber*, 607 F.2d 92, 98-100 (1979) (*en banc*), has ruled that, *as a matter of law*, willfulness cannot be established *regardless* of the

4

disagreement over the issue of beneficial ownership—the issue of who owns church property, a religious leader or his flock— inevitably impinges in this case on the exercise of religious liberty. Neither religious donors nor religious leaders should have to hazard a guess, on pain of criminal prosecution, as to the ownership and taxability of religious contributions.

II. MISCONCEIVING DEFENDANT'S FIRST AMEND-MENT ARGUMENTS, THE PANEL'S DECISION PLACES FEDERAL TAX PROSECUTIONS IN THIS CIRCUIT ABOVE THE RELIGION CLAUSES.

The panel repeatedly concedes that "the critical issue" in this case is an issue of property—whether the assets in question were owned by Reverend Moon or by the Unification Church movement. *See* Op.6376, 6379 n.1, 6413. But there is no *special* law of property for federal tax purposes. As both the majority and dissenting opinions recognize, Op.6393, 6436, "federal income tax liability follows ownership . . . [and] [i]n the determination of ownership, state law controls." *United States v. Mitchell*, 403 U.S. 190, 197 (1971). And, of course, whenever state property law determines *who* owns *what* in a religious community, it must do so within established Religion Clause constraints—constraints that limit the jury charge in criminal cases, *see United States v. Ballard*, 322 U.S. 78 (1944), no less than in civil. At least three such constraints were flouted here.

First, intra-church property disputes must be decided in accord with "neutral principles" calculated to "ensure that

defendant's subjective beliefs regarding taxability. *Cf. Harlow v. Fitzgerald*, 102 S.Ct. 2727, 2738-39 (1982) (absent "clearly established" prior law, even *civil* liability cannot be imposed on government officials, whatever their subjective beliefs may have been); *see also United States v. James*, 366 U.S. 213, 221-22 (1961). In *United States v. Ingredient Technology Corp.*, 698 F.2d 88, 97 (2d Cir.), *cert. denied*, 103 S.Ct. 3111 (1983), a panel of this Court refused to follow *Garber*. The conflict between the Fifth Circuit's *en banc* decision in *Garber*, and this Court's decisions here and in *Ingredient Technology*, presents a further compelling reason for rehearing *en banc*, especially warranted in this case to consider the chilling effects of uncertainty in a First Amendment context. *See* MB 55 n.80.

5

[the] dispute . . . will be resolved in accord with the desires of the members." *Jones v. Wolf*, 443 U.S. 595, 604 (1979); *see* MB 42, 45. Yet the panel concedes that, under the instructions here, the donors' intent was but one of *many* factors that the jury was left free to consider or not, as the jury saw fit. *See* Op.6396 (stating that all of the factors charged to the jury "were equally relevant to the jury's determination").[9] Thus, the jury was invited to ignore what even the majority recognized as the "testimony of three witnesses establishing that charitable *gifts* had been made *to the Church*." Op.6395 (emphasis added). *See also* T5521 (recognition by trial court that assets had been given to Reverend Moon "for a higher cause," by church members who "thought they were advancing the Unification Church's movement internationally").

Second, legal decisions turning on which uses of property advance the purposes of a religious body must be made on the basis of the religion's own criteria. *Holy Spirit Association v. Tax Commission*, 55 N.Y.2d 512 (1982); *see* MB 40-41, 42-44. Yet the panel implicitly acknowledges that the jury was left free to decide that a particular use of the property was not religious—and thus that the property was not church-owned— simply on the basis that the *jury* regarded the use as serving merely "business . . . or personal ends." Op.6398. The instructions thus permitted the jury wholly to disregard evidence that, from the *religion's* point of view, the uses in question were calculated to advance its cause.[10]

---

9   As Judge Oakes states in his dissent, "[t]he instruction as given allowed the jury to find against Moon on the issue of beneficial ownership without even considering the crucial issue of donors' intent." Op.6440.

10   The panel radically misstates defendant's argument when it says that "[u]nder the definition now advanced as the Church's, *any use* of these funds by Reverend Moon was for religious purposes." Op.6398 (emphasis in original). Reverend Moon has *never* claimed or suggested that *any* use of funds by him was *ipso facto* a religious use; his objection to the instructions is *not* that they permitted the jury to *distinguish* between religious and personal uses, but that they permitted the jury to do so *on whatever basis it wished*—without any regard whatever to the tenets or purposes of the Unification faith.

6

Third, because a religion's choices of organizational structures and practices are themselves religious matters, a religion cannot be penalized for those choices. *Serbian Eastern Orthodox Diocese v. Milivojevich,* 426 U.S. 696, 713, 721-22 (1976); *see* MB 41-42, 44-45; MRB 44. Yet the trial court listed as the very first factors the jury "should consider" in determining who owned the assets (a) "whether the Movement had a specific organizational structure . . . ," and (b) whether "other Unification Church corporate entities" existed. *See* Op.6438. This instruction clearly authorized inferences adverse to Reverend Moon based on the organizational choices of his religion.[11]

It follows from these three errors that the jury was unconstitutionally charged and the conviction must be reversed, *see* *Stromberg v. California*, 283 U.S. 359, 368-70 (1931); MB 44 n.61—unless the Religion Clauses are actually held to be *inapplicable* to this case. Astonishingly enough, that is precisely what the panel held, saying that the Religion Clause precedents *do not apply* "in a federal criminal tax prosecution." Op.6400; *see also id.* 6401 ("doctrine" of *Jones v. Wolf* "has no application").

It is difficult to fathom a basis for this extraordinary *ipse dixit*.[12] Perhaps it is the product of an unstated—and plainly erroneous—premise that, in federal income tax prosecutions, the Religion Clauses can be relevant, if at all, *only* by creating all-or-nothing immunity from tax liability. Why *else* would the

---

11   Nor, contrary to the majority's view, Op.6395-96, 6401 n.5, was this instruction cured by the later instruction that a movement *may* beneficially own property even if *not* incorporated. For an instruction permitting the jury to penalize the accused because of his religion surely cannot be cured by another instruction adding the qualification that the jury may also acquit the accused *despite* his religious affiliation.

12   Any such rule would impermissibly discriminate against religion. *See* MB 36-37 n.54, 49-50 n.69. *Cf. Minneapolis Star & Tribune v. Minnesota Commissioner of Revenue*, 103 S.Ct. 1365, 1372, 1376 (1983) (even without "[i]llicit . . . intent", singling out the press for "special tax" rules is impermissible). And, in any event, no such rule could be applied retroactively. *See Marks v. United States*, 430 U.S. 188, 196 (1977) (requirement of "fair warning" must be enforced with "special care" whenever case "implicates First Amendment values").

7

panel ignore Reverend Moon's claim that the Religion Clauses were breached by the *criteria* the jury was allowed to apply, and, instead, incorrectly attribute to Reverend Moon the claim that, "[s]ince the Unification Church movement can owe no taxes on income derived from church-related activities . . . . neither can Reverend Moon"? Op.6400. *No such claim has ever been made in this case.* In fact, as the trial court instructed the jury, *see* T6583, with the defendant's approval, T6117, nothing depends here upon whether the Church movement would *itself* owe income tax on the assets. Reverend Moon's position has always been that *his* lack of tax liability flows solely from the fact that *he* did not beneficially own the assets; the *movement* did.[13]

It bears emphasis that Reverend Moon's arguments under the Religion Clauses spring *not* from any claim of exemption from tax liability because of religion but rather from the simple propositions (a) that property ownership is a *constant,* and (b) that federal tax prosecutions turning on *who* owns *what* are as subject to *constitutional limits on resolution of property issues* as are all other governmental proceedings.[14] In its mistaken concern that Reverend Moon's instruction arguments would

---

13   The panel mistakenly suggests that, because "Moon personifies the church movement," he claims to be "indistinguishable from it." Op.6400. On the contrary, the only relevance of the fact that, in Unification theology, Reverend Moon is the "*spiritual* embodiment" of his faith, is "that a reference to 'Reverend Moon' [in describing various assets] was, understandably, interchangeable with a reference to that movement," MB 49 & n.67.

14   It would be absurd, and chaotic for tax planning and administration, for the law to say that an accused owns various assets for federal tax purposes, but that a religious body owns those same assets for such other purposes as state tax collection or inheritance by the accused's heirs. Yet such absurdity is precisely what the panel's ruling invites. Under that ruling, for example, it would seem that the "furnishings" purchased for East Garden from the Chase accounts, *see* Op.6383, belong to Reverend Moon and his heirs for federal income tax purposes but could well belong to the church for state tax purposes. To whom do they belong for purposes of inheritance law? For purposes of federal and state estate taxation? For purposes of debtor-creditor relations?

8

allow religious leaders to put themselves above federal tax law, Op.6401, the panel ends up adopting a rule that puts federal tax prosecutions in the Second Circuit outside the law of property and above the First Amendment.[15] Surely the Second Circuit cannot permit so extraordinary a holding to stand unreviewed.

---

15   In rejecting Reverend Moon's selective prosecution claim, the panel similarly puts federal tax *audits* above the First Amendment. For the panel finds no basis for holding that the Religion Clauses were violated here *even if*, as the trial court "acknowledg[ed]," Reverend Moon was singled out for tax audit because of his "status as a highly visible, religious leader." Op. 6405; *see also* MB 67.

To the extent that the panel bases this surprising finding on a view that the First Amendment does not apply as fully to investigations that precede criminal prosecutions as to criminal prosecutions themselves, it is in direct conflict with the Ninth Circuit, which recently stated that selective prosecution is established when it is shown that the government has focused its "*investigation* on [the defendant] because of his [protected First Amendment] activities," *United States v. Wayte,* 53 U.S.L.W. 2053 (9th Cir. July 19, 1983) (emphasis added).

To the extent that the panel bases its finding instead on the novel theory that the taint of an impermissibly motivated tax audit is necessarily dissipated by the government's "separate decision" to initiate a criminal prosecution, *see* Op. 6405, rehearing is also required. For, even if such a theory could ever have been colorable, it has, since oral argument, surely been laid to rest by the IRS's own policy, adopted in response to the Court's June 1983 decision in *United States v. Baggot,* 103 S.Ct. 3164 (1983), of dismissing tax audits as irrevocably tainted if they stem from any information obtained by the IRS unlawfully from the grand jury phase of a criminal prosecution. *See* "An Irrevocable Taint on Tax Cases?" *National Law Journal* (September 19, 1983). If wrongfully procured grand jury information irrevocably taints a *civil* audit, then *a fortiori,* wrongfully obtained civil audit information irrevocably taints a *criminal* prosecution.

Morever, even if such a taint could be dissipated, the unconstitutionality of the government's initial selective motivation for auditing Reverend Moon's taxes would, at the very least, impose on the *government* the burden of demonstrating that the taint was sufficiently attenuated—*i.e.*, that the government would have brought the criminal tax prosecution even in the absence of information gleaned from the unconstitutional tax audit. *Cf. United States v. Ceccolini,* 435 U.S. 268, 274-75 (1978). No such burden was met here.

9

III. THE PANEL'S DECISION REJECTS LONG-SET-TLED LAW BARRING DENIAL OF PRIVILEGES IN RESPONSE TO THE EXERCISE OF CONSTITU-TIONAL RIGHTS.

Reverend Moon contends that he was denied a bench trial, and thus forced to stand trial before a jury, because he had *spoken out in public* against the prosecution. The panel concedes that, even if he had no independent "right" to a bench trial, it would be impermissible to deny him such a trial—or, indeed, any other lawful procedural option—"for a reason that infringes [his] . . . First Amendment freedoms." Op. 6378. Nonetheless, the panel affirms the conviction, claiming to find no "*factual* predicate" for concluding that such impermissible denial occurred. Op.6379 (emphasis added). But its opinion plainly acknowledges *the sole fact necessary* to that conclusion—namely, that the prosecution's *overt reason* for insisting on and thereby securing a jury trial[16] over Reverend Moon's objection was to "defuse the public criticism that had been *leveled by Moon*" at the prosecution. Op.6377 (emphasis added).

Why, then, did the panel not reverse? Only three possibilities exist.

First, the panel might have assumed that the prosecution's stated reason for insisting on jury trial was *legitimate because not explicitly punitive.*[17] But such an assumption is flatly contrary to controlling Supreme Court precedents establishing that, even if the government's *motive* is not to "punish," it may not act with the *effect* of depriving someone of a benefit he would have enjoyed *but for* his exercise of a First Amend-

---

16 The record makes plain that, but for the *prosecution's* insistence on jury trial, the *trial judge* would have granted Reverend Moon's request for bench trial. *See* T1752, 1760-61.

17 *See* Op.6378 ("the defendant has presented no facts on this record that convince us that the government's *reason* for refusing to consent to a bench trial was impermissibly *to punish Moon* for exercising his First Amendment rights" (emphasis added)).

10

ment right. "Conditions upon [or denials of] public benefits cannot be sustained if they so operate, *whatever their purpose,* as to inhibit or deter the exercise of First Amendment freedoms." *Sherbert v. Verner,* 374 U.S. 398, 405 (1963) (emphasis added) (citing *Speiser v. Randall,* 357 U.S. 513 (1958); *see id.* at 518).[18]

Second, the panel might have assumed that the prosecution's stated reason for insisting on jury trial, however *illegitimate,* had not been sufficiently shown *by defendant* to have been the "but for" cause of the prosecution's insistence on jury trial.[19] It might have thought, for example, that the very existence of controversy surrounding this case contributed to the government's preference for jury trial. But no such contributing reason would matter in light of controlling Supreme Court precedent. For if protected expression has played *any* part in motivating government action injuring the person who engaged in that expression—as Reverend Moon's speech undeniably did, *see* A811-12, 1028-29; *see also* Op.6376-77—then it is the *government's* burden to show "by a preponderance of the evidence that it would have reached the same decision . . . even in the absence of the protected conduct." *Mt. Healthy Board of Education v. Doyle,* 429 U.S. 274, 287 (1977). *See MacFarlane v. Grasso,* 696 F.2d 217, 223 (2d Cir. 1982) (applying *Mt. Healthy* test). In violation of *Mt. Healthy,* the panel instead places the burden on *Reverend Moon* to show that the government would not have denied him a bench trial

---

18   The same principle has been applied to constitutional freedoms generally. *See, e.g., Shapiro v. Thompson,* 394 U.S. 618, 631 (1969) (penalty on travel); *United States v. Jackson,* 390 U.S. 570, 582-83 (1968) (penalty on pleading innocent and demanding jury trial); *Simmons v. United States,* 390 U.S. 377, 394 (1968) (penalty on asserting Fourth Amendment rights); *Griffin v. California,* 380 U.S. 609, 614 (1965) (penalty on asserting Fifth Amendment rights). *Cf. Brady v. Maryland,* 373 U.S. 83, 87 (1963) (suppression by prosecution of evidence favorable to accused violates due process "irrespective of the good faith or bad faith of the prosecution").

19 ·   *See* Op.6378 ("the defendant has presented *no facts on this record* that convince us that the government's reason . . . was impermissibly to punish Moon . . ." (emphasis added)).

11

absent his public speech against the prosecution.[20] Under the proper standard—that set forth in *Mt. Healthy*—the impermissible penalty on speech here requires reversal, for the government in this case has adduced *no* evidence, much less a preponderance, to show that it would have forced Reverend Moon to be tried by a jury *in any event*.[21]

Third, the panel might have assumed that, even if the prosecution's stated reason was illegitimate *and* the but-for cause of denial of a bench trial, such denial can *never* amount to punishment, because a jury trial is constitutionally presumed to be a good, not a harm.[22] This reasoning is likewise flatly irreconcilable with controlling Supreme Court precedent.

---

20   The panel might have been laboring under the impression that imposing such a burden on the party alleging retaliation was permissible in light of such cases as *NLRB v. New York University Medical Center,* 702 F.2d 284 (2d Cir. 1983), *cert. pending* (U.S. No. 82-1705), which placed just such a burden on employees alleging retaliation against union activism under the National Labor Relations Act. If so, then rehearing is certainly required, for the Supreme Court has, since oral argument in this case, forbidden precisely such an allocation, reversing a case in accord with *NYU Medical,* and expressly extending *Mt. Healthy* to cases involving retaliation against conduct protected by statute as well as by the Constitution. *NLRB v. Transportation Management Corp.,* 103 S.Ct. 2469, 2475 (1983) (reversing *NYU Medical* by implication, *see id.* at 2472 n.3).

21   The government indeed conceded the opposite: it reiterated to the panel, as it had argued to the trial judge, that its insistence on jury trial resulted, in fact, from controversy "of [Reverend Moon's] own making." *See* GB 68 & n.*. Where, as here, there is *no* contemporaneous "record revealing that legitimate alternative grounds for the decision existed, as there was in *Mt. Healthy*," the government is not entitled even to a remand for a factual hearing on causation, for that "would result in fictitious recasting of past conduct." *University of California Regents v. Bakke,* 438 U.S. 265, 320 n.54 (1978). *See* ACLU Brief at 8-16.
      Nor, of course, can the *accused* be penalized for not himself first suggesting—and then somehow producing "facts" to refute—such *post hoc* rationales.

22   *See* Op.6378-79 ("the defendant has presented no facts on this record that convince us that the government's reason . . . was impermissibly *to punish* Moon . . . [because] the prosecutor elected . . . to have this case tried in the constitutionally preferred manner" (emphasis added)).

12

For the very line of cases the panel concedes to be applicable focuses *not* on the *nature* of the benefit the government withholds, but on whether *withholding* the benefit has the *effect* of deterring protected expression[23] or of making its exercise substantially more costly.[24] And it would defy common sense to imagine that speech critical of the government is not inevitably deterred when its price is denial to a criminal defendant of a forum or procedure that both he and the trial judge believed would be fairer to him than what he got. *See* MB 18-29; MRB 5-9.[25]

Every conceivable reading of the panel's decision on this issue, therefore, conflicts starkly with settled Supreme Court precedents that prevent government from penalizing an individual in response to his constitutionally protected conduct or expression.

IV. IN HOLDING THAT IT WAS "FAIR" TO FORCE REVEREND MOON TO UNDERGO TRIAL BY JURY, THE PANEL NULLIFIES THE *SINGER* EXCEPTION FOR "COMPELLING CIRCUMSTANCES."

The panel purports to recognize the possibility of "circumstances . . . so compelling that . . . to countenance the government's insistence on a jury trial over the defendant's [objection] . . . would deny . . . a fair trial." Op.6379. But in finding that "[t]his is not such a case," *id.*, the panel effec-

---

23   *See Thomas v. Review Board,* 450 U.S. at 717-18; *Mt. Healthy City Bd. of Ed. v. Doyle,* 429 U.S. at 287; *Sherbert v. Verner,* 374 U.S. at 405; *Speiser v. Randall,* 357 U.S. at 518. *Accord, Regan v. Taxation with Representation of Washington,* 103 S.Ct. 1997, 2000 (1983) (dictum by the Court per Rehnquist, J.); *id.* at 2004 (Blackmun, J., concurring).

24   *Cf. Memorial Hospital v. Maricopa County,* 415 U.S. 250, 258-60 (1974); *Griffin v. California,* 380 U.S. at 614.

25   Nothing in *this* argument—that denial of bench trial impermissibly penalized Reverend Moon for exercising his right to *free expression*—depends on Reverend Moon's *separate* argument on appeal that trial before the jury in this case violated his right to fair trial. *See* § IV infra. The panel's contrary assumption, Op.6377, so substantially misconceives defendant's argument as to require rehearing on that ground alone.

13

tively negates that very proposition, and writes out of the law the exception the Supreme Court expressly left open in *Singer v. United States,* 380 U.S. 24, 37 (1965), discussed at MB 18-19. For if the trial of the founder and leader of an unorthodox religion, despised nationwide as a "cult" that is said to "exploit" for profit young people recruited through alleged "brainwashing," *see* MB 22-23 & n.33, is *not* a trial raising an intolerable risk of jury prejudice, then *no such trial is imaginable.*

The panel turns a blind eye to Reverend Moon's carefully documented argument that it was the endemic *religious* prejudice against him and his movement that made his request to avoid subjection to a jury trial compelling. *See* MB 20-27. The panel reduces his claim to "one of an atmosphere poisoned by a negative press," Op.6379-80, and thus capable of being cured by voir dire. But the atmosphere in which the prosecution of Reverend Moon took place—polluted not just by adverse publicity but by widespread *hatred* of Reverend Moon and his religion—was hardly so easily cured. Indeed, the trial judge still believed—*after* his conduct of careful voir dire— that, because of this entrenched religious prejudice, bench trial *would* have been fairer than trial by jury. *See* T1752, 1760-61.[26]

This Circuit has previously suggested that criminal defendants who make *no* effort to "procure a trial by a judge alone," *see United States v. Rosenberg,* 195 F.2d 583, 596 (2d Cir.), *cert. denied,* 344 U.S. 838 (1952), may simply have to swallow, as "one of the risks of trial by jury," *id.,* the risk that "jurors . . . may not be exempt from the general feelings prevalent in the society in which they live," *United States v. Dennis,* 183 F.2d 201, 226 (2d Cir. 1950) (L. Hand, J.), *aff'd,* 341 U.S. 494 (1951). But never before has this Circuit sanctioned imposition of an identical risk on a defendant who *has*

---

26   The trial judge proceeded with voir dire and with jury trial only because he thought *Singer* tied his hands. *See* T1752, S26. And he proceeded with a jury *after* voir dire only because he supposed that "this criminal case" would *not* put the Unification Church on trial. *See* T1758-59, MB 25. That this prognosis proved wrong, *see* MB 25-27; MRB 8-9, the panel totally ignores.

14

sought to substitute trial by a judge for trial by the "general feelings" of a jury.[27] The panel's decision, which gives *no weight at all* to the defendant's request for bench trial, should thus be overturned on rehearing.

V. IN BARRING AN ALIEN DEFENDANT FROM TES- TIFYING THROUGH HIS CHOSEN INTERPRETER, THE PANEL ABRIDGES THE CONSTITUTIONAL RIGHT TO DECIDE FREELY WHETHER TO TAKE THE STAND.

As construed by the panel, the Court Interpreters Act of 1978 thrusts an official court-appointed interpreter upon a non-English-speaking criminal defendant for any testimony he may wish to give, and prevents him from presenting his defense through the voice of his chosen interpreter, Op.6409, even where—as is undisputedly the case here—accuracy of transla- tion can be assured by less restrictive means.[28]

---

27   The "manifest prejudice" standard the panel imports without ex- planation, Op.6380-81, from cases such as *United States v. Brown,* 644 F.2d 101, 104 (2d Cir.), *cert. denied,* 454 U.S. 881 (1981)—cases involving *no religious prejudice* and *no requests for bench trial*—cannot properly be applied to a case where, as here, both those circumstances are involved. *See* MRB 8 n.12. Rehearing is required if only to overturn this radical extension of the scope of the "manifest prejudice" standard.

28   Although not mentioned by the panel, the record of this case makes overwhelmingly clear that the far less restrictive alternative of using a court-appointed interpreter *to monitor* the accuracy of the interpreter chosen by Reverend Moon not only was repeatedly offered by counsel at trial, P49-50, 51-52, 109-10, and urged on appeal, MRB 10, but also was *expressly recognized as an adequate alternative by the trial judge, see* P37,50,52—who rejected that alternative only because, in his view, the statute required him to do so as a matter of law, *see* P108-09.

In light of this record it is, indeed, inexplicable that the panel cites to "the legitimate public interest in . . . . accurate and unbiased translations of trial testimony," Op.6410, as if the very existence of that interest, without more, could justify a burden on the right at issue here. Even if the trial court's findings had not rendered such an argument wholly inapposite, the Supreme Court has specifically held that options which would otherwise fall within a defendant's rights—such as testifying *after* other defense witnesses have taken the stand, *Brooks v. Tennessee,* 406 U.S. 605, 612 (1972); or testifying *in response* to defense counsel's questions rather than in an unbroken

15

So construed and applied, the Interpreters Act not only needlessly impairs the ability of a non-English-speaking person to prepare, with the aid of counsel, his defense to criminal charges[29]; it also burdens gratuitously the right of such a defendant, again aided by counsel, freely to decide whether to take the witness stand in his own defense.[30] As the trial court

---

narrative, *Ferguson v. Georgia*, 365 U.S. 570, 596 (1961)—cannot be withheld on the rationale that such options might enable an accused unscrupulously to tailor his testimony to his advantage, at least where "[t]here *are other ways* to deal with the problem of possible improper influence on testimony or 'coaching' of a witness," short of restricting his rights. *Geders v. United States*, 425 U.S. 80, 89 (1976) (emphasis added) (holding that a defendant cannot, for similar reasons, be prevented from consulting with his own counsel during an overnight recess during his testimony).

29   A non-English speaking defendant could not, for example, even decide *whether* to testify or even "realistically assess . . . " his *proposed* testimony with his attorney, *see Brooks v. Tennessee*, 406 U.S. at 610, without either (a) piercing the privacy of the privileged attorney-client relationship by the presence and participation of the court-appointed interpreter; or (b) preparing with a chosen interpreter who would become useless in court and who would not even be able to inform the defendant or his attorney *what words* the court-appointed interpreter would actually speak to the jury. As is abundantly clear on the record of this case, in which the translations of Mr. Kamiyama's statements before the Grand Jury were the subject of so much dispute, not all interpreters interpret alike. *See also* judge's comments at, *e.g.*, P41-42, 52-53, 116-17, 119.

30   In *United States v. Bifield*, 702 F.2d 342, 349 (2d Cir.), *cert. denied*, 103 S.Ct. 2095 (1983), issued just before oral argument in this case, another panel of this Circuit held for the first time that this right—the right of an accused "to be heard *in person* at a federal criminal trial" (emphasis added)—is in itself a separate constitutional right that "may not be denied without violating the accused's Fifth and Sixth Amendment rights." *Bifield*, in sharp contrast to the panel's decision here, *see* Op.6409, correctly recognizes that *Brooks v. Tennessee* is not a narrow ruling restricted to burdens on the *timing* of a defendant's decision whether to take the stand, but rather holds broadly that "*whether* to testify is not only an important tactical decision for a defendant, but also a matter of constitutional right". 702 F.2d at 349 (emphasis added). *Accord, e.g., Geders*, 425 U.S. at 91; *Faretta v. California*, 422 U.S. 806, 819 n.15 (1975). Indeed, the *Brooks* Court itself relied expressly on *Ferguson v. Georgia* (holding unconstitutional a law that allowed the defendant to speak to the jury only through an unbroken narrative, and not through answers to questions posed by counsel),

16

expressly recognized, translation of one's statements is a highly individualistic matter,[31] best performed by one who knows the speaker well, see P52-53. An accused's translator must, therefore, be understood as a personal representation of the accused, not a mechanical extension of the court.

Thus it was no minor inconvenience to Reverend Moon to be told that the interpreter he and his counsel could *not* use was the one who had worked for him "for many years," see P37-38, 49, and the only one he *could* use was a court-appointed stranger. Just as "[a]n unwanted counsel 'represents' the defendant only through a tenuous and unacceptable legal fiction," *Faretta v. California*, 422 U.S. 806, 821 (1975), so an unwanted interpreter "speaks for" the defendant only in a similarly fictitious sense. Given the highly "personal character" of the right to make one's own defense, *id.* at 820, it was thus the height of unfairness to Reverend Moon—although the panel did not see it, see Op.6410—to rule that, if he wished to speak at all, he could do so only impersonally, through "an organ of the [government] interposed between [him] and his right to defend himself personally," *Faretta*, 422 U.S. at 820, thus thrusting upon him "not an assistant but a master," *id.* at 820-21.

Because the panel's construction of the Interpreters Act places substantial and readily avoidable obstacles in the path of aliens and their attorneys attempting to defend in American trials, it must be scrutinized with special care, see *Hampton v. Mow Sun Wong*, 426 U.S. 88, 102 (1976); and because, when so scrutinized, that construction cannot be reconciled with controlling Supreme Court precedent, reversal *en banc* is required.

---

which, of course, had nothing at all to do with the *timing* of a defendant's decision to testify but, like Reverend Moon's case, concerned only the *form* in which defendant's testimony could be presented.

31   The judge explained, ". . . a literal translation often loses meaning . . . . [as] . . . . there are phases that don't translate literally language-to-language, and you have to take the *intent* of the meaning of the expression to make an appropriate interpretation of it." P116-17 (emphasis added).

17

VI. IN HOLDING THE CONCEDEDLY ERRONEOUS ADMISSION OF SIMILAR ACTS EVIDENCE "HARMLESS" IN THIS CASE, THE PANEL REDUCES THE HARMLESS ERROR RULE OF THIS CIRCUIT TO A NULLITY.

The panel holds that the admission into evidence against Reverend Moon of the putatively false immigration documents as similar acts evidence, although "an abuse of discretion," Op.6411-12, was "*harmless*" error, Op.6412 (emphasis added). But this immigration evidence—particularly as it was *used* by the prosecutor in summation—was, in fact, the single most inflammatory piece of evidence against Reverend Moon that the government could have conjured up. It was evidence that the government characterized as showing that Reverend Moon had gained entry into this country under false pretenses; that the international Unification Church movement was a *non-existent fiction*; and that, accordingly, Reverend Moon's claim of having come to America to undertake a religious mission on behalf of that movement was a *sham. See* T6227, 6229; MB 65-66 & n.94; MRB 47-48 & nn.72, 73.

Thus abused, this evidence "proved" the very thing the jurors had "heard" about Reverend Moon in advance, *see* MB 21-22 & nn.31,33—that he is a *charlatan* whose very presence in America is simply intolerable. Thus abused, this evidence *confirmed* the public wish to rid this country of what the prosecution sought to portray as the scourge of Sun Myung Moon.[32]

---

32   It was surely not because "paying income taxes is . . . America's most popular national pastime," Op.6373, that there were cheers in the streets as headlines announced: "U.S. Set To Boot The Rev. Moon On Tax Charge," *New York Post* (Oct. 16, 1981); "Sun May Be Setting On Moonie Empire," *Calgary Sun* (May 19, 1982); "Judge Gives Moon Jail To Avoid A Public Outcry," *San Francisco Examiner* (July 16, 1982); "Take That, Rev. Moon," *The Tulsa Tribune* (July 19, 1982); "Bravo," *The Cleveland Plain Dealer* (July 25, 1982). Nor is it a coincidence that the government sought unsuccessfully to use Reverend Moon's conviction in this case as a basis for his expulsion from this country, either through deportation or through exclusion. *See* MB 66 n.95.

18

Plainly, this evidence—introduced by the government as its *coup de grace* on rebuttal and indeed as its *entire* rebuttal case, T6059-63, and dramatically emphasized in summation—"*must* have been in the forefront of the jurors' minds when they retired to deliberate." *See United States v. Ruffin*, 575 F.2d 346, 360 (2d Cir. 1978) (emphasis added). Thus reversal is required "*[r]egardless* of whether there were other independently sufficient evidence to convict the defendant." *United States v. Quinto*, 582 F.2d 224, 235 (2d Cir. 1978) (emphasis added).

Given the uniquely inflamatory use of this evidence—to fuel the very bias against Reverend Moon that even the trial court conceded lay simmering in the jury, *see* T1758-59; MB 21-22, 25—the panel's implicit conclusion that "the error did *not* influence the jury or had but very *slight* effect," *Kotteakos v. United States*, 328 U.S. 750, 746-65 (1946) (emphasis added); *Ruffin*, 575 F.2d at 359; *Quinto*, 582 F.2d at 235, promises to convert effective enforcement of this Circuit's rules about similar acts evidence, *see United States v. Figueroa*, 618 F.2d 934, 939 (2d Cir. 1980), into a pointless wrist-slapping exercise, making the commitment of those rules "a promise to the ear to be broken to the hope, a teasing illusion like a munificent bequest in a pauper's will." *Edwards v. California*, 314 U.S. 160, 186 (1941) (Jackson, J., concurring).

CONCLUSION

The panel struck an ominous note when it observed that this "will not be the last" occasion "when a controversial . . . religious figure [is] criminally prosecuted" in America. Op.6406. Lest such occasions end in religious persecution rather than secular justice, they demand the most scrupulous vigilance by the full bench of this Circuit. Because the panel's decision withers under any such scrutiny, it should be reconsidered, by the panel or *en banc*, and ultimately reversed.

Respectfully submitted,

LAURENCE H. TRIBE
1525 Massachusetts Avenue
Cambridge, Massachusetts 02138
(617) 495-1767

JEANNE BAKER
DAVID J. FINE
SILVERGLATE, GERTNER, BAKER & FINE
88 Broad Street
Boston, Massachusetts 02110

MORTIMER CAPLIN
CAPLIN & DRYSDALE, Chartered
1101 Seventeenth Street, N.W.
Washington, D.C. 20036

HAROLD R. TYLER, JR.
PATTERSON, BELKNAP,
  WEBB & TYLER
30 Rockefeller Plaza
New York, New York 10112

Of Counsel

CHARLES A. STILLMAN
STILLMAN, FRIEDMAN & SHAW, P.C.
521 Fifth Avenue
New York, New York 10175

Counsel for Appellant
Sun Myung Moon

PART II:
PETITION FOR CERTIORARI AND BRIEF IN OPPOSITION

Petition for Certiorari

i

QUESTIONS PRESENTED

1. Where the trial judge concurs with defendant that bench trial would be fairer than jury trial because of the depth of public hostility to defendant or the cause he represents, may trial by jury nonetheless be compelled for reasons demonstrably unrelated to achieving a fair result?

2. Do the Religion Clauses permit licensing a jury in a criminal case to substitute its lay views for the religious views of a church and its members as to how property and authority should be allocated within the church?

3. Does the Due Process Clause permit use of a criminal prosecution to pioneer a novel and debatable theory of federal tax liability?

iii

TABLE OF CONTENTS

v

TABLE OF AUTHORITIES

vi

PAGE

vii

viii

OPINIONS BELOW

This petition seeks review of a decision of a divided panel of the United States Court of Appeals for the Second Circuit, which is reported as *United States v. Moon*, 718 F.2d 1210 (2d Cir. 1983) (per Cardamone, J., and Winter, J.; Oakes, J., dissenting), and reprinted in the Appendix to the Petition for Certiorari, *infra* at App.1-74.[1] The underlying judgments of conviction in the United States District Court for the Southern District of New York (Goettel, J.), entered upon jury verdict, are unreported.

JURISDICTION

The decision of the United States Court of Appeals for the Second Circuit from which review is sought was entered on September 13, 1983. That decision affirmed, except with respect to one count against petitioner Kamiyama, judgments of conviction that were entered against petitioners Moon and Kamiyama in the United States District Court for the Southern District of New York, after jury trial, on July 16, 1982. Rehearings were denied on October 28, 1983, and November 1, 1983. By order dated November 22, 1983, Justice Marshall granted an extension of time in which to file a joint petition for certiorari to and including January 26, 1984. This Court has jurisdiction to review the judgment of the court of appeals under 28 U.S.C. § 1254(1).

---

1 Citations to the court of appeals opinions will be denoted "App. _____". Citations to the record as reprinted in the appendix submitted to the court of appeals will be denoted as follows: citations to pleadings and rulings, "A_____"; to pre-trial transcripts, "P_____"; to trial transcript, "T _____"; to post-trial transcript, "S_____"; to government exhibits, "GX _____"; and to defense exhibits, "DX_____".

2

CONSTITUTIONAL PROVISIONS INVOLVED

AMENDMENT I

Congress shall make no law respecting an establishment of religion, or prohibiting the free exercise thereof; or abridging the freedom of speech, or of the press . . . .

AMENDMENT V

No person . . . shall be . . . deprived of life, liberty, or property, without due process of law . . . .

AMENDMENT VI

In all criminal prosecutions, the accused shall enjoy the right to a speedy and public trial, by an impartial jury of the state and district wherein the crime shall have been comitted . . . .

STATEMENT OF THE CASE

Reverend Sun Myung Moon, the founder and leader of the Unification Church,[2] was convicted by a jury of filing false income tax returns—specifically, of failing to report as income the interest accrued on certain Chase Manhattan bank accounts openly held in his name, and the value of stock issued in his name in Tong Il Enterprises, a company run by members of his church.

Reverend Moon was also convicted, together with Takeru Kamiyama, a senior Unification Church member, of conspiracy to file false tax returns and to obstruct the tax investigation against Reverend Moon. Mr. Kamiyama was separately

---

2   The international Unification Church movement arose in Korea over a quarter of a century ago as one of a host of revivalist Christian religions flourishing in the aftermath of the 40-year Japanese occupation, and now involves "more than 120 national Unification Churches throughout the world propagating a common religious message under [Reverend Moon's] spiritual guidance." *Holy Spirit Association for the Unification of World Christianity* [Unification Church] v. *Tax Commission*, 55 N.Y.2d 512, 519 (1982).

3

convicted of related substantive counts, one of which was reversed.[3]

At issue in this petition is not the facts the government purports to have established, but the process—including the choice of tribunal and the charge to the jury—by which the government obtained the result it sought. To set in context the violations of fairness and religious freedom claimed by petitioners requires only the following exposition of the record.

A. How the Government Obtained Trial by Jury.

Prior to trial, Reverend Moon asked to stand trial before the bench rather than a jury. He did so on the ground that public hostility to him and the Unification Church was so deep-seated and pervasive that bench trial would be fairer than trial before twelve representatives of the public. Mr. Kamiyama joined this motion.

The government refused consent. The prosecution argued that jury trial was necessary to "defuse the public criticism that had been leveled by Moon" in a speech he had made after his arraignment. App.7. In that speech, Reverend Moon had criticized the prosecution as motivated by religious bigotry and racism. *Id.* The prosecution claimed that, once that speech had been made, only jury trial—the "normal and preferable" mode of criminal trial—could project the "appearance . . . of a fair trial," while sparing the judge from being placed in an " 'untenable' position." *Id.*

The judge expressed doubts about the logic of the government's argument and about the ability of any voir dire to flush out biases as deep as those against Reverend Moon. P381. Nonetheless, he proceeded with voir dire, which lasted seven days.

---

3   The jurisdiction of the district court was invoked under an indictment charging Reverend Moon with violation of 26 U.S.C. § 7206(1), Mr. Kamiyama with violations of 26 U.S.C. § 7206(2) and 18 U.S.C. §§ 1503, 1001, & 1623, and both defendants with conspiracy, 18 U.S.C. § 371, to violate 26 U.S.C. § 7206(1) and 18 U.S.C. §§ 1503, 1001, & 1623.

4

The jury selected was, as the judge recognized, "not totally free from bias." T1759.[4] Indeed, the judge stated after the jury selection that a bench trial would be "fairer" than trial before the jury selected. T1760-61. But he decided he had to acquiesce

---

4   Answers given by jurors who later sat at trial were in fact laden with negative preconceptions about Reverend Moon and his church:

—*Mary K. Nimmo*, forelady, had heard that the Unification Church was a "cult," "making money on young people," and "wouldn't have wanted [her] children to have been a part of it." T473; *see also* T449, 477-80.

—*Esperanza Torres* knew of a "deprogramming" controversy involving a Unification Church member and concluded "that the parents [of the member] are right . . . ," doubted Reverend Moon was a genuine spiritual leader, T847-48, and considered the Unification Church a "cult" involving "mostly young people," T857. *See* T849, 852, 858, 862-63, 871, 873-75.

—*Rosa Spencer* did not "think" it proper for religious groups to invest in businesses, and felt it improper for religious groups to "solicit funds" publicly. T1349-50; *see also* T1358.

—*Doris Torres* had heard that "some people think [Moon] is a god," T1391, and that the Unification Church "brainwashes" people, T1394.

—*Claudette Ange* had heard that Moon "was brainwashing some teenagers" and "has children selling . . . things . . . to get the money to buy property." T1514-15.

—*Maria Abramson* had not heard of Moon, but thought that religious cults brainwash young people, T1588, and believed religious groups "should collect their money in the church," not in public. T1587-88.

—*Paul Shanley* had heard about deprogramming and young people being "brainwashed" and "used for selling things." T1650; *see* T1631-32, 1636.

—*Freddie Bryant* thought churches should raise funds by donations from their own members and not by "go[ing] into a complete business." T1683-85.

—*Amerria Vasquez* had heard that the "Moonies" "indoctrinate the young people in the church," and "are taking over New York City." T2052.

—*Ernest Fetchko* had heard that the "Moonies" get members "by brainwashing them." T2106.

Thus, Reverend Moon's jury was truly a cross-section of the public—which, as reflected in a pre-voir dire opinion poll of 1,000 people, was over 76% negative in response to the very mention of the name "Reverend Moon," *see* A822. Indeed, almost 43% acknowledged that "[i]f [they] had the chance, [they'd] throw Reverend Sun Myung Moon *in jail*." A822-23 (emphasis added).

5

in the government's insistence on jury trial, T1761, because he thought that Reverend Moon's religion would not figure in the trial and thus that the jurors would be "by and large capable of putting aside the bias they have and deciding the case on the merits of the charges."[5] T1759.

B. How The Government Obtained Convictions By The Jury.

It was undisputed that the critical question at trial was who beneficially owned the Chase Manhattan bank accounts and the Tong Il stock: the Unification Church, or Reverend Moon himself.[6] Reverend Moon claimed that the church was the owner of the assets, for whose benefit he held and administered them; the government claimed these assets belonged to Reverend Moon personally. Contrary to the trial judge's prediction that nothing about Reverend Moon's religion would figure in the trial, the conflict between these two claims could not be properly resolved *without* consideration of Reverend Moon's religious relationship with his followers. For Reverend Moon's claim, quite simply, was that he had been given the assets *as* a religious leader, *by* his religious followers, *for* their religion.[7]

---

5   After trial, the judge reiterated "that this case would have been better tried without a jury, and if the discretion were solely mine, I would have given [defendants] a nonjury trial." S26.

6   The court of appeals majority called this issue "critical," App.6; the dissent called it not only " 'central,' " App.64, but "key," App.67, as had the trial judge in his instructions, *see* App.67 n.3.

7   As Judge Oakes explained in dissent:

[T]his case did *not* involve a claim that an ordinary, lay taxpayer held certain assets in a private trust for the benefit of another. On the contrary, the taxpayer here was the founder and leader of a worldwide movement which, regardless of what the observer may think of its views or even its motives, is nevertheless on its face a religious one, the members of which regard the taxpayer as the embodiment of their faith.

App.64-65.

6

The government did not overtly dispute, as it could not, that Reverend Moon was the leader of a *bona fide* religion,[8] or that the assets had been given to him by followers of his religion, who did so intending that the assets be used for that religion.[9] It simply proceeded with a theory that ignored Reverend Moon's religious relationship to his followers: a theory that Reverend Moon's ownership of the assets could be proved merely by showing that the assets were in Reverend Moon's name and under his control,[10] and that the assets had been used for what the government deemed Reverend Moon's personal investments and expenditures.[11] This theory treated the intent and religious identity of the assets' donors as wholly irrelevant, and relegated Reverend Moon to the role of an "ordinary, high-ranking businessman," A1905; *see* S60, 125—the very image the government continuously conjured up before the jury.

To counteract this filtering of religion from the case by the government, the defense sought to show that the uses of the

---

8   Reverend Moon's religion, "by any historical analogy, philosophical analysis, or judicial precedent . . . must be regarded as a bona fide religion." *Unification Church v. Immigration and Naturalization Service*, 547 F.Supp. 623, 628 (D.D.C. 1982).

9   As the court of appeals majority conceded, the only evidence at trial regarding donative intent was testimony by several church members that "they gave money to Moon, intending it as a donation to their church." App.23.

10   The defense never disputed the facts that the assets were in Reverend Moon's name and control, and that he had *legal* title to them; it simply argued that since a trustee, by definition, has legal title to and dominion and control over trust assets, such facts pointed as much to trusteeship as to beneficial ownership. *See* App. 64 (Oakes, J., dissenting).

11   But the only significant uses of the assets shown at trial, apart from direct transfers to church entities, *see, e.g.*, GX83, 85, 87, 88, were to assist in the purchase of real property titled in church entities, *see, e.g.*, T2865-66, 5922-23; to secure a loan to a church-related organization, *see* T2700-02; and to invest in businesses thought by church members to be good investments for the Unification Church's worldwide movement, *see, e.g.*, T5613-17, 5694-95. And *no* evidence showed that *any* use of the assets, even if for minor living expenses, conflicted with the religious aims of those who entrusted the assets to Reverend Moon.

7

assets which the government deemed non-religious in fact supported and advanced not Reverend Moon personally, but the aims and activities of the international Unification Church movement. The government had two responses. *First*, it insinuated that Reverend Moon had simply made up, after the fact, the explanation that the assets were owned by his church movement.[12] *Second*, it cut off defense efforts to show that uses which the government labeled merely "personal" or "business" in fact advanced the church. It did so by obtaining rulings of inadmissibility, *see, e.g.*, T5255-56, T5681, and issuing threats, echoed in warnings by the trial court, *see, e.g.*, T3042-45, 4818-20, 5256-57, 5759-60, that such evidence, if admitted, would "open the door" to the government's introduction of "negative things about the church," T5760. Nor were these threats idle, for when evidence about Reverend Moon's religion did "creep into the trial," App.43, the government made inflammatory use of it—for example, by arguing that church members' devotion to Reverend Moon signaled "mind control" that undermined church members' credibility on the stand. *See* T6184.

Caught between a government bent on portraying his religion as sinister when it could not excise it altogether from the case, and a jury predisposed to view Reverend Moon as a "charlatan" running a "cult" for his own profit, Reverend Moon was hardly free to present to the jury a full and accurate picture of his religious relationship to those who gave him the assets.[13] Nor was the defense that rested on that relationship—

---

12   Thus, the government told the jury that there was no such thing as the international Unification Church movement because, unlike other church entities, the "movement" was not incorporated, T6488-92; *see also* T5516-17, 5521, nor even listed in Reverend Moon's immigration papers, T6227, 6229—documents whose admission the court of appeals held a patent abuse of discretion, App.41-42, but deemed "harmless," App.42. And it told the jury that the movement could not have owned the assets because documents submitted to the IRS tracing some of the funds to particular church transactions had been backdated by Reverend Moon's aides, *see, e.g.*, T6193, 6205-18—even though the government never disputed that the assets came from church sources.

13   Post-trial the judge acknowledged that such a picture "would have been disastrous to [present] before a jury." S60.

8

namely, that Reverend Moon held the assets for the benefit of the international Unification Church movement and therefore was not their owner for tax purposes—properly put before the jury in the trial judge's instructions on beneficial ownership.

At the core of those instructions was a list of factors, each of which the jury was left free to give whatever weight it wished. *See* App.68 n.3.[14] This list submerged, among a host of factors requested by the government, *see* A1305-06, the defense proposition that assets placed by church members in a church leader's hands for church purposes belong to the church, *see* A1371-72. And, while the list included "the fact that the accounts were maintained under Reverend Moon's name," the instructions nowhere explained, as the defense requested, A1365-66, that to his followers Reverend Moon "personified" the church. Moreover, the list's first two factors—focusing on the "specific organizational structure[s]" of the church—invited the jury to find that the form in which the church chose to organize itself could alone be decisive of guilt.

Furthermore, instead of informing the jury that if those who gave the assets to Reverend Moon "intended [them] to be for the [i]nternational Unification Church movement," the assets could "be viewed as not . . . his but . . . the [m]ovement's," T6122-23, the instructions told the jury that there is no trust unless the donors, in placing the assets in Reverend Moon's hands, expressed a "clear and unambiguous" intent to place the assets in a trust, App.69 n.3. And, instead of informing the jury that "the fact that some of the funds were disbursed for Rev. Moon's benefit does not make the interest on the accounts income to him," A1372, *see also* A1423, the instructions directed the jury to find that "there is no trust if the person who receives the money is free to use it for his own benefit," App.69 n.3. Thus, the instructions permitted the jury to find that the assets belonged to Reverend Moon for tax purposes despite the donors' intent that he hold and use the assets for the church and have the freedom, customary for the clergy, to use a portion to meet his own needs.

14   The instructions on the central issue of ownership are reprinted in full at App.67-69 n.3.

9

C. How the Court of Appeals Affirmed the Convictions.

The court of appeals recognized that the defense had raised "troubling issues of religious persecution." App.3. It nonetheless rejected all of defendants' principal claims. As to the bench trial issue, the court simply ignored the trial judge's concession that bench trial would have been "fairer" than the jury trial demanded by the prosecution, and upheld the judge's acquiescence in that demand on the basis that it neither "punish[ed]" Reverend Moon, App.8, nor caused defendants "manifest prejudice," App.10. As to the instructions on beneficial ownership, the court rejected out of hand defendants' argument that those instructions violated Religion Clause principles, declaring those principles flatly inapplicable to this case. *See* App.28-31. And, as to defendants' argument that the instructions on beneficial ownership invited the jury to convict on a theory conflicting with settled federal tax authority as well as with New York trust law, the majority—citing no federal precedent, and over the dissent of Judge Oakes, App.62-74—disagreed, finding the instructions wholly unobjectionable, App.22-28.

SUMMARY OF ARGUMENT

Certiorari should be granted because, in at least three related respects, the government and the courts below violated not only First Amendment principles, but also elementary notions of fairness and the rule of law:

First, as this Court stated clearly in *Singer v. United States*, 380 U.S. 24 (1965), our Constitution does not permit the prosecution to insist on jury trial where to do so is to increase the probability of conviction, regardless of guilt, by throwing the defendant to the tribunal most likely to vent its hostility upon him. Our Constitution requires, rather, that any presumption in favor of jury trial be overridden where, as the trial court found here, that mode is *not* the one most likely to yield a fair result. *See id.* at 36-37. No case presented to this Court since *Singer* has shown so starkly the peril to fair trial of a

10

government licensed to convert jury trial—the ancient and honorable shield for defendants from oppressive officialdom—into a sword to be wielded freely against the unpopular minority or the outspoken dissident.

Nor, *second*, has any recent case so demonstrated the danger to religious liberty of a jury licensed to disregard the decisions of a church and the desires of that church's members in favor of its own lay instincts about how authority and property within a church should be allocated. As both the majority and the dissenting members of this Court made clear in *Jones v. Wolf*, 443 U.S. 595 (1979), the Religion Clauses forbid any secular tribunal from so second-guessing the internal decisions of a religious community—a commandment the jury was plainly invited to transgress by the instructions given and approved here. Whatever legitimate authority Congress and the IRS enjoy to protect the federal fisc by fixing clear rules that tell churches in advance what steps will ensure their retention of beneficial ownership of assets they choose to entrust to their leaders, it is plain that such federal authority does *not* encompass power to deputize juries to decide questions of church ownership without deference to the beliefs of church members, or to infer guilt from the entirely lawful organizational choices churches might make.

Third, contrary to the most basic principles of due process forbidding the minting of new theories of criminality on the brow of a defendant threatened with imprisonment, *see James v. United States*, 366 U.S. 213 (1961), the courts below unleashed a jury, already hostile to defendants' novel religion, not simply to assess a civil tax deficiency, but retroactively to impose criminal punishment upon Reverend Moon based on a novel theory of taxability—a theory in conflict with settled authority and announced for the first time on the very occasion it was first invoked.

11

REASONS FOR GRANTING THE PETITION

I. DEFERENCE TO THE PROSECUTION'S DEMAND FOR JURY TRIAL WHEN BENCH TRIAL WOULD BE FAIRER ABDICATES THE JUDICIARY'S DUTY TO ASSURE FAIR TRIAL.

It cannot seriously be disputed that Reverend Moon, the founder and leader of a small, new and unpopular religious denomination, is the target of profound public hostility in this country. Not only is it inconceivable that any "disciple of . . . the Reverend Moon [could be found] serving as the official chaplain in any state legislature," *Marsh v. Chambers*, 103 S.Ct. 3330, 3351 (1983) (Stevens, J., dissenting); it is even the case that some state legislatures, prompted by popular fear and loathing of the "Moonies," have tried to block the practice of their faith through legislation this Court has not hesitated to strike down as transparently unconstitutional, *see Larson v. Valente*, 456 U.S. 228, 255 (1982). It was out of fear that this widespread hostility would infect any jury empaneled to hear his case that Reverend Moon sought to waive his constitutional right to trial by twelve representatives of the public. And, for just that reason, the trial judge believed that the bench trial Reverend Moon requested would have been fairer than the jury trial to which the government's veto forced him instead.

To be sure, this Court held in *Singer v. United States*, 380 U.S. 24 (1965), that a federal criminal defendant, in the *ordinary* case,[15] need not be granted a bench trial over the government's veto. But *Singer* also held out the explicit promise that such a veto could not bar bench trial in "circumstances where a defendant's reasons for wanting to be tried by a judge alone are so compelling that the Government's insistence on trial by jury would result in the denial to a defendant of an impartial trial." *Id.* at 37. Denial of bench trial in Reverend Moon's case renders that promise a "promise to the ear to be broken to the hope," *cf. Edwards v. California*, 314 U.S. 160,

---

15 In *Singer*, the defendant sought bench trial merely to "shorten[ ] the trial." 380 U.S. at 25; *see id.* at 38.

12

186 (1941) (Jackson, J., concurring)—a broken promise that only review by this Court can restore. For in Reverend Moon's case, the reasons for seeking bench trial are indeed compelling—as they would be whenever popular hostility to the defendant, his cause, or his message[16] is so overwhelming that the trial judge himself concludes bench trial would be fairer.

The court of appeals found Reverend Moon's reasons for seeking bench trial uncompelling only because it thought the trial judge was obligated to accept any jury meeting the "manifest prejudice" test, App.10, that this Court has long set forth for juror bias in cases where defendants *demand* jury trial.[17] Thus, in the view of the court of appeals, there was no compelling reason to grant bench trial over the government's veto so long as defendants had not shown that the jurors selected were incapable of "set[ting] aside" their admitted bias. App. 10.[18]

To be sure, requiring such a showing where a defendant *demands* jury trial makes sense. For if a defendant could insist on being tried by "jurors . . . [who are] exempt from the general feelings prevalent in the society in which they live," *United States v. Dennis*, 183 F.2d 201, 226 (2d Cir. 1950) (L. Hand, J.), *aff'd.*, 341 U.S. 494 (1951), then any highly unpop-

---

16   A Communist likewise might have had compelling reasons to prefer bench trial during the McCarthy era, as would a civil rights worker in the South during the era of the struggle to end segregation there, or a woman accused of witchcraft in old Salem. As the court below itself observed, "This case is not the first occasion when a controversial political or religious figure has been criminally prosecuted; and if history teaches us anything, plainly, it will not be the last." App.36.

17   This stringent test for juror bias is derived from such cases as *Irvin v. Dowd*, 366 U.S. 717, 722-23 (1961), and ultimately from another case in which the defendants feared juror bias against their religion (the Mormon faith) but did not seek bench trial, *Reynolds v. United States*, 98 U.S. 145, 155 (1878).

18   The trial judge applied this same test when he reluctantly proceeded with jury trial on the theory that the jury, although "not totally free from bias," was "by and large capable of putting aside the bias [it had]." T1759.

13

ular defendant could assure the dismissal of his case simply by *insisting* on jury trial. Prosecutions cannot thus be allowed to lapse routinely whenever a pristine jury cannot be found to try an unpopular defendant who demands the jury mode of trial.

There is simply no similar danger of the prosecution lapsing, however, where, as here, a defendant affirmatively seeks trial before a *federal judge* rather than before a jury that is admittedly biased, but less than "manifestly prejudiced." To require a defendant to meet the "manifest prejudice" test where he seeks to *waive* a jury trial therefore turns the purpose of that test on its head and impermissibly burdens his efforts to seek what is, for him, the fairest mode of trial.[19] Here, Reverend Moon sought only to follow the advice of the Second Circuit, which itself observed, in one notorious Smith Act case where no bench trial was requested, that the risk of public hostility—however unavoidable in a jury trial—can be avoided if a defendant seeks instead "to procure a trial by a judge alone." *United States v. Rosenberg*, 195 F.2d 583, 596 (2d Cir.), *cert. denied*, 344 U.S. 838 (1952).

A far better test for granting bench trial over the government's objection is the one suggested by this Court in *Singer* and amply satisfied here. *Singer* rejected a claim of automatic right to a bench trial on the ground that the jury is the "tribunal which the Constitution regards as *most likely to produce a fair result.*" 380 U.S. at 36 (emphasis added). But *Singer* nowhere suggested that this presumption is irrebuttable; on the contrary, *Singer* expressly deemed it rebuttable in "compelling" circumstances, *id.* at 37—especially where " 'passion, prejudice . . . [or] public feeling' . . . may render

---

19   How a defendant who seeks to waive jury trial might ever go about showing "manifest prejudice" in all the *possible* jurors that an indefinitely extended voir dire or a change of venue might turn up surely strains the imagination. The government itself recognized the futility of any such effort when it facetiously defied the defense in this case to show that "in the whole Southern District of New York, there are not twelve people who will afford the defendants a [minimally] fair hearing of their case." A1036.

14

. . . unlikely an impartial trial by jury," *id.* Where, as here, the trial judge himself concurs with the defendants that bench trial would be *fairer* than jury trial because its outcome would be less vulnerable to rampant public hatred, then all the rebuttal *Singer* calls for is complete: as between the two modes, it is bench trial, not jury trial, which is "most likely to produce a fair result."

Unless the prosecution can show that the defendants and the trial judge are both wrong, and that in fact it is *jury* trial, not bench trial, that would be more likely to produce a fair result, acquiescence in the prosecution's preference for jury trial is a patent abdication to the executive branch of a core judicial function: namely, safeguarding the defendant's right to fair trial.[20] Here, the prosecution made no such showing. Indeed the justifications proffered by the government in this case for insisting on jury trial were, if viewed most charitably, irrelevant to the achievement of a fair result, and, if viewed any other way, constitutionally impermissible *per se.*

First, the prosecution said that jury trial was necessary to "defuse the public criticism that had been leveled by Moon." App.7. In aiming to silence speech critical of the government,[21]

---

20   Such an abdication is of course impermissible under our Constitution. *See Irvin v. Dowd*, 366 U.S. at 721 (statute could not properly be read to "condition" upon the consent of the prosecutor the "duty of the judiciary" to take steps to ensure fair trial); *Commonwealth v. Wharton*, 435 A.2d 158, 168 (Pa. 1981) (opinion in support of affirmance) (prosecutor's absolute veto over defendant's request for nonjury trial would unconstitutionally "restrict the exercise by trial court judges of their constitutional authority to conduct a fair trial").

21   Withholding bench trial in response to Reverend Moon's public criticism silences such criticism by penalizing it or, at the very least, exacting a substantial price for its exercise. This violates the long-settled doctrine that, even where one is not independently entitled to a benefit, such a benefit may not be conditioned on the sacrifice of a First Amendment liberty. *See, e.g., Regan v. Taxation with Representation*, 103 S.Ct. 1997, 2000 (1983); *id.* at 2004 (Blackmun, J., concurring); *Thomas v. Review Board*, 450 U.S. 707, 717-18 (1981); *Mt. Healthy City Bd. of Ed. v. Doyle*, 429 U.S. 274, 287 (1977); *Perry v. Sindermann*, 408 U.S. 593, 597 (1972); *Pickering v. Board of Education*, 391 U.S. 563, 574 (1968); *Sherbert v. Verner*, 374 U.S. 398, 404-05 (1963); *Speiser v. Randall*, 357 U.S. 513, 518 (1958).

15

and so to protect the government's reputation,[22] this proffered justification could not have more flagrantly violated the First Amendment. And even if subjecting Reverend Moon to jury trial did constitute the government's "answer" to his public outcry against bigotry and prejudice—albeit more in the spirit of censorship than of debate—it at best served extrinsic purposes wholly unrelated to assuring the "fair result" contemplated in *Singer*.

Second, the government claimed that, by so "defusing" Reverend Moon's speech, forcing him to jury trial would protect some public interest in the "appearance" of fairness. App.7. But even if the constitutionality of advancing this interest at the expense of fairness were not dubious,[23] and even if the interest could plausibly be served by projecting an image of a government that denies defendants trial by the tribunal both they and the judge think would be more fair, this interest is likewise wholly extrinsic to the fair *result* that is our Constitution's concern.

Third, the government claimed that jury trial was necessary to protect the trial judge from blame or criticism. App.7.[24] But

22   Because speech critical of the government is at the center of First Amendment values, *see Rosenblatt v. Baer*, 383 U.S. 75, 85 (1966); *Bridges v. California*, 314 U.S. 252 (1941), the government can claim no legitimate interest in protecting its reputation against such criticism, *see New York Times Co. v. Sullivan*, 376 U.S. 254, 272-73 (1964).

23   The government is without constitutional authority to increase the risk of serious injury to an innocent individual simply to make a point. *See Carey v. Population Services International*, 431 U.S. 678, 714-16 (1977) (Stevens, J., concurring). In any event, the public has no independent reason to prefer jury trial over bench trial as it does to prefer, for example, the fair appearance of open trial over the suspected unfairness of closed trial, *see Press Enterprise v. Superior Court*, 52 U.S.L.W. 4113, 4115 (U.S. Jan. 17, 1984). Indeed, this Court has stated that "it could hardly be seriously argued that a member of the public could demand a jury trial [over defendant's jury waiver] because of the societal interest in that mode of factfinding." *See Gannett Co. v. DePasquale*, 443 U.S. 368, 384 (1979).

24   In making this and the preceding claim, the government was evidently worried that, if it gave in to bench trial, the public would cry

16

this claim too is at once constitutionally dubious,[25] extrinsic to
the fairness of the result, and completely irrelevant in a case
where, as here, the judge was himself wholly willing to conduct
a bench trial and indeed believed it the fairer mode.[26]

And *fourth*, the government claimed that jury trial is the
"normal and preferable mode" of factfinding in criminal
cases, App.7, simply begging the very question *Singer* left
open: namely, whether jury trial, however "normal," is impermissible to force on a defendant when demonstrably less fair
than bench trial.[27] This case answers that question, for the
normal reasons for preferring jury trial are wholly absent
where, as here, defendant is deeply despised by the populace
for reasons far beyond the crime with which he is charged. The
jury, as a representative voice of the people, is hardly a
bulwark of protection for the accused, *cf. Duncan v. Louisiana*, 391 U.S. 145 (1968), when it is precisely oppression at

---

"whitewash" if the judge acquitted, and the defendants would cry "persecution" if he did not. Whatever is the case elsewhere in the world, our legal
system has long been proudly impervious to such cries, responding to public
suspicions that justice will not be done by opening the proceedings to public
view, not by relaxing the safeguards against unfair results.

25   Just as the interest of any public official in protecting himself from
public criticism can never outweigh a newspaper's right to print, *cf.* note 22
supra, it surely can never outweigh a defendant's right to a fair trial: "No
right ranks higher than the right of the accused to a fair trial," *Press
Enterprise*, 52 U.S.L.W. at 4115.

26   The trial judge in this case, moreover, expressly disclaimed any
personal sensitivity to public criticism or "blame," noting that "the framers
. . . took that into account 200 years ago" when they gave federal judges life
tenure. P371. *Cf. Craig v. Harney*, 331 U.S. 367, 376 (1947) ("judges are
supposed to be men of fortitude, able to thrive in a hardy climate" of public
criticism).

27   If jury trial were in fact the "transcending" mode the government
read this Court's opinion in *Patton v. United States*, 281 U.S. 276, 296-98
(1930), to deem it, *see* A811, the result in that case, which held jury waiver
permissible, would have gone the other way.

17

the hands of the people—through thinly veiled vigilanteism—that the defendant reasonably fears.[28]

II. LICENSING JURORS TO SUBSTITUTE THEIR LAY ALLOCATION OF CHURCH PROPERTY AND AUTHORITY FOR THAT OF THE CHURCH VIOLATES THE RELIGION CLAUSES.

The court of appeals was unanimous in recognizing that guilt or innocence in this case turned centrally on the question of who beneficially owned the funds and stocks placed by church members in Reverend Moon's hands—the Unification Church or Reverend Moon personally. *See* App.6, 64, 67.

It is beyond debate that, if this property question had arisen in the context of a dispute within the church over the issue of beneficial ownership, it would have been unconstitutional for a court simply to substitute its lay views, or those of a jury, for both the "desires of the members" of the church[29] and "the decisions of the church government agreed upon by the members"[30] to repose church property in Reverend Moon's hands. Such *ad hoc* substitution of lay standards for religious would profoundly violate the axiom that only government neutrality and deference toward determinations internal to churches and their membership are consistent with the religious freedom and the church-state separation contemplated by the Religion

---

28   Nor can a jury's capacity to reflect the average sentiments of the community—a capacity that is in some circumstances a jury's virtue—make a jury a "preferable" factfinder in a case where that very capacity is its vice: a case where the average sentiment of the community is implacable hatred of a defendant for leading a feared and detested new religion, *see* note 4 *supra.* "The jury may be an adequate reflector of the community's conscience, but that conscience is not and never has been very tolerant of dissent." Monaghan, *First Amendment "Due Process,"* 83 Harv. L. Rev. 518, 529 (1970).

29   *See Jones v. Wolf,* 443 U.S. 595, 597, 603-04 (1979) (such desires must be respected in resolving dispute over beneficial ownership of property acquired by "funds . . . contributed entirely by local church members").

30   *Id.* at 614 (Powell, J., dissenting).

18

Clauses.[31] Indeed, the core value underlying both the Free Exercise Clause and the Establishment Clause is that of facilitating spiritual volition by showing "no [government] partiality to any [religious] group" or view, but instead letting "each flourish [solely] according to the zeal of its adherents and the appeal of its dogma." *Zorach v. Clauson*, 343 U.S. 306, 313 (1952). *Cf. Torcaso v. Watkins*, 367 U.S. 488, 490 (1961); *Fowler v. Rhode Island*, 345 U.S. 67, 69-70 (1953).

The court of appeals, in approving instructions that gave the jury a veto over a church's organizational structures and property arrangements, *see* App.68 n.3, flatly rejected the relevance of this core Religion Clause value to this criminal trial. It held instead that the "doctrine" applicable to "the resolution of *intra*-church property disputes," App.31 (emphasis added), simply "has no application" to a case such as this: a case that pits the government against an *undivided* church. And, true enough, there was never any dispute here *among* church members that the property was given by religious followers to their religious leader to hold and use for purposes advancing their religion, and that the property had been so held and used.

But, contrary to the court's view, respect for the decisions of churches and their members as to the allocation of property and authority within a religious community is not less but *more* essential where all those members share the same view of the matter and it is the government that would substitute its view for theirs.[32] This is especially true in a criminal context, for

---

31   This case presents no occasion to revisit the issues that divided the *Jones* Court: *neither* the majority nor the dissenting view expressed in *Jones* is compatible with the *ad hoc* lay-for-religious substitution upheld in this case.

32   One perverse corollary of the reading given by the court below to the intra-church property dispute cases is that a religious community *united* would enjoy far less protection from second-guessing by a secular tribunal than would a religious community *in schism*. Indeed, had a property dispute within the Unification Church resulted in a state court declaration that the property at issue belonged beneficially to the international Unification Church or to one of its arms and *not* to Reverend Moon personally, Reverend Moon could hardly have been convicted for failing to report the property as his own. Surely petitioners cannot be jailed because their church *avoided* any such schism.

19

"[i]f one could be sent to jail because a jury in a hostile environment found [the views held within one's] religion false, little indeed would be left of religious freedom." *United States v. Ballard*, 322 U.S. 78, 87 (1944). It is thus the gravest constitutional error for a jury to be given unbounded license to discount, penalize, or simply to disregard the desires of church members and the decisions of the church itself in a case where, as here, those desires and decisions are logically and legally relevant to guilt or innocence.

Precisely such license was conferred by the courts below in this case. While conceding that Unification Church members had given the assets to Reverend Moon "intending [them] as a donation to their Church," App.23—"establishing that a charitable *gift* had been made *to the Church*," App.25 (emphasis added)—the court of appeals majority held that the trial judge would nonetheless have been free to omit *all* reference, in his charge to the jury, to the defense claim that it was in trust for his church, not for himself, that Reverend Moon held the assets, App.25. The majority accordingly found no error in the instructions the trial court *did* give—despite the fact that, as Judge Oakes observed without contradiction, those instructions freed the jury "to find against Moon on the issue of beneficial ownership without even considering the crucial issue of donors' intent," App.70 (dissenting opinion), and despite the fact that those instructions similarly freed the jury to reject "the Unification Church's definition of what constitutes a religious use or purpose" for that church, App.30 (majority opinion).

In expressly holding the jury "not bound to accept" church members' views of what uses of the assets were "religious," App.30, the court of appeals effectively licensed the jury to reject church beliefs on religious matters. In doing so, the majority wholly mischaracterized the defense claim as one that "*any use* of these funds by Reverend Moon was for religious purposes," App.28. Reverend Moon has never made any such extravagant claim; he claims only that it violates the Religion Clauses for a jury, in distinguishing between religious and personal uses for the purpose of deciding who owns property

20

contributed by church members, to deem "personal" those uses of the property which church members themselves fully ratify as advancing their religious mission.

Moreover, the court of appeals, in upholding the trial judge's refusal to instruct the jury that "Moon personifies the church movement," App.30, approved instructions that contained no reference at all to Reverend Moon's religious ministry, much less his special role as founder and leader of the Unification Church. But instructions that so fully filtered out religion, right down to the boilerplate admonition that "considerations of . . . religion must have no part in your deliberations," T6538—especially after a trial in which the government never ceased depicting Reverend Moon as merely an "ordinary, high-ranking businessman"—encouraged the jury to see Reverend Moon as running, in the judge's words, nothing beyond a "Fagin-like operation" with "hundreds of people collecting money and turning it over to him," *see* T4878, rather than as someone in whose hands it would be natural for members of his faith to place assets they desired to donate to the faith,[33] and by whose name it would be natural for them to refer to such assets.[34] A court or jury that cannot constitutionally

---

33   Such practices did not originate with these petitioners. As the founder of the Methodist Church, John Wesley, noted in his *Journal* of May 9, 1739, his followers in England had insisted on making their religious contributions not the ministry's trustees or "feoffees," but to Wesley himself, on the ground that "such feoffees always would have it in their power to control [him] and if [he] preached not as they liked, to turn [him] out of the [meeting house he] had built."

34   Reverend Moon has always made but one claim about the relevance of his special religious status to this case: that his pre-eminent role in the church he "personifies" explains why donations to the church would logically be placed in his name, and why references to the funds and stock as "Reverend Moon's" need not be seen as evidence that he or others ever "regarded [him] as owning the assets personally." *Cf.* App. 18. He has never made the radical claim the majority below wrongly attributes to him: namely, that the church "can owe no taxes," that Reverend Moon is "indistinguishable" from the church, and that therefore Reverend Moon can owe no taxes either. *See* App.30. Quite to the contrary, Reverend Moon has freely conceded that the church may owe taxes on its investment income, and that he may owe taxes on income he receives from the church for personal

21

defrock a minister, *see Serbian Orthodox Diocese v. Milivo-jevich*, 426 U.S. 696 (1976), surely cannot be permitted, in a prosecution to which the minister's religious status is crucially relevant, simply to suppress that status as though it did not exist.

Finally, the trial judge's instructions, as approved by the court of appeals, invited the jury to draw adverse inferences from the way in which the international Unification Church chose to organize itself. For the jury was told that, in deciding "whether. . .the international Unification Church movement existed"—and thus could have been the beneficial owner of the assets—the jury "should consider" "whether the Movement had a specific organizational structure, written charter or constitution" and "the existence of other Unification Church corporate entities during the relevant time period," App.68 n.3—as well as considering the church's decision to have Reverend Moon personally, rather than any of those subordinate corporate entities, hold and "administer[ ]" the funds, *id.*[35] In short, the very existence of this international religious movement—and, *a fortiori*, the claim that this movement owned the assets—was to be deemed suspect if the jury thought it more suitable for church assets to be entrusted to one of the church's incorporated worldly branches than to the church's leader. Such "searching and therefore impermissible inquiry into church polity," *Serbian Orthodox Diocese*, 426 U.S. at 723, becomes particularly offensive when used, as it was here,

---

consumption—taxes of the sort he in fact *did* pay, *see, e.g.*, GX590, 591, 597, 800; T3729-30, 3735, 3812-13, 4094, 4982-98; DXH. His only claim has been that, because the income at issue here was owned not by him but by the church—a claim turning wholly on the two *being* distinguishable—*he* owed no tax on that income.

35   Nor, contrary to the majority's view, App. 26, 31 n.5, was this instruction cured by the later instruction that a movement may beneficially own property even if *not* incorporated. For an instruction permitting the jury to penalize the accused because of his religion surely cannot be cured by another instruction adding the qualification that the jury may also acquit the accused *despite* his religion.

22

to displace the "power [of religious bodies] to decide for themselves, free from state interference, matters of church government. . .," *Kedroff v. St. Nicholas Cathedral*, 344 U.S. 94, 116 (1952).

*   *   *   *   *

Properly instructed under the Religion Clauses, a jury would have been bound to defer to whatever decision had been made by church members as to where and how to repose property they intended for church benefit. The instructions instead invited the jury to exercise a lay veto of that religious decision. Such free-wheeling veto power is anathema to the Religion Clauses, for it permits a jury to convict on criteria by which church members could not have been guided in advance—on the basis of jurors' subjective approval or disapproval of the choices a religious community has made internally, permitting prosecution to "degenerate into religious persecution," *see United States v. Ballard*, 322 U.S. at 95 (Jackson, J., dissenting).[36] And such veto power is likewise anathema to due process, for a jury empowered to ignore "legally fixed standards," and to penalize defendants instead "based upon [the jury's] own notions of what the law should be," is a jury loosed to be "arbitrary and discriminatory" in violation of our most fundamental norms of fairness, *see Giaccio v. Pennsylvania*, 382 U.S. 399, 402-03 (1966).[37]

---

36   To be sure, some may not be uncomfortable with setting so roving a commission at large. After all, as noted above, note 4 *supra*, almost half of the 1,000 people polled prior to voir dire said that, "[i]f [they] had the chance, [they'd] throw Reverend Sun Myung Moon in jail." *See* A822-23.

37   If a *per se* rule, neutral and mild enough to survive First Amendment scrutiny, had been promulgated in advance by Congress or the IRS making the funds in this case taxable to Reverend Moon—say, by making legal title automatically dispositive of beneficial ownership absent formal trust instruments—the ability of church members to plan their conduct in accord with their religious wishes would arguably have reconciled such a rule with the Religion Clause value of respecting volition and the due process value of the rule of law. But not even the government here claims the pre-existence of any such fixed *per se* rule, *see, e.g.*, A1305-06, 1309, 1310. Thus this case, unlike *Jones v. Wolf*, necessarily "involve[s] a claim that retroactive [and *ad hoc*] application of [a jury's lay preferences] infringes free-exercise rights," *see* 443 U.S. at 606 n.4.

23

III. A CRIMINAL CONVICTION BASED ON A NOVEL AND DEBATABLE THEORY OF FEDERAL TAX LIABILITY VIOLATES DUE PROCESS.

The court of appeals majority gave full approval to instructions permitting a finding that, for federal tax purposes, funds placed in a religious leader's hands by members of his church as "a charitable *gift*. . .to the Church", see App.25, belong to the leader and not to the church, so long as the members, in making that "gift," failed to "clear[ly] and unequivocal[ly]" express an intent "to create a *trust*," App.23 (emphasis added), *or* the leader, in receiving that gift, was "free to use" even a portion for his own personal benefit, App.28, *cf.* App.73. In so doing, the majority upheld the convictions in this case on a wholly novel theory of federal tax liability: a theory that, far from being settled at the time the taxpayer acted, not only rests on a reading of underlying New York state trust principles so uncertain as to be ground for dissent within the panel, but squarely conflicts with all relevant federal tax precedents.

Indeed, prior to the decision in this case, federal courts considering the taxability of property in the hands of an individual for a charitable or similar purpose have universally recognized that, while use of a portion of the property for the recipient's personal purposes may make *that portion* taxable as his income,[38] the remainder—so long as held idle or used for the intended purpose—is not taxable to him. Nor is any of the interest earned on those idle funds taxable to him.

Court decisions involving the transfer and holding of funds in a wide variety of factual settings—including such contexts as transfers intended to benefit another individual,[39] a legal en-

---

38   If the donors intended that the recipient be free to use a portion for his personal benefit, the portion so used may, however, be a non-taxable gift. *See* Internal Revenue Code § 102; *Commissioner v. Duberstein*, 363 U.S. 278 (1960).

39   *E.g.*, *Brittingham v. Commissioner*, 57 T.C.91, 100-01 (1971), *acq.*, 1971-2 C.B. 2.

24

tity,[40] or simply a "cause," such as a charity[41], political campaign[42] or religious work[43]—reflect this rule. So do published IRS determinations,[44] which the IRS expressly encourages taxpayers to follow in preparing their returns, see Revenue Procedure 78-24, 1978-2 C.B. 503,505. Given the donors' intent, expressed or implied, that the transferred funds be used for a charitable or similar purpose, in none of these authorities has the result ever turned—as the courts below made it turn here—on whether the donors "mentioned the word 'trust' " or otherwise displayed a "clear and unequivocal" intent to "create a trust,"[45] or on the recipient's freedom to make personal use

---

40   E.g., Herbert v. Commissioner, 377 F.2d 65 (9th Cir 1967); cf. Broussard v. Commissioner, 16 T.C. 23 (1951).

41   Cf. Pierce Estates Inc. v. Commissioner, 3 T.C. 875, 893-94 (1944) acq., 1944 C.B. 22 (trust for medical treatment of the poor and needy).

42   E.g., O'Dwyer v. Commissioner, 266 F.2d 575, 585-86 (4th Cir.), cert. denied, 361 U.S. 862 (1959) (political campaign); Stratton v. Commissioner, 54 T.C. 255, 282 (1970), acq. in relevant part, 1970-2 C.B. xxi (political campaign); Seven-Up Co. v. Commissioner, 14 T.C. 965 (1950), acq., 1950-2 C.B. 4 (conduit for advertising fund).

43   Cf. Winn v. Commissioner, 595 F.2d 1060, 1065 (5th Cir. 1979) (fund for missionary work); Morey v. Riddell, 205 F.Supp. 918, 921 (S.D. Cal. 1962) (contribution to informally organized church).

44   See, e.g., Revenue Ruling 74-23, 1974-1 C.B. 17 (interest earned on idle campaign funds held by a candidate is reportable only as income earned in a fiduciary capacity, rather than as personal income of the candidate); Revenue Procedure 68-19, 1968-1 C.B. 810, 811.

45   Indeed, when the recipient of funds is one who has held himself out as the representative of a cause, not even direct evidence of the donors' intent to benefit that cause has previously been deemed necessary. Rather, federal tax law has always presumed, absent evidence to the contrary, that a donor making a gratuitous transfer to the representative of a cause intends to benefit the cause. United States v. Scott, 660 F.2d 1145, 1164 (7th Cir. 1981), cert. denied, 455 U.S. 907 (1982). See also Revenue Procedure 68-19, supra note 44 ("The Service will presume in the absence of evidence to the contrary that contributions to a political candidate are political funds which are not intended for the unrestricted personal use of such a recipient" (emphasis added)).

25

of some portion of the property donated. On the contrary, the rule has consistently been applied regardless of whether the donation establishes a "trust", an "agency," or even an unlabeled fiduciary relationship[46]—and even where the recipient is expected to make personal use of a portion of the property.[47] Had the settled rule been applied in this case, none of the Chase interest—all of which was earned on funds donated "to the church," and earned, of course, while those funds were idle—would have been taxable income to Reverend Moon.

Nor, prior to the majority's decision in this case, was there any clear, certain rule under New York law deviating from the rule settled by the federal tax authorities. Indeed, the majority cited no direct authority for its view that, in New York, evidence of intent to make a charitable donation to a cause is insufficient to permit a finding of charitable trust[48]; and it ignored closely analogous New York authority, cited by Judge Oakes, that intent to make a gift for "charitable or religious purposes" is in fact sufficient. See App.66; see also App.70-72. As demonstrated by Judge Oakes' forceful dissent, it is at best doubtful that the New York Court of Appeals would in fact agree with the majority's interpretation of New York law.[49]

---

46   Compare, e.g., *Pierce Estates* (gift for charitable purposes created an informal oral trust) and *Brittingham* (recipient of funds held them as agent for transferror) *with Broussard* and *Herbert* (no characterization of relationship between holder of property and beneficial owners).

47   E.g., *Morey v. Riddell*, 205 F.Supp. at 921 (pastors received and held money as a donation to their church with the understanding that they would be free to use a portion for their personal support).

48   While the principle invoked by the majority—that intent "to create a trust" must be unequivocally expressed—has been applied by New York courts to decide whether a charitable trust was restricted to specific uses, *see* App.24, it has never been applied by *any* court to conclude that property donated for charitable purposes could be deemed to *belong* to the recipient.

49   Among other things, the majority's novel trust-law interpretation would perversely free faithless trustees—simply by persuading donors to avoid using the word "trust" or by making personal use of part of the assets entrusted to them—to divest the trust's beneficiaries of all claim to beneficial ownership of *any* of the trust assets.

26

But even if it were to do so, its ruling would break new ground in New York and would be inconsistent with the mainstream of federal tax authorities. And, unlike a diversity case or other civil suit in which federal courts might properly anticipate a previously unannounced state ruling, this is a *criminal* proceeding—a proceeding in which a novel interpretation may not be newly announced without running headlong into the prohibition of the Due Process Clause, which "mandate[s] that no individual be forced to speculate, at peril of indictment, whether his conduct is prohibited . . ." and forbids "punishment for actions that [were] not " 'plainly and unmistakably' proscribed." *Dunn v. United States*, 442 U.S. 100, 112 (1979).

That mandate was wholly ignored here. For the theory of taxability used to obtain conviction in this case was not "plainly and unmistakably" the law; indeed it was an entirely novel theory. And such a theory, announced for the first time on the very occasion on which it is first invoked—and departing sharply from the standards of prior cases—suffers from precisely the vice that may render a vague rule unconstitutional on its face. *Cf. Shuttlesworth v. Birmingham*, 394 U.S. 147, 150-53 (1969). Like a rule that is written in an ink visible only to the prosecutor, judge, and jury, a newly announced theory of liability not only fails to give fair notice in advance of the conduct for which punishment will be imposed. It also fails to prevent the prosecutor from creating the "crime" to fit the accused, *see United States v. Evans*, 333 U.S. 483 (1948); *United States v. L. Cohen Grocery Co.*, 255 U.S. 81 (1921)[50] —from engaging in *ad hoc*, arbitrary, and discriminatory prosecution and conviction, *see, e.g., Kolender v. Lawson*, 103 S.Ct. 1855, 1858-59 (1983); *Grayned v. City of Rockford*, 408

---

50   *See Bouie v. City of Columbia*, 378 U.S. 347, 354 (1964) ("[T]he vice in [a vague criminal statute] cannot 'be cured in a given case by a construction in that very case placing valid limits on the statute.' "); *Marks v. United States*, 430 U.S. 188, 191-92 (1977) (ban on applying novel standard of criminal liability in *ex post facto* manner must be enforced with "special care" whenever case "implicates first amendment values").

27

U.S. 104, 108-09 (1972).[51] And this Court has treated the risk of such discrimination as least tolerable when its victims might be religious minorities. *See, e.g., Kunz v. New York*, 340 U.S. 290, 295 (1951); *Cantwell v. Connecticut*, 310 U.S. 296, 305-07 (1940).[52]

Tax cases enjoy no immunity from these due process principles. Twenty-three years ago in *James v. United States*, 366 U.S. 213 (1961), five justices of this Court, in two separate opinions,[53] decided that, as a matter of law, a taxpayer may

---

51   Nor can a conviction obtained on the basis of a novel rule be saved from a due process challenge simply on the ground that the government must prove, as an element of its case, that the defendant acted willfully. For while a defendant's subjective belief that he was committing a crime may be relevant to ensuring adequate notice, it is wholly irrelevant to the prevention of discriminatory prosecution. And, as the Court recently emphasized in *Kolender*, 103 S.Ct. at 1858-59, it is the prevention of discriminatory prosecution, regardless of the defendant's subjective intent—the prevention of a "standardless sweep [that] allows policemen, prosecutors, and juries to pursue their personal predilections"—that is the central thrust of the void-for-vagueness doctrine.

52   As the trial judge himself observed post-trial, the investigation of Reverend Moon's taxes would have been less likely if he had been the leader of a less controversial religion. A536-57; *see* App. 35. This case thus illustrates that careful adherence to the requirements of precision and prospectivity would have served an important policy against selective prosecution, the soundness of which the Solicitor General has recently acknowledged: "[W]hen the decision to prosecute is based upon an impermissible criterion, such as race or religion or the exercise of constitutional rights, the general rule [of discretion] must yield to an exception." Brief for the United States at 10, *Hobby v. United States*, No. 82-2140, *cert. granted*, 52 U.S.L.W. 3460 (U.S. Dec. 13, 1983). To the extent that the ban on retroactive application of novel rules is used to police this exception preventively, courts and litigants will be relieved from the need to face the thorny factual issues that arise when, as in this case, defendants seek discovery and a hearing to explore *actual* prosecutorial motive in the context of a claim of selective prosecution. *See* App.33-37.

53   Chief Justice Warren, joined by Justices Brennan and Stewart, announcing the judgment of the Court, 366 U.S. at 220; Justice Black, joined by Justice Douglas, concurring in part, dissenting in part, *id.* at 224.

28

not be convicted on the basis of a new theory of taxability that was at best uncertain at the time the taxpayer acted.[54] Since then, three circuits, following *James'* lead, have declared their view that, while a "pioneering interpretation of tax liability" may be appropriate to impose in a *civil* tax proceeding, it may not be imposed in a *criminal* prosecution, "with attendant potential loss of freedom . . ." *United States v. Critzer*, 498 F.2d 1160, 1162 (4th Cir. 1974) (holding conviction for tax evasion barred "as a matter of law" where taxability "highly debatable," *id.* at 1162); *United States v. Dahlstrom*, 713 F.2d 1423, 1428 (9th Cir. 1983) (holding "[d]ue process," *id.* at 1427, precludes tax fraud convictions where legality of tax shelter program "was completely unsettled by any clearly relevant precedent on the dates alleged in the indictment," *id.* at 1428); *see United States v. Garber*, 607 F.2d 92, 100 (5th Cir. 1979) (en banc).[55] In reaching this conclusion, all three of these circuits recognized that, when the "obligation to pay is . . . problematical . . . , defendant's actual intent is irrelevant." *Critzer*, 498 F.2d at 1162; *Garber*, 607 F.2d at 98; *see Dahlstrom*, 713 F.2d at 1428.

The decision of the Second Circuit in this case, upholding the defendants' convictions on what must be recognized as "a pioneering interpretation of tax liability"—"novel and unsettled by clearly relevant precedent," *Garber*, 607 F.2d at 100—

---

54   As Justice Black, anticipating the Court's reasoning in *Marks v. United States, supra* note 50, explained, "[e]ven though the *ex post facto* provision of the Constitution has not ordinarily been thought to apply to judicial legislation," the theory of taxability newly announced by the Court in *James* should not be made "applicable to past conduct" as a matter of "good, governmental policy." 366 U.S. at 224. And, in any event, "a criminal statute that is so ambiguous in scope that . . . [a new] interpretation of it brings about totally unexpected results . . . raises serious questions of unconstitutional vagueness." *Id.* at 224.

55   Although the holding in *Garber* was to remand for a new trial to correct the errors in excluding expert testimony on the "uncharted" area of tax law involved in that case, and in failing to instruct the jury that uncertainty of law was relevant to criminal intent, *id.*, at 99, in reaching that result the *en banc* majority firmly stated that where "the tax question was completely novel and unsettled by clearly relevant precedent . . . [a] criminal proceeding . . . is . . . inappropriate," *id.*, at 100.

29

plainly conflicts with the *James* line of cases.[56] Indeed, the Second Circuit's decision in this case is the *only* federal decision in the 23 years since *James* to affirm a criminal tax conviction over a dissent as to the underlying theory of taxability of the income in question.

Conclusion

The court of appeals correctly observed that "[t]his . . . is not the first occasion when a controversial political or religious figure has been criminally prosecuted." App.36. But it does appear to be the first in which such a figure has been forced to stand trial before a jury that he sought to waive so as to avoid pervasive prejudice against him as a political or religious figure. It is surely the first time a conviction by a jury has been affirmed despite the trial court's conclusion that a non-jury trial would have been fairer, and despite the appellate court's concession that a non-jury trial would have been permitted absent defendant's public protest at being singled out for

---

56   Although the circuit court's opinion does not *explicitly* reject defendants' argument that, in light of the *James* line of cases, criminality cannot properly be found where the underlying theory of taxability has not been clearly established in advance, it must in fact be read to reject that argument as one of the supposedly "minor points [the court] consider[ed] wholly without merit," *see* App.4. For the colloquy at oral argument before the circuit court—in which Judge Oakes stated explicitly that the Second Circuit's decision in *United States v. Ingredient Technology*, 698 F.2d 88 (2d Cir.), *cert. denied*, 103 S.Ct. 3111 (1983), "rejects the *Garber* test of intent" grounded in *James*—made plain that the court entertained defendants' argument, but rejected it out of hand as foreclosed by *Ingredient Technology*. Transcript of Oral Argument, at 16-17 (2d Cir., Mar. 23, 1983).

Nor does this Court's denial of certiorari in *Ingredient Technology* foreclose the argument petitioners here advance. *First*, the decision in *Ingredient Technology* did not reject this argument, but merely found "no lack of clarity in the law" challenged there, 698 F.2d at 96 n.8. *Second*, the only ruling in *Garber* actually rejected by *Ingredient Technology* concerned an issue not relevent here: namely, the admissibility of expert testimony about the debated theory of taxability of the income in question.

This case, therefore, squarely presents for the first time the issue whether the retroactive application of a novel theory of taxability in a criminal case violates due process—a question that now divides the Second Circuit from at least the Fourth and Ninth, if not also the Fifth.

30

prosecution. If these petitioners go to jail, they will indeed be the first religious leaders since the ratification of the Constitution to be imprisoned because of the way they and their followers chose to organize their church's internal affairs—and the first defendants in a federal criminal tax prosecution in at least a quarter century whose convictions have been affirmed over a dissent as to the underlying theory of the income's taxability.

To permit such extraordinary results without plenary review by this Court would be troublesome even if it could safely be predicted that what befell these petitioners would not befall others. But such predictions are notoriously unsafe, and the court of appeals may well have been right in its prophesy that Reverend Moon's case "plainly. . . will not be the last" of its type, *id.* That, at least, must be the estimate of the many and diverse *amici*—friends not of these petitioners, surely, but of this Court and of religious and civil liberty—who join in urging review by the Court on the merits of this case.

For these and all the foregoing reasons, petitioners accordingly pray that a writ of certiorari issue so that such review may take place.

Respectfully submitted,

LAURENCE H. TRIBE
Counsel of Record
KATHLEEN M. SULLIVAN
1525 Massachusetts Ave.
Cambridge, Massachusetts
(617) 495-1767

HAROLD R. TYLER, JR.   JEANNE BAKER
  Patterson, Belknap,   DAVID J. FINE
    Webb & Tyler   Silverglate, Gertner, Baker & Fine

CHARLES C. RUFF   MORTIMER CAPLIN
  Covington & Burling   RICHARD C. TIMBIE
                                 Caplin & Drysdale
ANDREW C. LAWLER

January 26, 1984

App. 1

UNITED STATES COURT OF APPEALS

FOR THE SECOND CIRCUIT

Nos. 755, 765, 766, 1153—August Term, 1982

Cal. No. 1630

(Argued March 23, 1983   Decided September 13, 1983)

Docket Nos. 82-1275, 82-1279, 82-1277,
82-1357, 82-1387

UNITED STATES OF AMERICA,

Appellee,

—v.—

SUN MYUNG MOON and TAKERU KAMIYAMA,

Defendants-Appellants.

Before:

OAKES, CARDAMONE and WINTER,
Circuit Judges.

Appeals from judgments of the United States District
Court for the Southern District of New York (Goettel, J.)

App. 2

convicting appellant Moon of conspiracy and filing false tax returns and appellant Kamiyama of aiding and abetting the filing of false returns, obstruction of justice, and perjury.

Affirmed in part, reversed in part.

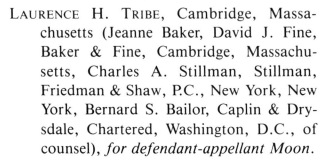

LAURENCE H. TRIBE, Cambridge, Massachusetts (Jeanne Baker, David J. Fine, Baker & Fine, Cambridge, Massachusetts, Charles A. Stillman, Stillman, Friedman & Shaw, P.C., New York, New York, Bernard S. Bailor, Caplin & Drysdale, Chartered, Washington, D.C., of counsel), *for defendant-appellant Moon.*

ANDREW M. LAWLER, New York, New York (Maurice M. McDermott, Dennis E. Milton, Anne T. Vitale, Andrew M. Lawler, P.C., New York, New York, Barry A. Fisher, Robert C. Moest, David Grosz, Fisher & Moest, Los Angeles, California, of counsel), *for defendant-appellant Kamiyama.*

JO ANN HARRIS, Assistant United States Attorney, New York, New York (William M. Tendy, Acting United States Attorney for the Southern District of New York, Gary G. Grindler, Gerard E. Lynch, Walter P. Loughlin, Assistant United States Attorneys, New York, New York, Martin Flumenbaum, Special Assistant United

App. 3

States Attorney, New York, New York, of counsel), *for appellee.*

SAMUEL E. ERICSON, Springfield, Virginia (Edward Larson, Springfield, Virginia, of counsel), *for the Center for Law and Religious Freedom, Amicus Curiae.*

STEVEN R. SHAPIRO, New York, New York, *for the American Civil Liberties Union and New York Civil Liberties Union, Amicus Curiae.*

EARL W. TRENT, JR., Valley Forge, Pennsylvania, *for National Ministries, American Baptist Churches in the U.S.A., Amicus Curiae.*

————————★————————

CARDAMONE, *Circuit Judge:*

Reverend Sun Myung Moon and Takeru Kamiyama appeal from judgments of conviction entered on July 16, 1982 in the United States District Court for the Southern District of New York following a six-week jury trial before Judge Gerard L. Goettel. Moon was charged basically with filing false income tax returns and Kamiyama with obstructing the investigation of those returns.

Paying income taxes is not America's most popular national pastime. But, most accept the certainty of taxes as part of the price of modern life. Tax fraud prosecutions usually do not present the myriad of constitutional problems involved here. Yet in this case the defense raises troubling issues of religious persecution and abridgment of free speech that are interwoven with other grounds for objection to the judgments below. In reducing this huge record and the veritable avalanche of arguments presented to what we hope is comprehensible form, we have divided this opinion into five major sections—Denial of Bench Trial, Sufficiency of the Evidence, Jury Instructions, Miscellaneous Issues, and Kamiyama's Claims. Most of the issues raised have been addressed. Those not discussed are minor points that we consider wholly without merit.

We commend the manner in which Judge Goettel presided in this especially lengthy trial. Such errors as inevitably crept in were skillfully unearthed by counsel. Of course, defendants are only entitled to "a fair trial but not a perfect one." *Lutwak v. United States*, 344 U.S. 604, 619 (1953). Defendants did receive a fair trial and we affirm their convictions on all counts, except Kamiyama's conviction on Count Seven which is reversed.

BACKGROUND

The main indictment upon which Reverend Moon and Mr. Kamiyama were tried charged them in Count One with conspiracy, 18 U.S.C. § 371, to file false federal income tax returns, 26 U.S.C. § 7206(1), to obstruct justice, 18 U.S.C. § 1503, and to make false statements to government agencies, 18 U.S.C. § 1001, and to a federal grand jury, 18 U.S.C. § 1623. Counts Two, Three and Four charged Moon with filing false tax returns for 1973, 1974 and 1975, in violation of 26 U.S.C. § 7206(1). Counts Five and Six charged Kamiyama with aiding and abetting the filing of the false 1974 and 1975 returns, 26 U.S.C. § 7206(2). The remaining counts (Seven through Thirteen) charged Kamiyama with the substantive of-

App. 5

fenses of obstruction of justice through the submission of false documents to the grand jury, 18 U.S.C. § 1503, submitting false documents to the Department of Justice, 18 U.S.C. § 1001, and five counts of perjury, 18 U.S.C. § 1623. A separate indictment charged Kamiyama with an additional count of perjury.

At the conclusion of the trial on May 18, 1982 the jury returned guilty verdicts against both defendants on all counts. Moon was sentenced to concurrent terms of 18 months in prison on Counts One through Four and fined $25,000 plus costs. Kamiyama was sentenced to concurrent terms of six months in prison on all counts of which he was convicted and fined $5,000. Both sentences have been stayed pending this appeal.

Defendants moved in September 1982 for a new trial, alleging juror misconduct. After holding hearings on this issue, Judge Goettel denied the motion by order dated October 13, 1982 and issued an order on November 5, 1982 restraining all parties and their agents from communicating with the trial jurors without prior consent of the court. Defendants appeal from these two post-trial orders as well as from their convictions.

The case focused principally on bank accounts held in Reverend Moon's name in the Park Avenue office of the Chase Manhattan Bank. On March 27, 1973 Reverend Moon walked into the Chase branch and opened a personal checking account and a savings account. During the next nearly three years over 1.7 million dollars was deposited in these accounts in Moon's name, all but $200,000 of which was in cash. A substantial portion of the funds were transfered to high-yielding Chase time deposits held in Moon's name. During the years 1973-1975 these investments earned more than $100,000 in interest, not reported as income on Moon's tax returns

App. 6

for the years in question. Also at issue was $50,000 worth of stock issued to Moon in 1973 in Tong Il Enterprises, Inc., a corporation organized in New York in 1973 by Moon and Kamiyama which was engaged in the business of importing products from Korea. The receipt of this stock, which the government apparently views as a dividend, also was not reflected as income on Moon's tax return.

The critical issue is whether, as the government claims, Moon owned these assets and was therefore required to pay income taxes on the bank interest and the value of the stock or, as the defense urges, Moon held these assets merely beneficially or as a trustee for the Unification Church. Before entering upon a discussion of this central issue, we first address contentions raised by the defendants as a result of the government's refusal to consent to defendants' request for a bench trial.

I

DENIAL OF BENCH TRIAL

A. As a Denial of the First Amendment
Right to Free Speech

It is the view of the defense that the government's reason for opposing the defendants' request for a bench trial is unconstitutional, so that the judge's acceptance of it was error of constitutional dimension mandating reversal. The factual background may be simply stated. At a rally in New York City's Foley Square on October 22, 1981 following his arraignment, Moon made a speech which was partially reprinted as a full page advertisement in the New York Times of November 5, 1981. He stated:

App. 7

I would not be standing here today if my skin were white or my religion were Presbyterian. I am here today only because my skin is yellow and my religion is Unification Church. The ugliest things in this beautiful country of America are religious bigotry and racism.

In response to defense efforts to waive a trial by jury, the prosecutor wrote a letter to Judge Goettel dated March 11, 1982 stating her opposition and, referring to the excerpt quoted above, adding that defendants had raised—and circulated worldwide—questions about "the integrity and motives of this prosecution." It was the prosecutor's conclusion that a single factfinder would be placed in an "untenable" position and that there was an overriding public interest in the appearance as well as the fact of a fair trial, which could be achieved only by a jury. The government insisted that employing this normal and preferable mode of disposing of fact issues in a criminal trial would defuse the public criticism that had been leveled by Moon.

The defense argues that, on the contrary, insistence upon a jury trial had the effect of punishing Moon for exercising his First Amendment right of free speech. The punishment, so the argument runs, took the form of denying Moon a benefit, i.e., a nonjury trial, that he would otherwise have been entitled to. The underlying rationale for this argument is that Moon and his followers had received such negative press that, regardless of the government's protestations, it was impossible to obtain a fair trial with a jury and that this state of affairs was only exacerbated by Moon's speech.

Trial by jury is a constitutional right provided in Article III Section 2 of the Constitution. The Sixth Amendment

App. 8

guarantees that "[i]n all criminal prosecutions, the accused shall enjoy the right to a speedy and public trial, by an impartial jury of the State and district wherein the crime shall have been committed." Nothing in the Constitution guarantees one the right to select his own tribunal or the right to a speedy and public trial by a fair and impartial judge. The right to trial by jury is a benefit granted an accused, *see Gannett Co., Inc. v. DePasquale*, 443 U.S. 368, 380 (1979), which a defendant has the power to waive. But before a waiver can be effective, the consent of the prosecutor and the sanction of the court must be obtained. *See Patton v. United States*, 281 U.S. 276, 312 (1930); Fed. R. Crim. P. 23(a). The ability to waive the benefit does not import a right to claim its opposite. And the Supreme Court has stated that because of "confidence in the integrity of the federal prosecutor, Rule 23(a) does not require that the Government articulate its reasons for demanding a jury trial at the time it refuses to consent to a defendant's proffered waiver." *Singer v. United States*, 380 U.S. 24, 37 (1965).

Conclusive as that statement might appear, it does not end the matter. For the Supreme Court has also held that even though one has no right to a government benefit, such benefit may not be denied and when granted may not be conditioned or later revoked for a reason that infringes an individual's constitutional rights, especially First Amendment freedoms. *See, e.g., Perry v. Sindermann*, 408 U.S. 593, 597 (1972); *Sherbert v. Verner*, 374 U.S. 398, 405 (1963). But the defendant has presented no facts on this record that convince us that the government's reason for refusing to consent to a bench trial was impermissibly to punish Moon for exercising his First Amendment rights. Instead, it appears that the public prosecutor elected, as was her right and based upon the

App. 9

reasons she gave, to have this case tried in the constitutionally preferred manner. Without the factual predicate to support his argument, the defendant's claim of error evaporates.

B. *As the Denial of the Right to a Fair Trial*

Moon also contends that prior to the voir dire there was an unacceptable risk that a fair jury could not be selected and therefore that the denial of a bench trial violated his right to a fair trial.[1] This argument, like the previous one, urges that there was a reasonable likelihood in advance that public animosity toward Moon and his religion would prevent a fair trial. In our view this debatable contention could be satisfactorily resolved only upon the voir dire of prospective jurors. *See Application of Cohn*, 332 F.2d 976, 977 (2d Cir. 1964). Ordinarily, insisting that a defendant undergo a jury trial against his will does not run afoul of a defendant's right to due process and a fair trial. *Singer v. United States*, 380 U.S. at 34-36. Certainly we recognize, though, that there might be cases where the circumstances are so compelling that for the court to countenance the government's insistence on a jury trial over the defendant's request to be tried by a judge alone would deny the defendant a fair trial. *See Singer v. United States*, 380 U.S. at 37. This is not such a case. Compelling circumstances are not demonstrated simply by claims of an atmosphere poisoned by a negative

---

1   Appellants also contend that the subject matter of this tax fraud prosecution, together with the sheer volume of complicated exhibits, turned this trial into one of mesmerizing complexity. We believe the case was not so complex as to be beyond the grasp of the jury. While the trial lasted over six weeks and there were hundreds of exhibits introduced, very few of them were complicated. The jury's task came down to deciding the basic issue of ownership of the Chase accounts and the Tong Il stock.

App. 10

press. The validity of such claims is properly shown upon a voir dire of prospective jurors. The trial court, wisely recognizing that this was a safer avenue to follow in order to ascertain whether a fair jury could be obtained, properly reserved until after the voir dire its option to overrule the government's refusal to waive a jury trial.

Additionally, review of the transcript of the seven painstaking days of jury selection, involving the interrogation of 63 out of 200 veniremen for the panel and 17 for the six alternate positions, convinces us of the accuracy of the trial court's finding after selection was completed that "we have gotten a jury which is, if not totally free from bias, by and large capable of putting aside the bias they have and deciding the case on the merits of the charges." Jurors need not be totally ignorant of a defendant in order to be fair and unbiased. *See Dobbert v. Florida*, 432 U.S. 282, 302 (1977); *Murphy v. Florida*, 421 U.S. 794, 798-800 (1975). Even where a prospective juror has formed some preconceived opinion as to the guilt of the accused in the case on trial the juror is sufficiently impartial if he or she can set aside that opinion and render a verdict based on the evidence in the case. *Murphy v. Florida*, 421 U.S. at 799-800; *Irwin v. Dowd*, 366 U.S. 717, 722-23 (1961); *United States v. Murray*, 618 F.2d 892, 899 (2d Cir. 1980). Significantly, defense counsel only challenged one of the 12 jurors for cause, and the denial of that challenge is not raised on appeal. *See Beck v. Washington*, 369 U.S. 541, 557-58 (1962) (failure to challenge for cause prospective jurors is strong evidence defendant considered jurors not biased). Absent a clear abuse of the trial court's discretion, one that results in manifest prejudice to defendants, the finding made by the trial judge that the jury was fair and unbiased must be upheld. *See United States v. Brown*,

App. 11

644 F.2d 101, 104 (2d Cir.), *cert. denied*, 454 U.S. 881 (1981).

II

SUFFICIENCY OF THE EVIDENCE

A. Counts Two Through Six

Defendants argue that the evidence presented was insufficient to find them guilty beyond a reasonable doubt on the substantive tax offenses charged in Counts Two through Six. To find defendants guilty of fraud in the filing of Moon's income tax returns, the jury had to find that statements contained in the returns which were verified as true were in fact false, and that these false statements were willfully made. Viewing the evidence in the light most favorable to the government and considering that all questions of credibility are within the exclusive province of the jury, there was ample evidence to find that Moon willfully filed false tax returns for the years 1973-75 and that Kamiyama willfully aided and abetted in the false 1974 and 1975 filings.

(1) Falsity

(a) Moon's Financial Picture

We examine first the evidence regarding falsity. In order to do so we sketch briefly defendants' financial picture. In November 1972 when Reverend Moon visited the United States he was already a successful businessman, being founder and chairman of the boards of eight publishing and manufacturing companies in his native Korea. The Unification Church of New York had begun purchasing and importing ginseng tea and marble vases

App. 12

from some of Moon's Korean companies. In June 1973 Kamiyama incorporated Tong Il Enterprises in New York which purchased and sold these items. Moon subscribed to 500 shares for $50,000 which, according to some of the corporation's records, he paid for. His wife subscribed to 200 shares for $20,000 and Kamiyama subscribed to 100 shares for $10,000, all from an original issue of 1005 shares. Thus, Moon and his wife had 70 percent control of the company and Moon was elected chairman of its board. Although 500 shares were issued to Moon, he did not actually pay for them, as he had originally obligated himself to do. Instead the stock was issued to him without payment in 1973, apparently in exchange for various assets transferred to Tong Il by other corporations which Moon controlled. In the spring of 1974 Moon began drawing a salary from this enterprise as a "business consultant" and at the same time opened a checking account, known as the "household account," in the Chase Manhattan Bank into which his salary was deposited.

As noted, about a year earlier, Moon had opened a different personal checking account ("checking account") and an individual savings account at the Chase Manhattan Bank. Subsequently, on April 9, 1973, Moon personally deposited $100,000 into the checking account. During the three-year course of his relationship with the bank approximately $1,724,774 was deposited into Moon's various accounts. Commencing in late 1973 he transferred from the checking and savings accounts, and directly deposited, a substantial portion of the $1.7 million in high-yielding Chase time deposits. These time deposits were also held in Moon's name, and on his instructions they, together with the interest earned on them, were rolled-over. The total interest earned on all the

App. 13

Chase accounts in the relevant years, 1973-75, was approximately $106,650.

With respect to living expenses, the household account at Chase was used by Moon primarily to pay the private school expenses of his children. Ordinary personal and household expenses were paid for by the Holy Spirit Association for Unification World Christianity (HSA-UWC), incorporated in California in 1961 as the American branch of the Unification Church.

Having outlined the Tong Il stock and Chase accounts transactions, we complete Moon's financial picture by describing the real estate dealings pertinent to this case. A month before Moon's November 1972 arrival in the United States HSA-UWC purchased "Belvedere," the 20 acre Bronfman estate in Tarrytown, New York, for $750,000. The seller took back a $550,000 mortgage and the $200,000 balance was paid by HSA-UWC. When Moon came in 1972 he occupied the main house on this estate. In the fall of 1973 an adjoining estate became available. It was purchased that October in the name of HSA-UWC for $631,827. To complete the purchase Moon loaned HSA-UWC $361,827 from the checking account at Chase. He also issued his personal check to Sotheby Park Bernet for $51,160 to pay for furnishings in the estate, which he named "East Garden." In late 1973 Moon's family came from Korea. He and his staff moved out of Belvedere and, together with his family, took up residence in East Garden.

(b) Evidence

Under the government's theory of the case, Moon failed to report interest income earned on the Chase Manhattan Bank accounts that he purportedly owned and income recognized as a result of a distribution of Tong Il

App. 14

stock to him at no cost.[2] Appellants' principal contentions at trial were that the Chase accounts and Tong Il stock belonged to the Church, that Moon merely held these assets as the nominee, agent, and/or trustee of the Church, and that therefore he was not taxable on either the Chase interest or Tong Il stock distribution.

In concluding that the jury properly found the Chase accounts and Tong Il stock to be Moon's personal property, we start first with the fact that the Chase accounts and Tong Il securities were maintained in Moon's name and controlled by him. Second, some funds clearly destined for Church entities were put in existing Church bank accounts which were owned and controlled by church corporations. Third, from his handling of the Chase accounts and Tong Il stock Moon seemingly regarded them as his own, not as belonging to the Church. Fourth, high ranking members of the Church were told that the Chase funds belonged to "Father," not to the Church.

The government introduced evidence that Moon actually considered the Chase accounts to be his own property rather than the Church's, and that he used funds from the accounts for expenditures which the jury could have concluded were personal in nature. Several examples will suffice. In September 1975 Moon and Kamiyama purchased shares in a new bank, Diplomat National Bank in Washington, D.C., $80,000 worth of stock for Moon

---

2   Since the defendant's only argument regarding the Tong Il stock is that it belonged to the Church rather than to Moon, it appears that he concedes the taxability of the distribution if in fact the stock belonged to Moon personally. The defendant did not assert below and does not assert now that the distribution constituted a gift to him from Tong Il, which gift of course would not be subject to the federal income tax. The jury could well have found that the whole transaction amounted to an indirect dividend to Moon from the companies under his control which transferred assets to Tong Il.

App. 15

and $75,000 for Kamiyama. The funds used to pay for the stock were derived from one of Moon's time deposits at Chase and transferred into the household account, and later a check drawn on that account was made payable to the Diplomat National Bank.

In 1973, when HSA-UWC purchased East Garden, Moon loaned HSA-UWC $361,827 from the checking account to complete the $631,827 purchase. This transfer was carried on HSA-UWC's books as a personal loan from Moon. Later, when HSA-UWC was unable to meet mortgage payments on the $500,000 mortgage on "Belvedere," Moon broke a Chase time deposit and loaned $175,000 to the Church organization. HSA-UWC repaid Moon $70,000 of this loan, writing off the $105,000 balance as a personal contribution from Moon. The jury might well have inferred from the bookkeeping entries concerning these transactions that HSA-UWC considered the Chase funds Moon's exclusive property.

In November 1973 Moon directed that title to East Garden be transferred to him because he had supplied most of its purchase price from his personal funds, i.e., the Chase accounts. But before Moon's subordinates could complete this transfer they were informed by Church lawyers that Moon would have to pay the estate's fair market value of $700,000 in order to avoid adverse tax consequences for himself and the Church. To create this $700,000 consideration, loans to HSA-UWC from Moon amounting to $361,827 were falsely increased on the Church books to $700,000. Moon then signed a Release and Cancellation of Indebtedness Agreement covering the $700,000 purchase price for East Garden. Even though this document was never actually used, by signing it Moon implicitly acknowledged that the $361,827 used

App. 16

to pay for the property, which had come from the Chase accounts, was his own.

Finally, the documents given by the defendants to the Justice Department to support their theory that Moon held the Chase funds and Tong Il stock other than individually were revealed to be fraudulently backdated. To understand how this came about it is helpful to capsulize Moon's finances at the beginning of 1974. At that time Moon had $556,000 in Chase time deposits, an outstanding loan of $361,827 to HSA-UWC made in connection with the purchase of East Garden, $50,000 and $4,000 in his Chase checking and savings accounts respectively and $50,000 worth of Tong Il stock. East Garden had $51,160 worth of furnishings purchased from Sothebys. These assets had a value in excess of a million dollars. At this point the leaders of HSA-UWC consulted a Washington law firm regarding a number of business and financial matters, including the transfer of East Garden into Moon's own name. The leaders were advised by counsel to keep Moon's assets separate from those of the Church, that Moon had to file a personal income tax return, that as a resident alien he was taxable on all income to him from whatever source, and that the custom of providing substantial gifts to Reverend Moon in kind or cash should be terminated.

After meeting with lawyers and accountants on January 3 and 4, 1974 it was decided not to have these professionals handle Moon's 1973 tax return. Instead, Kamiyama was to be in charge, preparing the return under Moon's instructions. Records were produced to account for the nearly 1.8 million dollars deposited into the Chase Manhattan Bank and to show these as the Church's assets rather than Moon's. Three hundred and fifty thousand dollars was accounted for as "loans" from

App. 17

leaders of Unification organizations in England, France, Germany, Italy and the Netherlands. Each loan, signed by Kamiyama, bore a date and amount which matched, or in combination matched, a deposit into the Chase account in 1973. Another 1.2 million of cash deposited into Chase was accounted for by Japanese church members who, it was said, carried this money into the United States in amounts of three or four thousand dollars each. A ledger was kept—the Japanese Family Fund Ledger—with hundreds of entries showing a name, date of contribution and amount. The ledger also showed disbursements labelled "donations" which matched precisely the deposits into the Chase accounts.

With respect to the loans from the European leaders ostensibly made and entered into a loan ledger in 1973, a watermark expert established at trial that the paper on which these 1973 transactions occurred had not been manufactured until 1974. The Japanese Family Fund Ledger was also shown to be manufactured after the fact. Because some of the bank deposits consisted not of cash but of checks from sources other than Japanese donors, the government was able to demonstrate the falsity of the ledger. A comparison of Chase deposit slips, which included checks not reflected in the ledger, with the Japanese Family Fund Ledger revealed "donation" disbursements on the same date in the exact amount of each Chase deposit. A discrepancy appeared because the ledger disbursement indicated that the entire deposit in the same amount as the deposit slip was cash, while the proof at trial demonstrated that the deposit was partly in checks. Thus unravelled it appeared that Kamiyama's aide, Yukiko Matsumura, had constructed the ledger simply by working backwards from Moon's bank statements and deposit slips to create fictitious cash sources to account

App. 18

for all of the deposits at Chase. Since she mistakenly thought each deposit was all cash the ledger entries and the total amount deposited into the bank accounts matched perfectly. When checks were included in the totals, however, the fraudulently backdated nature of the ledger was clearly revealed.

In sum the government presented evidence at trial that Moon controlled the Chase accounts and Tong Il stock, held them in his own name, considered the Chase accounts his own, used the accounts in a seemingly personal manner, and was regarded by other Church figures as owning the assets personally. Additionally, the documents produced by the defendants to show that the assets were in fact Church property proved to be backdated and false. Viewing this evidence in the light most favorable to the government, it is sufficient to establish that Moon owned the Chase accounts and Tong Il stock in a personal capacity. Because he owned the assets, he should have reported the interest and stock distribution income on his tax returns. Since he failed to do so, his 1973-75 returns were false.

(2) Willfulness

We turn to the evidence that Moon willfully filed income tax returns for the 1973-75 tax years knowing that these returns contained false information and that Kamiyama willfully aided and abetted the 1974 and 1975 filings. Willfulness in tax fraud cases has become equated with bad faith, want of justification or knowledge that the taxpayer should have reported more income than he did. *See United States v. Bishop*, 412 U.S. 346, 360 (1973). The Supreme Court collected the formulations cited in *Bishop* and reduced them to the statement that willfulness in the context of filing a false income tax

App. 19

return "simply means a voluntary, intentional violation of a known legal duty." *United States v. Pomponio*, 429 U.S. 10, 12 (1976).

The evidence presented on this issue, although circumstantial, was sufficient to sustain the jury's verdict. The salient points follow. Moon signed his 1974 and 1975 returns, acknowledging that he had read them and that they were accurate, and he signed an RSC-12 form giving similar assurances as to his 1973 return; Moon and Kamiyama both knew of Moon's interest income at Chase and income from the distribution of Tong Il stock; Moon actively supervised all of his personal financial matters and never signed anything until he understood it; Moon's 1973 "personal income tax matters [were] being handled under his instructions by Mr. Kamiyama" (quoting from a wire communication sent by a Unification Church official); Kamiyama participated in the completion of Moon's 1973 returns directly; and the public accounting firm that prepared Moon's 1974 and 1975 returns was provided with false information and fraudulently backdated documents. As an example of this last point, the preparers of the 1974 return were shown the "loans" ledger of transactions from the European Church leaders to Kamiyama. These "loans" amounted to $200,000. The ledger then reflected that Kamiyama made a loan to Moon (backdated and signed by both defendants) for the $200,000. The accountants were advised that these loan agreements evidenced the fact that the funds on deposit in the Chase Manhattan Bank earning interest in Moon's name were not his funds, but were held by him only as nominee for the Church. Noteworthy is the fact that appellants' initial tax attorneys informed HSA-UWC leaders prior to the filing of Moon's 1973 return that he would have to pay taxes on all of his

App. 20

United States income, from whatever source it was derived. No interest income was declared on the 1973 return, and only small amounts the two succeeding years. For example, Moon's 1973 return declared $14,458 income from the Unification Church of New York and no interest earned, although there was earned interest of $3,208 on the Chase accounts. On the 1974 return, reported income was $20,520 from Tong Il and $254 interest earned, although the deposits at Chase earned $59,079. On the 1975 return Tong Il income was reported at $37,080 and interest of $267, although the accounts at Chase earned $43,841. Moon apparently knew that the interest he *reported* in 1974 and 1975 on the small savings account at Chase was income to him; thus it seems reasonable for the jury to conclude that he also knew that the interest on his time deposits at the same bank, which came from withdrawals from the checking and savings accounts, was also income to him. We are unable to accept defendants' argument that as new residents of the United States they were unfamiliar with tax law. Not only are both defendants sophisticated businessmen, but they had at their disposal a small army of tax attorneys and accountants whose advice, unfortunately, was not sufficiently heeded.

Finally, Moon's signing of the aborted Release of Indebtedness on the East Garden transfer, discussed earlier, was an acknowledgment by him that the Chase accounts in his name were actually his funds and at the same time evinced his willingness to sign a false document to escape personal income tax liability.

App. 21

B. The Conspiracy Count (Count One)

Moon next argues that the government presented no evidence that he personally entered into or participated in a conspiratorial agreement to file false tax returns or obstruct the tax fraud investigation against him. The facts adduced at trial contained ample evidence that several subordinates of Moon engaged in a continuing and agreed upon course of conduct amounting to a conspiracy to file false returns and obstruct justice. Included among these was Kamiyama, whose participation in the preparation of the 1973 return and whose part in the false and backdated "loan" agreements submitted to the accountants for preparation of the 1974 and 1975 returns has already been recounted. Viewed in the light most favorable to the government, Moon's argument of lack of involvement is unpersuasive. Not only was Moon the person with the greatest personal stake in the success of the acts in question, but there was proof that he exerted close scrutiny over his own personal affairs and was aware of the information contained in his tax returns. He signed one of the postdated loan agreements (the $200,000 loan from Kamiyama to Moon) which was later submitted to the IRS in connection with the audit of his returns. Finally, Moon and his associates, through Moon's personal lawyers, submitted to the Justice Department in 1981 the same falsely backdated documents that had earlier been submitted to the IRS and to Moon's accountants. In short, there was ample evidence for the jury to find that Moon participated in a conspiracy to file false tax returns and/or obstruct justice.

App. 22

III

JURY INSTRUCTIONS

Moon objects to the trial court's instructions to the jury in three particular areas. First he contends that the instructions on the law of trusts were erroneous and incomplete. Second, he argues that certain instructions violated the First Amendment's Religion Clauses. And third he questions the instructions on intent. Although specific objections overlap to some extent, we will deal with them separately.

A. Charge on Trusts

Perhaps the most crucial area concerns the trial judge's charge on the law of trusts. Despite the fact that Moon did not, until late in the trial, clearly raise the claim that he was holding the assets in question in trust for the International Unification Church movement, the district court saw fit to instruct the jury on this defense theory. The defendant now objects to what he claims are errors and omissions in this charge. We believe that defendant's contentions fail, first, because the trial court was not required to charge the jury on the trust issue and, in any event, because the trust instructions were neither erroneous nor prejudicial.

As a preliminary matter, it is essential to inquire as to who had the burden of proof on the trust issue. Of course, the government must prove every element of the offense charged beyond a reasonable doubt. One of those elements is that Moon had income from the Chase accounts and the Tong Il stock distribution that he failed to report. Defendant may then present an "affirmative defense," one which does not rebut an element of the crime,

App. 23

or some other defense which rebuts an element of crime. If defendant asserts an affirmative defense he bears the burden of proof on it. Here, since the defense theory that Moon was acting only as a trustee rebuts the "ownership" element of the crime charged, it was not an affirmative defense. Hence, the only burden on Moon was to present a prima facie case that he held the assets in trust. If the defense had successfully introduced into evidence this prima facie rebuttal of the element of ownership, the trial court would have been obliged to instruct the jury on the law of trusts and the government would still have had to prove beyond a reasonable doubt that Moon "owned" the assets.

A careful review of the evidence, however, reveals no proof that Moon actually held the subject funds in trust. In order to establish the defense of trusteeship, defendants would have had to produce evidence of the donors' intent to create a trust. Yet the only evidence even remotely touching on this issue was the testimony of Church members Matsumura and Porter and German Unification Church leader Werner who simply stated that they gave money to Moon, intending it as a donation to their church. They never mentioned the word "trust" or, more importantly, gave any indication that they intended to create a trust relationship. Accordingly, this evidence only demonstrated the charitable intent of the contributors, not the clear expression of intent necessary to create a trust.

Under New York law, which governs the issue of ownership, it is well settled that a donor's intent to create a trust must be clear and unequivocal. This rule is not limited to private trusts, as defendant claims, since the creation of a charitable trust also requires a clear expression of intent. *See, County of Suffolk v. Greater New*

App. 24

York Councils, Boy Scouts of America, 51 N.Y. 2d 830, 832-33 (1980); *Lefkowitz v. Cornell University*, 35 A.D.2d 166, 173 (4th Dep't 1970) (while no particular words are required to create a charitable trust, the words relied upon to create such a trust must be unequivocal), *aff'd*, 28 N.Y.2d 876 (1971); 4 *Scott on Trusts* § 348, at 2769-70 (3d ed. 1967) (as with a private trust, person creating a charitable trust must manifest by his words or conduct an intention to create it); *Restatement (Second of Trusts* § 351 (1959).

The dissenting opinion, unfortunately, obscures the intent requirement, focusing instead on a totally distinct and, for purposes of this analysis, inapposite issue—the policy of upholding charitable trusts whenever possible by construing their terms liberally. For this proposition, the dissent cites *In re Price's Will*, 264 A.D. 29 *aff'd* 289 N.Y. 751 (1942) and *In re Durbrow's Estate*, 245 N.Y. 469 (1927), neither of which controls here. Each of these cases involved a written will which plainly expressed the testator's intent to create a trust. More specifically, *Price's Will* applied the *cy pres* doctrine and held that a charitable trust already in existence survived even after its primary purpose had terminated. Similarly, *Durbrow's Estate* held that a charitable trust will not fail for want of a definite beneficiary. It is true, therefore, that both of these cases support the policy of upholding charitable trusts; however, neither stands for the proposition that a charitable trust comes into being absent the clearly expressed intent to create it. Since the intent to create such a trust was clearly indicated by the written wills in *Price's Will* and *Durbrow's Estate*, the question of intent to create a charitable trust was not in issue.

Contrast these cases with the present one. Here, there is no evidence of intent to create a *trust*, only the vague

App. 25

testimony of three witnesses establishing that a charitable *gift* had been made to the Church. Although we agree with the dissent's assertion that charitable trusts must be liberally upheld, there is no rule of law that presumes simply from a charitable gift the donor's intent to create a trust.

Thus, since defendants failed to make a prima facie case that Moon held the Chase accounts and Tong Il stock in trust, the trust issue was one that need not have been charged to the jury in the first instance. Any purported errors or omissions in the instructions were therefore harmless.[3]

In any event, we find that the defendant's objections to the trust instructions are without merit. Moon challenges the use of what he terms a "laundry list" of factors which the trial court instructed the jury to consider in determining whether a trust existed. He now asserts that important factors were omitted from this list, the vital issues of source of funds and donor's intent were buried in this extensive list, and some factors were misleading.

The claim of omissions is spurious, as all the factors alleged to be omitted were clearly charged. In connection with the first of these factors, i.e., whether the International Unification Church movement "had a specific organizational structure, written charter or constitution," the dissent believes that Judge Goettel should have said that a specific organizational structure was not a prerequisite to the existence of a charitable trust. But, the record reveals that immediately following the list of factors, Judge Goettel did so charge in the following language:

---

3   The instructions on the law of trusts were essentially correct, as discussed *infra*, and occupied only a very small portion of the jury charge. Therefore, even though these instructions were not required, their inclusion could not have confused or misled the jury.

App. 26

As I have mentioned, you may consider whether the International Unification Church Movement had a specific organizational structure in making your decision. *However, the lack of a formal corporation does not prevent a religious movement from being the beneficial power of property held in the name of another* (emphasis supplied).

It ill-behooves an appellate court to engage in word-by-word parsing of a jury charge, *Cupp v. Naughten*, 414 U.S. 141, 146-47 (1973), substituting its own choice for those equally appropriate words already in the charge. With regard to the last two objections, the dissenting opinion is also critical of the trial court, not for its failure to charge correctly, but for its failure to instruct the jury to accord the greatest weight and thereby emphasize the factor of the "intent of the parties" who gave property to Moon. Each of the factors referred to was correctly stated by the trial court and all of them were equally relevant to the jury's determination. Undue emphasis on any was not required. The "list" was slightly over one half a page; it was hardly extensive and no important factor was buried.

Moon and the dissent also object to the "if-then" language in the following instruction on the ground that it impermissibly shifts the burden of proof to the defense to show that the interest on the Chase accounts was not taxable to him:

If you find that the funds in the Chase accounts were the property of International Unification Church Movement or were held in trust by Moon for the International Unification Church Movement and used for church purposes and that the interest on those funds also belonged to the International Unifi-

App. 27

cation Church Movement and were used for it, then that interest would not be taxable income to Moon.

This "if-then" formulation did not shift the burden of proof to defendants to prove their innocence. First, the charge contained 30 separate instances properly stating the burden of proof, and read as a whole and in context, the charge on this particular issue clearly states the correct burden. Second, the implication, if any, is even stronger in Moon's own written request to the trial judge[4] which contained, in addition to this subject, five other "if-then" formulations. Third, since no objection was made to the trial court's charge as given, it was waived. *See United States v. Praetorious*, 622 F.2d 1054, 1061-62 (2d Cir. 1979), *cert. denied*, 449 U.S. 860 (1980). This belated argument is thus totally without merit.

Moreover, we find no error in the charge that trust property diverted is taxable to the extent diverted. The objections raised are that this "diversion" theory was not contained in the indictment, no instruction was given on partial diversion, and there was no explanation by the trial judge of what "diversion" means. Since diversion was not an element of the crime charged, it was not required to be included in the indictment. The crucial point is that Moon was indicted, tried and convicted for his false and fraudulent failure to report taxable income. Further, in response to the trust defense raised at trial, the court did properly instruct the jury on partial diversion when it charged that the funds diverted to Moon's per-

---

[4]   If you find that the Chase time deposits and the Tong Il stock were in fact the property of the international Church Movement, rather than the personal property of Rev. Moon, then the exclusion from Rev. Moon's tax returns of the interest earned by the time deposits and the Tong Il stock was proper, and did not make those returns false.

App. 28

sonal use became taxable "to the extent so diverted." Obviously, the word "divert" is in common enough use and understandable by ordinary jurors, so as to require no explanatory charge. *Cf. United States v. Valencia*, 645 F.2d 1158, 1167 (2d Cir. 1980) (term "hesitation" did not need to be clarified).

Finally, the trial judge properly charged that "there is no trust if the person who receives the money is free to use it for his own benefit." This instruction was in accord with familiar law that the same person may not at one and the same time be the sole trustee and sole beneficiary of a trust. *In re Phipps*, 2 N.Y.2d 105, 108 (1956); 61 N.Y.Jur., *Trusts* § 214, at 395 (1968); *Restatement (Second) of Trusts* § 341(1) (1959).

B. Religion Clauses Objections

Moon objects to instructions that permitted the jury to find that if he used the Chase funds for his own business investments or personal ends—that is for other than religious purposes—such use would indicate the lack of a trust relationship. The defense urges that this instruction violated the First Amendment Religion Clauses because the trial court was obligated to charge that the jury must accept as conclusive the Unification Church's definition of what it considered a religious purpose. Under the definition now advanced as the Church's, *any use* of these funds by Reverend Moon was for religious purposes.

This argument overstates the scope of the protections afforded by the Religion Clauses. The term "religion" was defined by the Supreme Court nearly 100 years ago in *Davis v. Beason*, 133 U.S. 333, 342 (1980) as having reference to a person's views of his relations to his Creator. This definition seems unduly narrow today. In every religion there is an awareness of what is called

App. 29

divine and a response to that divinity. 7 *The Encyclopedia of Philosophy* 143 (1972). But, there are religions which do not positively require the assumption of a God, for example, Buddhism and the Unitarian Church. Hence, a broader definition of the word religion—one which we think more accurately captures its essence—is that formulated by the pre-eminent American philosopher, William James, who said religion means: *"the feelings, acts, and experiences of individual men in their solitude, so far as they apprehend themselves to stand in relation to whatever they may consider the divine."* W. James, *The Varieties of Religious Experience* 31 (1910). In referring to an individual's relation to what he considers the divine, Professor James used the word "divine" in its broadest sense as denoting any object that is godlike, whether it is or is not a specific deity. *Id.* at 34. Therefore, under the Religion Clauses, everyone is entitled to entertain such view respecting his relations to what he considers the divine and the duties such relationship imposes as may be approved by that person's conscience, and to worship in any way such person thinks fit so long as this is not injurious to the equal rights of others. "It was never intended or supposed that the amendment could be invoked as a protection against legislation for the punishment of acts inimical to the peace, good order and morals of society." *Davis v. Beason*, 133 U.S. at 342. The Supreme Court continued, "however free the exercise of religion may be, it must be subordinate to the criminal laws of the country, passed with reference to actions regarded by general consent as properly the subjects of punitive legislation." *Id.* at 342-43. To foreclose a court from analyzing a church's activities as needed to determine whether those activities violated a statute, on the ground that the First Amendment forbids such inquiry,

App. 30

would mean that there are no restraints or limitations on church activities. *See Christian Echoes National Ministry, Inc. v. United States*, 470 F.2d 849, 856 (10th Cir.), *cert. denied*, 414 U.S. 864 (1973). The "free exercise" of religion is not so unfettered. The First Amendment does not insulate a church or its members from judicial inquiry when a charge is made that their activities violate a penal statute. Consequently, in this criminal proceeding the jury was not bound to accept the Unification Church's definition of what constitutes a religious use or purpose.

Holy Spirit Association v. Tax Commission, 55 N.Y.2d 512, 518 (1982), is inapposite. That case dealt with the inquiry that a court may conduct when determining whether a religious organization is entitled to a real property tax exemption under New York law. The principles there enunciated upon which appellant relies are relevant in that context and do not serve as precedent in a federal criminal tax prosecution.

Moon also argues that an omission from the charge— the so-called "Messiah" defense—permitted the jury to look at the assets held in his name "secularly," in violation of the First Amendment. Counsel asserts that Moon's worldwide followers believe him to be "potentially the new Messiah." From this theological premise the argument is made that Moon personifies the church movement and is indistinguishable from it. Since the Unification Church movement can owe no taxes on income derived from church-related activities, the defense argues that neither can Reverend Moon.

We do not accept this defense. The fact that Moon is the head of the Church does not mean that the Church itself is not a distinct and separate body. Moon's spiritual identity as leader of the Unification Church movement and his legal identity as a taxpayer are not the same. He is

App. 31

the spiritual leader of the Church, as the Pope is the spiritual leader of the Roman Catholic Church, but he also has a legal identity as a distinct, individual human being. It is in this latter capacity that he, or the Pope, could have taxable income. It has long been held that a church may hold property legally free from government interference because such inference would violate the First Amendment. *Terrett v. Taylor*, 13 U.S. (9 Cranch) 43, 51-52 (1815). But where property held individually and used personally gives rise to income, that income is subject to taxation. To allow otherwise would be to permit church leaders to stand above the law, a view we have previously rejected.

Finally, contrary to defendant's argument, the failure to charge that assets which came from church sources to be used for church purposes are not taxable to Moon, did not violate the "neutral principles" approach outlined in *Jones v. Wolf*, 443 U.S. 595 (1979). In *Jones* the Supreme Court held that the First Amendment prohibits the resolution of intra-church property disputes by civil courts interpreting religious doctrine, and required that civil courts defer the resolution of such issues to the highest hierarchical church organization. This "neutral principles of law" approach is one of several approved methods of resolving church property disputes between groups within the church. *Id.* at 602. The doctrine has no application to the facts of this case.[5]

---

5   Contrary to the defendant's contention, the trial judge *did* instruct the jury that lack of a formal organizational structure would not prevent the Unification Church movement from being the beneficial owner of the property in question.

App. 32

C. Charge on Intent

The final jury charge objections deal with the issue of intent in two particulars. First, Moon objects to the "if-then" formulation contained in the following instruction:

> *If* you find that Moon provided the person who prepared the tax return with full and honest information as to his income and that Moon then adopted, signed and filed the tax returns as prepared in the belief that the return contained the full and honest information he had provided to the preparers regarding income, *then* you must find defendant Moon not guilty.

(emphasis added). This objection is rather surprising, in light of the fact that the defendant requested the following charge:

> *If* you find Rev. Moon and his representatives acted in good faith in providing the information that they believed to be relevant to the determination of Rev. Moon's tax liability and that they responded fully and candidly to Peat, Marwick's requests for additional information relating to the Chase accounts, *then* you must find defendant Rev. Moon not guilty of the false return counts for 1974 and 1975.

(emphasis added). Needless to say, the defendant cannot now be heard to complain of the same "if-then" formulation he requested. In fact, this requested language was preceded by a sentence which shifted the burden of proof even more emphatically to the defendant than did the charge given by the court.

Second, the intent charge gave the jury factors to consider in evaluating defendant's state of mind. Among

App. 33

those mentioned as an affirmative act designed to conceal consciousness of wrongdoing was "dealing in cash." Moon claims that dealing in cash is a common practice in the Orient and could not, therefore, be interpreted as evidence of intent to conceal. In tax fraud cases evidence tending to show misconduct through extensive dealings in cash is properly admitted into evidence, *see United States v. White*, 417 F.2d 89, 92 (2d Cir. 1969), *cert. denied*, 397 U.S. 912 (1970). It is, therefore, properly chargeable. And, in any event, the "dealing in cash" language was immediately followed by a balancing charge that "openness in conduct" could give rise to the inference that the taxpayer believed he had done nothing wrong and "had nothing to hide."[6]

IV

MISCELLANEOUS ISSUES

A. Selective Prosecution

Both appellants contend that the prosecution mounted against them was impermissibly motivated by hostility toward their religion and that the district court erred in denying their request for discovery and a hearing on the issue of selective prosecution. In this Circuit, a defendant who advances a claim of selective prosecution must do so in pretrial proceedings, *see United States v. Taylor* 562 F.2d 1345, 1356 (2d Cir.), *cert. denied*, 432 U.S. 909 (1977). The person asserting such a claim bears the burden of establishing *prima facie* both:

---

6   Moon also contends that this language contravened the Religion Clauses by inviting the jury to treat the Church's practice of soliciting cash contributions from the public as suspect. But the charge clearly refers to *Moon's* conduct and not Unification Church practices.

App. 34

(1) that, while others similarly situated have not generally been proceeded against because of conduct of the type forming the basis of the charge against him, he has been singled out for prosecution, and (2) that the government's discriminatory selection of him for prosecution has been invidious or in bad faith, i.e., based upon such impermissible considerations as race, religion, or the desire to prevent his exercise of constitutional rights.

United States v. Berrios, 510 F.2d 1207, 1211 (2d Cir. 1974). No evidentiary hearing or discovery is mandated unless the district court, in its discretion, *see id.* at 1212, finds that both prongs of the test have been met. *See United States v. Ness*, 652 F.2d 890, 892 (9th Cir.), *cert. denied*, 454 U.S. 1126 (1981); *United States v. Catlett*, 584 F.2d 864, 866 (8th Cir. 1978); *Berrios*, 501 F.2d at 1211. We cannot say on this record that the district court abused its discretion in holding that appellants failed to demonstrate the necessary factual predicates for their claim of selective prosecution.

The only evidence offered pretrial in support of appellants' assertion of selective prosecution was to the effect that Congress had previously conducted an investigation into Korean-American relations (Koreagate), that such investigation had touched upon the Unification Church, and therefore that the government's prosecution of Moon could be seen to have stemmed from impermissible religious and/or political hostility. No other evidence was submitted in support of the motion. The proof before the trial court was wholly insufficient to mandate further inquiry or a hearing and the court's rejection of the claim of selective prosecution at that point was clearly proper.

Following the trial, and in an arguably untimely manner, appellants submitted additional "evidence" of selec-

App. 35

tive prosecution. Specifically, they presented affidavits from four individuals who, while disavowing any knowledge of the government's motive in this case, asserted that they held church funds in their own names and did noi pay taxes on interest earned on the funds. Moon also submitted a copy of a letter from United States Senator Robert Dole to the IRS requesting that it look into the Unification Church's tax exempt status. While acknowledging that Moon's status as a highly visible, religious leader may well have led to the audit of his tax returns, the district court reasoned that the government's decision to institute criminal rather than civil charges was a wholly separate decision and that the additional evidence of improper prosecutorial motive submitted by appellants still failed to satisfy the requirements of *Berrios.* We need not decide here whether appellants' post-trial submission of evidence regarding selective prosecution was too late; even considering that evidence, the district court correctly concluded that it was insufficient to meet the *Berrios* standard.

With respect to the first requirement of *Berrios*—proof that "others similarly situated" have not been prosecuted—the four above-mentioned affidavits of other church leaders did not adequately prove *Berrios'* first prong for two reasons. First, the government's theory against Moon was that the funds he held were his own personal property and that therefore any interest earned on the funds was taxable to him. By contrast, the submitted affidavits describe situations involving persons who claim to hold church funds, as opposed to personal funds, in their own names and pay no taxes on interest earned by the funds. While Moon still contends that the funds he held were church property, at the time of this post-trial motion the jury had squarely rejected this

App. 36

theory. Second, this case also involved charges of perjury and obstruction of justice. Reference to these charges is totally ignored in appellants' analysis of whether similarly situated individuals have been prosecuted. In short, appellants simply failed to provide the necessary *prima facie* evidence that others similarly situated have not been prosecuted.

As for the second prong of *Berrios*—proof that the government's decision to prosecute was based on impermissible considerations of race and/or religion—appellants rely heavily on the above-mentioned letter from Senator Robert Dole to the IRS. That letter merely requested an audit of the Unification Church's tax exempt status. It did not request an audit of Moon's personal tax status, suggest that he be criminally prosecuted, or indicate any racial or religious bias. Thus, we fail to see how the letter can be said to constitute *prima facie* evidence that the decision to prosecute Moon was the product of an impermissible motive. Appellants have therefore failed to satisfy either prong of *Berrios*.

We recognize that Moon is a controversial public figure who has been subjected to extensive media attention, much of it critical, and that his church may perhaps be viewed by the general public in an unfavorable light. These facts naturally tend to foster suspicion that the motive behind this prosecution might have been improper. That naked suspicion cannot serve as a substitute for the evidentiary showing mandated by *Berrios*. This case is not the first occasion when a controversial political or religious figure has been criminally prosecuted; and if history teaches us anything, plainly, it will not be the last. By their very nature, such highly visible cases will always engender some suspicion with respect to the government's *bona fides*. But to engage in a collateral inquiry respect-

App. 37

ing prosecutorial motive, there must be more than mere suspicion or surmise. If a judicial inquiry into the government's motive for prosecuting could be launched without an adequate factual showing of impropriety, it would lead far too frequently to judicial intrusion on the power of the executive branch to make prosecutorial decisions. Unwarranted judicial inquiries would also undermine the strong public policy that resolution of criminal cases not be unduly delayed by litigation over collateral matters.

B. Interpreters Act

The next issue raised concerns the Court Interpreters Act of 1978, 28 U.S.C. § 1827 (Supp. V 1981). It provides in pertinent part that:

> The presiding judicial officer . . . shall utilize the services of the most available certified interpreter . . . in any criminal or civil action initiated by the United States in a United States district court . . . if the presiding judicial officer determines . . . that [a] party (including a defendant in a criminal case), or a witness who may present testimony in such action—
>
> > (1) speaks only or primarily a language other than the English language; or
> >
> > (2) suffers from a hearing impairment (whether or not suffering also from a speech impairment)
>
> so as to inhibit such party's comprehension of the proceedings or communication with counsel or the presiding judicial officer, or so as to inhibit such witness' comprehension of questions and the presentation of such testimony.

28 U.S.C. § 1827(d) (Supp. V 1981). The Act further provides that persons, "other than witnesses," may waive,

App. 38

with the court's permission, their entitlement to a court-appointed interpreter and use their own translator instead. 28 U.S.C. § 1827(f) (Supp. V 1981).

During pretrial proceedings, Moon moved pursuant to § 1827(f) to waive the use of a court-appointed interpreter and to employ instead his own personally-selected translator. The district court ruled that Moon was free to use the interpreter of his own choice for purposes of translating the proceedings of the trial to him; but, that if Moon elected to testify, his testimony would have to be translated by a court-appointed, certified interpreter. Moon elected not to testify at his own trial.

While it was not argued below that the use of a court-appointed translator would impinge upon Moon's ability to communicate effectively with the jury, he now argues that the district court incorrectly construed § 1827(f) to preclude him from waiving the use of an appointed interpreter if and when he elected to testify. Specifically, he asserts that if he had testified, he would have been a party-witness, that a party-witness is not a "witness" within the meaning of § 1827(f), and that he therefore should have been allowed to waive the use of a court-appointed interpreter.

Moon's premise—that party-witnesses are somehow different from other witnesses for purposes of § 1827(f)—is untenable. The express language of subsection (f) makes no such distinction. While § 1827(d) does refer to "parties" and "witnesses" separately, this language does not create a distinction that must be carried over to subsection (f). The legislative history of § 1827(f) indicates that its purpose was to prevent *parties* from using untrustworthy translators. For example, the House Judiciary Committee Report in discussing the waiver provision refers to the danger of allowing "an individual to

App. 39

waive use of a certified interpreter and then to substitute their own personal interpreter [which] might create an opportunity for a *party* to use an unscrupulous interpreter." H.R. Rep. No. 95-1687, 95th Cong., 2d Sess. 5, *reprinted in* 1978 U.S. Code Cong. & Ad. News 4652, 4656. (emphasis added). To interpret the § 1827(f) term "witness" so narrowly as not to include party-witnesses, as Moon now suggests, would seriously undermine Congress's scheme of using independent interpreters to insure accurate translations. Thus, the district court correctly ruled that under § 1827(f), if Moon elected to testify, he would have to speak through a certified, court-appointed interpreter.

Moon further argues that requiring him to testify through a court-appointed interpreter impermissibly burdened his Fifth and Sixth Amendment rights to present a full defense. Citing *Brooks v. Tennesee*, 406 U.S. 605 (1972), he asserts that by depriving him of the opportunity to testify through an interpreter of his own choosing, the district court unconstitutionally restricted his decision as to whether or not he would testify. *Brooks* dealt with a state requirement that a defendant choosing to testify must testify at the beginning of the defense case before any other testimony is heard. This restriction is different from that now at issue. By forcing a defendant to decide whether he will testify at a point in the trial where a realistic assessment of the value of his testimony is difficult, the condemned state provision in *Brooks* restricted the privilege to remain silent because it put the defendant at an unfair tactical disadvantage in deciding whether to exercise his privilege. *Id.* at 610-11. The Interpreters Act does not make the assertion of the privilege similarly costly; it simply ensures that whatever testimony a defendant gives is honestly reported.

App. 40

Moreover, even were requiring Moon to use a court-appointed interpreter to be viewed as some restriction on his ability to present a full defense, we observe that not all restrictions on a defendant's right to testify are *per se* impermissible. *See e.g., United States v. Bifield*, 702 F.2d 342, 350 (2d Cir.), *cert. denied*, 51 U.S.L.W. 3826 (U.S. May 5, 1983). For example, certain evidentiary and procedural restrictions are sanctioned where reasonably necessary to the achievement of a fair trial. *See id.* There is no evidence here that use of a court-appointed interpreter would have been unfair to Moon and he has not suggested why it would have been. We regard § 1827 as reasonably designed to further the legitimate public interest in the fair administration of criminal trials. Such interest necessarily requires accurate and unbiased translations of trial testimony. Since the statute does not force a defendant who elects to testify to do so at any unfair disadvantage, we hold that the district court's application of § 1827 did not impermissibly restrict Moon's constitutional right to present a full defense.

C. *Evidentiary Problems*

Both defendants raise questions regarding the admissibility of certain evidence at trial. Moon contends that the district court erred in allowing the government to introduce various immigration documents as similar act evidence. Kamiyama complains that the prejudice created by this evidence infected his trial by "spilling over." Additionally, Kamiyama challenges the admission during the government's rebuttal of evidence concerning his failure to file income tax returns in 1973 and 1974. Finally, both defendants claim that the government presented improper evidence to the jury regarding the religious practices of

App. 41

the Unification Church which they claim permitted them to be tried by religious innuendo.

After the defense rested, the government introduced documents relating to Moon's and his wife's applications for permanent residence in the United States. Contained in these documents were what the government maintained were false representations concerning the Moons' income for 1972 and 1973. The government argued that such evidence was probative of Moon's intent and knowledge because it was relevant on the question of absence of mistake regarding the preparation of the tax returns.

We acknowledge the long held view of this Circuit that the trial judge is in the best position to weigh competing interests in deciding whether or not to admit certain evidence. *See United States v. Birney*, 686 F.2d 102, 106 (2d Cir. 1982). Absent an abuse of discretion, the decision of the trial judge to admit or reject evidence will not be overturned by an appellate court. *Id.* In reviewing the district court's determination we turn to Federal Rule of Evidence 401 which states that relevant evidence "means evidence having any tendency to make the existence of any fact that is of consequence to the determination of the action more probable or less probable than it would be without the evidence." The government argues now, as it did at trial, that the submission of false immigration documents was relevant to Moon's intent in filing the false tax returns. We do not see how the submission of the false immigration papers to the Immigration and Naturalization Service in one instance is relevant to the defendant's intent to submit unrelated false papers to the IRS in another. *Cf. United States v. Halper*, 590 F.2d 422, 432 (2d Cir. 1978) (submission of false tax return not relevant as to whether defendant intended to submit false Medicaid claims, and vice versa). Admission of this irrelevant

App. 42

evidence constituted an abuse of the trial court's discretion. Nevertheless, in light of the strong evidence relating to Moon's intent to file false tax returns, see Section II A.(2) *supra*, the error must be deemed harmless. *See United States v. Quinto*, 582 F.2d 224, 235 (2d Cir. 1978).

With respect to Kamiyama's claim of spillover, the trial court's charge contained the cautionary instruction that the immigration documents were to "have no bearing on the case against [Kamiyama]." This instruction, coupled with the fact that the government made no claim that Kamiyama had any connection with the Moons' immigration papers, was sufficient to safeguard adequately against impermissible prejudice. *See United States v. Reed*, 639 F.2d 896, 907 (2d Cir. 1981).

Kamiyama's major claim of evidentiary error relates to the admission of an IRS certificate indicating that there was no record of Kamiyama having filed federal income tax returns for the years 1973 and 1974. It was the government's contention that the certificate was relevant on the issue of Kamiyama's motive to create the Family Fund Ledger. Purportedly, Kamiyama paid $10,000 cash for 100 shares of Tong Il stock in 1973 and $110,000 cash for 1,100 shares of Tong Il stock in 1974. The government argued that this "untraceable" cash was income and that to cover up the source of this money Kamiyama concocted the Family Fund Ledger. Since precisely the same scenario was established to account for the cash deposits in Moon's Chase accounts, the jury was entitled to infer from Kamiyama's conduct, so the government argues, that his handling of Moon's returns was with the requisite criminal intent and knowledge.

Nonetheless, there was no proof that Kamiyama had income sufficient to require him to file a tax return for the years in question. Simply purchasing stock with cash

App. 43

is not proof that Kamiyama had taxable income, since the cash might have come from some other source, *see Marcus v. United States*, 422 F.2d 752, 755 (5th Cir. 1970). Lacking a proper foundation, *see Dupree v. United States*, 218 F.2d 781, 784 (5th Cir.), *reh'g denied*, 220 F.2d 748 (5th Cir. 1955), the IRS certificate was not relevant evidence and it was improperly admitted. We note that the certificate and the testimony accompanying it were admitted in the government's case on rebuttal and that this proof occupied an insignificant portion of the trial record, was not raised in summation, and was not in the trial court's instructions to the jury. Balanced against the other evidence of Kamiyama's guilt, we find this error harmless.

With respect to trial by religious innuendo, concededly there was testimony that members of the Unification Church lived and worked together, donating their earnings to their church.[7] The central issue for the jury to decide was whether the Tong Il stock and Chase Manhattan Bank accounts belonged to the Church or to Moon personally. In probing that issue, it was inevitable that some Unification Church practices would creep into the trial in order to illustrate Moon's control over the activities of other church officials. The question before us is whether evidence of Church practices, although relevant, should have been excluded because "its probative value [was] substantially outweighed by the danger of unfair prejudice," Fed. R. Evid. 403. The trial judge from his superior vantage point is in the best position to weigh these competing interests. *See United States v. Robinson*,

---

7   We note that the Unification Church members' mode of living, evidence of which appellants claim amounts to religious innuendo, is also prevalent in certain centuries-old orders of Christians and Buddhist monks.

App. 44

560 F.2d 507, 514 (2d Cir. 1977) (en banc), *cert. denied*, 435 U.S. 905 (1978). Absent an abuse of his broad discretion, the decision of the trial judge to admit the challenged evidence of religious practices must stand. To find such abuse, we must conclude that the trial judge acted arbitrarily or irrationally; to avoid acting arbitrarily a court must make a conscientious assessment when weighing probative value against the risk of unfair prejudice. *United States v. Birney*, 686 F.2d at 106. A thorough review of the record reveals no abuse of the district court's discretion.

D. Post Trial Proceedings

After the trial was concluded claims surfaced of improper influences on the jury. These allegations arose when a Unification Church member, attorney David Hager, was contacted by a man named Bruce Romanoff who was apparently attempting to sell tape recordings of phone conversations between Romanoff's associate, John Curry, and former trial juror Virginia Steward, a personal friend of Curry. On these tapes Steward made various statements indicating that the jury might have been exposed to extraneous prejudicial information and improper outside influences. After conducting a hearing where Romanoff, Curry, Steward and two other potentially knowledgeable jurors, forelady Mary Nimmo and John McGrath, were questioned, the trial court concluded that no grounds existed to believe that the jury had been exposed to improper outside influences or extraneous prejudicial information and that there was no need to continue the inquiry.

It hardly bears repeating that courts are, and should be, hesitant to haul jurors in after they have reached a verdict in order to probe for potential instances of bias, miscon-

App. 45

duct or extraneous influences. As we explained in *United States v. Moten*, 582 F.2d 654, 666-67 (2d Cir. 1978), a trial court is required to hold a post-trial jury hearing only when reasonable grounds for investigation exist. Reasonable grounds are present when there is clear, strong, substantial and incontrovertible evidence, *King v. United States*, 576 F.2d 432, 438 (2d Cir.), *cert. denied*, 439 U.S. 850 (1978), that a specific, nonspeculative impropriety has occurred which could have prejudiced the trial of a defendant. A hearing is not held to afford a convicted defendant the opportunity to "conduct a fishing expedition." *United States v. Moten*, 582 F.2d at 667. Although the circumstances in the decided cases are instructive, each situation in this area is *sui generis*. *United States v. Barnes*, 604 F.2d 121, 144 (2d Cir. 1979), *cert. denied*, 446 U.S. 907 (1980).

This same standard, which applies to a trial judge's determination of whether to hold a post-verdict hearing, is also useful in ascertaining whether the scope of a hearing that has been held is adequate. While the breadth of questioning should be sufficient "to permit the entire picture to be explored," *United States v. Moten*, 582 F.2d at 667, that picture is painted on a canvass with finite boundaries. Therefore, in the course of a post-verdict inquiry on this subject, when and if it becomes apparent that the above-described reasonable grounds to suspect prejudicial jury impropriety do not exist, the inquiry should end.

Moon asserts that the district court improperly curtailed defense attempts to conduct a more thorough inquiry and that at the post-trial hearings three areas should have been explored further. First, he claims it was error to block defense efforts to find out whether the jurors discussed Moon's request not be tried by a jury.

App. 46

This fact was allegedly reported at the end of a newspaper article which concerned a *different* topic that had apparently been mentioned by Nimmo and discussed among the jurors. But all the jurors questioned stated that they had not read the article, and the two found to be credible by the court below noted that the main subject of the article was mentioned only casually and was passed-off lightly. None even indirectly intimated that Moon's request concerning a jury trial was known to them, let alone a topic of conversation before the jury at large. Moreover, Moon has not shown how he would be prejudiced even were the jurors aware of his desire to be tried without a jury.

Second, Moon claims that the trial court erred by refusing to call additional jurors to explore the issue of newspapers in the jury room. The fact that there were newspapers in the jury room is an insufficient predicate for conducting a post-verdict inquiry. The jurors were instructed not to read articles concerning the case before them; they were not absolutely precluded from looking at newspapers. All of those questioned indicated that they had not read articles about the case, did not know of any jurors who had, and had not heard other jurors discussing such articles (other than the one alluded to above). One said she did not look at the newspapers, another said she only played the "Wingo" game, and the third said he and others cut out articles about the case, but he was saving these to read after the trial. There has been no showing, let alone a substantial one, that any of the jurors read prejudicial newspaper accounts of the case. Moon's claim that some juror *might* have done so is a speculative argument insufficient to justify further inquiry.

App. 47

Third, Moon argues that it was necessary to call juror Esperanza Torres to the stand and to explore the circumstances surrounding the firing of a shot through Torres's window during the trial. Steward testified that Torres had been upset one day because a shot had been fired through her window the night before, and that Torres intimated to Steward that the incident might be connected to her jury service. Steward also related that Torres told her the police had investigated, found no bullet, and concluded that the hole in Torres's window was most likely caused by a BB shot by "just some fresh kids . . . fooling around." Steward apparently thought little of the incident since Torres lived in a bad neighborhood, and when Torres had been similarly upset after her car was hit from behind, Steward told her not to be silly and that it was just a coincidence. Nimmo confirmed having heard second-hand of the BB incident and that it was probably due to the nature of Torres's neighborhood, but she had not heard that Torres attributed it to the trial. McGrath, who sat next to Torres in the jury box, heard nothing about these events.

Given these facts it was unnecessary for the district court to probe any further into the event since, unlike the circumstances in *Remmer v. United States*, 347 U.S. 227 (1954), *appeal following remand*, 350 U.S. 377 (1956) and *United States v. Gersh*, 328 F.2d 460 (2d Cir. 1964), there was no rational basis to connect these outside incidents with the trial. Moreover, even if Torres had been interrogated, she could only have been questioned about "whether any outside influence was improperly brought to bear upon" her, and could not have been asked about "the effect of [the incident] upon [her] mind or emotions as influencing [her] to assent to or dissent from the verdict," Fed. R. Evid. 606(b). The most she could have

App. 48

done was to repeat the story about the BB shot, but it would violate Rule 606(b) to have her juxtapose the incident with her jury service and have her testify that it influenced her vote. *See United States v. Beltempo*, 675 F.2d 472, 481 (2d Cir.), *cert. denied*, 102 S. Ct. 2936 (1982). Without calling Torres the court had sufficient information from which it could conclude that there was no outside influence improperly brought to bear upon her, and that any supposed connection between the two events and the trial was not and could not be supported factually.

Of course, "[t]he safeguards of juror impartiality, such as *voir dire* and protective instructions from the trial judge, are not infallible" and "it is virtually impossible to shield jurors from every contact or influence that might theoretically affect their vote." *Smith v. Phillips*, 455 U.S. 209, 217 (1982). It is up to the trial judge to determine the effect of potentially prejudicial occurrences, *id.*, and the reviewing court's concern is to determine only whether the trial judge abused his discretion when so deciding. Whether or not we, sitting in the trial judge's place, might have called Torres to testify is not the issue. We cannot say that Judge Goettel abused his discretion by ending the post-trial inquiry when he did.

At the conclusion of the post-verdict jury inquiry, the district judge also ordered, on pain of contempt,

> that the defendants . . . and their agents, the defense attorneys and their agents, and the Government attorneys and their agents, are restrained from communicating with, or contacting in any manner whatsoever any juror, alternate juror, or . . . prospective juror in the [instant] case, without prior consent of the Court.

App. 49

Defense counsel argue that this amounts to a gag order which violates the First Amendment because, when read in conjunction with the court's accompanying memorandum decision, it placed a prior restraint on all Unification Church members, forbidding them from communicating with the media on the subject of jury prejudice in Moon's case. Aside from the fact that the memorandum does not say this, such a reading of the clear, unambiguous language of the restraining order is far-fetched. While the accompanying memorandum sheds light on the court's reasons for imposing and power to impose the restraint against jury contact, it is gratuitous insofar as the content of the order itself is concerned. Moreover, we lack appellate jurisdiction to review this order and mandamus is inappropriate where, as here, the district court's power to act as it did is unquestionable. *See Miller v. United States* 403 F.2d 77 (2d Cir. 1968) (no appellate jurisdiction, and virtually identical order condoned).

V

KAMIYAMA CLAIMS

A. Intent to Impede the Grand Jury Investigation

Kamiyama contends that his conviction for knowingly submitting false and misleading documents to the grand jury with intent corruptly to impede its investigation, in violation of 18 U.S.C. § 1503 (Supp. V 1981), must be set aside. Specifically, he asserts that he only submitted the documents in question (the Family Fund Ledger and European Loan Agreements) to the grand jury because it had subpoenaed them and that there was insufficient evidence that he intended to impede its investigation. In response to this challenge, the government answers that

App. 50

Kamiyama's corrupt intent was adequately demonstrated by the facts that he could have resisted production of the documents on Fifth Amendment grounds and that he vouched for the accuracy of the documents in his testimony before the grand jury. Specific intent to impede the administration of justice is an essential element of a § 1503 violation, *United States v. Ryan*, 455 F.2d 728, 734 (9th Cir. 1972) (citing *Pettibone v. United States*, 148 U.S. 197 (1893)), which the government must establish beyond a reasonable doubt. Viewing the evidence in the light most favorable to the prosecution, we are unpersuaded that Kamiyama's corrupt intent was adequately proved.

In examining the evidence underlying this Count, we may look only to that evidence actually introduced before the petit jury. There would be no problem with the government's contention had it introduced proof before the petit jury to the effect that Kamiyama had not only produced the questionable documents, but had also affirmatively vouched for their accuracy. Similarly, the government's case would be more persuasive were there any evidence that Kamiyama had submitted the documents with the knowledge that, had he chosen, he could have resisted production on the grounds of self-incrimination. On both of these points the government fails to direct us to any portion of the trial record in which such evidence was brought to the petit jury's attention. Nor have we, after reviewing the actual trial transcript, found any such evidence.

What remains to be answered is whether the petit jury could still properly infer corrupt intent from the fact that Kamiyama submitted the false documents to the grand jury knowing that the documents were material to that jury's investigation. Intent to obstruct justice is normally

App. 51

something that a jury may infer from all of the surrounding facts and circumstances. *See United States v. Haldeman*, 559 F.2d 31, 115-16 (D.C. Cir. 1976), *cert. denied*, 431 U.S. 933 (1977); *cf. United States v. Dibrizzi*, 393 F.2d 642, 644 (2d Cir. 1968) (dealing with intent to embezzle). Were it not for the fact that the documents were subpoenaed, such an inference would doubtless have been permissible in this case. But here the ledger and loan agreements were produced pursuant to subpoena and even though there was ample proof of their being falsely backdated, there was no evidence of Kamiyama's corrupt intent in producing them. Whether or not Kamiyama could have resisted production, as the government argues, evidence of this government theory was not before the trial jury. Without it, a reasonable doubt as to Kamiyama's *mens rea* exists. Therefore, his Count Seven conviction must be reversed.

B. *False Declarations Before the Grand Jury*

Kamiyama also attacks his convictions under Counts Eleven, Twelve and Thirteen of the main indictment and the only count of the additional indictment (No. 194). As earlier noted, those counts charged Kamiyama with making false declarations to a grand jury, in violation of 18 U.S.C. § 1623 (Supp. V 1981). That statute provides in pertinent part that "[w]hoever under oath . . . in any proceeding before or ancillary to any . . . grand jury of the United States knowingly makes any false material declaration" shall be guilty of a crime. 18 U.S.C. § 1623(a). Before addressing the precise issues raised some background information is necessary.

In March 1981 Kamiyama appeared before the June 1980 Additional Grand Jury for the Southern District of New York (Grand Jury) but refused, on Fifth Amend-

App. 52

ment grounds, to testify. In July 1981 Kamiyama changed his mind and testified before both the Grand Jury and a substitute grand jury which was filling in for the Grand Jury while its members were on vacation. Counts Eleven, Twelve, Thirteen and No. 194 involve statements initially made and recorded before this substitute grand jury and later presented to the Grand Jury in accordance with the latter's instructions.

Prior to trial appellant moved to dismiss the perjury counts arising from his testimony before the substitute grand jury on the ground that this testimony was not material to any investigation being conducted by the substitute grand jury. In a published decision, the district court agreed that Kamiyama's statements to the substitute grand jury technically were not material to any investigation then being conducted by it. *United States v. Moon*, 532 F. Supp. 1360, 1371 (S.D.N.Y. 1982). Nevertheless, the district court refused to dismiss the subject counts, reasoning that § 1623(a) extends to proceedings ancillary to those of a grand jury and that at the time Kamiyama testified before the substitute body it was acting in such an ancillary capacity. *Id.* On that basis the trial judge found that Kamiyama's substitute grand jury testimony was material to an investigation being conducted by the Grand Jury. The petit jury thereafter impiedly found by its conviction of defendant on Counts Eleven through Thirteen and No. 194 that Kamiyama gave the testimony knowing it to be false.

Kamiyama now challenges the district court's materiality finding. He argues that the substitute grand jury could not, as a matter of law, constitute an ancillary proceeding; that there was no evidence that the substitute grand jury was ancillary; that the district court erred in ruling on the ancillary proceeding question rather than submit-

App. 53

ting it to the petit jury; and that the district court impermissibly amended the indictment by relying on the ancillary proceeding theory which was not set out in the indictment. Moreover, he contends that there was insufficient evidence that his misstatements were material to the Grand Jury which eventually heard them. For the reasons discussed below these arguments are of no avail.

Section 1623 proscribes false declarations made before a grand jury where those declarations are "material," i.e., made in response to questions within the purview of matters that the grand jury is investigating. *United States v. Berardi*, 629 F.2d 723, 727 (2d Cir.), *cert. denied*, 449 U.S. 995 (1980); *see United States v. Mulligan*, 573 F.2d 775, 779 (2d Cir.), *cert. denied*, 439 U.S. 827 (1978). Whether or not a false declaration is material to a grand jury investigation is a question of law that must be determined by the court, not the jury. *Sinclair v. United States*, 279 U.S. 263, 298-99 (1929) (dicta); *Berardi*, 629 F.2d at 728; *Mulligan*, 573 F.2d at 779. Materiality is demonstrated if the question posed is such that a truthful response could potentially aid the inquiry or a false answer hinder it. *Berardi*, 629 F.2d at 728. Because materiality is a question of law, an appellate court may substitute its judgment for that of the lower court on the issue of whether the materiality element has been met. *See Berardi*, 629 F.2d at 728-29 (holding that the district court erred in finding false declaration immaterial).

Because we disagree with the district court's holding that Kamiyama's statements "technically" were not material when made to the substitute grand jury, we need not reach or decide the numerous questions regarding whether the substitute grand jury was conducting an ancillary proceeding. The district court's finding that Kamiyama's statements were immaterial to the substitute

App. 54

grand jury is at odds with the only evidence in the record on this point. There is uncontradicted, direct testimony in the record by Assistant United States Attorney Martin Flumenbaum that both the Grand Jury and the substitute grand jury were investigating Moon for possible tax violations. For example, Flumenbaum testified that the substitute grand jury was "charged with investigating the same matters that [the Grand Jury] was doing." This testimony was supported by affidavit evidence to the effect that: the Grand Jury approved in advance the procedure by which Kamiyama testified before the substitute grand jury, which was advised as to the substance of the on-going investigation of Moon and informed of the context in which Kamiyama was testifying; on two occasions the substitute grand jury heard testimony from another witness in this case; and the substitute grand jury actively participated in the proceedings by asking numerous questions relating to the handling of Moon's tax and business affairs and by requesting the production of documentary evidence. If the substitute grand jury cannot be said to have been investigating Moon's tax affairs when it was asking Kamiyama about those affairs, it is difficult to perceive exactly what it was doing.

Since both grand juries were investigating Moon's tax affairs, it seems somewhat illogical to say that Kamiyama's answers were immaterial when given to the substitute grand jury, but material, as the district court found they were, when repeated verbatim to the indicting Grand Jury. Our examination of the questions and responses in issue further strengthens our conviction that they were material to both grand juries' inquiries. The questions and answers set forth in Counts Eleven, Twelve, Thirteen and No. 194 do not deal simply with tangential matters of no relevance to the instant prosecution. Instead, they are

App. 55

concerned with the sources of Moon's Chase accounts funds, the Family Fund Ledger, the acquisition of the Tong Il stock, and the manner in which Moon conducted his business affairs. These matters were at the very heart of both grand juries' inquiries and related to the critical issues at trial. As a matter of common sense, we do not believe there is any basis to label them immaterial.[8]

C. Claimed Translation Inaccuracies

Kamiyama further contends with respect to his perjury convictions that he was impermissibly indicted and convicted for statements he did not give. Because his principal language was Japanese, he addressed the grand juries through an interpreter. At the request of counsel tape recordings were made of Kamiyama's grand jury statements. After being indicted for perjury in October 1981, Kamiyama received copies of the tape recordings of his testimony. After they were reviewed by defense counsel Kamiyama moved to dismiss certain specifications contained in Counts Ten through Thirteen on the ground that the allegedly perjurous language did not accurately reflect what he had actually said to the grand jury. He also requested that a court-appointed translator review the accuracy of the challenged language. Before the trial court ruled on Kamiyama's motion, a superseding indict-

---

[8] Our decision on the materiality issue does not intrude on appellant's double jeopardy rights under the Fifth Amendment since it neither necessitates a retrial nor has the effect of setting aside a judgment of acquittal on the merits. *See Berardi*, 629 F.2d at 730; *cf. Whalen v. United States*, 445 U.S. 684, 688 (1980) (double jeopardy protects against a second trial for the same offense); *United States v. Scott*, 437 U.S. 82, 91 (1978) (judgment of acquittal may not be appealed and terminates prosecution when reversal would necessitate new trial). We have merely adopted another basis for affirming the district court's conclusion that Kamiyama's substitute grand jury statements were material.

App. 56

ment was returned which omitted two of the allegedly inaccurate specifications in Count Ten.

The trial court ultimately appointed an interpreter to translate the tape recording of those portions of Kamiyama's grand jury testimony included in the indictment. Judge Goettel also requested defense counsel to "specify the particular portions of the translation that [were] in dispute." This was done at a pretrial hearing held on March 5, 1982. With respect to the objections to Counts Ten and Eleven, the district court found no significant difference between Kamiyama's testimony as set out in the superseding indictment and the court-appointed translator's interpretation of the recordings of that testimony. It did agree with Kamiyama's claims that certain Count Twelve testimony had been translated inaccurately and it dismissed all of that Count's specifications objected to by Kamiyama. With regard to Count Thirteen, the court found that the appointed translator's version of what Kamiyama had said agreed with the language quoted in the indictment, and counsel for Kamiyama accepted those translations as being accurate. The government later obtained a superseding Count Twelve indictment which omitted the previously objected to language.

At trial Kamiyama did not argue that the translation of the testimony set forth in the remaining false declaration counts was inaccurate. After the close of the evidence, the district court granted Kamiyama's request to make the court translator's translation an exhibit which the jury could see, if requested. Although the jury was so informed, apparently it did not request the exhibit.

On appeal Kamiyama now asserts that "all specifications" in the perjury counts were erroneously translated and fatally ambiguous.[9] Close examination of appellant's

---

9   Citing *United States v. Estepa*, 471 F.2d 1132, 1137 (2d Cir. 1972), Kamiyama also contends that the prosecution abused the grand jury

App. 57

contentions reveals that some of the points raised actually relate to sufficiency of the evidence as to falsity, not to accuracy of translation. In any event we address appellant's "translations" contentions one count at a time.

With respect to Count Nine, appellant asserts that while he was indicted for answering in the negative the question "did" Reverend Moon sign any documents dealing with stock, the question actually posed was whether Reverend Moon ever "had" to sign such documents. This claim of inaccurate translation was not raised in defendant's pretrial motion to dismiss; nor did he attempt to bring the purported infirmity to the attention of the court or jury at trial. Consequently, the objection to Count Nine has not been preserved for appeal. *See United States v. Bonacorsa*, 528 F.2d 1218, 1222 (2d Cir.), *cert. denied*, 426 U.S. 935 (1976).

The testimony underlying Count Ten, as set out in the indictment, is as follows:

[False declarations or answers are underlined.]

"Q. Did Reverend Moon carry the check book with him?

A. *He doesn't, because I managed it.*

Q. You carried the check book with you from the very beginning of the account?

A. *Yes, I kept it myself from the beginning.*

Q. Did you sign any of the checks for Reverend Moon's account?

---

process by not having it reevaluate all of the perjury counts in light of the court-appointed translator's findings. This claim is meritless; even Kamiyama concedes that the translator's findings generally accorded with the allegedly perjurous language set forth in the indictment. Where there were material variances, for example in Count Twelve, the government did resubmit its case to the grand jury.

App. 58

A. I never signed it myself, although I asked him for signature, and I made a request, but I never signed myself.

Q. Reverend Moon signed all the checks?

A. That's correct.

Q. And did Reverend Moon write out the other portions of the check other than his signature?

A. *No, no, he didn't do it.*

Q. You prepared all the checks for him?

A. *That's correct.*

*   *   *

Q. Did Reverend Moon ever write any portion of the checks on the Chase Manhattan account other his signature?

A. *He never wrote anything other than his own signature as far as I remember.*

*   *   *

Q. So, to your knowledge, he never wrote anything but the signature; is that correct?

A. *To the best of my knowledge, Reverend never affixed anything other than the signature in the book, in the check.*

With respect to the first two allegedly false answers, Kamiyama's objection goes not to the accuracy of the translation, but to the sufficiency of the government's proof at trial. He claims that his answers stated only that Moon does not presently carry the Chase account checkbook; that while the government proved at trial that Moon previously carried the checkbook, it did not prove that he presently does so; and that, therefore, Kamiyama's answers were not shown to be literally false at trial.

App. 59

We disagree. Viewing the first two answers in sequence and in context, *see Bonacorsa*, 528 F.2d at 1221, they plainly state that Moon "did" not carry the checkbook. This assertion was indisputably proved not to be true at the trial. Kamiyama's remaining contentions regarding Count Ten were either waived or are wholly without merit.

Moving to Count Eleven, the specifications of perjury were as follows:

[False declarations or answers are underlined.]

Q. Now, what was the largest deposit, single deposit that was made into Reverend Moon's account?

A. I think it was around four hundred thousand dollars.

Q. Who deposited that money?

A. I don't remember who I asked to do so. One thing is for sure, I didn't do it myself.

Q. And where did you get the money, that four hundred thousand dollars, to deposit in Reverend Moon's account?

A. *From family fund.*

Q. And where was the money actually at the time before you deposited it into Moon's account?

A. I wasn't physically in charge for that fund. But, I may have asked Miss Tomoko Torii, T-o-m-o-k-o T-o-r-i-i, but without clear recollection.

Q. Well, where did the four hundred thousand dollars—how did you get the four hundred thousand dollars that you deposited into Moon's account?

A. *Over the years, our brethren from Japan, who came to USA, they contribute, and it was accumu-*

App. 60

lated. I remember that there are at least about seven hundred brethren coming to the USA.

Q. Was any of the money in the family fund ever used to pay expenses for the Japanese members who had come to New York?

A. No. We never did that.

Q. So why didn't you put this money in a bank account?

A. Part of which was put into the bank, and the balance was kept.

Q. Well, did you have a bank account in the name of the family fund?

A. No.

Q. Why did you use Reverend Moon's name for the family fund?

A. *As the money came from overseas*, and part of that money may become necessary as expenses to take care of the brethren, we put it in Reverend Moon's name, who legitimately represents International Unification Church.

Kamiyama argues that the first two answers, although not alleged to be false, were inaccurately translated and somehow cast the third answer in a misleading context. Even assuming inaccuracies with respect to the interpretation of the first two answers, we fail to see any relationship between them and the third answer, the one alleged to be false. With respect to the second allegedly false answer, Kamiyama's claim that it was inaccurately translated is unpersuasive since the version set out in the indictment is in substantial agreement with the appointed translator's version. Kamiyama also argues that the third

App. 61

allegedly false answer—"As the money came from overseas"—resulted from an inaccurate translation by the interpreter. Comparing this language used in the indictment with the version of the court-appointed translator—"the money from overseas"—we see no material difference.

As for Count Twelve, none of the alleged mistranslations, ambiguities, or other purported infirmities complained of now was raised below. Thus, these claims are waived. Similarly, while he now asserts that the two questions underlying Count Thirteen were translated in a fatally "vague and ambiguous fashion," appellant abandoned his Count Thirteen translation objections during the pretrial hearing on his motion to dismiss. Moreover, there is nothing unduly vague or ambiguous about the Count Thirteen colloquy, which reads as follows in the indictment:

> "Q. Did you ever tell Michael Warder [a lower echelon Unification Church official] to tell government investigators that he got $5000 to purchase stock in Tong Il from relatives or friends? Did you ever tell him to give that explanation to anyone?
>
> A. *I didn't do it.*
>
> Q. Did you ever tell Mike Warder to give a false explanation as to how he paid for his stock in Tong Il?
>
> A. *No, I didn't.*

Appellant further argues with respect to Count Thirteen that the government failed to prove the falsity of his answers. Specifically, he contends that the government demonstrated at trial only that he "suggested" or "recommended" that Warder give a false explanation as to the

App. 62

Tong Il stock's origin, which is not the same as "telling," and, therefore, that his answers to the grand jury questions were not proven false. Viewing the evidence in the light most favorable to the government, the jury could have concluded that when Kamiyama recommended to Warder that he do something he was telling him to do it. Appellant makes no specific claims with respect to the translation of colloquy underlying count No. 194. Nor does he argue that the government's evidence on that count was insufficient.[10]

Accordingly, the judgments of conviction are affirmed on all counts except Count Seven, on which Kamiyama's conviction is reversed. The mandate of the court shall issue forthwith, provided that the mandate shall be stayed for the purpose of and for so long as is permissible to perfect and determine timely appeals from this decision.

---------★---------

OAKES, *Circuit Judge* (dissenting):

While fully concurring in the other portions of Judge Cardamone's lucid and careful opinion, I am required to dissent to that portion of it relating to the trial judge's charge on the law of trusts. Majority op. IIIA. Contrary to the Government's brief and the majority's view that "Moon did not raise until late in the trial" the claim that

---

10   Kamiyama's final contentions regarding his perjury convictions are: (1) that the government breached some obligation on its part to insure at the grand jury level that Kamiyama's erroneous answers were in fact intentional lies rather than mere negligent mistakes; and (2) that his false answers underlying Counts Nine and Ten were immaterial because the grand jury already had in its possession information contradicting his testimony. The district court rejected these arguments in its published decision *see* 532 F. Supp. at 1371-72, 1374, and we agree with that rejection for the reasons stated in the district court's opinion.

App. 63

he was holding the assets in question in trust, this was his position in the pretrial motion to dismiss as well as during argument on the midtrial motion for a judgment of acquittal. The trial judge quite properly acknowledged his obligation to charge on the law of trusts and did so no fewer than three times in the space of six pages of transcript.[1] The Government's assertion that defendants made "no claim . . . that [they] wanted, much less were entitled to, any of the specific instructions on the law of trusts which are claimed to be so crucial on appeal" simply does not hold water. The Reverend Moon submitted detailed instructions with supporting memoranda of law both on the general issue of beneficial ownership (No. 16) and on the specific issue whether an unincorporated religious association can be the beneficiary of a charitable trust (No. 15). Similarly, counsel pressed and elaborated upon his requests at the charging conference and made plain his disagreement with the proposed instruction submitted by the Government. Furthermore, counsel lodged specific objections to the instructions as given and in doing so specifically renewed the request for proposed instructions. The defense position was clear and consistent throughout the proceedings. *See United States v. Kelinson*, 205 F.2d 600, 601-02 (2d Cir. 1953) (Fed. R. Crim. P. 30 "does not require a lawyer to become a chattering magpie").

---

1   For example:

> But I do think you have got to get before the jury the notion that if the jury believes that the people who gave the money intended it to be for the International Unification Church Movement, and if Moon believed he was holding it for that purpose, and if he believed he was using them for that purpose, even though he may have in a few instances made bad investments or used some of it for himself, that the monies could still be viewed as not being his but being the Movement's.

T. 6122.

App. 64

Even if objections were not properly preserved, however, the issue of beneficial ownership was one "central to the determination of guilt or innocence" in the case, *United States v. Alston*, 551 F.2d 315, 321 (D.C. Cir. 1976). Thus, any defects in respect to the charge on this central issue would constitute plain error and require reversal. *See Connecticut v. Johnson*, 51 U.S.L.W. 4175, 4178 (U.S. Feb. 23, 1983).

Before discussing in detail what I believe were the errors in the trust instructions, I wish to put them in context because it is only then that their importance becomes apparent. In the first place, whether the Chase Manhattan Fund and the Tong Il stock held in Moon's own name were church property or Moon's personal property was the critical issue in the case. The Government went to great lengths to establish a fact that was really conceded from the beginning, that the assets were held in Moon's own name. But the law is clear that dominion and control over funds does not by itself establish taxability, at least where funds are beneficially owned by another. *See, e.g., Brittingham v. Commissioner*, 57 T.C. 91 (1971); *Seven-Up Co. v. Commissioner*, 14 T.C. 965 (1950). *See also Poonian v. United States*, 294 F.2d 74 (9th Cir. 1961). Thus, it was essential that the court's instructions precisely state the law on the creation of a trust relationship and the implications of the jury's finding that such a relationship existed in this case.

In the second place, this case did *not* involve a claim that an ordinary, lay taxpayer held certain assets in a private trust for the benefit of another. On the contrary, the taxpayer here was the founder and leader of a worldwide movement which, regardless of what the observer may think of its views or even its motives, is nevertheless on its face a religious one, the members of which regard

App. 65

the taxpayer as the embodiment of their faith. Because Moon was the spiritual leader of the church, the issue whether he or the church beneficially owned funds in his name was not as crystal-clear as might seem at first glance to be the case.

It appears that the assets in question came to Moon largely from members of his faith, and there was some evidence that the donors intended their contributions to be used by him for religious purposes. The religious context involved gives the case a special color. As noted in cases such as *Winn v. Commissioner*, 595 F.2d 1060, 1065 (5th Cir. 1979), funds donated for the use of an individual involved in religious work may be considered gifts to the religious organization with which the individual is affiliated. In *Winn*, for example, it was held that where money was given to the taxpayer's cousin, a missionary, in response to a church-sponsored solicitation, for deposit ultimately to her personal account, and was used, as intended, to support her mission work, it was sufficiently established that the funds were donated "for the use of" the church(es) to permit the contributing taxpayers to claim deductions for contributions. Similarly in *Morey v. Riddell*, 205 F. Supp. 918, 921 (S.D. Cal. 1962), it was held that where money contributed to a totally unorganized religious association by way of checks to individual "ministers" was used to meet expenses of the church, including the ministers' living expenses, deductions for religious contributions would be permitted. *But see Cox v. Commissioner*, 297 F.2d 36 (2d Cir. 1961) (not deductible when intent was to make bequest to individual). The Reverend Moon's claim that he held the Chase Funds and the Tong Il stock as trustee for the Unification Church movement likewise raised the question whether the donors intended this property to be used for religious

App. 66

purposes. In this context, then, I think it was incumbent
upon the court to make certain that the trust charge not
only properly state the factual elements that were involved, but that it also clearly emphasize that the Government had the burden of proof beyond a reasonable doubt
on this difficult issue.

Moreover, as we are referred to state law in respect to
ownership, *see United States v. Mitchell*, 403 U.S. 190,
197 (1971); *United States v. Manny*, 645 F.2d 163, 166 (2d
Cir. 1981); *see also* Treas. Reg. § 301.7701-4 (1974), the
instructions must be viewed in light of New York law
pertaining to assets given to a religious leader for use by
the trust. While I by no means agree with the appellants'
contention that New York law establishes a presumption
that any assets given to a religious leader are held by him
in a charitable trust, it at least permits of a finding to this
effect.

This conclusion stems from the following facts. First,
the law favors charitable trusts and will draw reasonable
inferences and resolve ambiguities to find and uphold
them. *In re Price's Will*, 264 A.D. 29, 35 N.Y.S.2d 111,
114-15, *aff'd*, 289 N.Y. 751, 46 N.E.2d 354 (1942); *In re
Estate of Nurse*, 35 N.Y.2d 381, 389, 362 N.Y.S.2d 441,
446, 321 N.E.2d 537 (1974). *See* N.Y. Est. Powers &
Trusts Law § 8-1.1 (McKinney 1967). Second, when a gift
appears to have been made for charitable or religious
purposes, the gift may be found to have been made in
trust even if no trust language has been used and even if
the gift was in form absolute. *In re Durbrow's Estate*, 245
N.Y. 469, 477, 157 N.E. 747, 749 (1927); *see also New
York City Mission Society v. Board of Pensions*, 261
A.D. 823, 823, 24 N.Y.S.2d 395, 396 (1941). Third, there
are numerous cases holding that a minister or other
church official who held title to property in his own name

App. 67

did so as trustee for the church. *See, e.g.*, *Sears v. Parker*, 193 Mass. 551, 79 N.E. 772 (1907) (fund for widows and orphans of church ministers); *Jones v. Habersham*, 107 U.S. 174, 182 (1882) (devise to church trustees to benefit of poor and feeble churches in state). *See* 4 A. Scott, *The Law of Trusts* §§ 371.3, at 2885 & n.4, 351 at 2797-98 (3d ed. 1967). Finally, where the source of the assets is a church source, added to the fact that the donee is a religious official, a trust may be imposed. *See Fink v. Umscheid*, 340 Kan. 271, 19 P. 623 (1888) (Catholic bishop using money supplied by congregation to purchase land in his own name for a church and school, later attempting to sell property; land concededly held in trust). *See also Archbishop v. Shipman*, 79 Cal. 288, 21 P. 830 (1889). Thus the key issue was whether the funds were given to Moon for his own use or for that of his international church movement, and whether, even though some of the funds were utilized for his own living purposes, the donors intended to permit such use.[2]

I reprint in the margin[3] the instructions on the "key issue" or the "central question" as the judge in his

---

[2] I note here that Moon was indicted, and the case was tried, on the theory that the funds were never in trust to begin with, and not on the theory that he had "diverted" to his own use funds originally given in trust.

[3]   The key issue is whether or not the bank accounts at the Chase Manhattan Bank and the Tong Il stock issued in Reverend Moon's name belonged to Reverend Moon.
     The defense contends that these funds and stock were beneficially owned by the International Unification Church Movement which supported the activities of the various national church entities in the United States and elsewhere.
     The government contends that these funds belong to Reverend Moon.
     This is the crucial issue of fact for you to decide.
     If you find that the funds in the Chase accounts were the property of International Unification Church Movement or were held in trust by Moon for the International Unification Church

App. 68

instructions to the jury termed it. The ensuing discussion relates to this material. In my view those instructions

Movement and used for church purposes and that the interest on those funds also belonged to the International Unification Church Movement and were used for it, then that interest would not be taxable income to Moon. You should not consider whether that interest income would be taxable to anyone other than Moon; that is, you should not concern yourself with whether the International Unification Church Movement had any tax liability for the interest earned by the time deposits, because that is not an issue in this case.

In determining whether in 1973, 1974 and 1975 the International Unification Church Movement existed and whether the Movement owned the funds in the Chase accounts and Tong Il stock or whether Reverend Moon owned them, you should consider all the evidence, including such factors whether the Movement had a specific organizational structure, written charter or constitution, the existence of other Unification Church corporate entities during the relevant time period, the fact that the accounts were maintained under Reverend Moon's name, the source of the funds, the intent of the parties who caused the stock and funds to be transferred to Reverend Moon's name, evidence of any agreements as to how the funds would be used, the manner in which the stock and funds were administered and whether there is any evidence Moon ever accounted to anyone for the use of the funds.

This list is by no means exhausted. You should consider all the evidence in making your determination.

In consider[ing] the evidence, there are a number of related issues which may occur to you. I want to briefly instruct you on the law applicable to these issues.

As I have mentioned, you may consider whether the International Unification Church Movement had a specific organizational structure in making your decision. However, the lack of a formal corporation does not prevent a religious movement from being the beneficial owner of property held in the name of another.

Now, the defendants contend, among other things, that Moon held the Tong Il stock and the funds of the Chase accounts as trustee for the International Unification Church Movement. Let me briefly explain to you the essentials of a trust in order for you to evaluate these contentions.

A trust is created when a person is given money or property to be held and used for the benefit of someone else. The person holding the property is called the trustee.

The person who transfers the property to the trust is referred to as a "settler"; the person who holds the property is the "trustee"; and the person or entity on whose behalf it is held is the "beneficiary."

Whether a trust is created depends on the intent of the person giving the property at the time of the transfer, and that intent must

App. 69

contained errors which, because they were on the crucial issue of the case, must be considered prejudicial.

First, in referring to the fact that the jury should consider all the evidence on the issue whether the Unification Church movement existed and whether the move-

be clear and unambiguous. A trust can be created orally or by the conduct of the parties. The trust need not be reflected in a written document.

In order for a trust to exist, the trustee must be obligated to use the property for the benefit of the beneficiaries; a gift with a mere request or expectation that the property would be used a particular way does not create a trust. There is no trust if the person who receives the money is free to use it for his own benefit. If a trust does exist and the trustee diverts trust property to his own use, the funds diverted become taxable to him at the time and to the extent so diverted.

In determining whether a trust relationship existed, you should, as I have already mentioned, consider all the evidence before you.

It is unnecessary for there to be a written agreement between Reverend Moon and the International Unification Church, providing he held the time deposits and the Tong Il stock on behalf of the church. All that is required is that both parties to the relationship understand that the first person is holding the property for the benefit of the second, and you can find such an understanding on the basis of the party's conduct.

Also the mere fact that Reverend Moon exercised control over the funds and the stock is not necessarily indicative of his personal ownership. A person who holds property on behalf of another may be given broad authority and discretion to deal with that property as long as he does so in a manner consistent with the purpose for which he was given title to the property in the first place.

I would like to say a few final words on the subject of religious movements.

Such organizations can invest and conduct businesses. While the income from such businesses is taxable, this fact does not make taxable the religion's income from other sources, including interest it earns on funds it has on deposit.

There is no legal requirement that a religious society be incorporated prior to making business investments. It is legal for an unincorporated church or religious association to be the beneficial owner of property held for its use in the name of others.

A religious organization can properly pay the living expenses of [its] leaders or ministers in order to allow them to pursue its religious purposes and can make loans to its ministers or leaders on arm's length terms.

T. 6583-88.

App. 70

ment or the Reverend Moon owned the funds in the Chase accounts and Tong Il stock, the court listed eight factors as set forth in Paragraph Six of the footnote. Listed among these, but not emphasized, was "the intent of the parties who caused the stock and funds to be transferred to Reverend Moon's name." Rather than simply including intent as one of the things for the jury to consider, the court in my view should have advised the jury to accord the greatest weight to this factor. The church source of the funds and Moon's role as church leader were likely to cast light on the issue of the donors' intent, and accordingly the charge should have specifically directed the jury's attention to them. The instruction as given allowed the jury to find against Moon on the issue of beneficial ownership without even considering the crucial issue of donors' intent. *See Sandstrom v. Montana*, 442 U.S. 510 (1979).

Secondly, though the issue was whether funds were given to a religious trust, the charge was that the intent to create it must be "clear and unambiguous," as in the case of private trusts. I recognize that the majority believes this portion of the charge to be correct under New York law, but the cases it cites for that proposition do not support it. *County of Suffolk v. Greater New York Councils, Boy Scouts of America*, 51 N.Y.2d 830, 832-33, 433 N.Y.S.2d 424, 425, 413 N.E.2d 363, 364 (1980), dealt only with the issue when a donation to a charitable organization, concededly subject to charitable trust restrictions, will be subject to additional specialized restrictions on use narrower than the organization's general charitable purpose; the court reversed a holding that a bequest to the Queens County Council of the Boy Scouts had to be used forever for a particular Boy Scout camp as distinct from the Boy Scouts generally. *Lefkowitz v.*

App. 71

Cornell University, 35 A.D.2d 166, 173, 316 N.Y.S.2d 264, 271 (1970), *aff'd*, 28 N.Y.2d 876, 322 N.Y.S.2d 717 (1971), held that a trust was not created by the donee's actions. Relying upon *In re Fontanella*, 33 A.D.2d 29, 30, 304 N.Y.S.2d 829, 831 (1969), the court held that the evidence was insufficient to show that the donee ever intended to create a trust. *Fontanella* simply involved a private trust, not a religious trust, and the donee was not the leader of a religious group.[4]

Thus, there appears to be no good basis for finding that "clear and unambiguous" intent is necessary to create a charitable trust under the law of New York. The strong policy of New York trust law and of trust law generally is to uphold charitable trusts whenever possible and to construe their terms liberally. *See, e.g., In re Price's Will*, 264 A.D. at 29, 35 N.Y.S.2d at 111; *In re Durbrow's Estate*, 245 N.Y. at 469, 157 N.E. at 747. In light of this fact, it is anomalous to require "clear and

---

4   The majority is equivocal in saying, on the one hand, that the only burden on Moon was to present a prima facie case that he held the assets in trust, and not to establish this as an affirmative defense and, on the other, that a review of the evidence reveals no proof that Moon actually held the subject funds in trust. The majority states that "the only evidence presented was the testimony of three church members who simply stated that they gave money to Moon intending to donate it to their church. Nothing was said about creation of a trust." This statement runs contrary to the New York and other trust law I have cited above. It was not necessary that the creation of a trust be mentioned. *See* N.Y. Est. Powers & Trusts Law § 8-1.1 (McKinney 1967); Restatement (Second) of Trusts § 351 comment b (1959) ("No particular form of words or conduct is necessary for the manifestation of intention to create a charitable trust. Compare, as to private trusts, § 24(2). A charitable trust may be created although the settlor does not use the word 'trust' or 'trustee.' ").

In this connection the trial court and I agree. There was evidence sufficient, though by no means conclusive, to present the question to the jury. The majority and I agree that, if this were the case, the burden of proof beyond a reasonable doubt remained upon the Government. But the majority thinks there was not enough evidence to present the issue to the jury at all.

App. 72

unambiguous" proof of the donor's intent to establish a charitable trust.

The second crucial error in the instructions lies in the charge that the jury should consider as the very first factor whether the International Unification Church movement "had a specific organizational structure, written charter or constitution . . . ." (*See supra* note 3, ¶ 3.) The Government concedes that it is a cardinal rule of trust law that a charitable trust cannot fail for lack of a specific beneficiary. The court should have said that a specific organizational structure was *not* a prerequisite to the existence of a charitable trust because in fact no beneficiary of a charitable trust need be designated at all. *See* N.Y. Est. Powers & Trust Law § 8-1.1 (McKinney 1967).[5] *See* 4 A. Scott, *The Law of Trusts* § 364, at 2838-39 (3d ed. 1967).

Moreover, the court's instructions regarding the use or misuse of trust funds were at the very least confusing. (*See supra* note 3, ¶ 14.) First, while it may be correct as a matter of law that a trustee who diverts trust property to his own use is taxable to the extent of the diversion, diversion was not charged in the indictment. Thus, evidence of diversion was irrelevant to the case. The diversion instruction, given over defense objection, was at variance with the theory on which the Reverend Moon was indicted and on which the entire case was tried.

---

5   N.Y. Est. Powers & Trusts Law § 8-1.1(a) (McKinney 1967) reads as follows:

> No disposition of property for religious, charitable, educational or benevolent purposes, otherwise valid under the laws of this state, is invalid by reason of the indefiniteness or uncertainty of the persons designated as beneficiaries. If a trustee is named in the disposing instrument, legal title to the property transferred for such a purpose vests in such trustee; if no person is named as trustee, title vests in the court having jurisdiction over the trust.

App. 73

Second, a trust may exist even though the trustee is endowed with the freedom to use for his own personal benefit a portion of the funds he holds in trust and such use will not nullify the existence of the trust. *United States v. Scott*, 660 F.2d 1145, 1166 n.38 (7th Cir. 1981), *cert. denied*, 455 U.S. 907 (1982); Rev. Rul. 71-449, 1971-2 C.B. 77. This is particularly true in the case of monies held in trust by religious leaders, since often use of such funds to pay a leader's living expenses are within the scope of the church's religious purposes. *See, e.g., Morey v. Riddell*, 205 F. Supp. at 918. Moreover, the instruction failed to explain that, even if the Reverend Moon had improperly diverted some of the Chase funds to a nontrust use, such partial diversion could not make the entire corpus, and thus the interest thereon, taxable to him. *United States v. Scott*, 660 F.2d at 1145; *see also Herbert v. Commissioner*, 377 F.2d 65 (9th Cir. 1967). The inclusion of the phrase "to the extent so diverted" in the diversion portion of the charge could not have conveyed this concept at all.

Finally, in my view the instructions shifted to the defendant the burden of proof on the issue of beneficial ownership. The jury was charged that "if" it found the Chase funds were the property of the International Unification Church movement or were held in trust by Moon for the movement, "then" the interest "would not be taxable income to Moon." The implication of this instruction was that Moon had to convince the jury that the property belonged to the movement. *See Notaro v. United States*, 363 F.2d 169, 175-76 (9th Cir. 1966) (condemning an "if/then" instruction as obscuring the locus of the burden of proof). By saying that the donor's intent must be "clear and unambiguous," not only was the law of charitable trusts being misstated, but the burden of

App. 74

proof improperly placed upon the defendant was made heavy indeed. I do not believe that the mention of "beyond a reasonable doubt" at the tail end of this discussion overcame the improper language within the curative concept of *Cupp v. Naughten*, 414 U.S. 141, 146-47 (1973).

Thus in a case where the crucial issue, and indeed the only real factual question, was whether property unquestionably held in Moon's own name was beneficially owned by him personally or was held by him on behalf of his international church movement, the charge fell short in several respects.

While often a charge is simply a way to achieve rough justice with the help of a jury, when a critical issue separating criminal conduct from civil is involved, in my view it must be accurate in *all* respects. This charge, I believe, was not.

Supplemental Brief for Petitioners

Table of Authorities

CASES

STATUTES

MISCELLANEOUS

No. 83-1242

In the
Supreme Court of the United States

OCTOBER TERM, 1983

SUN MYUNG MOON AND TAKERU KAMIYAMA,
PETITIONERS,

v.

UNITED STATES OF AMERICA,
RESPONDENT.

ON PETITION FOR CERTIORARI TO THE UNITED STATES COURT
OF APPEALS FOR THE SECOND CIRCUIT

Supplemental Brief for Petitioners

This supplemental brief is filed by petitioners Moon and
Kamiyama pursuant to Rule 22.6 of this Court. Petitioners wish to
call to the attention of this Court the fact that, since the filing of
their petition on January 26, 1984, the United States has filed a
petition for certiorari in a case raising a legal issue closely related

2

to the third of the questions presented by the *Moon* petition[1] —
namely, *United States* v. *Dahlstrom, 713* F.2d 1423 (9th Cir.
1983), *petition for cert. filed,* No. 83-1297 (February 6, 1984; opposition due April 11, 1984) (hereinafter, "Dahl. Pet.").

In *Dahlstrom,* the court of appeals held that proof of willful violation of 26 U.S.C. § 7206(2) was insufficient because, in the
court's view, the supposed illegality of tax-shelter transactions ad-
vocated by the defendants "was completely unsettled by any
clearly relevant [prior] precedent." 713 F.2d at 1428. In *Moon,*
petitioners contend that the instructions to the jury impermissibly
invited conviction under 26 U.S.C. § 7206(1) on a substantive
theory of taxability that was not only unsettled by prior precedent,
but was altogether pioneering in light of prior rulings affirmatively
suggesting that property acquired as petitioner Moon acquired the
assets at issue here would *not* be taxable to him. *See* Moon Pet. at
23-26. Thus both cases raise parallel questions about when
novelty or uncertainty in interpretation of the tax laws should preclude criminal conviction for willful violations of the Internal Revenue Code — questions that have been raised in a variety of cases
attempting, without notable success, to explicate the splintered
opinions of this Court in *James* v. *United States, 366* U.S. 213
(1961). *See* Moon Pet. at 27-29. But the *Moon* case raises those
questions in a context far more sympathetic to the taxpayer's position and, more to the point of this Court's exercise of its discretionary jurisdiction, does so in a context far more conducive to a
holding broadly resolving the "confusion" the government concedes, *see* Dahl. Pet. at 18 n.15, *James* and its progeny have
spawned.

Even if *Dahlstrom* were to be reviewed and reversed for the
reasons the government plausibly urges, such a decision would

---

[1] The third question presented by the *Moon* petition is the following: "Does the
Due Process Clause permit use of a criminal prosecution to pioneer a novel and
debatable theory of tax liability?" *See* Petition for Certiorari in *Moon and
Kamiyama* v. *United States,* No. 83-1242 (hereinafter, "Moon Pet."), at i.

3

wholly fail to resolve the issues left open by the *James* series of decisions and squarely posed in *Moon,* for any *holding* by this Court in *Dahlstrom* would of necessity be too narrow, in at least four respects, to shed light on the basic dilemma of the taxpayer facing criminal prosecution for failing to report, as his own income, holdings of a sort previously characterized by government as nontaxable to him.

1. In *Dahlstrom,* the Government contends that the only novelty involved in the prosecution was that the precise version of sham transaction newly devised by the defendants had not yet been denounced as illegal in a prior ruling expressly directed to just such a scam. *See* Dahl. Pet. at 10-11, 29. In *Moon,* by contrast, petitioners contend not only that the taxpayer's treatment of the income as not reportable by him involved no such variation on a well-settled illegal theme, but indeed that prior rulings had strongly suggested the affirmative *legality* of that treatment. *See* Moon Pet. at 23-25.

2. In *Dahlstrom,* any novelty conceivably present in the tax theory invoked by the government went at most to a legal issue "wholly collateral" to the central issue of whether the transactions in question were a sham. *See* Dahl. Pet. at 19-22. In *Moon,* by contrast, the alleged novelty unmistakably goes to the admitted heart of the criminal prosecution — namely, to whether the property in question was beneficially owned by Reverend Moon rather than by the church he leads. *See* Moon Pet. at 23.

3. In *Dahlstrom,* the government contends that any due process danger arising from the unsettled illegality of various transactions should be negated by sufficient proof of subjective intent to create those transactions — as a sham — for the very purpose of evading taxes. *See* Dahl. Pet. at 20-21. In *Moon,* by contrast, the substantive tax violation itself is not defined in terms of any sham transaction, with the result that proof of subjective intent could at most negate a claim of insufficient notice, not a claim of undue government power to shape the criminal law to fit the accused

4

through a theory of liability that is radically novel at its core — as was the theory invoked by the government in *Moon*. *See* Moon Pet. at 26-27 & n.51.

4. The extent to which retrospective application of a novel and debatable theory of taxability poses special danger to activity protected by the First Amendment is an issue far more starkly posed in *Moon* than in *Dahlstrom*, as even the most cursory review of the plainly misguided First Amendment holding in *Dahlstrom* makes clear. *Compare* Moon Pet. at 27 & n.52 *and* 17-22 *with* Dahl. Pet. at 23-28.

So manifest are these distinctions between the two cases that no resolution of *Dahlstrom* could settle the issue presented in *Moon*, much less illuminate the broad issues left open by *James* and its offspring.

For these reasons, the very policy of clarity and consistency in national standards of tax law enforcement which the government seeks certiorari in *Dahlstrom* in order to promote, *see* Dahl. Pet. at 28-30, would be far better served by this Court's consideration of both *Moon* and *Dahlstrom* than by its review of *Dahlstrom* alone. For the differences that separate the two cases ensure that resolution solely of the narrow issue in *Dahlstrom* would give little guidance to federal prosecutors, the Internal Revenue Service, or the criminal tax bar, in resolving related issues.[2] Should this Court grant certiorari in *Dahlstrom*, therefore, it would advance the in-

---

[2] That the *individuals* involved in *Moon*, and the religious beliefs that generated the unusual prosecution leading to their conviction, may seem *sui generis* should not be allowed to obscure the generality of the predicament that this conviction, and the circuit court ruling upholding it, lays bare. The very multitude of *amicus* briefs in support of plenary review herein, and the diversity of the groups represented, testifies to the difficulty of treating Reverend Moon as a containable class of one.

5

terests of economy and efficiency in the use of the dramatically overburdened resources of this Court for certiorari to be granted in *Moon* as well.[3]

Conclusion

Accordingly, the intervening filing of the Government's petition in *Dahlstrom* strongly supports granting certiorari with respect to the third issue in *Moon*.

Respectfully submitted,

LAURENCE H. TRIBE, *Counsel of Record*
KATHLEEN M. SULLIVAN
1525 Massachusetts Avenue
Cambridge, Massachusetts 02138
HAROLD R. TYLER, JR.   (617) 495-1767
PATTERSON, BELKNAP, WEBB
& TYLER   JEANNE BAKER
New York, New York   DAVID J. FINE
                              SILVERGLATE, GERTNER, BAKER & FINE
CHARLES C. RUFF   Boston, Massachusetts
COVINGTON & BURLING
Washington, D.C.   MORTIMER CAPLIN
                              RICHARD TIMBIE
ANDREW C. LAWLER, P.C.   CAPLIN & DRYSDALE, Chartered
New York, New York   Washington, D.C.

April 5, 1984

---

[3] Given the differences between *Moon* and *Dahlstrom*, *denial* of certiorari in *Dahlstrom a fortiori* would not counsel against a grant of certiorari in *Moon*. Indeed, should this Court leave standing the decision in *Dahlstrom*, the conflict between the Second and Ninth Circuits would call even more clearly for a grant of certiorari in *Moon*.

Brief for the United States in Opposition

QUESTIONS PRESENTED

1. Whether the district court properly denied petitioners' request for a bench trial.

2. Whether the district court's instructions to the jury were consistent with the Religion Clauses of the First Amendment.

3. Whether under the Due Process Clause, legal uncertainty, if any, regarding the correctness of the district court's instructions on the creation of a charitable trust precluded prosecution of petitioners.

TABLE OF CONTENTS

TABLE OF AUTHORITIES

Cases:

(III)

IV

In the Supreme Court of the United States

OCTOBER TERM, 1983

No. 83-1242

SUN MYUNG MOON AND TAKERU KAMIYAMA, PETITIONERS

v.

UNITED STATES OF AMERICA

*ON PETITION FOR A WRIT OF CERTIORARI TO THE
UNITED STATES COURT OF APPEALS
FOR THE SECOND CIRCUIT*

BRIEF FOR THE UNITED STATES IN OPPOSITION

OPINIONS BELOW

The opinion of the court of appeals (Pet. App. 1-74) is reported at 718 F.2d 1210. The district court judgments of conviction are not reported.

JURISDICTION

The judgment of the court of appeals was entered on September 13, 1983. Petitions for rehearing were denied on October 28, 1983, and November 1, 1983. On November 22, 1983, Justice Marshall extended the time within which to file a joint petition for a writ of certiorari to and including January 26, 1984, and the petition was filed on that date. The jurisdiction of this Court is invoked under 28 U.S.C. 1254(1).

STATEMENT

After a jury trial in the United States District Court for the Southern District of New York, petitioners were convicted of various charges in connection with the filing of false income tax returns for petitioner Moon in the years 1973, 1974, and 1975, and the preparation and presentation of fabricated documents in support of the

(1)

2

returns. The 13-count indictment charged both petitioners, under 18 U.S.C. 371, with conspiring to defraud the United States by impeding and obstructing the Internal Revenue Service in the computation, assessment and collection of income taxes due and owing from petitioner Moon, as well as with conspiring to make and subscribe false federal income tax returns, in violation of 26 U.S.C. 7206, to obstruct justice, in violation of 18 U.S.C. 1503, to make false statements to government agencies, in violation of 18 U.S.C. 1001, and to make false statements to the grand jury, in violation of 18 U.S.C. 1623. Petitioner Moon was also charged in three substantive counts with filing false personal federal income tax returns for the years 1973, 1974, and 1975, in violation of 26 U.S.C. 7206(1). Petitioner Kamiyama was also charged with aiding in the filing and preparation of Moon's false tax returns for the years 1974 and 1975, in violation of 26 U.S.C. 7206(2), obstruction of justice through the submission of false documents to the grand jury, in violation of 18 U.S.C. 1503, submission of false documents to the Department of Justice, in violation of 18 U.S.C. 1001, and perjury, in violation of 18 U.S.C. 1623. A separate indictment charged Kamiyama with an additional count of perjury. Pet. App. 4-5.

Petitioners attempted to waive their right to a trial by jury in favor of a bench trial, but the government withheld its consent pursuant to Fed. R. Crim. P. 23(a). After voir dire, the district court rejected petitioners' motions for bench trial, finding the impanelled jury capable of rendering an impartial verdict (Tr. 1751-1761). Upon trial, petitioners were found guilty on all counts. Petitioner Moon was sentenced to four concurrent terms of 18 months' imprisonment and fined $25,000 plus costs. Pet. App. 5. Petitioner Kamiyama was sentenced to seven concurrent terms of six months' imprisonment and fined $5,000 (*ibid.*).

1. The court of appeals affirmed the convictions with the exception of petitioner Kamiyama's conviction for obstruction of justice (Pet. App. 4, 49-51). The court

3

unanimously rejected petitioners' claims, inter alia, that the prosecution was impermissibly motivated by hostility toward petitioner's religion (*id.* at 33-37), that the trial by jury violated their due process rights (*id.* at 6-11), that the evidence was insufficient to support conviction (*id.* at 11-21), and that the jury instruction violated the Religion Clauses (*id.* at 28-32). On a divided vote, the court rejected petitioners' contention that the instructions on the creation of a charitable trust conflicted with applicable New York trust law (*id.* at 22-28). The court concluded that no such instruction had been required under the facts of the case (*id.* at 22-25) and, as a separate alternative holding, that the instructions as given were correct (*id.* at 25-28).

2. Petitioner Moon is the founder and leader of the Unification Church, incorporated in the United States in 1961 as the Holy Spirit Association for the Unification of World Christianity (HSA-UWC) (Pet. 2; Pet. App. 13). He is also a successful businessman; at the time of his initial visit to the United States in 1972 he was founder and chairman of the board of eight Korean publishing and manufacturing companies (Pet. App. 11; GX 570).

The principal issue at trial concerned ownership of bank accounts in the Chase Manhattan Bank and stock in a corporation, Tong Il Enterprises, Inc. The government contended that the funds and the stock were petitioner Moon's personal property, while petitioners contended that Moon held them for the "international Unification Church Movement"—an entity whose very existence the government questioned—as a nominee, agent, or trustee. The evidence at trial, which must be viewed in the light most favorable to the government (*Glasser* v. *United States*, 315 U.S. 60, 80 (1942)), may be summarized as follows.

a. *The Tong Il stock.* In June 1973, petitioner Kamiyama incorporated Tong Il Enterprises, a firm that purchased and imported ginseng tea and marble vases (Pet. App. 11-12; GX 401A). Petitioner Moon and his wife

4

received 70% of the corporation's stock; petitioner Kamiyama received 10% (Pet. App. 12). Although originally he had agreed to pay for his shares, petitioner Moon did not do so; but various assets were transferred to Tong II by other corporations that Moon controlled (*ibid.*). As the court of appeals observed (*id.* at 14 n.2), "[t]he jury could well have found that the whole transaction amounted to an indirect dividend to Moon from the companies under his control." Petitioner Moon did not report income attributable to the stock distribution (*id.* at 13-14). There was no other evidence regarding the source of the shares, and no evidence at all suggesting that the Unification Church viewed itself at the time as the beneficial owner of the shares held in petitioner Moon's name. Indeed, an official of the church organization, HSA-UWC, told lawyers for that organization that HSA-UWC had no connection with Tong Il other than as a purchaser of ginseng tea (GX 456).

b. *The Chase Manhattan bank accounts.* On March 27, 1973, petitioner Moon walked into the Chase Manhattan Bank's international office in New York City and opened a personal checking account and a personal savings account in his name (Tr. 2241-2267). The initial checking account deposit was of three checks totalling $82,400, made out to Sun Myung Moon (GXs 4A, 4B, 4C). Although petitioner Moon identified himself to the Bank as the founder of HSA-UWC (GX 2), he did not mention the "international Unification Church Movement," in whose beneficial interest he now claims to have opened the account, or otherwise indicate that the account was not his personally (Tr. 2302). Had he done so, the Bank would have required the name on the account (Tr. 2303).

By the end of 1975, more than $1.7 million had been deposited in these accounts. All but $200,000 of the deposits were in cash. Pet. App. 5; GX 2006. A substantial portion of these funds was transferred to high-yield Chase time deposits in petitioner Moon's name (Pet. App. 5; GX 2005). From 1973 through 1975, these investments earned more than $100,000 in interest, which was

5

not reported on Moon's tax returns for the prosecution years (Pet. App. 5; GX 2018). It is undisputed that the funds were held in petitioner Moon's name, and evidence showed, in the trial court's words (S. 13), "that he treated the entire sum of money as his and used it for whatever purposes he wanted to, some personal and some more business-related, and that all of it was treated by him as being his own." The defense theory, however, was that it could be inferred from the source of the funds that they were actually held in trust for the international Unification Church Movement.

The actual source of most of the funds (and, accordingly, their intended use) was and remains unknown, as the government demonstrated at trial (see S. 16; Tr. 6222). The evidence indicated both that there were alternative sources of the funds—petitioner Moon's international and domestic business activities—and that Unification Church members had a "custom of providing gifts of substantial value" to petitioner Moon "personally" (GX 456B, at E1881). As described more fully below, petitioners created documents purported to show that the *ing* funds in question were derived from foreign Unification Church loans and donations. The government conclusively showed these documents to be fabrications. Three witnesses, members of the Unification Church whose testimony was seriously impeached,[1] testified that they gave sums totalling $172,000 (out of a total of about $1.7

---

[1] Two of the witnesses, for example, were shown to be participants in the manufacture of the phony Japanese Family Fund ledger (Yukiko Matsumura) and the backdated "loan agreements" from foreign Unification Churches (Paul Werner). See pages 11-13, *infra*. Moreover, the testimony of the witnesses was in fact contradictory to the defense theory that the funds were intended to be used for nonspecific Church purposes at the discretion of petitioner Moon; both Marion Porter (alleged donor of $37,400) and Paul Werner (alleged donor of $135,000) stated that the funds were raised to support a series of speaking tours then being undertaken by petitioner Moon (Tr. 3124, 3405-3406). Instead of being used for that purpose, the funds were deposited to personal accounts held in petitioner Moon's name.

6

million in the accounts) to petitioner Moon, intending them as a donation to their church. They did not state that they communicated any such intention to petitioner Moon.[2]

The only evidence concerning the view of petitioners and Unification Church officials *at the time of the events in question* on the ownership of the funds were various statements that the funds were petitioner Moon's own.

---

[2] We thus feel constrained to point out that petitioners' assertion in their statement of facts (Pet. 6 (footnote omitted)) that "[t]he government did not overtly dispute, as it could not, * * * that the assets had been given him by followers of his religion, who did so intending that the assets be used for that religion" (see also, to similar effect, Pet. 7 n.12), is not the case. See Tr. 6222-6224 (government's summation to the jury); Gov't C.A. Br. 8-9, 94. The government frankly does not *know* where the funds came from, but is disinclined to accept the explanation that petitioners' fabricated documents and perjured grand jury testimony purported to establish. Similarly, the court of appeals did not "conced[e]," as petitioners assert (Pet. 19), "that Unification Church members had given the assets to Reverend Moon 'intending [them] as a donation to their church' " (quoting, out of context, Pet. App. 23). See also Pet. 6 n.9. What the court said (Pet. App. 23 (emphasis added)) was:

> In order to establish the defense of trusteeship, defendants would have had to produce evidence of the donors' intent to create a trust. Yet *the only evidence even remotely touching on this issue was* the testimony of Church members Matsumura and Porter and German Unification Church leader Werner who simply stated that they gave money to Moon, intending it as a donation to their church.

For purposes of appellate review, a convicted defendant is not entitled to treat as established fact a proposition contested by the government and supported only by a few interested witnesses whose testimony was evidently not believed by the jury. Yet in addition to suggesting that the government and the court of appeals concede the truth of their dubious view of the facts, petitioners repeatedly refer in their Petition to the alleged gifts by church members for religious purposes, without acknowledging that no such facts have been established. See Pet. 6, 7 n.12, 17 & n.29, 18, 19-20, 23, 25; but cf. *id.* at 5, 8, 20 n.34 (acknowledging, at least implicitly, ʌhat the source and intended use of the funds were controverted "claim[s]" or "proposition[s]" of the defense).

7

His banking transactions were invariably accompanied by written authorizations signed by himself, referring to the accounts in personal terms, such as "my account," "my money," and "my Time Deposit" (see, *e.g.*, GXs 89, 100, 110, 111, 113, 116, 118, 120, 123, 143, 146, 150, 158, 161, 182F, 186, 230, 234, 236, 251, 252, 263, 264, 273, 276, 277, 278, 282). Although informed by accountants that if he held funds in his name on behalf of someone else he should file IRS Form 1087, petitioner Moon did not do so (Tr. 4190-4191; see *id.* at 6666-6667). Evidence showed that in discussions with lawyers and accountants in January 1974, Unification Church officials described the funds at issue as petitioner Moon's personal property, totally separate from Church property. See pages 10-11, *infra*. Moreover, on several occasions when a Unification Church official proposed using the Chase funds for various important Church projects, Kamiyama told him that the funds were "Father's money" and that they were "not accessible" (Tr. 5185-5186).

In October 1973, HSA-UWC, the Church corporation, purchased a 26-acre estate (East Garden) for petitioner Moon's use as a home for himself, his family, and his staff (Pet. App. 13, 15; Tr. 3017). Petitioner Moon provided the church corporation $361,827 from the disputed checking account at Chase to complete the cash purchase of the estate for $631,827 (Tr. 2863-2866; GXs 76, 76B, 76C, 444, 445).[3] HSA-UWC issued a promissory note for $361,827, signed by Neil Salonen, Acting President, and made out to the order of "Reverend Sun Myung Moon" (GX 445). This transfer of funds was carried on the Church corporation's books as a personal loan to the Church from Moon (Pet. App. 15; Tr. 5842-5844; GX 500).[4] Later, when HSA-UWC was unable to

---

[3] Petitioner Moon also issued a check for $51,160 to pay for furnishings in the estate (Pet. App. 13).

[4] A financial and legal official of HSA-UWC later prepared a list of all loans outstanding from petitioner Moon to HSA-UWC, in-

8

meet mortgage payments on a $500,000 mortgage on another Church property, known as "Belvedere," Moon broke a Chase time deposit and lent $175,000 to the organization (Pet. App. 15; GX 86). HSA-UWC repaid petitioner Moon $70,000 of this loan and wrote off the $105,000 balance as a "special contribution[]" from Moon (GX 513, at E1983; see Pet. App. 15; GX 511).[5]

In November 1973, petitioner Moon directed that title to East Garden be transferred to him. The HSA-UWC president explained to another Church official that "Father wanted East Gardens transferred into his own name because it was his personal money" (Tr. 2870-2872; see Pet. App. 15). However, before the transfer could be completed, HSA-UWC lawyers informed petitioner Moon's subordinates that a simple transfer would result in substantial personal tax liability to Moon because the value of the estate transferred would be personal income to him. The transfer would also, according to the lawyers, jeopardize HSA-UWC's tax exempt status. To avoid these consequences, petitioner Moon would have to pay the estate's fair market value of $700,000 to HSA-UWC. Petitioner Moon's loans to HSA-UWC were then falsely increased on the church organization's books to $700,000, and Moon signed a Release and Cancellation of Indebtedness Agreement covering the $700,000 purchase price for East Garden (Pet. App. 15; GXs 471, 472). After the deed to East Garden had been executed, but before it was filed, the transaction was reversed on advice of counsel and the documents ordered destroyed (GXs 436, 475). The court of appeals observed that petitioner Moon, by signing the false release and cancellation of indebtedness, "implicitly acknowledged that the

cluding those in connection with East Garden (GX 478). The list was prepared for petitioner Kamiyama, expressly for use "in the handling of Father's *personal* records" (GX 478, at E1940 (emphasis added)).

[5] HSA-UWC accountants considered treating petitioner Moon's contribution as a transfer from "an ass ciated entity," but decided instead that it was properly treated as a "contribution" (GX 638A).

9

$361,827 used to pay for the property * * * was his own" (Pet. App. 15-16, 20); if petitioner Moon had simply been acting on behalf of a related Church entity, rather than himself personally, the transfer could have been accomplished without any personal tax consequences whatsoever.

The government introduced evidence of a number of business and personal transactions engaged in by petitioner Moon with the disputed funds.[6] The purpose of this evidence was not to show that the uses of the funds were not "religious" in nature—a church can legitimately engage in business transactions—but that the transactions were personal to petitioner Moon. In none of the transactions did any contemporaneous document or other credible evidence suggest that petitioner Moon was acting on behalf of an "international Unification Church Movement," or indeed, on behalf of any one other than himself.[7]

The very existence of an "international Unification Church Movement" was an issue at trial. Petitioners contended (Tr. 5432, 5513-5515, 6304; see Defendant Moon's Proposed Instruction No. 15, at C.A. App. 1365) that the "international Unification Church Movement" was an unincorporated association, the predecessor entity to the "Unification Church International." The latter, in-

---

[6] For example, in September 1975 petitioners Moon and Kamiyama obtained $155,000 from one of Moon's time deposits at Chase for purchase of stock in Diplomat National Bank in Washington, D.C., in the names of Moon and Kamiyama (Pet. App. 14-15; Tr. 3498). After the IRS investigation began, petitioner Moon redeemed his shares (Tr. 3509-3511; GX 556). The defense conceded at trial that these shares were "a personal investment" for petitioner Moon, but contended, without evidentiary support, that the money used was a loan to petitioner Moon from the international Unification Church Movement (Tr. 6335-6336, 6345).

[7] Two defense witnesses, senior Unification Church officials, stated the opinion that two particular business ventures were entered on behalf of the Churcn (Tr. 5658 (Choi), 5818-5819 (Kim)). However, both witnesses admitted that they had no personal knowledge of the Chase accounts or the financing of the transactions (Tr. 5664-5666 (Choi), 5787, 5806 (Kim)).

10

corporated in 1977, is a *taxable* entity that holds Church business properties. See Tr. 4649-4652, 5939. The government contended that the "international Unification Church Movement" never existed as an entity, but was created after the fact to justify petitioner Moon's failure to pay taxes on personal income (Tr. 6488-6492). During the period from early 1973 to early 1974, petitioners and the Unification Church set up a number of church organizations. Each was separately incorporated, and had its own bank account or accounts in its own name. See, *e.g.*, Tr. 5792-5798; GX 972. Thus, in addition to a total absence of any direct contemporaneous evidence that the "international Unification Church Movement" existed as an entity, the government showed that such an amorphous financial and organizational arrangement would have been inconsistent with Unification Church practice.

In an intensive two-day meeting in January 1974, leaders of HSA-UWC, including its President, Neil Salonen, consulted a Washington law firm and an accounting firm about a number of business and financial matters, including the loans from Moon for the purchase of East Garden and the intended transfer of East Garden to Moon (Pet. App. 16; GXs 454A, 456B). The discussions concerned a wide array of Unification Church entities, both incorporated and unincorporated. No mention of an "international Unification Church Movement" was made, and the obvious premise of the legal advice sought was that the funds in question belonged to petitioner Moon personally. Memoranda and letters prepared by counsel on the basis of the information provided at the meeting by the Church leaders were introduced into evidence in redacted form as proof of the contemporaneous understanding of the Unification Church concerning petitioner Moon's finances and the funds in question. In a letter to Salonen dated January 11, 1974, counsel advised (GX 454A, at E1845):

It is important to stress what may be obvious: to the extent that Rev. Moon has separate assets

11

which are to be maintained as such, it is vital to maintain that separateness in all respects. Therefore, if the Church borrowed funds from Rev. Moon, or vice versa, for the purchase of one of the properties, that amount should be repaid. Furthermore, such transactions between the Church and Rev. Moon should be avoided in the future.

A memorandum summarizing the meeting makes it even clearer that in his treatment of the Chase funds and the East Garden transaction, petitioner was acting as an individual, not as an agent or trustee for the Church (GX 456B, at E1881):

We discussed the affairs of Rev. Moon and his and their relationship to the Church because Rev. Moon has monies of his own having no relationship with HSA-UWC and those monies are involved in the purchase of property which might be used in Church activities. * * *

If title to the East Garden property is to be transferred to Rev. Moon, there would have to be an accounting and repayment to the Church of any monies which it advanced toward the purchase price. Otherwise, there would be a diversion of tax exempt funds for private gain.

The memorandum also revealed that Unification Church members had made substantial gifts to petitioner Moon personally (*id.* at E1881-E1882):

We suggested also the termination of the custom of providing gifts of substantial .value to Rev. Moon on various occasions, in kind or in cash. To the extent that members cannot be dissuaded from making gifts to Rev. Moon, then Rev. Moon should indicate that he wishes the gift to be made to HSA-UWC in his honor rather than to himself personally.

c. *The false documents and returns.* Soon after this meeting, petitioner Kamiyama was put in charge of the preparation of petitioner Moon's tax returns under Moon's own direction (Pet. App. 16; GX 463A). Any reference in the evidence at trial to the "international

12

Unification Church Movement" as beneficial owner of the funds, or to petitioner Moon as agent, nominee, or trustee, originated after this point (see Tr. 3863, 3866, 4182-4186, 4186, 4189-4190). During this period, records were created to account for the more than $1.7 million deposited into the Chase accounts and to create the impression that these funds were Church assets (Pet. App. 16).[8] Three hundred and fifty thousand dollars was accounted for as loans from Unification Church organizations in Europe, and $1.2 million was accounted for as funds purportedly brought to the United States in amounts of $3000 to $4000 by Japanese Unification Church members (*id.* at 16-17). These latter amounts were included in a ledger called the "Japanese Family Fund Ledger" (*id.* at 17). The loan agreements and this ledger were manufactured after the fact; the ledger was created after the IRS investigation had begun, by a Kamiyama aide, Yukiko Matsumura, who worked backwards from Moon's bank statements and deposit slips and created fictitious sources to account for the deposits (*id.* at 17-18).[9] The petitioners later gave these documents to the Justice Department, claiming that they were contemporaneous documentary evidence that petitioner Moon held the Chase funds and the Tong Il stock as an agent, nominee, or trustee of the Unification Church (*id.* at 16).

---

[8] The evidence of the document fabrications and their use by petitioners to mislead their own accountants and lawyers, the IRS, the Department of Justice, and the grand jury is so extensive and occupies such a large part of the 15 volumes of exhibits and transcripts in the printed record, that we have not provided specific citations to record evidence. The government's brief in the court of appeals contains a detailed summary. See Gov't Br. 25-43.

[9] Petitioners refer discreetly to these manufactured documents as having been merely "backdated" (Pet. 7 n.12) and complain that the government used these documents before the jury to "insinuate[]" (Pet. 7) that "Reverend Moon had simply made, after the fact, the explanation that the assets were owned by his church movement." That, of course, was the government's theory of the case, strongly supported by the evidence, which was apparently credited by the jury.

13

The government introduced evidence of numerous false and conflicting statements and explanations, mostly based upon these fabricated documents, made by petitioners to their accountants and lawyers, the IRS, the Department of Justice, and the grand jury. This evidence of deliberate misstatements of fact and manufacture of phony documents formed the core of the government's case that the false statements in petitioner Moon's tax returns were willful, as well as for the related charges of perjury and submission of false documents. See Pet. App. 11-21.

ARGUMENT

1. Petitioners contend (Pet. App. 11-17) that the district court erred in rejecting their attempt to waive a jury trial and be tried by the judge sitting alone. The general principle that a criminal defendant is not entitled to insist upon a bench trial over the prosecution's objection is well settled, and indeed flows naturally from the provision of Section 2 of Article III that "[t]he Trial of all Crimes, except in Cases of Impeachment, shall be by Jury." Petitioners' claim that they come within a possible exception to this principle raises an infrequently litigated issue that has produced no division of opinion among the circuits, is not well rooted in the specific facts of this case, and does not warrant review by this Court.

a. Denial of petitioners' attempted waiver of a jury trial was in full accord with Fed. R. Crim. P. 23(a), which provides that "[c]ases required to be tried by jury shall be so tried unless the defendant waives a jury trial in writing with the approval of the court and the consent of the government." See *Singer* v. *United States,* 380 U.S. 24 (1965); *United States* v. *Houghton,* 554 F.2d 1219, 1226 (1st Cir.), cert. denied, 434 U.S. 851 (1977); *United States* v. *Wright,* 491 F.2d 942, 945 (6th Cir.), cert. denied, 419 U.S. 862 (1974); *United States* v. *Farries,* 459 F.2d 1057, 1061 (3d Cir. 1972), cert. denied, 410 U.S. 912 (1973); *United States* v. *Ceja,* 451 F.2d 399 (1st Cir. 1971); *United States* v. *Abrams,* 357 F.2d 539, 549-550 (2d Cir. 1966). "A de-

14

fendant's only constitutional right concerning the method of trial is to an impartial trial by jury." *Singer*, 380 U.S. at 36.

Petitioners rely on the following dictum in *Singer*, 380 U.S. at 37-38 (citation deleted):

> We need not determine in this case whether there might be some circumstances where a defendant's reasons for wanting to be tried by a judge alone are so compelling that the Government's insistence on trial by jury would result in the denial to a defendant of an impartial trial. Petitioner argues that there might arise situations where "passion, prejudice . . . public feeling" or some other factor may render impossible or unlikely an impartial trial by jury. However, * * * this is not such a case, and petitioner does not claim that it is.

Petitioners assert that public hostility toward Reverend Moon constituted the kind of compelling circumstance referred to in *Singer*.

As the court of appeals correctly recognized (Pet. App. 9-10), the validity of a claim that a fair trial cannot be had because of public hostility can be resolved definitively only upon a voir dire of prospective jurors. Here, at the conclusion of a seven-day voir dire (Tr. 1-2121), the district court expressly rejected petitioners' claims that a fair and unbiased jury could not be, and had not been, selected (Tr. 1751-1761). The court stated (Tr. 1759):

> I have reasonable faith in the lack of bias in this jury. * * * I think that we have gotten a jury which is, if not totally free from bias, by and large capable of putting aside the bias they have and deciding the case on the merits of the charges.

After the trial, the court was even more emphatic in once again rejecting the petitioners' view of the jury. At the same time, the court, citing *Singer*, indicated that it would have ordered a bench trial had it in fact found pervasive bias against petitioners (S. 26):

15

If we had gotten to a position in the jury selection where I did not believe that we had a pool of unbiased jurors, I would have exercised almost unprecedented discretion of saying you would have to go without a jury. But I became convinced by the time we got to a pool of about 36 that a jury could be selected that would be sufficiently unbiased, and there is nothing more you can say in that regard that is going to change my view on it.

As the court of appeals unanimously determined (Pet. App. 10), these findings were amply supported by the record of the extensive voir dire undertaken by the trial court and were in accord with the settled principle that a juror is considered sufficiently impartial if he can set aside any opinions he holds and render a verdict based on the evidence in the case. *Murphy* v. *Florida*, 421 U.S. 794, 798-800 (1975); *Irvin* v. *Dowd*, 366 U.S. 717, 722-723 (1961).[10] The findings of two courts, both of them citing the *Singer* standard, that the jury was fair and impartial need not be reviewed by this Court.

b. Petitioners contend (Pet. 14), however, that a defendant should be entitled to a bench trial whenever the trial judge indicates that such a trial would be "fairer" than a jury trial and the prosecution does not make an adequate showing to the contrary. No such finding was made by the district court.[11] But even if the court had

---

[10] Petitioners were granted 20 peremptory challenges—twice the usual number. Approximately 20 jurors were excused for bias, and only six or eight of petitioners' challenges for cause were denied by the trial court. Tr. 1752-1753. And, as the court of appeals noted (Pet. App. 10), defense counsel challenged only one of the 12 actual jurors for cause, and did not raise the denial of that challenge on appeal. See *Beck* v. *Washington*, 369 U.S. 541, 557-558 (1962) (failure to challenge prospective jurors for cause is strong evidence defendant considered jurors not biased). Any requirement that a defendant's objections to prospective jurors be accorded particular consideration when he has attempted to waive jury trial (Pet. 12 n.17) was satisfied by the trial court's liberal grant of peremptory challenges and challenges for cause.

[11] Contrary to petitioners' claims (Pet. 14), the district judge did not actually determine in any formal sense that a bench trial would

16

made such a finding, petitioners' conclusion could not be squared with *Singer*. Under *Singer*, a bench trial may be required not where it would be "fairer," but where "the Government's insistence on trial by jury would result in the denial to a defendant of an *impartial trial*." 380 U.S. at 37 (emphasis added). Petitioners' view would eliminate the government's right under Rule 23 (a) to insist upon a jury trial; the government's "consent" would be reduced to the right to argue to the trial judge that he would not be "fairer" than a jury. There is no precedent for such a conclusion, and neither Rule 23(a) nor anything in the Constitution requires it.

c. Petitioners also contend (Pet. 14-15) that a reason given by the government for withholding consent to a bench trial violated their First Amendment right to free speech. This contention lacks merit.

The government's position on jury trial was set forth in a letter to the district judge dated March 11, 1982 (C.A. App. 811-812).[12] One of the reasons for the government's objection to petitioners' request was the "overriding public interest in the appearance as well as the fact of a fair trial" (C.A. App. 812). The government referred to various public statements of petitioner Moon and his supporters charging that this prosecution was motivated by "religious persecution and racial bigotry" (C.A. App. 811) and noted that the Constitution seeks to

---

be "fairer" than a jury trial. It is true that the judge commented at one point: "I would have thought it fairer to have this case tried without a jury" (Tr. 1760) and "[b]ut I do think I would feel better about the fairness from the position of the defendants had they been granted a non-jury trial" (Tr. 1761). However, he later made it clear that those statements were informal remarks and not "findings." During a post-trial hearing the judge stated to defense counsel (S. 40-41): "Keep in mind I did not say it would be fairer not to have a jury but it would be better. * * * * * You are putting into my mouth words that were put forward as debate and not as finding."

[12] The government is not required to provide a reason for refusing to consent to a bench trial. *Singer*, 380 U.S. at 37.

17

defuse such "attempt[s] to create a public atmosphere of distrust for our system" by assigning primary responsibility for deciding controversial criminal cases to a jury drawn from the lay community (C.A. App. 812).

The government's concern was legitimate. It has long been recognized that it is vital to our system of justice not only that justice be done, but that it appear to be done. See *Globe Newspaper Co.* v. *Superior Court*, 457 U.S. 596, 606 (1982); *Gannett Co.* v. *DePasquale*, 443 U.S. 368, 429 (1979) (Blackmun, J., concurring). Since the jury is "the tribunal which the Constitution regards as most likely to produce a fair result" (*Singer*, 380 U.S. at 36), the government had reason to believe the public would better accept the results of a jury trial. But even if this belief was wrong, it is difficult to understand petitioners' contention (Pet. 14 n.21) that the government's refusal to consent to a bench trial should be regarded as "penalizing" their expressions of criticism. After all, as this Court observed in *Singer*, the effect is "simply that the defendant is subject to an impartial trial by jury—the very thing that the Constitution guarantees him" (380 U.S. at 36).

2. Petitioners contend (Pet. 17-22) that jury instructions given by the district court and approved by the court of appeals violated the Religion Clauses of the First Amendment.[13] They claim (Pet. 17) that the jurors were "licens[ed] * * * to substitute their lay allocation of church property and authority for that of the church." The general principles invoked by petitioners are central to this nation's heritage of religious liberty and must be protected; their charge that those principles were violated in this case is, however, entirely without foundation.

Petitioners concede, at least in this Court, that petitioner Moon's finances must be viewed as separate and

---

[13] Although the Petition does not so state, we assume that the second and third questions presented by petitioners have no bearing on petitioner Kamiyama's convictions for perjury and submission of false documents.

18

distinct from those of the Unification Church (Pet. 20-21 n.34). It seems obvious—and we think it is undisputed —that the jury must therefore be "licensed" to decide whether funds held in petitioner Moon's name were held for his personal use or for church purposes. And it would seem just as obvious that the jury is not required to "defer" (Pet. 22) to statements by petitioners and other Church officials concerning who owned particular property. The jurors are entitled to disbelieve the defendants' version of the facts; and in this case they did.[14] It should not be forgotten that all of the contemporaneous evidence before the jury showed that petitioners and other Unification Church leaders treated the funds as, and understood them to be, the personal property of petitioner Moon, and that there were powerful reasons to doubt the credibility of the few witnesses who testified, after the fact, to the contrary.[15] Thus, there was ample basis for the jury to decide against petitioners on the controlling factual issues. See Pet. App. 11-23. Since petitioners rely on a *contrary* set of factual assumptions (see note 2, *supra*) as the predicate for their constitutional arguments, we submit that their second and third questions presented are not properly raised on this record.

Moreover, although the second and third questions petitioners ask this Court to review relate to the trial court's jury instructions, petitioners did not, with one minor exception,[16] raise their arguments in a timely

---

[14] Petitioners hint darkly (Pet. 7) that the government "cut off" the presentation of evidence by the defense by "obtaining rulings of inadmissibility" and "issuing threats" concerning rebuttal evidence. Petitioners do not raise these allegations as issues for this Court's review, and it is therefore appropriate to assume (as we believe to be the case) that petitioners had a full and fair opportunity to introduce all relevant evidence in their own defense.

[15] Petitioners themselves did not testify at trial. Moreover, the entire testimony that the funds had been intended as donations to the Church—even if believed—accounted for only about ten percent of the Chase Manhattan funds.

[16] Petitioners objected to the district court's instruction regarding proof of the existence of the "international Unification Church

19

fashion in trial court or properly preserve them for appeal. See Fed. R. Crim. P. 30; *Henderson* v. *Kibbe*, 431 U.S. 145, 154 (1977).

In any event, the court of appeals unanimously rejected petitioners' claim that the jury instructions were in violation of the First Amendment.[17] We believe that petitioners' specific criticisms of the instructions reflect nothing more than a misunderstanding of them and do not raise legal issues warranting review by this Court.[18]

Petitioners claim that under the instructions the jury could reject the defendants' explanation that petitioner Moon held the funds in trust for the Church "if," in petitioners' words, "the jury thought it *more suitable* for church assets to be entrusted to one of the church's incorporated worldly branches than to the church's leader" (Pet. 21 (emphasis added)). This is simply not an accurate reading of the instruction. The jurors were not charged with deciding how petitioners and the Unification Church *should have* organized their affairs, but only with deciding how they actually *did* organize them. Petitioners quote nothing, and we can find nothing, in the instructions to support their reading.

Petitioners assert (Pet. 19) that "the court of appeals effectively licensed the jury to reject church beliefs on

Movement" as an unincorporated association, properly preserving the issue for appeal (Tr. 6660-6661). Even so, the argument at trial bears little resemblance to petitioners' argument here. Compare Tr. 6660-6661 with Pet. 21-22.

Petitioners intially attempted to "except generally" to the jury instruction "insofar as it does not specifically adopt the language of [their] requests" (Tr. 6658), but the district court correctly advised them that they could not "do it that way" (*ibid.*). Petitioners had submitted a lengthy proposed instruction on trust law (Defendant Moon's Proposed Instruction No. 16, at C.A. App. 1369), but defense counsel subsequently made no specific objection to the court's instructions on that subject as proposed or given.

[17] Judge Oakes' dissent went solely to issues of New York trust law.

[18] The relevant instruction is quoted in full at Pet. App. 67-69 n.3, and is found at Tr. 6583-6588.

20

religious matters" by "expressly holding the jury 'not bound to accept' church members' views of what uses of the assets were 'religious.' " But petitioners at trial neithei presented evidence of Unification Church doctrine or "religious uses" of assets nor requested a jury instruc tion concerning the weight to be given the Church's defi nition of religious use. The jury instructions referrec only to the *defense theory* that the funds "were held ii trust by Moon for the International Unification Churcl Movement and used for *church purposes*" (Pet. App. 67- 68 n.3 (emphasis added)).[19] The term "church purposes" was proposed by petitioners themselves for use in the instructions on this point (Defendant Moon's Proposed Instruction No. 16, at J.A. 1371-1372; see also Tr. 6340 (defense summation)), and fairly captures the distinc- tion between personal funds and funds held for institu- tional—or "church"—purposes.[20] The jury was not asked to decide whether expenditures actually made by a church were for "religious purposes." Rather, in the absence of any direct evidence that a trust relationship, whether ex- press or implied, had been created, the jury was properly invited by both defense and prosecution to treat peti- tioner Moon's uses of the funds as evidence of whether he and the Unification Church regarded the funds at the time as the property of the international Unification Church Movement, or of Moon personally. Resolution of this question required the jury neither to accept nor to reject—nor to undertake any inquiry concerning—the religious beliefs or mission of the Unification Church.

Indeed, however religious the motivation or purpose of the Church donors (if Church donors were the source of the funds) may have been, the interest on the funds

----

[19] That the court of appeals used the term "religious use or pur- pose" in this context (Pet. App. 30) does not affect the propriety of the jury instruction.

[20] The trial court expressly instructed the jury that religious organizations can legitimately invest and conduct busines ses, and can pay the living expenses of their leaders. Pet. App. 69 n.3.

21

could still have been taxable income to petitioner Moon. Devoted believers have been known to make personal gifts to religious leaders. Evidence showed that Church members had the "custom of providing gifts of substantial value" to petitioner Moon "personally" (GX 456B, at E1881). Interest on personal gifts to Moon—as opposed to the Church—would be taxable to him quite without regard to any questions of religious doctrine.

Petitioners also claim that the jury instructions "invited the jury to draw adverse inferences from the way in which the international Unification Church chose to organize itself" (Pet. 21), apparently because the jury was instructed to consider, among other factors, "whether the Movement had a specific organizational structure, written charter or constitution" (Pet. App. 68 n.3), "the existence of other Unification Church corporate entities during the relevant time period" (ibid.), "the fact that the accounts were maintained under Reverend Moon's name" (ibid.), and the "manner in which the stock and funds were administered" (ibid.).[21] Petitioners assert (Pet. 21 n.35) that this instruction "permitt[ed] the jury to penalize the accused" because of the organizational choices of the Church.

Petitioners gravely misapprehend the question. A church is free to organize itself as it sees fit, but the First Amendment does not preclude a factfinder from determining how a church has organized itself and drawing appropriate factual inferences from that structure. Tax consequences may (and often do) flow from a church's organizational decisions. Here, petitioners have put forward a defense that is totally undocumented (more precisely, fraudulently documented), involving an alleged entity that uncharacteristically had no documentary evidence for its existence. This understandably placed them at some disadvantage in explaining their actions. But religious leaders, no less than the average taxpayer, must

---

[21] The court also instructed the jury that "the lack of a formal corporation does not prevent a religious movement from being the beneficial owner of property held in the name of another" (Pet. App. 68 n.3).

22

assume the risk when they engage in undocumented transactions that the jury may not believe their account of the events. See *United States* v. *Garguilo*, 554 F.2d 59, 62 (2d Cir. 1977). To look at the quality of a taxpayer's proof hardly violates the First Amendment.

The jury instruction in question simply set forth commonsense, objective factors that the jury could rationally consider in determining whether the alleged international Unification Church Movement existed as an entity (as the defendants contended and the government contested at trial), and whether the assets in question were held for it in trust. Evidence that the Unification Church ordinarily incorporated its entities and maintained bank accounts in the institutional name, and that there were other Church entities that, in the ordinary course of Unification Church affairs, would be expected to hold Church funds, was obviously probative evidence.

Petitioners claim (Pet. 19, quoting the dissenting opinion, Pet. App. 70) that the jury instructions "freed the jury 'to find against Moon on the issue of beneficial ownership without even considering the crucial issue of donors' intent.'" But the court expressly instructed the jury that it "*should* consider all of the evidence, *including* such factors as * * * the intent of the parties who caused the stock and funds to be transferred to Reverend Moon's name" (Pet. App. 63 n.3 (emphasis added)). The instruction went on to emphasize that [w]hether a trust is created depends on the intent of the person giving the property at the time of the transfer," and to explain how that intent could be manifested (*ibid.*). The jury was thus clearly instructed that it should consider donors' intent (if any could be discerned). Petitioners' claim, as stated, thus has no basis in fact.

Perhaps petitioners mean to argue that the instruction on donors' intent, while correct, was not sufficiently prominent. But this amounts to no more than fine-tuning a trial judge's instructions. See *Cupp* v. *Naughten*, 414 U.S. 141, 146-147 (1973). It certainly raises no First Amendment issue.

Petitioners' complaint that the trial court made "no reference at all to Reverend Moon's religious ministry"

23

(Pet. 20)—and indeed "fully filtered out religion" (*ibid.*) —is the most curious of all. To be sure, the trial court and the government were scrupulous in ensuring that petitioners' religion would not be an issue in the case— either for them or against them.[22] The jury was more than amply informed of petitioner Moon's relationship to the Unification Church—the whole case turned on it—but irrelevant and potentially inflammatory religious concepts were properly excluded from the case, as petitioners repeatedly requested at the time (see Tr. 2544, 2548-2550, 5117, 5720; see S. 24). This was consistent with the "neutral principles" approach of *Jones* v. *Wolf*, 443 U.S. 595 (1979).[23] Further discussion of why petitioner Moon's religious status might "explain[] why donations to the church would logically be placed in his name" (Pet. 20 n.34) would not be an issue of law to be explained by the judge, but an avenue of argument for the defense.

3. Petitioners contend (Pet. 23-29) that the "theory of federal tax liability" in this case, as reflected in the trial court's instructions to the jury on the law of the formation of charitable trusts, was so "novel and debatable" that its application in a criminal prosecution violated due

---

[22] The court's statement to the jury that "considerations of [race or] religion must have no part in your deliberations" (Tr. 6538, quoted at Pet. 20 (material in brackets deleted)) was a standard admonition against racial or religious bias. Petitioners did not object to it at trial, and we find it incredible that they find fault with it now.

[23] Petitioners disagree (Pet. 18-19) with the court of appeals' conclusion (Pet. App. 31) that *Jones* v. *Wolf, supra*, was not directly pertinent here. This case does not involve competing claims to control of property that is established as belonging to a church. Rather, it involves whether certain income-producing property is owned, for federal tax purposes, by an individual. See pages 28-29, *infra*. But even assuming *Jones* applies in this somewhat different context, there plainly was nothing in the district court's instructions that violated the "neutral principles" approach of *Jones*. The instructions simply referred to "objective, well-established concepts of trust and property law" with no need for "inquiry into religious doctrine" (443 U.S. at 603).

24

process. Petitioners do not ask this Court to decide whether the jury instruction on trust law was erroneous. For purposes of evaluating this contention, therefore, this Court may assume the instruction was legally correct.[24] Nor do petitioners challenge the jury's factual conclusion that petitioners prepared and filed the disputed tax returns with full knowledge of their illegality. See Pet. App. 18-20. They also do not suggest that their false filings were predicated on any actual good faith reliance on prior precedent (cf. *United States* v. *Bishop*, 412 U.S. 346, 361 (1973), explaining *James* v. *United States*, 366 U.S. 213 (1961)) or mistake of law (cf. *United States* v. *Brown*, 411 F.2d 1134, 1137 (10th Cir. 1969)). Rather, they apparently contend that to prosecute them violated due process solely because of an asserted uncertainty in law that did not affect their conduct.

We would dismiss petitioners' theory as being plainly contrary to precedents of this Court (e.g., *United States* v. *Bishop, supra*; *Boyce Motor Lines, Inc.* v. *United States*, 342 U.S. 337 (1952); *Screws* v. *United States*, 325 U.S. 91 (1945)), as well as common sense—as the court of appeals unanimously did [25]—were it not for *United States* v. *Dahlstrom*, 713 F.2d 1423 (9th Cir. 1983), petition for cert. pending, No. 83-1297.[26] In *Dahlstrom*, the Ninth Circuit held that the absence of a prior statute, regulation, or court decision directly establishing the illegality

---

[24] Petitioners assert that the court of appeals' holding on the instruction "squarely conflicts with all relevant federal tax precedents" (Pet. 23). Nonetheless, they do not seek reversal of that holding; their sole complaint before this Court is that it was "novel and debatable" (Pet. i). Their position therefore must be that no conviction could be sustained on the basis of the instruction, even assuming it was correct.

[25] Dissenting Judge Oakes agreed with the implicit holding of the majority on this point, as he stated during oral argument. See Pet. 29 n.56. Petitioners' theory is inconsistent with Second Circuit precedent. *United States* v. *Ingredient Technology Corp.*, 698 F.2d 88 (1983), cert. denied, No. 82-1526 (June 20, 1983).

[26] Petitioners have been provided copies of the Petition in *Dahlstrom*.

25

of a tax evasion scheme precludes prosecution of the promoters, even where there is ample evidence of willfulness
and no evidence that any lack of clarity in the law had
an actual impact upon the promoters' actions. We believe
the holding of *Dahlstrom* is clearly incorrect, as our petition for a writ of certiorari explains in detail. But even
if the *Dahlstrom* decision were correct, petitioners' more
extreme claim would still be without merit.[27] Petitioners
have no basis for claiming legal uncertainty here, and the
holding of *Dahlstrom* would not in any event stretch so
far.

As an initial matter, we find it difficult to identify any
significant difference between petitioners' legal position
and the trust instruction. It seems to us that the instruction, taken as a whole, was substantially in accord with
petitioners' theory of the law. Indeed, petitioners lodged
no specific objection to the trust instruction when it was
given. See note 16, *supra*. This casts considerable doubt
on their claims of prejudice here, if they can raise the
argument at all. See *Henderson* v. *Kibbe*, 431 U.S. at
154.

Petitioners point out (Pet. 23 (emphasis in original;
footnote omitted)) that, once a trust is created, "use of a
portion of the property for the recipient's personal purposes may make *that portion* taxable as his income," but
that "the remainder * * * is not taxable to him." So did

---

[27] The other decisions cited by petitioners (Pet. 27-29) neither
create a conflict nor otherwise justify granting certiorari. *James*
v. *United States*, 366 U.S. 213 (1961), has subsequently been explained by this Court as holding merely that "[t]he requirement of
an offense committed 'willfully' is not met * * * if a taxpayer has
relied in good faith on a prior decision of this Court." *United States*
v. *Bishop*, 412 U.S. at 361. Similarly, in *United States* v. *Critzer*,
498 F.2d 1160 (4th Cir. 1974), the taxpayer relied in good faith on
the advice of a government agency with responsibility for supervis-
ing her affairs. *United States* v. *Garber*, 607 F.2d 92 (5th Cir.
1979) (en banc)—though wrongly decided, in our view—dealt with
the right c. a taxpayer to introduce expert evidence bearing on
the asserted uncertainty of the law. The holdings of these cases
have no bearing on the issue here.

26

the instruction.[28] Petitioners point out (Pet. 24-25 (footnote deleted)) that, to create a trust, there is no requirement that the donors "mentioned the word 'trust' or otherwise displayed a 'clear and unequivocal' intent to 'create a trust.'" So did the instruction.[29] Petitioners point out (Pet. 24-25) that the existence of a trust does not turn on "the recipient's freedom to make personal use of some portion of the property donated." The instruction was not to the contrary—so long as it is understood that, to be a trustee, the recipient must be under *some* legal constraint in his use of the funds.[30] In short,

---

[28] "If a trust does exist and the trustee diverts trust property to his own use, the funds diverted become taxable to him at the time and to the extent so diverted" (Pet. App. 69 n.3).

[29]   Whether a trust is created depends on the intent of the person giving the property at the time of the transfer, and that intent must be clear and unambiguous. A trust can be created orally or by the conduct of the parties. The trust need not be reflected in a written document.

* * * * *

All that is required is that both parties to the relationship understand that the first person is holding the property for the benefit of the second, and you can find such an understanding on the basis of the party's conduct.

Pet. App. 68-69 n.3. The "clear and unambiguous" intent mentioned in the instruction is not, as petitioners apparently believe (Pet. 23-25), an intent to create a juristic entity known as a "trust," but— as the full instruction makes clear—intent that one party hold the property for the benefit of another. The court of appeals' imprecise reference to "evidence of intent to create a *trust*" (Pet. App. 24 (emphasis in original)) may be the source of petitioners' misunderstanding; but since the trial court's instruction was correctly worded, the court of appeals' dictum does not create an issue warranting review.

[30]   In order for a trust to exist, the trustee must be obligated to use the property for the benefit of the beneficiaries; a gift with a mere request or expectation that the property would be used a particular way does not create a trust. There is no trust if the person who receives the money is free to use it for his own benefit.

* * * * *

Also, the mere fact that Reverend Moon exercised control over the funds and the stock is not necessarily indicative of his

27

unlike in *Dahlstrom*, the uncertainty here is, at most, over minor variations in language of a jury instruction, such as might arise in any criminal trial. Petitioners have identified no uncertainty in the law that might cast doubt on the constitutionality of their convictions.[31]

Moreover, the instruction in question was in accord with settled principles of both New York trust law and federal tax law. In *Lefkowitz* v. *Cornell University*, 35 A.D.2d 166, 173, 316 N.Y.S.2d 264, 271 (1970), aff'd, 28 N.Y.2d 876, 271 N.E.2d 552, 322 N.Y.S.2d 717 (1971), property was given to a charitable organization, but the court concluded that no trust had been created (*id.* at 172-173):

> While a charitable trust may be created by a dec-
> laration of the owner of the property that he holds
> it upon a charitable trust (Restatements, Trusts 2d,
> § 349), no trust is created unless the donor mani-

personal ownership. A person who holds property on behalf of another may be given broad authority and discretion to deal with that property as long as he does so in a manner consistent with the purpose for which he was given title to the property in the first place.

* * * * *

A religious organization can properly pay the living expenses of [its] leaders or ministers in order to allow them to pursue its religious purposes and can make loans to its ministers or leaders on arm's length terms.

Pet. App. 69 n.3. There is, therefore, no conflict between the instructions and the holding in *Morey* v. *Riddell*, 205 F. Supp. 918 (S.D. Cal. 1962). See Pet. 25.

[31] Petitioners seek to magnify the importance of the issue by asserting (Pet. 25) that "[h]ad the settled rule been applied in this case, none of the Chase interest—all of which was earned on funds donated 'to the church' * * * —would have been taxable income to Reverend Moon." They conveniently forget (see note 2, *supra*) that the jury was entitled to disbelieve their account of the origin of the funds—undermined, as it was, by their fabrication of documents—and that there was no credible evidence whatsoever that petitioner Moon intended to hold the funds on behalf of the Church. Given the evidence in this case, it is highly unlikely that minor alterations in the jury instructions would have resulted in a different verdict.

28

fests an intent to impose enforceable duties. (Restatement, Trusts 2d, § 351.) While no particular words are required to create the trust, "the words and acts relied upon must be unequivocal in nature and admit of no other interpretation than that the property is held in trust". (*Matter of Fontanella*, 33 A.D.2d 29, 30.)

Accord, Restatement (Second) of the Law of Trusts § 351 (1959) ("A charitable trust is created only if the settlor properly manifests an intention to create a charitable trust")[32]; *Cox* v. *Commissioner*, 297 F.2d 36 (2d Cir. 1961); *Estate of Barry* v. *Commissioner*, 34 T.C. 160 (1960).[33] The New York cases cited by the dissenting judge (Pet. App. 66), and relied on by petitioners (Pet. 25),[34] are not in point. In none of them was the intent to create a trust at issue. They stand for the well-established principle that courts should apply reasonable inferences to uphold charitable trusts where the requisite intent was manifested; they do not support petitioners' view that a trust may be found even in the absence of intent clearly manifested at the time the transfer of property is made.

Moreover, the question of "ownership" for purposes of federal tax law does not depend upon refinements of title under state trust law: the question is one of actual command over property and realization by the taxpayer of

---

[32] See Restatement, *supra*, comment d: "If property is transferred to a person, with no restrictions upon his disposition of the property, a charitable trust is not created merely because the transferor states * * * that he is making the transfer from a motive of promoting charity. If the transferee is authorized to dispose of the property in any manner or to any person he may select, he takes the property for his own benefit."

[33] Special rules for political campaign contributions, relied on by petitioners (Pet. 24 & nn.42, 44, 45), do not apply to charitable or religious trusts. See *United States* v. *Scott*, 660 F.2d 1145, 1164 (7th Cir. 1981), cert. denied, 455 U.S. 907 (1982); Rev. Proc. 68-19, 1968-1 C.B. 810, 811.

[34] *In re Will of Price*, 264 A.D. 29, 32, 35 N.Y.S.2d 111, 114-115 (1942); *In re Durbrow*, 245 N.Y. 469, 474, 157 N.E. 747, 749 (1927); *In re Estate of Nurse*, 35 N.Y.2d 381, 388-389, 321 N.E.2d 537, 540, 362 N.Y.S.2d 441, 446 (1974).

29

economic value from the property. *Rutkin* v. *United States*, 343 U.S. 130, 136-137 (1952); *Burnet* v. *Wells*, 289 U.S. 670, 678 (1933); *Corliss* v. *Bowers*, 281 U.S. 376, 378 (1930); see 26 U.S.C. 678(a). For tax purposes, a person may even be deemed the owner of property to which he does not have a legal right. See *James* v. *United States*, 366 U.S. 213 (1961) (embezzled funds taxable); *Rutkin* v. *United States*, *supra* (extorted money held to be taxable income). Accordingly, if petitioner Moon had unfettered power to use the assets in question for his own personal benefit and enjoyment, even if he appropriated such power without consent of the putative donors, he was the "owner" of the assets for tax purposes.[35]

Therefore, even under the test in *Dahlstrom*, petitioners have not made out a colorable due process violation. Even the *Dahlstrom* court would permit criminal prosecution where, as here, a "court decision gave fair warning" (713 F.2d at 1429) of the law. But even assuming that petitioners have correctly identified a relevant uncertainty in the law, it would require a significant and unreasonable expansion of the principle of *Dahlstrom* to preclude prosecution here.

In *Dahlstrom* the legal uncertainty held to preclude prosecution purportedly related to the government's case in chief—*i.e.*, to whether the government's evidence supported a finding of a violation of the tax laws.[36] Here, in contrast, the government's case is simple and straightforward: all the evidence shows petitioner Moon owned the property; he paid no taxes on the interest or on the receipt of stock; therefore, he violated the law. There is absolutely no uncertainty about the proposition that if the property belonged to Moon personally, he was obliged

---

[35] This would not, of course, preclude prosecution of an errant trustee for embezzlement or diversion of trust funds. See Br. for State of Hawaii, et al., as amici curiae.

[36] As we explain in the Petition in *Dahlstrom* (at 19-22), we do not believe the court of appeals was correct in holding that the asserted legal uncertainty there was material to the government's case.

30

to pay income taxes on the income it reflected or produced. The supposed uncertainty in this case arises solely with respect to the defense proposition—supported by evidence so marginal that the court of appeals concluded that petitioners had not established a prima facie case on their theory (Pet. App. 23-25)—that the property was held in trust. Whatever the merits of the *Dahlstrom* principle with respect to pioneering government theories of liability, there is no merit in petitioners' view that a criminal defendant may not be prosecuted for a crime if his lawyers are clever enough to propound a theory for the defense that involves, as one of its elements, an unsettled proposition of law.

4. Quite apart from the correctness of the decision below, the Petition raises no issue of general importance warranting this Court's review. On the first issue—denial of bench trial—petitioners seek nothing short of invalidation of Rule 23(a) of the Federal Rules of Criminal Procedure and reversal of the principles established in *Singer* and applied, without deviation or apparent problem, in each of the small handful of circuit court decisions addressing the problem since *Singer*. And on the second and third issues, petitioners seek a detailed reexamination of the nuances of a jury instruction essentially unique to this case. Such an examination has already been performed by the court of appeals in a lengthy and painstaking opinion. We well recognize that the prominence of petitioner Moon has attracted unusual attention to this case; the legal issues raised, however, are of little significance beyond these unusual circumstances,[37] and were dealt with fully and responsibly by the courts below.

---

[37] This prosecution for willful violations of the tax laws and related offenses was precipitated and the proof largely supported by petitioners' massive and undisputed effort to deceive the tax authorities by document fabrications, false explanations, and perjury. Contrary to the fears expressed by the numerous religious individuals and groups appearing as amici curiae (none of whom manifests an awareness of the evidence that supported conviction of petitioners), informal financial arrangements maintained by churches in good faith are not in jeopardy.

31

CONCLUSION

The petition for a writ of certiorari should be denied.

Respectfully submitted.

REX E. LEE
Solicitor General

GLENN L. ARCHER, JR.
Assistant Attorney General

MICHAEL W. MCCONNELL
Assistant to the Solicitor General

MICHAEL L. PAUP
ROBERT E. LINDSAY
ALAN HECHTKOPF
Attorneys

APRIL 1984

Reply to Brief in Opposition

TABLE OF CONTENTS

ii

TABLE OF AUTHORITIES

INTRODUCTION

The government uses fully half its brief to make what amounts to a jury summation to this Court. The government's factual assault seeks to convey an image of a Watergate-style cover-up of tax crimes triggered by the initial tax investigation itself. *See, e.g.,* Opp. 12 n.8, 30 n.37. It clearly hopes thus to convince the Court that this is hardly a case in which any due process or first amendment protection for "good faith" religious leaders (Opp. 30 n.37) need be proclaimed. This image, however, is as false as it is irrelevant.

First, this prosecution was precipitated *not,* as the government claims, by a "massive and undisputed effort to deceive the tax authorities" (Opp. 30), but rather, as the trial judge found, by a tax audit triggered by "Moon's status as a highly visible, religious leader" (App. 35). Had Reverend Moon been less controversial, the trial judge expressly concluded, this investigation would have been less likely. *See* A536-37; Pet. 27 n.52. *Second,* what the government portrays as a massive "cover-up" was simply an understandable attempt by loyal followers of Reverend Moon to construct documents and "shuffl[e] around . . . papers here and there" to memorialize prior transactions "to conform . . . to the[ir] lawyer's view of American tax laws." T5522 (Goettel, J.). And the massive "deception" the government dramatizes consisted simply of mistakes in that reconstruction *not* about the key fact that the funds came from church sources, but about whether they came by cash or by check, from abroad or from the streets of America. *See* note 4 *infra.*

Such mistakes may be regrettable, but they do not prove what the government tells this Court: namely, that the entire Unification Church movement for which Reverend Moon contends he held the assets was conjured up in hindsight to justify Reverend Moon's non-payment of taxes. Evidence that this movement "existed" long before the "cover-up," and that Reverend Moon acted as its trustee, is indeed ample in the record. *See* note 7 *infra.*

In any event, invocation of the "cover-up" evidence before this Court is simply beside the point. For the true issues raised here are whether the defense was wrongly left to the mercy of an improper factfinder, which in turn

2

was impermissibly left to apply novel and improper rules. Indeed, the "cover-up" is most relevant here, if at all, as a reminder of the danger of permitting the government to pursue religious figures, secure in the knowledge that it may hand-pick the most favorable tribunal, invite that tribunal to wink at a religion's own allocations of property and authority, and make up its law as it goes along. For any government so omnipotent could keep *every* religious group on the run, forcing each to leave a paper trail —designed to meet the changing demands of those in power—that, on the government's theory, would never be "clean" enough for the plight of such groups to merit this Court's attention. It is no surprise, therefore, that dozens of religious groups support a grant of certiorari to consider the questions that this case clearly poses even if the government succeeds in giving a sinister cast to the facts the jury heard at trial.

Certiorari should be granted to vindicate the primacy of fairness as the criterion for choosing between jury trial and bench trial, and to assure religious groups that their informal financial arrangements will not be caught in nets the prosecution is free to cast as it sees fit.

A. There Could Be No Better Case for Deciding When the Constitution Entitles an Accused to Bench Trial.

Opposing petitioners' argument that this is the ideal case for deciding when due process may entitle an accused to a bench trial, the government suggests only that this issue has long been foreclosed from further inquiry by this Court. It argues that, under a "well-settled" "general principle," a defendant has no right "to insist upon bench trial" (Opp. 13), while the government has a "right to insist upon a jury trial" under Rule 23(a) (Opp. 16). This argument cannot be squared with *Singer* v. *United States*, 380 U.S. 24 (1965), or any other decision of this Court. *Singer* plainly rested *not* on any "general principle" that the *prosecution* has a right to insist on *jury* trial, but rather on the general principle, rooted deeply in our Constitution and not merely in a rule of procedure, that a criminal *defendant* has a right to a *fair* trial —a right that, as an historical matter, jury trial had been

3

most likely to vindicate. *Id.* at 34-37. No asserted prose-cutorial "right" could possibly outweigh that right. For, as this Court recently reiterated, "[n]o right ranks higher than the right of the accused to a fair trial." *Press-Enterprise Co.* v. *Superior Court,* 104 S.Ct. 819, 823 (1984).

It is thus of critical importance to the administration of criminal justice to decide whether the prosecution's insistence on trying a gravely unpopular defendant by jury may violate the Fifth Amendment right to fair trial. This issue was explicitly left open in *Singer. See* Pet. 11. The government's wish to dodge this issue as "infrequently litigated" (Opp. 13) must fail since its significance cannot be measured by counting the published opinions on the matter. Nor is there any reason to suppose that resolution of this issue would in fact have narrow rather than "general importance" (*see* Opp. 30). On the contrary, concern that due process was violated by the forced jury trial in this case has been powerfully voiced in this Court by an array of groups especially concerned with protecting defendants who face analogous intense popular hostility in a wide variety of contexts—*e.g.*, the Southern Christian Leadership Conference (SCLC), the American Civil Liberties Union (ACLU), the National Emergency Civil Liberties Committee (NECLC), the Spartacist League, and the Institute for the Study of American Religion (ISAR).

The bench trial issue is thus a uniquely appropriate one for review by this Court—provided it is fairly presented here. The government suggests it is not, relying on the findings of both courts below that the jury, while biased, met the minimum standard of impartiality that this Court, in order to prevent rampant dismissals, has applied when defendants *demand* jury trial under the Sixth Amendment. Opp. 15; *see* Pet. 12-13. But those findings cannot foreclose the bench trial issue here because, even if correct, they are simply irrelevant to the Fifth Amendment due process claim of defendants who seek to *waive* jury trial. *See* Pet. 12-13; *see also Amicus* Briefs of the ACLU, NECLC, ISAR. The government offers not one word of analysis to refute this conclusion. Indeed, as the government nowhere denies, the Fifth Amendment bench trial issue presented here could arise *only* in a case where, as

4

here, a jury *could* be empaneled that would satisfy the minimum Sixth Amendment standard. For if a circumstance ever arose in which such a jury could *not* be empaneled, any well-counseled defendant would not voluntarily seek a trial before a judge, but would insist on a jury trial and demand to have his case dismissed. *See* Pet. 12-13; *Amicus* Brief of ACLU at 6 n.3.

Not only is the bench trial issue thus fairly presented here, but this case is a particularly well-suited vehicle for its review. *First,* petitioners' contention that bench trial would have been fairer here than jury trial is unusually well-grounded in light of the trial judge's identical conclusion.[1] *Second,* the record in this case forecloses any confident conclusion that a judge would have reached the same result the jury did.[2] Thus the government's flat denial that imposition of a jury trial could ever be a "penalty" (*see* Opp. 17) is unfathomable. *Third,* the reasons the government explicitly gave for insisting on jury trial here, far from being "legitimate" (Opp. 17), were, under the circumstances, absurd. *See* Pet. 14-16.[3] In particular, the

---

[1] *See* Pet. 4-5 & n.5. Nothing in petitioners' argument turns on the presence or the absence of any "formal . . . 'findings' " by the district court regarding the relative fairness of bench and jury trial, as the government wrongly suggests (*see* Opp. 15-16 & n.11).

[2] After all, this jury was a cross-section of a public nearly half of which acknowledged that, given the chance, it would "throw Reverend Sun Myung Moon in jail". *See* Pet. 4 n.4. Despite the government's contrary "assum[ption]" (Opp. 18 n.14), the imposition of this jury did prevent petitioners from presenting "a full and accurate picture of Reverend Moon's religious relationship to those who gave him the assets" (Pet. 7; *see Amicus* Briefs of National Council of Churches *et al.* at 11-17; Bishop Unterkoefler *et al.* at 6-7; The Freemen Institute at 4, 8-9). The trial judge himself acknowledged as much when he remarked after conviction that a picture of Reverend Moon as his religion's messiah "would have been disastrous to [present] before a jury." S60. Petitioners' entire defense was in fact constrained in an attempt to avoid "be[ing] sent to jail because a jury in a hostile environment [might find their religious] teachings false," *United States* v. *Ballard,* 322 U.S. 78, 87 (1944). Thus no one can know what a trial of this case before a judge would even have looked like, much less what its outcome would have been.

[3] One government reason—to "defuse the public criticism that had been leveled by Moon" (App. 7)—also transgressed First Amendment values. But nothing whatever in petitioners' bench

5

government could not, as it claims, have projected to the public the "appearance of fairness" (Opp. 17) by *denying* petitioners the very tribunal they desperately sought and forcing them to appear instead before a tribunal the petitioners were confident harbored irreducible hostility. To be sure, a public that predominantly despises a defendant may well "better accept the results of [such] a jury trial" (*see* Opp. 17)—provided it results in conviction. But no such public satisfaction has ever been blessed by this Court. There is truly "no precedent" (*see* Opp. 16) for the government's self-interested surmise (Opp. 17) that the public would think a bench trial disturbingly unfair. Certiorari is essential to ensure that such a surmise cannot suffice as a pretext for the government to obtain the more favorable rather than the fairer tribunal.

B. Granting Certiorari Will Also Present a Valuable Opportunity to Assure Compliance With the Religion Clauses in Cases That Turn on the Allocation of Church Property.

The need for such assurance is created by the holding below that Religion Clause cases "do not serve as precedent in federal criminal tax prosecutions" (App. 30)—a holding that will, unless set aside, "li[e] about like a loaded weapon ready for the hand of any authority" willing to invoke it. *Korematsu* v. *United States,* 323 U.S. 214, 246 (1944) (Jackson, J., dissenting). The government offers no innocent interpretation of that ruling. It says only that "good" religions need have no fear (*see* Opp. 30 n.37) since the gun will not go off at *them,* and that the gun did not go off even at these petitioners, as their religion was "scrupulous[ly]" not considered "for them or against them" at their trial (*id.*). Such reassurance may be acceptable in a criminal case where religion has no bearing on the defense. But as the government concedes, "th[is] whole case turned on" Reverend "Moon's relationship to the Unification Church" (Opp. 23), and the *only* evidence introduced as to the *source* of the assets, as Judge Oakes found, was that they "came to Moon largely from members of his faith"

---

trial argument turns on the presence or absence of an *independent* First Amendment violation here, as the government wrongly suggests. *Compare* Opp. 16-17 *with* Pet. 14-15.

6

(App. 65). *See, e.g.,* T2164, 2770, 3117-20, 3124-25, 4280-84, 4605-08.[4]

Given this evidence, what counts for constitutional purposes, as this Court held in *Sandstrom v. Montana,* 442 U.S. 510, 517 (1979), is whether the jury "could well have interpreted" the instructions in an unconstitutional manner.[5] Here, the jury surely *could* have interpreted them the way petitioners, Judge Oakes, and many *amici* did. Specifically, the jurors could have decided that, even if the assets *had* come from church members,[6] the jury need not consider whether or how those donors wished to restrict use of the assets in Reverend Moon's hands (*see* App. 70). These jurors, after all, had heard that Reverend Moon "brainwashes" church members, that his "cult" thinks him "a god," and the like. *See* Pet. 4 n.4. They could well have decided that, whatever these "Moonies" intended for their church money, it was *really* Moon's because the ways he used it did not strike *them* as "constitut[ing] a religious use or purpose" (App. 30)—a judgment the court below delegated to the jury (*id.*). Or the jurors could have decided the money was really Moon's because real church money would more likely be placed in an entity with a "specific organizational structure" (App. 68 n.3), than given to Moon to hold for the church

---

[4] Contrary to the government's suggestion, there was *no* evidence that the assets came from "petitioner Moon's international and domestic business activities" (Opp. 5) ; nor did the government ever make that argument to the jury (*see* T6222-24, misleadingly cited at Opp. 6 n.2). Indeed, the government's "theory of the case" at trial was that the funds came mostly from members' collections "on the streets" (T5520-21, Goettel, J.) ; and although the government now conjectures that the jury "disbelieve[d]" that theory (Opp. 18), literally *nothing* in the record contradicts Judge Oakes' conclusion that the assets came from church sources.

[5] The claim that the "second and third questions presented are not properly raised on this record" (Opp. 18) because petitioners waived their objections to the instructions (Opp. 18-19 n.16, 25) is nonsense, flatly foreclosed by portions of the record the government conveniently omits to cite. *See* T6119, 6121, 6123, 6129-31, 6157-59, 6531-37, 6650, 6656, 6663, 6664, 6666, 6667, 6677.

[6] Due process would preclude affirming this conviction on the new ground that the assets came not from church members but from an alternate source such as "business activities" (*see* note 4 *supra*). *See Cole v. Arkansas,* 333 U.S. 196, 201 (1948).

7

movement.[7] So much for the right of a church to make its *own* decisions about how it should be organized and what should be done with its resources.[8]

To reassure the several State *amici* that this disregard of church donors' intent will not undermine enforcement of charitable trusts, the government says States can still rely on that intent to prosecute a religious leader like Reverend Moon "for embezzlement or diversion of trust funds" (Opp. 29 n. 35) if he should ever treat those funds as his own against the donors' wishes. In the meantime, *federal* authorities can tax the leader as though his use of the assets were *not* in fact so restricted.[9] True, the government concedes, it would not so treat a *political* leader who held "campaign contributions" under his name, dominion and control. Opp. 28 n.33. For a politician would enjoy the presumption that such contributions would be unavailable for his "unrestricted personal use"—even absent any direct evidence of donors' intent to that effect. *Id.; see* Pet. 24 n.45. But *religious* leaders, the government inexplicably proclaims, are different; they enjoy no such presumption. Opp. 28 n.33.

---

[7] The remarkable assertion that the movement was an afterthought, and that there was a "total absence of any direct contemporaneous evidence" of its existence (Opp. 10), is flatly contradicted by the record. Not only did a church official testify that in "early . . . 1973" Reverend Moon had told him, in reference to the Chase funds, "that the money was coming from our movement overseas and was to be put into an account here to be used for the work of our International Church" (T4089-90); but documentary evidence shows that at least by the outset of 1974, Reverend Moon was being formally addressed by public officials as the head of the "Unification Church International" (*see* AA2, AA3, AA5, *see also* DXAA1, AA4). Indeed, a letter from then-President Nixon, on White House stationery, dated December 11, 1973, addresses Reverend Moon with that title.

[8] On threats to church ministries implicit in the decision below, *see Amicus* Briefs of Catholic League at 6; Church of Latter-Day Saints at 7; American Ass'n. of Christian Schools at 1-2, 5, 10-11; American Coalition of Unregistered Churches *et al.* at 10; Center for Judicial Studies at 18; Senator Orrin Hatch at 13-14.

[9] Although the government now suggests Reverend Moon might have "appropriated . . . power" over church assets "without consent of the putative donors" (Opp. 29), no such diversion was alleged or proved (*see* App. 72 Oakes, J.). To affirm on this new theory would again violate due process. *See* note 6 *supra*.

8

Whether this "rule" for religion, announced for the first time in the Brief in Opposition on April 9, 1984, is good for Reverend Moon only or for *all* religious leaders is left to the Court's imagination. If the former, there is a denominational preference violative of the Establishment Clause. *Larson* v. *Valente,* 456 U.S. 228 (1982). If the latter, there is a discrimination against religious speech violative of the Free Speech Clause. *Widmar* v. *Vincent,* 454 U.S. 263 (1981). Should the Court agree to hear this case, the government may choose between those positions —or attempt to formulate yet another. But, should this Court decline review, the many for whom this case has caused concern will rightly wonder who the next victims of the government's cavalier approach, sanctioned by both courts below, will be.

C. The Government's Unveiling of New Theories of Guilt Underscores the Importance of Assuring That the Basis for Criminal Tax Liability Be Clearly Settled in Advance.

The government completely misses the thrust of the third Question Presented[10] when it challenges petitioners to show that, despite the jury's finding of willfulness, the "asserted uncertainty in law . . . affect[ed] their conduct." Opp. 24. Petitioners do maintain that they were affirmatively misled by the well-settled tax rules previously applicable to funds gratuitously transferred to a representative of a cause.[11] The presence or absence of such reliance, however, is irrelevant to the rule, traceable to *James* v. *United States,* 366 U.S. 213 (1961), that the basis for criminal liability must be clearly defined *before* the alleged crime has been committed. The central purpose of the *James* rule, wholly independent of protecting surprised innocents, is to prevent zealous prosecutors from shaping

---

[10] As to the government's frivolous suggestion that the question is not "properly raised" (Opp. 18, 25), *see* note 5 *supra.*

[11] Petitioners had always supposed that such funds were presumed to be held on behalf of the cause without regard to evidence of intent to create a "trust" as such, and that such funds were not taxable to the representative unless and until used personally. Pet. 23-26. Consistent with that supposition, Reverend Moon paid tax on assets he personally used (Pet. 20-21 n.34)—a fact the government does not deny.

9

"crimes" to fit those they would accuse—thereby engaging in low-visibility discriminatory prosecution. *See* Pet. 26-27 & nn.51-52 (invoking, *inter alia, Kolender v. Lawson,* 103 S.Ct. 1855, 1858-59 (1983)). That purpose, to which the government does not even refer, has nothing at all to do with the defendant's state of mind—which is precisely what the Fourth Circuit held in *United States* v. *Critzer,* 498 F.2d 1160, 1162 (1974), the Fifth said in *dictum* in *United States* v. *Garber,* 607 F.2d 92, 98 (1979) (en banc), and the Ninth held in *United States* v. *Dahlstrom,* 713 F.2d 1423, 1428 (1983), *cert. pending,* No. 83-1297.[12] Since the government treats the Second Circuit as having held the contrary here (*see* Opp. 24 n.25), an important conflict among the circuits is squarely presented.

Each time the government—whether below or in this Court, *see* notes 4, 6, 9 and page 8, *supra*—has redefined the tax principle that Reverend Moon supposedly violated when he treated the assets entrusted to him as church property, it has underscored the importance of a ruling by this Court clarifying the *James* line of cases.[13] Because *Dahlstrom* is too limited a vehicle for that purpose, *see* Pet. Supp. Brief (April 5, 1984), this case should be heard on the merits in tandem with *Dahlstrom*—or alone.[14]

---

[12] The government indefensibly asserts that the *James* rule is inapplicable to an accused's defense. Opp. 29-30. Even if that were so, to withhold the presumption that petitioners had always supposed was available would plainly affect the government's burden, not just the defense.

[13] Several of the *amici* likewise express concern at the novel and *ad hoc* nature of the criteria used below to permit a jury to find the income at issue taxable to Reverend Moon. *See, e.g., Amicus* Briefs of Coalition for Religious Freedom *et al.* at 7-10; Bishop Unterkoefler *et al.* at 13-20; Spartacist League at 12, 16, 22; States of Hawaii, Oregon and Rhode Island at 5-12.

[14] The distinction between the fair notice aims of the *James* line of cases, and the anti-discrimination purposes served in those cases, is badly blurred in a case like *Dahlstrom,* where the very illegality claimed by the government was the concoction of sham transactions whose sole purpose was tax evasion. In that context, whether the government had made up a new crime, and whether the accused's actions were not willful, turn out to be the same question. In *Moon,* however, the supposed "effort to deceive the tax authorities by document fabrications, false explanations, and perjury" by followers of Reverend Moon (Opp. 30 n.37) all came after, and were independent of, the alleged illegality of Reverend Moon's

10

Indeed, it is hard to imagine a better context for clarifying this important area than one in which the risk of discriminatory enforcement threatens religious minorities (*see* Pet. 26-27), and in which—as the government has been unable to deny—the Court would have before it the *only* criminal tax conviction in the quarter century since *James* to be affirmed over a dissent as to the underlying theory of the income's taxability to the accused.

CONCLUSION

At bottom, it is the *rule of law* that the prosecution and conviction in this case challenge. At stake is whether government should be able to pick the more favorable rather than the fairer tribunal, free the factfinder of First Amendment inhibitions, and even shape the law itself to fit the accused. Few matters could more clearly merit this Court's plenary attention.

---

conduct in treating certain assets as church property for purposes of his 1973, 1974 and 1975 tax returns. In this context, a jury might reason backwards from subsequent cover-up to initial willfulness, even if the rules making the underlying conduct objectively illegal were *not* in fact sufficiently settled in advance to meet due process standards. Only if the Court has this type of case before it can the most basic confusion of the *James* line be sorted out. Ironically, therefore, the nature of the cover-up alleged in this case argues *for* rather than *against* a grant of certiorari.

11

Respectfully submitted,

LAURENCE H. TRIBE
Counsel of Record
KATHLEEN M. SULLIVAN
1525 Massachusetts Ave.
Cambridge, Mass. 02138
(617) 495-1767

HAROLD R. TYLER, JR.
  Patterson, Belknap,
  Webb & Tyler

CHARLES F. C. RUFF
  Covington & Burling

ANDREW M. LAWLER

JEANNE BAKER
DAVID J. FINE
  Silverglate, Gertner, Baker &
  Fine

MORTIMER CAPLIN
RICHARD E. TIMBIE
  Caplin & Drysdale

April 16, 1984

PART III:
BRIEFS AMICI CURIAE

The American Coalition of
Unregistered Churches, and The
Religious Freedom International

TABLE OF CONTENTS

Page

ii

TABLE OF AUTHORITIES

IN THE
Supreme Court of the United States
OCTOBER TERM, 1983

No. 83-1242

SUN MYUNG MOON and TAKERU KAMIYAMA,
Petitioners,

v.

UNITED STATES OF AMERICA,
Respondent.

On Petition for Certiorari to the United States
Court of Appeals for the Second Circuit

BRIEF AMICUS CURIAE
FOR THE AMERICAN COALITION OF
UNREGISTERED CHURCHES AND THE
RELIGIOUS FREEDOM INTERNATIONAL
IN SUPPORT OF PETITION FOR CERTIORARI

Consent for filing this brief has been obtained from
both parties. Their original letters have been filed with
the Clerk of this Court pursuant to Rule 36.

INTEREST OF THE *AMICI*

The American Coalition of Unregistered Churches is a
voluntary association of fundamentalist churches comprising approximately 5000 independent congregations;
likewise, the Religious Freedom International is a volun-

2

tary association of holiness churches comprising approximately 2000 independent congregations. Therefore, both organizations are vitally interested in maintaining separation of church and state, believing that Christ is the head of the Church as to all matters.

Moreover, they believe that Christianity pervades the entire realm of human experience, and the scope of traditional Christian principles embraces education, the family, social outreach, youth, the elderly, and innumerable other activities which, if separated from their religious context, might well be considered "secular" activities.

Amici's current concern springs particularly from recent and highly controversial attempts by state government to regulate Christian education as a mere secular activity. The Supreme Court explicitly recognized that education is "an integral part of the religious mission" of certain churches in *Lemon v. Kurtzman*, 403 U.S. 602, 616 (1971); *see NLRB v. Catholic Bishop of Chicago*, 440 U.S. 490 (1979); *Pierce v. Society of Sisters*, 268 U.S. 510, 534-35 (1925); and so it is for these *amici*.

SUMMARY OF ARGUMENT

If the Supreme Court does not hear this case, the precedent which will be left by the Second Circuit's decision in *United States v. Moon*, 718 F.2d 1210 (1983), will seriously limit and re-define the permissible ministries and activities of churches. If the prosecution and courts are allowed to ignore a church's sincerely held definition of its religion, then they will certainly not be bound to accept the church's definition of the nature and extent of its ministry. Many activities now viewed by churches as an integral part of their ministries will be susceptible to being artificially labelled as independent non-related activities if this precedent is left standing. Once these activities are separated out and branded as "secular" they are shorn of their sacrosanct character and become vul-

3

nerable to increased government regulation, intervention and taxation.

Amici fear that the Court of Appeals' holding in the instant case gives rise to precedent legalizing undue government intrusion in religious ministries. The Second Circuit ruled that "in this criminal proceeding, the jury was not bound to accept the Unification Church's definition of what constitutes a religious use or purpose." 718 F.2d at 1227. This contradicts fundamental First Amendment principles. If it becomes legitimate for the government and the courts to tangle themselves in consideration of the expenditures of a church, without due consideration and deference to that church's *bona fide* belief as to the "religiousness" of such expenditures and allocations of funds, *Lemon v. Kurtzman* will essentially be overruled. For besides embracing religious education with First Amendment protections as a religious ministry, *Lemon v. Kurtzman* also held that the government could not examine a school's records "to determine how much of the total expenditures is attributable to secular education and how much to religious activity. This kind of state inspection and evaluation of the religious content of a religious organization is fraught with the sort of entanglement that the constitution forbids." 403 U.S. at 620.

It is this same sort of government evaluation as to what was a secular as opposed to a religious use of funds which *amici* finds so offensive in the instant case. If the principle of *Lemon v. Kurtzman* applies to church ministries, it certainly has an even more obvious application to the expenditures of the church itself. The central issue to be determined in the *Moon* case was whether the assets involved belonged to Moon personally, as the government claimed, or to the Unification Church, although held in trust by Moon, as the defense claimed. As the dissenting judge recognized, in regard to the way funds were spent, the jury was left free to decide that any given use of property was not religious, and thus that the property

4

was not church-owned, simply because the jury regarded
the use as serving merely "business . . . or personal
ends." The instructions given to the jury said that in
order for a trust to exist, the assets had to be used "for
church purposes" but then left it at that, permitting the
jury to distinguish between church and personal uses on
whatever basis it wished, without regard to the tenets or
purposes of the Unification faith. This permitted the
jury to disregard evidence that, from the religion's point
of view, the uses in question were calculated to advance
its cause.

The holding in the *Moon* case offends the Religion
Clauses of our Constitution in at least two fundamental
respects: First, in finding that the Religion Clauses did
not apply to "federal criminal tax prosecutions," the
Court of Appeals overlooked this Court's prior holdings in
such landmark cases as *United States v. Ballard*, 322
U.S. 78 (1944), *Wisconsin v. Yoder*, 406 U.S. 205 (1972)
and *United States v. Seeger*, 380 U.S. 163 (1975). All
of these were *criminal* cases, and in each of them this
Court established a constitutional duty to respect the defendant's own religious views, provided that they were
sincerely held. The Court of Appeals' decision in the
Moon case has far-reaching implications, given the reality
today when practicing Christians have been criminally
prosecuted and jailed in essence for what they sincerely
believe to be their obligation to give their children a
totally religious education. *Amici* fear that the decision
in this case may seriously undercut the principles established in *Ballard, Yoder, Seeger* and other decisions.

Second, the Court of Appeals, by affirming the trial
court's instructions and evidentiary rulings artificially separating religion out from the underlying events, seriously
misinterpreted the separation of church and state mandated by the Constitution. The trial judge characterized
the issue in the case as one of whether Reverend Moon
could "simultaneously be a businessman and a religion".

5

T.5520.[1] Yet, it ignored this Court's holdings in such cases as *Murdock v. Pennsylvania*, 319 U.S. 105 (1943) and *Larson v. Valente*, 456 U.S. 228 (1982), which recognized the right of churches to sustain themselves through financial activities which might otherwise look to be solely secular business activities. Although the public or the prosecutors may have feelings about the business practices of churches, this does not make church investments any less legal or valid. Nor do the jury's own religious predilections make the defendant's beliefs any less sincere.

It is in these two respects that the Court of Appeals decision most directly impinges on *amici's* religious freedom in the field of education. If in this case, the activities and expenditures of a church, which it sincerely believes to be religious, may be improperly detached from the church as a whole, examined and henceforth regulated as mere secular activities, the same danger is posed for our Christian schools and those who administer them.

Even conceding the state police power over matters of health and safety, and even the government's responsibility to see that basic education takes place, the line must be drawn as to the permissible extent of government entanglement in religious affairs. *Lemon v. Kurtzman*, 403 U.S. at 602.

ARGUMENT

I. CERTIORARI SHOULD BE GRANTED IN ORDER TO CLARIFY THE ROLE OF THE RELIGION CLAUSES IN FEDERAL CRIMINAL TAX PROSECUTIONS

In this case the government brought a criminal prosecution against a minority religious leader under circumstances which would arguably initiate merely a taxpayer

---

[1] Citations to trial transcripts will be to "T. ——"; citations to post-trial hearing transcripts will be to "S. ——."

6

interview or at most a civil suit. By simply labeling the proceedings "criminal" the Court of Appeals justified itself in its refusal to apply the Religion Clauses.

In the resolution of church property disputes, the courts are certainly bound to give effect to the intent of the donors, or take a "neutral principles of law approach", giving deference to the church's definition of religiousness, *Jones v. Wolf*, 443 U.S. 595 (1979). *See*, Ellman, *Driven from the Tribunal: Judicial Resolution of Internal Church Disputes*, 69 Calif. L.R. 1378, *particularly* 1437-44 (1981). That the constitutional underpinnings of these decisions apply equally well to criminal prosecutions can be seen in the constitutional reasoning behind the church property dispute holdings: "To permit civil courts to probe deeply enough into the allocation of power within a church so as to decide . . . the [appropriate] use of church property would violate the First Amendment in much the same manner as civil determinations of religious doctrine," *Maryland and Virginia Churches v. Sharpsburg Church*, 396 U.S. 367, 369 (1970) (Brennan, J., concurring) ; "the hazards are ever present of inhibiting the free development of religious doctrine and of implicating secular interests in matters of purely ecclesiastical concern." *Serbian Eastern Orthodox Diocese v. Milivojevich*, 426 U.S. 696, 710 (1976), *quoting Presbyterian Church v. Hull Church*, 393 U.S. 440, 449 (1969).

Undisputedly, the government has a legitimate interest in the collection of tax revenue, but "[f]orbidding church leadership to use contributed funds for a purpose authorized by the donors surely requires the presence of some important policy of overriding concern." Ellman, *supra*, at 1439. While whenever a criminal investigation is involved "the state's interest unquestionably is strong," *Surinach v. Pesquera de Busquets*, 604 F.2d at 80; *see Cantwell v. Connecticut*, 310 U.S. 296, 306 (1940), Moon's holding of church funds in an account

7

in his own name and spending those funds on behalf of his church—a practice followed by other religious leaders and the common practice of which the judge recognized pretrial as undisputed, P. 99, 104—falls somewhat short of an act "inimical to the peace, good order and morals of society." 718 F.2d at 1227, *quoting Davis v. Beason,* 133 U.S. 333, 342 (1890). While defendants should not be allowed to be insulated from the court's analysis of their "church's activities as needed to determine whether those activities violated a statute," [2] 718 F.2d at 1227, the Constitution does require that those activities be viewed in their religious context.

Despite the government's interest in the enforcement of criminal laws, the courts were nonetheless required to consider the defendant's sincerely held religious views as this Court did, for instance, in the *Ballard, Yoder* and *Seeger* cases. The Court of Appeals should not have stopped its analysis by the mere labeling of the prosecution as a "criminal proceeding". The Court of Appeals erroneously upheld the trial judge's instructions to the jury which effectively stated that they needn't pay attention to whether the donors had a religious purpose in giving their money, nor to whether Moon acted in accordance with their wishes in spending the money. *Amici* urge that this

---

[2] The Court of Appeals' recognition that it is the *church's* activities that are being questioned reflects an inconsistency in its opinion and detracts from its contention that this was simply a case of an individual's liability for tax reporting. 718 F.2d at 1227-28. While individuals should not be allowed to avoid liability by hiding behind the First Amendment, so, too, the government, once it grants tax exemption to *bona fide* religious organizations, cannot attempt to get around *that* status by charging the religious leaders with the income. The Unification Church was granted federal tax exempt status in 1963 and has received judicial recognition as a *bona fide* religious group. *See, e.g., Unification Church v. Immigration and Naturalization Service,* 547 F.Supp. 623 (D.D.C. 1982). "[B]y any historical analogy, philosophical analysis, or judicial precedent . . . [the Unification Church] must be regarded as a *bona fide* religion." *Id.* at 628.

8

disturbing and apparently novel rule be given full review by this Court.

Ignoring the petitioners' beliefs as to "religiousness" is as erroneous in the *Moon* case as it would have been in the *Ballard* case to tell the jurors to decide whether the content of the literature the Ballards sent through the mail was true, and if not, to convict them of mail fraud. In *Ballard*, this Court ruled that the determination of guilt or innocence had to be based on what the Ballards sincerely believed.

The Second Circuit's decision in the *Moon* case would seem to say that the jury in *Wisconsin v. Yoder*, 406 U.S. 205 (1972), could have been told that it needn't worry that Mr. and Mrs. Yoder thought it was crucial to their religion to keep their children home from school; rather the jury could decide on any criteria it wished that it was not a good idea to keep the Yoder children home from school, and could therefore convict the parents for doing so.

Similarly, by instructing the jurors in the *Moon* case that the "religion . . . of the defendants is of no consequence whatsoever", T. 6538, and by failing to instruct them or give them any guidance as to how to make a legally sound determination as to church purposes, the court effectively overruled *United States v. Seeger*, 380 U.S. 163 (1975). The Supreme Court ruled in *Seeger*, the conscientious objector case, that if Seeger's beliefs were sincere and occupied a position that he believed to be religious, then the government and courts must respect them in the same way it did traditional religious beliefs. Applying the standard which was applied in the instant case would have allowed Mr. Seeger's jury to send him not simply to jail, but possibly to war, despite his sincerely held belief.

Clearly the Religion Clauses do apply to federal criminal prosecutions. The Court of Appeals offered no legitimate grounds for carving out an exception to this rule in the prosecution of Reverend Moon.

9

II. CERTIORARI SHOULD BE GRANTED TO RE-AFFIRM THE SANCTITY OF A CHURCH'S OWN DEFINITION OF ITS RELIGIOUS ACTIVITIES AND MINISTRIES

An issue squarely presented by the *Moon* case is whether the government can filter out the religious dimension of a church's efforts to survive and grow by making economic investments without "excessive government entanglement with religion." *Walz v. Tax Commisison*, 397 U.S. 664, 674 (1970). In the *Moon* case the jurors were prevented from hearing defense evidence "with respect to the relationship between church and business", T. 5254, and that the investments in question were made for religious purposes, T. 5618. In addition, the judge failed to properly explain the legal standard the jury should apply in determining "church purposes", a determination which he told them they would have to make in order to determine whether or not a trust existed. In the absence of appropriate instructions it is impossible to predict upon what basis the jury reached its verdict, nor whether they simply discounted expenditures of the funds in question as being "secular", despite the fact that the defendants believed them to be religious. This was all despite the well-settled principle in *Lemon v. Kurtzman*, 403 U.S. at 621-22, that it is constitutionally impermissible for a government body, be it the prosecution or the courts, "to determine which expenditures are religious and which are secular."

The question this case presents is whether the government can ignore a church's sincere definition of its own ministry. As the government openly declared, "we undertook to try Reverend Moon . . . like any ordinary person charged with tax fraud," S. 65, and the court confirmed that the trial proceeded on this basis when the judge acknowledged that Reverend Moon was "treated as anyone else would be without any consideration of his re-

10

ligious beliefs." S. 133. *See also,* S. 24, T. 2163, 6281, 6471-73. Perhaps in a misguided effort to show deference to the principle of the separation of church and state, the court imposed secular standards exactly where the *Ballard* line of cases established that deference should be given to religious beliefs.

By permitting the jury to superimpose its own standards, be they secular or eevn those of the religion of *their* own choosing, the government excessively entangled itself with the Unification religion and denied that Church and its members their right to free exercise. As education was held to be "an integral part of the religious mission", so, too, the "ability to make decisions concerning the recruitment, allocation and expenditure of their funds is intimately bound up in [the church's religious] mission . . . and thus is protected by the free exercise clause of the First Amendment." *Surinach v. Pesquera de Busquets,* 604 F.2d 73, 78 (1st Cir. 1979).

As *amici* read the Court of Appeals' decision, its precedent will certainly have a chilling effect on the constitutionally sanctioned practice of almost all major religions of holding stock or other investments in properties or profit-making corporations for the benefit of the church, out of fear that such investments might trigger criminal investigations or the loss of tax exempt status and its accompanying tax-deductible donations. Moreover, of more immediate concern to this *amici*, the door has been shoved open for the government to impose secular standards and reject the church's own sincerely held belief in the "religiousness" of an activity or decision. This would hold true not only in the broad terms of the expenditure of church funds, but it might also be used to justify government intrusion without a compelling state interest—perhaps merely with the prelitigated label of "criminal"—in even the routine administration of church ministries, including religious schools.

11

CONCLUSION

As our society becomes more and more secularized, safeguards must be taken that we do not eradicate the protection of the First Amendment for those it was originally drafted and demanded to protect. When it comes to activities and decisions that a church views as integral to its mission, be it spending decisions or the education of its youth, the government should certainly not be allowed to knock those activities down from the status of "integral" to that of "secular" in one fell swoop. Although the free exercise of religion is "subordinate to the criminal laws of the country", 718 F.2d at 1227, *quoting Davis v. Beason*, 133 U.S. at 342-43, the factfinder's ultimate determination as to criminality must, in accordance with the Constitution and precedents set by this Court, at least consider the sincerely held religious beliefs of the defendant when those beliefs are relevant to the issues being tried. To separate out the various activities of a church in total disregard of the beliefs and practices of the religion carries the separation of church and state to an extreme that clearly violates the First Amendment.

The Court of Appeals' decision in *United States v. Moon* raises far-reaching implications for the sanctity of all religions and religious ministries. *Amici* therefore respectfully request that this Court take jurisdiction over the case by granting certiorari.

Respectfully submitted,

ALAN L. CRAPO
3035 South Keystone Ave.
Indianapolis, Indiana 46237
(317) 783-7769
Attorney of Record
for Amici Curiae

March, 1984

The American Association of
Christian Schools

TABLE OF CONTENTS

ii

TABLE OF AUTHORITIES

iii

TABLE OF AUTHORITIES—Continued

No. 83-1242

SUN MYUNG MOON and TAKERU KAMIYAMA,
Petitioners,

v.

UNITED STATES OF AMERICA,
Respondent.

On Petition for Certiorari to the United States
Court of Appeals for the Second Circuit

BRIEF OF AMICUS CURIAE AMERICAN ASSOCIATION
OF CHRISTIAN SCHOOLS IN SUPPORT OF
PETITION FOR CERTIORARI

INTEREST OF AMICUS CURIAE

Both parties have consented to the filing of this brief pursuant to Rule 36 of the Rules of this Court. Their consents are on file with the Clerk of the Court.

The American Association of Christian Schools (AACS) consists of more than 1,130 member schools from across the nation. These member schools engage in practices that are similar or identical to some of those involved in this case. Many of them accumulate funds over periods of years to carry out religious ministries. Some-

2

times these funds are held in the name of a single individual, as they were in this case. Moreover, many of the reasons given by the courts below to justify treating the income from religious gifts as taxable to Rev. Moon could be applied to various AACS members—the lack of a formal organizational structure, for example. The AACS therefore has a vital interest in the proper disposition of this important case because the decision of the courts below, if permitted to stand, has the potential of generating extremely adverse effects upon its members.

SUMMARY OF ARGUMENT

Certiorari should be granted in this case for two reasons.

First, the rulings of the courts below have a vast potential for imposing onerous burdens upon the free exercise of religion by many Americans. These rulings permit the government to ignore the doctrines and structures of religious organizations, and to disregard the conscientious and sincere beliefs of members of those organizations, in determining whether a given activity is secular or religious. They pose a particular hazard to the AACS because its principal activity is the establishment and maintenance of Christian schools. That activity can be regarded as secular under the decisions below, which permit religious doctrine and sincere beliefs to be held for naught. Moreover, many members of the AACS are especially vulnerable to charges of shortcomings of the kind which the courts below held to justify treating certain activities as secular; shortcomings such as the lack of formal organizational structure, and the absence of a "clear and unambiguous" intent to create a trust. The number of organizations subject to these potential hazards to free exercise is huge.

Second, the rulings of the courts below are inconsistent with doctrine this Court has established in Free Exercise Clause cases.

3

ARGUMENT

I. The Rulings of the District Court and the Opinion of
the Court of Appeals Approving Them Have a Vast
Potential for Imposing Onerous Burdens Upon the
Free Exercise of Religion by Countless Numbers of
People and Therefore Cry Out for Plenary Review by
This Court.

The undisputed issue in this case is deceptively simple:
did the bank accounts and other assets held in Rev.
Moon's name belong to him personally, or were they
rather church property held by him as a trustee? All
four judges in the courts below agreed that this was
the central issue.[1]

The courts below resolved this issue by focusing on two
distinct, but overlapping questions: Was a trust created
at the time the assets were donated? And were the uses
which Rev. Moon made of the assets personal or
religious?

As to the trust question, the jury was given a list
of "factors" it could consider. Conspicuous among these
factors was "the fact that the accounts were maintained
under Reverend Moon's name" (a fact which was never
denied), and "whether the Movement had a specific organizational structure, written charter or constitution."
Petn. App. 68 n.3.[2] But the jury also was instructed
that religion had nothing to do with the resolution of
this question. T. 6538. The Court of Appeals then went
even further; it held that the District Judge would not
have been required to instruct on the law of trusts at all.
Petn. App. 25.

---

[1] We adopt the statement of the case contained in the Petition for
Certiorari, and supplement it only when necessary.

[2] Our citations to the opinions of the Court of Appeals in this
case will be to the Appendix contained in the Petition for Certiorari,
as follows: "Petn. App. ——." Our few references to the trial
transcript are denoted "T. ——."

4

The rulings of the trial judge and the opinion of the Court of Appeals together result in a threefold burdening of the free exercise of religion. *First*, they put a religious organization at the peril of losing its constitutional benefits if a jury second guesses it and concludes that its "organizational structure" is inappropriate to carry out its religious missions. *Second*, they disregard as irrelevant whether the religion's "organizational structure" was influenced or dictated by religious doctrine or practices. Moreover, they relegate to the status of a "factor to be considered" the religious intent of the donors of the assets—which means, of course, that the jury is free to disregard that factor if it chooses to do so. *Third*, as dissenting Judge Oakes pointed out, they impose upon the religious organization the burden of proving that its "organizational structure" is appropriate to its mission while at the same time they deny the organization the opportunity to show that its structure was influenced or dictated by its religious doctrines or practices. Petn. App. 73-74.

As to the uses made of the assets (whether they were "personal" or "business" rather than religious), the courts below held that this question could be resolved without considering the obviously religious context in which the donations were made, or the purposes which the church considered to be within its religious mission. The jury was given virtually no guidance on this question.[3] Instead it was allowed to decide, in its uncon-

---

[3] Only two paragraphs of the lengthy set of instructions dealt with this question, and they were ambiguous at best:

> Also the mere fact that Reverend Moon exercised control over the funds and the stock is not necessarily indicative of his personal ownership. A person who holds property on behalf of another may be given broad authority and discretion to deal with that property as long as he does so in a manner consistent

5

trolled discretion, whether the activities supported by the use of the assets were religious or not.

These rulings have an enormous potential for imposing onerous burdens upon the free exercise of religion by the members of the AACS. Three characteristics of Christian schools are especially significant in evaluating their potential effects.

First, members of AACS conscientiously and sincerely believe that founding Christian schools is a religious mission that serves a religious purpose. Dr. Paul A. Kienel recently put the matter succinctly when he testified before a congressional committee:

> These beliefs of ours have one consequence of special relevance to your Committee today; we are *required* by our religious convictions to found and maintain Christian schools. Put differently: our Christian schools exist *solely* because of our Christian faith. They have no other reason for being. We obviously do not found Christian schools for secular purposes—just to assure, for example, that children will learn mathematics, English or other "basics." While superior academics is not our primary purpose we are pleased, of course, that the achievement level of our students is one full grade level ahead of the nation's public schools. [Testimony of Paul A. Kienel, Executive Director, Assn. of Christian Schools International, at Hearing Before United States Senate Committee on Finance on Mandatory Social Security Coverage for Employees of Religious Organizations, Washington, D.C., December 14, 1983, p. 2 (emphasis in original).]

---

with the purpose for which he was given title to the property in the first place.

    * * * *

A religious organization can properly pay the living expenses of [its] leaders or ministers in order to allow them to pursue its religious purposes and can make loans to its ministers or leaders on arm's length terms.

Petn. App. 69 n.3.

6

But most Americans think of education as a secular activity. If juries are free to determine that such activities are secular in disregard of conscientious and sincere religious beliefs, as the courts below held they are, the consequences to members of AACS, and to the thousands of Americans who believe as they do but who are not its members, will be earth shaking.

It is easy to discern why most Americans think of education as a secular activity. Under a long line of widely publicized decisions from this Court, they are *required* to think of *public* education as secular. E.g., *Abington School Dist. v. Schempp*, 374 U.S. 203 (1963); *Epperson v. Arkansas*, 393 U.S. 97 (1968); *Stone v. Graham*, 449 U.S. 39 (1980). But this is not a case, like those just cited, in which the Establishment Clause requires courts to distinguish the areligious from the secular. This is not even the case in which the issue is whether collecting a certain tax is a sufficiently compelling governmental interest to override a legitimate Free Exercise Clause claim. Cf., *United States v. Lee*, 455 U.S. 252 (1982). Rather, the issue in this case is whether a legitimate free exercise claim can be overridden by a jury's unguided and *ex post facto* conclusion that a religion's "organizational structure" is inappropriate, or that its members' intention to create a trust is not sufficiently "clear and unambiguous," *in the absence of any indication by government*, by way of the statute or other positive law, *that it has any interest whatsoever* in regulating the kinds of organizations that churches must establish or specifying the clarity of intent that must be shown when members make a religious donation.

Second, although most of the schools associated with AACS are owned by churches, some of them are independent of any church. The latter are organized by small groups of individuals whose bond is a shared belief

7

in the authority of the Bible. The religious character of the Christian schools rests upon an especially strong belief in a Biblical and historical foundation for the conclusion that education is a religious enterprise:

> The word "church" in English comes from the Greek "ecclessia" which is the Greek form of two Hebrew words meaning congregation and assembly. Now, in the Old Testament the church or congregation had two facets, priestly and levitical. The levitical function as supplied in all of Deuteronomy and summed up in Deuteronomy 33:10 is instruction. With the atonement of Christ fundamentalists believe that the priestly function came to an end. In all forms of Western Christianity, including those churches such as the Catholic and Anglo Catholics who call their clergy priests, the basic function of the clergy is still levitical. In the Eastern churches, because of the influence of the Byzantine State which insisted on the rigid control of religious rights, the instructional aspect, the levitical function, of the clergy was lost. As a result, there has been a stultification and a lack of growth in the life of the Eastern churches because they have been limited to a liturgical function. In Western Christianity, the basic function of the church is levitical or instructional. Whenever that instructional aspect has been restrained or has declined through decadence in the church, the life of the church has become minimal and the faith has receded. The fundamentalists very strongly emphasize the levitical or instructional aspect of the life of the church as central (V, 41-41). [R. J. Rushdoony in Goodell and Lee, Government's Golden Image: Kentucky (Christian Heritage Ministries, Louisville, KY, 1980), 83.]

Such small groups are particularly vulnerable to second-guessing about the inadequacies of their "organizational structures," and about their faith and confidence in the individuals they have chosen to spearhead their efforts to found a Christian school.

8

Third, the number of people potentially affected by the lower courts' rulings is enormous. AACS has more than 1,130 member schools. Moreover, Christian day schools, which provide full-time elementary or secondary education, are the fastest growing segment of private education. One analysis, published in 1979, described their growth as follows:

In the 1950s, 91 percent of all children in America attended tax-supported public schools. Today, only 74 percent of the nation's children are still enrolled in public schools. The rest are in private schools. Even more important, the fastest growing segment of private school enrollment is among evangelical Christians. There are now well over one million schoolchildren attending over 5,000 Christian (evangelical) elementary and high schools. *Two new Christian Schools are being established every twenty-four hours.* "In the past ten years our Christian School Movement has more than tripled," says Reverend Arno Weniger, executive vice president of the American Association of Christian Schools. The growth in Christian schools is truly one of the most significant cultural phenomena of the decade. By and large the students come from lower-middle-class families whose incomes lie in the ten thousand to fifteen thousand dollar range. Despite the often heard criticism that Christian school growth has been motivated by racial prejudice, the reality is just the opposite. Less than 5 percent of these private schools are segregationist oriented. The overwhelming majority are deeply committed to fostering integration between the races.

* * * *

There is no doubt that the mushrooming growth in evangelical believers, evangelical communications and evangelical infrastructures is the most significant cultural phenomenon in American life today. [Jeremy Rifkin, The Emerging Order: God in the Age of Scarcity (1979), 122, 126 (emphasis in original).]

9

Later estimates have placed the number of such schools even higher. One recent study concluded that, ". . . between eight and ten thousand Christian day schools have been established since the mid-1960s, with a current enrollment of approximately one million students." Carper, The Christian Day School Movement, 1960-1982, 17 Educ. F. 135 (1983).

The intrinsic relation of the Christian school to the other ministries of the church was described by Rev. Guy G. Goodell, one of the plaintiffs in *Kentucky State Board v. Rudasill*, 589 S.W.2d 877 (Ky., 1979):

> The relationship is a very integral one. The school is not a separate entity. It is one of the arms and ministries of our church. For example, we have a ministry for the shut-ins in Frankfort, Kentucky; we have a ministry for people who are unable to provide transportation to church, and we have an extension ministry to help them and bring them in. We have a visitation ministry. We have a counseling ministry for people who are having marital problems. And then we feel, in order to prohibit or to prevent any future difficulties in the lives of children growing up and marrying, that we need to have some type of ministry to them in obedience to bible command. We have a school that takes the child at the very youngest age and begins to provide the teaching, inculcating of the Bible doctrine in his heart and mind at that age. We operate under the same board that our church operates under; that is, in other words, our deacons and trustees in the church are the leaders of the school and, as pastor of the church, I am Pastor and also principal of the school. We follow a curriculum plan of teaching the Word of God through the academic material that we use, and we comply with the absolute standards of the Word of God concerning the teaching ministry. [Goodell and Lee, Government's Golden Image: Kentucky (Christian Heritage Ministries, Louisville, KY 1980) 47.]

10

Other religious groups share this view that education is an exercise of religious ministry. See *Lemon v. Kurtzman*, 403 U.S. 602, 616 (1971) (The District Court concluded that the parochial schools constituted 'an integral part of the religious mission of the Catholic Church.' The various characteristics of the schools make them "a powerful vehicle for transmitting the Catholic faith to the next generation."); *Westbury Hebrew Congregation, Inc. v. Downer*, 59 Misc.2d 387, 388, 302 N.Y.S.2d 923, 925 (Sup. Ct., N.Y. Co. 1969), (The court indicated its approval of plaintiff's contention that "the parochial school use for the teaching of additional secular subjects is an integral part of the functions and activities of synagogue use and is accessory thereto.")

In light of these facts, the potentially pernicious effects of the rulings of the courts below on the free exercise of religion by countless Americans can be made even clearer.

Literally thousands of people who donate money for the purpose of establishing Christian schools may discover that, despite their intentions, their contributions were ineffectual—perhaps because the "organizational structure" of their group is found by hindsight, as permitted by the courts below, to have been inadequate; or because, never having heard of "trusts" and having no idea how to create one, their intentions were not made "clear and unambiguous," as required by the courts below; or because, as authorized by the courts below, a jury is permitted to decide that establishing a school is a secular rather than a religious purpose. The same reasons may justify denying them the right to deduct their contributions from their income tax liabilities. Since many of these people have only modest incomes (see Rifkin, *supra*), and many of them comply with the Biblical injunction to "tithe" their organizations, they may lose the only tax benefits for which they qualify.

It frequently happens that funds must accumulate for years before they reach a level sufficient to accomplish

11

one or another of the religious missions of Christian schools, such as the construction or purchase of a suitable building. It is not unusual for such funds to be held in the name of a single individual, as they were in this case. The decision of the courts below imperil this practice in a number of ways. First, if the income that accumulates from these funds is taxable to the person in whose name they are deposited, as the courts below held it may be, then the total accumulation is depleted pro tanto. Similarly, the result reached by the courts below cannot help but encourage the government, in its endless quest for additional revenue, to claim the right to tax such income. The accumulation thus will be depleted by the costs of fending off the claim even when the defense is successful.

Moreover, it is a long-standing practice of congregationally governed Christian churches to provide their ministers with "parsonage" and transportation allowances. Under the decision below, such allowances obviously may be viewed as "personal" rather than religious. The courts below went even further: they clearly held that juries may be permitted to decide that the total corpus of the fund from which these allowances are derived—not just the allowances themselves—may be considered to be secular. And lying just below the surface of the decision below is the implication that jurors are especially entitled to treat such funds as secular if the standard of living the congregation provides its minister is too lavish for their tastes.

The most disturbing element of the opinion below is its holding that juries may be permitted to decide, without regard to religious doctrine or structure, that certain activities are secular rather than religious. Our most obvious concern is the danger that establishing Christian schools will be found to be a secular activity. But we have other concerns too. As the Rev. Goodell pointed out in the abstract quoted above, many Christian organiza-

12

tions establish counselling ministries to assist married couples who are encountering difficulties. Many Christian schools establish summer camps to provide their children with opportunities of a kind usually associated with scouting. These camps typically have paid directors and staffs. The decision below opens the door to an ex post facto characterization of all of these activities as secular, despite the sincerely held belief of our members that they are essentially religious.

These few examples, which could be multiplied many times, only begin to suggest how drastic the implications of the decision below are for the free exercise of religion by the members of the AACS.

II. The Rulings of the District Court and the Opinion of the Court of Appeals Approving Them are Inconsistent With Free Exercise Clause Principles Established by This Court.

The Court of Appeals ruled that, "The central issue for the jury to decide was whether the Tong IL stock and Chase Manhattan Bank accounts belonged to the Church or to Moon personally." Petn. App. 43. The answer to this question, however, depended upon determining the purpose for which the funds were given to Rev. Moon and whether his use of the funds was within that purpose. The jury was permitted to decide this issue according to its own lights and with no requirement that it accept or even consider the Unification Church's own definition of its religious purposes. This is the major error with which Amicus is concerned.

No evidence was presented in this case that any of the money involved was given to Rev. Moon for any purpose other than what the donors regarded as the religious purposes of the Unification Church. Yet the jury was not required to accept or even to consider the good-faith belief of the donors and of the Church that the purposes and activities involved were religious. Instead, the jury was

13

permitted to decide that those professedly religious purposes and activities were not religious, as the Church and
its members believed them to be, but were instead secular.
And the jury decided that since, as the jury believed, some
of the uses to which Rev. Moon put the funds were secular, therefore the entire fund had been given to him for
secular rather than religious purposes and it belonged to
him rather than to the Church.

Not only was the jury not instructed to accept or even
to consider the Church's own conception of its religion, but
the trial judge explicitly emphasized that religion had
nothing to do with the case. The charge by the trial
judge warned the jurors that:

> It is also your duty to appraise the evidence calmly
> and objectively and to reach your verdict in this case
> without prejudice or sympathy or any consideration
> of race, religion or ethnic origin. I have told you
> before and I repeat it again, that the race, religion
> and ethnic origin of the defendants is of no conse-
> quence whatever. They are on trial in an American
> court before American jurors under the Constitution
> of the United States and considerations of race or
> religion must have no part in your deliberations."
> [T. 6538.]

This case required the jury "to resolve a religious
controversy." *Jones v. Wolf*, 443 U.S. 595, 604 (1979).
The ownership issue depended on whether the purposes
involved were religious or secular. "The Supreme Court
has been especially sensitive to an entanglement which
requires the state to distinguish between and thus determine what is religious and what is secular." *Surinach
v. Pesquera de Busquets*, 604 F.2d 73, 78 (1st Cir. 1979).
In *Lemon v. Kurtzman*, 403 U.S. 602, 620 (1971), the
inspection and evaluation procedures involved in the program of state aid to parochial education were held to
create an unconstitutional entanglement of government
with religion because they could require "the govern-

14

ment to examine the school's records in order to determine how much of the total expenditures is attributable to secular education and how much to religious activity. This kind of state inspection and evaluation of the religious content of a religious organization is fraught with the sort of entanglement that the Constitution forbids. It is a relationship pregnant with dangers of excessive government direction of church schools and hence of churches." Similarly, this Court held in *NLRB v. Catholic Bishop of Chicago*, 440 U.S. 490 (1979), that to construe the applicable statute to authorize National Labor Relations Board jurisdiction over Catholic school teachers "would implicate the guarantees of the Religion Clauses" (440 U.S. at 507) because "the schools had responded that their [alleged unfair labor practices] were mandated by their religious creeds. The resolution of such charges by the Board, in many instances, will necessarily involve inquiry into the good faith of the position asserted by the clergy-administrators and its relationship to the school's religious mission. It is not only the conclusions that may be reached by the Board which may impinge on rights guaranteed by the Religion Clauses but the very process of inquiry leading to findings and conclusions." 440 U.S. at 502.

The inquiry process found objectionable by this Court in *Lemon v. Kurtzman* and *Catholic Bishop* is comparable to the process involved in this case. The jury evaluated, pursuant to criteria of its own devising, the includability of certain purposes and activities within the religious mission of the Unification Church. And it did so without regard to the Church's own conception of that mission. The vice in this sort of process was accurately described by the New York Court of Appeals in *Holy Spirit Ass'n v. Tax Comm.*, 55 N.Y.2d 512, 450 N.Y.S.2d 292, 435 N.E.2d 662 (1982):

> [The taxing agencies and the lower court] each asserted the right of civil authorities to examine the

15

creed and theology of the Church and to factor out what in its or his considered judgment are the peripheral political and economic aspects, in contradistinction to what was acknowledged to be the essentially religious component. Each then took the view that beliefs and activities which could be objectively accurately described by knowledgeable outsiders as "political" and "economic" were by that fact precluded from being classified as "religious." As stated it is not the province of civil authorities to indulge in such distillation as to what is to be denominated religious and what political or economic. It is for religious bodies themselves, rather than the courts or administrative agencies, to define, by their teachings and activities, what their religion is. The courts are obliged to accept such characterization of the activities of such bodies, including that of the Church in the case before us, unless it is found to be insincere or sham. [55 N.Y.2d at 527-28.]

The decision in this case subjects Christian schools to the kind of factoring out process condemned by *Holy Spirit*. Courts will have a practically unlimited power to decide that Christian schools are not religious at all and that therefore they do not enjoy the special protection of the Free Exercise Clause of the First Amendment.

The Christian schools are entitled to constitutional protection in their own right (See *Pierce v. Society of Sisters*, 268 U.S. 510 (1925); *Norwood v. Harrison*, 413 U.S. 455, 462 (1973)) and by reason of "the rights of parents to direct the religious upbringing of their children." *Wisconsin v. Yoder*, 406 U.S. 205, 233 (1972). *Pierce* was described by the Court in *Yoder* as "a charter of the rights of parents to direct the religious upbringing of their children." 406 U.S. at 233. See also *Committee for Public Education v. Nyquist*, 413 U.S. 756, 788 (1973).

As long as Christian schools are recognized by the courts as a religious activity, they are protected by the

16

requirement that an infringement upon the free exercise of religion must be justified by a "compelling state interest . . . . It is basic that no showing merely of a rational relationship to some colorable state interest would suffice; in this highly sensitive constitutional area, '[o]nly the gravest abuses, endangering paramount interests, give occasion for permissible limitation.' *Thomas v. Collins*, 323 U.S. 516, 530 . . . ." *Sherbert v. Verner*, 374 U.S. 398, 406-407 (1963). Also, "The state may justify an inroad on religious liberty by showing that it is the least restrictive means of achieving some compelling state interest. However, it is still true that '[t]he essence of all that has been said and written on the subject is that only those interests of the highest order . . . can overbalance legitimate claims to the free exercise of religion.' " *Thomas v. Review Board*, 450 U.S. 707, 718 (1981), quoting *Yoder*, 406 U.S. at 215.

If the conduct of a Christian school is held to be a secular rather than a religious activity, the claim of a right to participate in that sort of school will be viewed as merely a claim of a right to participate in a certain type of secular education. But since an infringement upon the right to education is not an infringement upon a fundamental right, it will not trigger the highest level of scrutiny (*San Antonio Independent School District v. Rodriguez*, 411 U.S. 1 (1973)) and the validity of that infringement will be determined by a less stringent criterion.

The Christian schools are concerned about regulations as to curriculum, education and other matters which are far from incidental, and which impose a direct and crippling burden on the free exercise of their religious ministry. Many court decisions, correctly applying principles developed by this Court, have recognized Christian schools as an exercise of religious ministry and, on that basis, have prevented the imposition on Christian schools of burdensome state regulations. See, for example, *State*

17

v. Whisner, 47 Ohio St.2d 181, 351 N.E.2d 750 (1976); *State v. LaBarge*, 134 Vt. 276, 357 A.2d 121 (1976); *Kentucky State Board v. Rudasill*, 589 S.W.2d 877 (Ky. 1979); *State ex rel. Nagle v. Olin*, 64 Ohio St.2d 341, 415 N.E.2d 279 (1980); *Baingor Baptist Church v. Maine* (U.S. District Court, District of Maine, Dec. 20, 1983); *Sheridan Road Baptist Church v. Michigan Dept. of Education* (Michigan Cir. Ct., Ingham County, Dec. 29, 1982, 3 Religious Freedom Reporter 10 (1983)).

However, the recognition that Christian schools are an exercise of ministry does not immunize them from all regulation since a court may still decide that a particular regulation is justified by a compelling state interest. See, for example, *State v. Shaver*, 294 N.W.2d 833 (N.D., 1980); *State ex rel. Douglas v. Faith Baptist Church*, 207 Neb. 802, 301 N.W.2d 571 (1981). Nevertheless, the recognition by the courts of the Christian school as an exercise of religious ministry is an important safeguard against abuse, since that recognition would require that any restriction on that religious ministry be justified by a compelling state interest, and that it be the least restrictive alternative available to protect that interest.

CONCLUSION

The rulings of the District Court and the opinion of the Court of Appeals approving them break new ground in Free Exercise Clause doctrine. They do so in a way that permits the imposition of onerous burdens upon the free exercise of religion by countless Americans, that is inconsistent with principles developed by this Court, and that conflicts with many lower court decisions that have conscientiously and correctly applied this Court's principles.

These rulings pose a particularly severe hazard to the establishment and maintainance of Christian schools, the

18

fastest growing segment of private education in the nation.

The rulings therefore cry out for plenary review by this Court. The thousands of people involved with Christian schools and the lower courts are entitled to an authoritative resolution of these crucial issues.

Accordingly, Amicus Curiae AACS joins in the Petitioners' prayer that a writ of certiorari issue.

Respectfully submitted,

JULES B. GERARD
Counsel of Record
Box 1120
Washington University
St. Louis, Mo. 63130
314/889-6427

The American Civil Liberties Union
and the New York Civil Liberties
Union.

MOTION FOR LEAVE TO FILE
BRIEF AMICI CURIAE

Amici respectfully move, for the reasons set forth in the Interest of Amici Curiae, for leave to file the within brief amici curiae. Petitioners have granted written consent to the filing of this brief. While Amici anticipate that respondent will consent, written consent has not yet been received by counsel.

_____
BURT NEUBORNE
Counsel for Amici Curiae

February 22, 1984

QUESTION PRESENTED

Did the court below err in declining to
permit petitioners to be tried before a
judge instead of a jury in view of the
petitioners' pervasive unpopularity and the
District Judge's recognition that a bench
trial would be "fairer"?

INDEX

ii

TABLE OF CASES

iii

SUMMARY OF ARGUMENT

When a pervasively unpopular defendant faces trial before a jury which he reasonably believes may harbor a degree of hostility toward him, three alternatives are possible. First, the government may forego criminal prosecution. Such an alternative is, of course, unpalatable in the extreme because it might permit a defendant to escape trial merely because his crimes are universally abhorred. Second, the court may empanel the fairest jury possible, recognizing that it may be impossible to assemble a wholly untainted jury. When a criminal defendant demands a jury trial, the constraints of practicability weigh heavily in favor of selecting the fairest jury possible rather than foregoing prosecution. Thus, a criminal defendant who

iv

demands a jury trial may be forced to appear before a jury which harbors hostility toward him.

However, when a defendant is prepared to waive trial by jury in order to avoid the impact of pervasive commmunity hostility, no basis exists to force that defendant to be tried before a tainted jury. Thus, in the absence of a showing of compelling need for a jury determination, procedural due process of law requires that an unpopular defendant be permitted to opt for a bench trial in order to avoid the impact of widespread community hostility.

INTEREST OF AMICI CURIAE

The American Civil Liberties Union is a nationwide, non-partisan organization of over 250,000 members dedicated to the protection of fundamental liberties guaranteed by the Constitution. The New York Civil Liberties Union is the New York State affiliate of the American Civil Liberties Union. The right of a pervasively unpopular defendant to a fair and impartial finder of fact in a criminal trial which· turns on highly subjective considerations is at the core of procedural due process of law. Ordinarily, of course, the imperative of a fair and impartial fact-finder in a criminal case is satisfied by compliance

with the commands of the 6th Amendment.
When, however, a defendant has reason to
fear that his pervasive unpopularity may
taint the deliberations of a jury selected
in compliance with traditional 6th Amendment
standards, amici believe that the Due
Process Clause of the Fifth Amendment
guarantees such a defendant the right to be
tried before a judge, especially when the
judge believes that a bench trial would be
"fairer" to the highly controversial
defendant.

This brief amici curiae is respectfully
submitted in support of petitioners'
application for a writ of certiorari in the
hope that the Court will utilize this
opportunity to clarify the circumstances
under which a pervasively unpopular
defendant enjoys a due process right not to
be tried before a cross-section of the
community which fears and despises him.

STATEMENT OF THE CASE

Reverend Sun Myung Moon may well be among the most unpopular figures in the United States.[1] As founder and leader of a small controversial religious denomination which seeks to appeal to the young; which engages in vigorous prosyletization; and which purports to exercise considerable control over the daily lives of its adherents, Rev. Moon has incurred the hostility of mainstream religious groups and has triggered an outpouring of fear from the general public, many of whom view him as the leader of a dangerous cult which preys on the young.

When the government charged Rev. Moon with knowingly filing false income tax

---

1. This brief is submitted in support of Rev. Moon's petition for certiorari, as well as the petition of Takeru Kamiyama, one of his close aides. The relationship between Rev. Moon and Mr. Kamiyama is such that Mr. Kamiyama bears the same burden of hostility as Rev. Moon.

returns because he failed to report

approximately $100,000 in interest on funds

held openly in his name in an account at

Chase Manhattan Bank,[2] it raised two

critical factual questions:

> (1) Was Rev. Moon holding the
> funds for his personal use
> or for the use of the church?

> (2) Did Rev. Moon willfully fail
> to report the interest as tax-
> able income, or was he acting
> pursuant to a good faith belief
> that, as church funds, the
> interest was not income to him?

In order to have answered those questions, a

finder of fact must, of necessity, have

passed upon Rev. Moon's credibility and

integrity, as well as his role in -- and

relationship to-- the Unification Church.

Given the pervasively negative perception of

---

2. The indictment also charges a failure to
report the receipt of shares of stock in
Tong II Enterprises as a taxable stock
dividend. Since the issues surrounding the
interest on the Chase Manhattan accounts and
the Tong II stock are identical, discussion
is confined to the Chase Manhattan interest
in order to simplify the brief.

both Rev. Moon and the Unification Church in

the community, and given the highly

subjective nature of the necessary factual

determinations, petitioners harbored

understandable fears that even the most

conscientious juror could not help but be

influenced by a latent hostility toward Rev.

Moon in making the delicate factual

judgments made necessary by the government's

indictment. Accordingly, each petitioner

waived the 6th Amendment's guaranty of trial

by jury and sought instead to be tried

before a judge. The government, claiming

that public confidence in the fairness of

the proceedings could be assured only by the

participation of a jury, declined to consent

to a bench trial. The District Judge,

despite his belief that a bench trial would

be "fairer" and despite his skepticism

concerning the government's ostensible

reason for opposing a bench trial, deemed

himself bound by Singer v. United States,

380 U.S. 24 (1965), to deny petitioners'

request for a bench trial in the absence of

the government's consent.[3] With respect,

however, Singer holds merely that a

defendant is not entitled to a bench trial

over the government's objection simply to

serve his personal convenience. When, as

here, a defendant seeks a bench trial, not

to advance his personal convenience, but

because he reasonably believes himself to be

widely feared and disliked in the community,

Singer fully supports a defendant's right to

---

3.   The Second Circuit, in affirming,
similarly viewed Singer as giving the
government an absolute veto over a
defendant's request for a bench trial unless
a defendant could show that it was
impossible to empanel a jury which met
minimum 6th Amendment standards. Why a
defendant who is able to show that it is
impossible to empanel a jury to try him
would voluntarily seek a trial before a
judge, as opposed to demanding an outright
dismissal, is a mystery that neither the
District nor the Circuit Court chose to
explore.

a bench trial, at least in the absence of a

compelling showing of need for a trial by

jury.

REASONS FOR GRANTING THE WRIT

This Court has lavished considerable

attention on assuring that the criminal

fact-finding process remains scrupulously

fair. Whether it has been concerned with

the size,[4] placement[5] and satisfaction[6] of

the burdens of proof, the composition of the

jury;[7] or the effect of prejudicial

publicity,[8] this Court has been careful to

assure an accused access to an impartial

fact-finder capable of treating the

---

4.   Eg. In re Winship, 397 U.S. 358 (1970).
5.   Compare, Mullaney v. Wilbur, 421 U.S.
684 (1975) with Patterson v. New York, 432
U.S. 197 (1977).
6.   See generally, Leary v. United States,
395 U.S. 6 (1969) and Jackson v. Virginia,
443 U.S.307 (1979).
7.   Eg. Castaneda v. Partida, 430 U.S. 482
(1977); Taylor v. Louisiana, 419 U.S. 522
(1975); Ballew v. Georgia, 435 U.S. 223
(1978).
8.   Sheppard v. Maxwell, 384 U.S. 333
(1966).

defendant as innocent until proven guilty
beyond a reasonable doubt. Ordinarily,
careful voir dire coupled with conscientious
jurors combine to produce juries which are
both impartial and fully prepared to deflect
error in accordance with the constitutional
presumption of innocence. Occasionally,
however, a defendant is so notorious that
empanelling a wholly untainted jury is all
but impossible.

One alternative to the use of such a
partially tainted jury would be to forego
the prosecution altogether. However, such
an approach might well permit notorious
criminals to escape prosecution merely
because their crimes are universally
abhorred.

A second and more practical response
would be to empanel the fairest jury
possible, recognizing that while some taint
may exist, so long as a tolerably neutral

fact-finder can be assembled, the

alternative of no trial at all is

unacceptable. See Dobbert v. Florida, 432

U.S. 282 (1977); Murphy v. Florida, 421 U S

794 (1975); Irwin v. Doud, 366 U.S. 717

(1961). Thus, if Rev. Moon had demanded a

jury trial, the constraints of

practicability would have made it impossible

for him to have demanded a wholly untainted

jury.

A third alternative, however, should be

available to a defendant who reasonably

fears that even the fairest available jury

is saturated with conscious or unconscious

bias, making it virtually impossible for the

presumption of innocence to operate

properly. Instead of being forced to stand

trial before a tainted jury, such a

vulnerable defendant should be able to waive

trial by jury and seek, instead, a bench

trial. Singer v. United States, 380 U.S.

24, 37-38 (1965). When such an unpopular defendant reasonably fears that a jury trial is a tainted trial, no legitimate basis exists to deny him access to the fairest available fact-finder. Certainly, the justifications proferred by the government do not make out a case for denying an unpopular defendant's request to be tried before a judge.

The government argued below that its opposition to a bench trial was necessary to preserve the integrity of the institution of trial by jury. However, the recognition of a narrow class of widely unpopular defendants who may seek a bench trial in no way threatens the institution of the jury, which would remain the finder of fact in the vast bulk of criminal settings. Indeed, the government's objection appears to confuse means and ends. A jury is not an end in itself, but the means by which a fair and impartial factual determination may be

reached. When, because of the pervasive

unpopularity of a defendant, genuine doubt

exists about the fairness of using a cross-

section of the community as a fact-finder,

it would be self-defeating to argue that a

jury must be used, even when a judge agrees

with a defendant that a bench trial would be

fairer.

The government's other justifications

for blocking a bench trial are similarly

unpersuasive. Solicitude for the trial

judge's reputation cannot possibly justify

the government's refusal to accede to a

bench trial, especially when the judge was

perfectly willing to accept the

responsibility.

Concern over public acceptance of the

verdict is certainly a legitimate concern of

a prosecutor, but it is difficult to see how

the public's sense that justice was done can

be enhanced by forcing an overwhelmingly unpopular defendant to be tried before a jury in spite of his request to be tried before a willing judge.

Finally, opposing a bench trial because the defendant has claimed that the indictment was politically motivated is both irrational and violative of the First Amendment. If anything, the government's insistence on a jury when both the defendant and the judge believe that a bench trial would be fairer simply reinforces public suspicion that Rev. Moon was the target of religious persecution, to say nothing of inflicting a serious penalty on Rev. Moon for having dared to criticize the prosecutor.

CONCLUSION

For the above-stated reasons, amici urge that a writ of certiorari be granted herein or, in the alternative, that petitioners' convictions be summarily

reversed and remanded for a bench trial.

Respectfully submitted

BURT NEUBORNE
American Civil Liberties Union
 Foundation
132 West 43 Street
New York, New York 10036
(212) 944-9800

STEVEN R. SHAPIRO
New York Civil Liberties Union
84 Fifth Avenue
New York, New York 10011
(212) 924 7800

February 22, 1984

Bishop Ernest L. Unterkoefler; Clare
Boothe Luce; Eugene J. McCarthy;
Robert Destro; and a Coalition of
Catholic Laymen

i

TABLE OF CONTENTS

ii

TABLE OF AUTHORITIES

iii

Table of Authorities Continued

Page

iv

Table of Authorities Continued

Page

v

Table of Authorities Continued

IN THE

Supreme Court of the United States

OCTOBER TERM, 1983

———

No. 83-1242

———

SUN MYUNG MOON and TAKERU KAMIYAMA,
Petitioners,

v.

UNITED STATES OF AMERICA,
Respondent.

———

On Petition For Certiorari To The United States
Court Of Appeals For The Second Circuit

———

BRIEF AMICI CURIAE FOR
BISHOP ERNEST L. UNTERKOEFLER
CLARE BOOTHE LUCE
EUGENE J. McCARTHY
ROBERT DESTRO AND A COALITION OF
CATHOLIC LAYMEN

———

Pursuant to Rule 36.1 of the Rules of this Court, the individual *amici* listed below file this brief in support of the petition
for certiorari. Consent for filing this brief has been obtained in
writing from the attorneys of record for the parties in this case.
Their original letters are filed together with this brief.

INTEREST OF AMICI

Bishop Ernest L. Unterkoefler, Clare Boothe Luce, Eugene
J. McCarthy, Robert Destro, Hurd Baruch, Joseph McPher-
son, Ralph McInerny, Paul Finney, Edward S. Szukelewicz,
Joseph McGrath, Joseph Crumlish, and Edward Canfield are
members of the Roman Catholic Church. The *amici* by profession and calling include a member of the hierarchy of the

2

Roman Catholic Church, a former United States Ambassador, a former United States Senator, business executives, a publisher, lawyers, teachers, former members of the Executive Branch, veterans of the armed forces, married and single, male and female Catholics.

Amici are appalled by the treatment afforded Reverend Moon in this case because, as the Second Circuit majority acknowledged, Reverend Moon "is the spiritual leader of the [Unification] Church, as the Pope is the spiritual leader of the Roman Catholic Church." *United States v. Moon*, 718 F.2d 1210, 1227 (2d Cir. 1983). Moreover, the manner in which property is held in the Unification Church—an issue of critical significance in Reverend Moon's case—is similar in many respects to the manner in which property is held in the Roman Catholic Church. Finally, the intolerance and persecution encountered by the Unification Church in this country is all too reminiscent of the experience of Catholics in 19th century America, the bitter traces of which linger to this day. Because the above-named *amici* believe Reverend Moon to have been dealt a serious injustice by the courts below, and because of the parallels between the practices and precepts of his church that were condemned in this case and the practices and precepts of theirs, *amici* share a particularly keen interest in this Court's review of the judgment below.

Although *amici* do not claim to represent the views of all Catholic laymen, they believe that their views would fairly represent a sizeable segment of the Catholic lay community. Catholic lay persons number in the millions and are under an obligation in conscience to express their position on issues which could seriously affect the practice of their religion.

While there are many significant differences between Unification theology and the tenets of the Roman Catholic Church, the similarities—centering around the trust placed by the members in the head of the Church—are at the heart of this case and are of vital interest to the *amici*. Consequently, *amici* believe that the legal issues in this matter deserve an expression of their concern.

3

STATEMENT OF THE CASE

Amici adopt the statement of the case set forth in the petition for certiorari, insofar as the facts set forth therein are relevant to the arguments below.

SUMMARY OF THE ARGUMENT

The First Amendment to the Constitution prohibits "excessive government entanglement with religion." *Lemon* v. *Kurtzman*, 403 U.S. 602 (1971). The far-reaching decision of the court below invites this type of entanglement in several respects. Specifically, the court approved of certain jury instructions utilized in the trial court which permitted the jury to determine whether the funds at issue in this case were used for religious purposes without reference to the doctrine of the Unification Church as to what its religious purposes embraced. Further, the court refused to recognize the crucial significance of the ecclesiastical role of Reverend Moon within the Unification Church in its determination of the ownership of such funds.

In this connection, *amici* call the Court's attention to the description of the Unification Church and its theology offered by the New York Court of Appeals in *Holy Spirit Association* v. *Tax Commission*, 55 N.Y.2d 512, 524-25, 450 N.Y.S.2d 292, 296-97, 435 N.E.2d 662, 666-67 (1982):

> According to Unification theology, the 'great promise of Christianity' is 'the return of Christ' . . . Through the Resurrection, the Church believes, Jesus brought 'spiritual salvation,' but the physical institutions of this world—beginning with the family—remained unredeemed; in the Church's view, it is for the new Messiah to restore a Bride and establish the True Family serving as the foundation for ending 'the existence of evil in the world,' and to accomplish 'not only spiritual but also physical' salvation for mankind. Adherents of the Unification faith look to Reverend Moon to accomplish this task.

Amici submit that had the court properly considered these doctrines of Unification theology, including the special role of Reverend Moon within this theology, and the special status of

4

religion under the Constitution, the court could not have found Reverend Moon to be the beneficial owner of the funds at issue herein.

Amici concur with the Petitioners that the donative intent of the various contributors of the funds in question is of overriding significance in determining the ownership of those funds. Nevertheless, *amici* do not believe that interest income on funds contributed into the hands of a church leader, by church members for church purposes, can be treated as income to the church's leader unless those funds have been improperly diverted and used *primarily* for the personal benefit of that leader, rather than for purposes which are consistent with the stated objectives of the church.

For these and other reasons discussed below, *amici* believe that Reverend Moon's petition for certiorari should be granted by this Court.

I. THE DECISION OF THE SECOND CIRCUIT INVITES AN UNCONSTITUTIONAL ENTANGLEMENT OF CHURCH AND STATE

The distinction between church and state in America did not suddenly emerge in the 18th century.[1] Rather, it had its genesis in the concept of the freedom of the church enunciated by church fathers after the fall of the Roman Empire.[2] The concept of two orders, each supreme within its own jurisdiction, persists to this day.

---

[1] *See* L. Pfeffer, *Religious Freedom* 3 (1977).

"The dual principle of the First Amendment—that Congress shall make no law respecting an establishment of religion or prohibiting the free exercise thereof—was not invented in 1791 when the amendment was added to the newly established United States Constitution. For Centuries before then philosophers, religious leaders, and statesmen had asserted that men should be free of governmental coercion in their beliefs and in the expression of their beliefs in matters of religion."

[2] *See* J. C. Murray, *We Hold These Truths* 196 (1964).

"Two there are, august Emperor, by which this world is ruled on title of original and sovereign right—the consecrated authority of the priesthood and the royal power. [Pope] Gelasius I to Emperor Anastasias I, 404 A.D.

5

By trial and error a compromise and equilibrium has been attained in the United States between the freedom to worship and the power of the state. Certain relationships are the concern of both the religious and secular orders, although for different purposes. But control over the religious order, through an unwarranted extension of power granted by the people to the secular order, would be a constitutional disaster. The solution our founding fathers developed to avoid possible conflicts between the body politic and the various forms of religious belief is found in the First Amendment to the Constitution which provides that "Congress shall make no law respecting an establishment of religion . . ."[3]

The current test for determining whether state actions are consistent with the Establishment Clause was set forth in *Lemon* v. *Kurtzman, supra* wherein the court stated:

> The law in question must, first, reflect a clearly secular legislative purpose, second have a primary effect that neither advances nor inhibits religion, and, third avoid excessive government entanglement with religion."

For the reasons stated below, *amici* believe that the decision of the Second Circuit invites an excessive entanglement of church and state.

> **A. The Second Circuit Improperly Refused To Recognize Reverend Moon's Ecclesiastical Role Within His Religion, A Crucial Factor In The Determination Of His Guilt Or Innocence.**

In urging the Internal Revenue Service to undertake an investigation of Reverend Moon and the Unification Church— a request that ultimately led to the prosecution of Reverend Moon in this case—Senator Robert Dole, a member of the Senate Finance Committee, stressed the identification of Reverend Moon and the Unification Church. "Since many members of the [Church] perceive Mr. Moon to be the embodiment

---

[3] U.S. Const. Amend. I.

6

of the Church," Senator Dole wrote, "the appearance is that his stated intentions are not simply the goals of a private individual but the stated purposes of the [Church]."[4]

Nevertheless, in upholding Reverend Moon's conviction, the Second Circuit concluded that Reverend Moon's ecclesiastical status was *beside the point* in considering his individual responsibilities as a taxpayer. *See United States* v. *Moon, supra.* Thus, although it recognized that Reverend Moon "is the head of the [Unification] Church" and the "leader of the Unification Church movement," *Id.* at 1227, the court below, over Judge Oakes's dissent, *Id.* at 1245, sustained the trial court's failure to direct the jury's specific attention to Reverend Moon's role as leader and founder of his Church, *Id.* at 1227. Such instructions, had they been given, would surely have made a difference to the jury in deciding whether Reverend Moon had been given the disputed funds to hold in trust for his followers, thus personally owing no taxes on the interest on those funds. For example, the Second Circuit recognized that the jury based its verdict, at least in part, on evidence that "high ranking members of the Church were told that the Chase funds belonged to 'Father.' " *Id.* at 1220. However, the references to Reverend Moon as "Father" are not unlike references to the Pope as "Holy Father."[5] If only the jury's attention had been focused by the trial judge on the deeply religious significance of such

---

[4] Senator Dole's letter to the IRS, noted by the Second Circuit, *see* 718 F.2d at 1229, is reproduced as Appendix A to this brief; it appears in the record below at A1816.

Citations herein to the pleadings will be denoted "A__"; references to the trial transcript will be denoted "T__".

[5] The title "Pope" itself derives from the classical Greek word "pappas" or father, and denotes "spiritual paternity." 11 *New Catholic Encyclopedia* 572 (1967). It should be noted that Reverend Moon certainly occupies no more exalted a place within the Unification Church than the place occupied by the Pope in the Roman Catholic Church; the Pope is regarded as having "supreme and universal power over the whole Church, a power which he can always exercise unhindered." Vatican Council II, *Dogmatic Constitution on the Holy Roman Catholic Church, Lumen Gentium,* 21 November 1964, *reprinted in* Vatican Council II, *The Conciliar and Post Conciliar Documents* 372 (Flannery ed. 1975). The Dogmatic Constitution provides that

7

references, far from supporting the view that Reverend Moon held the Chase Manhattan Bank funds as his *own*, this terminology, would have supported his claim that he held the funds beneficially for his *followers*. The poet's query, "What's in a name?" could scarcely have greater meaning than in a case such as this.

If permitted to stand, the principle upheld by the Second Circuit could readily be applied against those who hold office in the Roman Catholic Church, as well as against leaders of other hierarchical religions. The weapon fashioned by the government in this case—hailing a religious leader into court in part *because* of his ecclesiastical office,[6] and then denying the significance of that office when it sheds critical, exonerating light on actions taken by the religious leader and his followers, is a weapon that this Court, faithful to the precepts of the Religion Clauses, must not permit civil authorities to wield.

> B. The Practice For Which Reverend Moon Was Condemned—Taking And Holding In His Own Name Property Given To Him For Church Purposes—Is A Long-Established Practice Of The Roman Catholic Church And Of Other Religions In America

Since the Edict of Constantine, civil authorities have recognized the validity of bequests to the Catholic Church;[7] and,

---

"the Roman Pontiff does not utter a pronouncement as a private person, but rather does he expound and defend the teaching of the Catholic faith as the supreme teacher of the universal Church, in whom the Church's charism of infallibility is present in a singular way." *Id.* at 380.

[6] The trial judge expressly acknowledged that the investigation of Reverend Moon's taxes would have been less likely if his religion had been less "controversial," A536-37; and the Second Circuit, noting that the trial judge had so acknowledged, nonetheless accepted the trial court's incredible conclusion that the government's decision to prosecute Reverend Moon was a "separate" decision. 718 F.2d at 1229.

[7] Edict *reprinted in* P. Coleman-Norton, *Roman State and Christian Church* 85-86 (1966). The power of the Roman Catholic Church in America to hold property was expressly recognized by the Attorney General of the United States in 1822. 1 Op. Att'y. Gen. 563-64 (1822). *See also Municipality of Ponce v. Roman Catholic Apostolic Church*, 210 U.S. 269, 318 (1908).

8

throughout this Nation's history, the Catholic Church and other religious bodies have held property through individual spiritual leaders, constituted as "corporations sole."[8] The corporation sole is a form of property ownership tracing its origin to colonial times; judicial decisions recognizing it appeared as early as 1807.[9] As Justice Story recounted in *Terrett* v. *Taylor*, "the minister of the parish was, during his incumbency, seized of the freehold of its inheritable property, as emphatically *persona ecclesiae*, and capable, as a sole corporation, of transmitting that inheritance to his successors." 13 U.S. (9 Cranch) 43, 46 (1815).[10]

Ironically, the Roman Catholic Church in America at first encountered sharp resistance to its use of corporations sole as a form of property ownership—for reasons strikingly similar to those which caused the trial judge to casually dismiss the notion in this case that Reverend Moon could be "a walking unincorporated association." T6119. The reason was that the Catholic Church "had a hierarchical structure that many found offensive."[11] To many 19th century Americans, the hierarchical character of the Roman Catholic Church "meant government by a foreign sovereign."[12] Thus, for many years the church, although favoring the use of the corporation sole, "was generally unsuccessful in its efforts to have the corporation sole adopted."[13] Indeed, "legislation tended to discriminate against

---

[8] *See* Kauper & Ellis, *Religious Corporations and the Law*, 71 Mich. L. Rev. 1499 (1973); P. Dignan, *A History of the Legal Incorporation of Catholic Church Property in the United States (1784-1932)* (1935).

[9] *See e.g., Inhabitants of the First Parish* v. *Dunning*, 7 Mass. 445, 447 (1811); *Weston* v. *Hunt*, 2 Mass. 500 (1807).

[10] *See also Town of Pawlet* v. *Clark*, 13 U.S. (9 Cranch) 292 (1815).

[11] Kauper & Ellis, *supra*, at 1520.

[12] *Id., citing Dignan, supra*, at 192-95. The assets, real and personal, which pertain to the Holy See, dioceses, religious orders, and parishes in America are ecclesiastical property and "are indirectly and directly subject to the authority of the Holy See." A. Maida, *Ownership, Control and Sponsorship of Catholic Institutions* 18 (1975).

[13] Kauper & Ellis, *supra*, 1523-24.

9

the Catholic Church, since it was feared that, with its hierarchical control, it would accumulate wealth and power incompatible with the American idea of democracy."[14]

As prejudice has been overcome, several states today specifically allow the incorporation of bishops of the Catholic Church
as corporations sole,[15] and ownership of church property
through the corporation sole is provided by statute in at least
15 states.[16] As Kauper & Ellis note, the corporation sole "is

---

[14] *Id.* at 1536.

[15] *E.g.*, Ala. Code § 10-4-1 (1980); Cal. Corp. Code § 10002 (West 1977);
Mich. Stat. Ann. 21.1691-2 (1983). For a clergyman or minister to hold title to
church property for religious purposes, the New York Court of Appeals long
ago held that "there [need be] no declaration of trust," *Baxter* v. *McDonnell,*
155 N.Y. 83, 49 N.E. 667, 668 (1898); *see also* N.Y. Relig. Corp. Law ¶ 91,
note 1 (McKinney 1952), and § 436 of N.Y.R.P.T.L. (McKinney Supp. 1983-
1984) which specifically provides that "[r]eal property held in trust by a
clergyman or minister of a religious denomination for the benefit of the
members of his incorporated church or unincorporated church shall be entitled to the same exemption from taxation, special ad valorem levies and
special assessments" as real property owned by a religious corporation or
association under N.Y.R.P.T.L. § 420-a (McKinney Supp. 1983-1984). *See
Town of Hardenburgh* v. *State,* 52 N.Y.2d 536, 540, 439 N.Y.S.2d 303, 304,
421 N.E.2d 795, 796, *appeal dismissed,* 454 U.S. 958 (1981); *In re Kimberly,*
27 A.D. 470, 50 N.Y.S. 586, 590 (N.Y. App. Div. 1898); *In re Smith,* 77 Mun.
134, 28 N.Y.S. 476, 477 (N.Y. App. Div. 1894); *Wolek* v. *New York,* 131 Misc.
37, 225 N.Y.S. 669, 671-72 (N.Y. Mun. Ct. 1927).

[16] Ala. Code §§ 10-4-1 to 9 (1980); Alaska Stat. §§ 10.40.010-.150 (1968 &
1983 Supp.); Ariz. Rev. Stat. Ann. §§ 10-421 to 10-427 (1977); Cal. Corp.
Code §§ 10000-15 (West 1977 & 1983 Supp.); D.C. Code Ann. §§ 29.501 *et seq.*
(1981 & 1983 Supp.); Hawaii Rev. Stat. §§ 419-1 to 9 (1968); Mich. Stat. Ann.
§§ 21.1691-.2016 (1983); Mont. Rev. Codes Ann. §§ 35-3-101 to 209 (1982);
Nev. Rev. Stat. §§ 84.010-.080 (1979); N.H. Rev. Stat. Ann. § 306.4 (1966)
(not clear that such a corporation could be formed in New Hampshire, but
nothing says otherwise); N.C. Gen. Stat. § 61-5 (1982); Ore. Rev. Stat.
§ 61.055 (1969); Utah Code Ann. §§ 16-7-1 to 11 (1953); Wash. Rev. Code
¶¶ 24.12.010-040 (1969); Wyo. Stat. Ann. §§ 17-80109 to 117 (1977).

10

exactly what it name implies—a one man corporation," a form of property ownership that "follows from the very nature of" hierarchical religious institutions.[17]

Thus, in holding in his own name, and under his control, property given for religious purposes, Reverend Moon followed a practice as old as the Republic. This practice would have been followed by the Roman Catholic Church even more widely, but for the very type of religious bigotry reflected in the government's failure in this case to respect the method chosen by members of the Unification movement for assuring the proper use of their property. The Second Circuit's notion that Reverend Moon's ecclesiastical office was essentially irrelevant in determining the status of property held by him in his own name and under his control rejects the witness of history. The judgment below can only be regarded as a denial of the legitimacy of his religion—an impermissible basis for assessing criminal liability under the Religion Clauses.

C. **The Second Circuit Disrupted The Traditional Equilibrium Between Church And State By Refusing To Recognize The Unification Church's Definition Of Its Religious Purposes.**

The distinction between church and state in purposes, methods, and manner of organization has been one of Christianity's cardinal contributions to Western political tradition.[18] When recognition of this distinction has been denied, the result

---

[17] Kauper & Ellis, *supra*, at 1540. *See also* A. Maida, *supra*, at 22. *See Bolshanin v. Zlobin*, 76 F.Supp. 281, 288 (D. Alaska 1948) ("Conveyance of the legal title [to property] to the spiritual head of [a] church is a fairly common practice.").

[18] R. W. Carlyle, I *A History of Medieval Political Theory in the West* 193 (1928).

> In the fathers, then, we see clearly the first development of those difficult questions concerning the relations of the temporal and spiritual authorities in society, round which so much of medieval political theory was to take shape. There can, we think, be little doubt that in the end nothing contributed so much to emancipate the judgment of theologians from the tendency to recognize an absolute authority in the monarch, as the clearly felt necessity of defending the independence of the Church.

11

has been an infringement of man's freedom of religious faith, or his freedom as a citizen, or both. The broad American drive toward freedom has naturally included the traditional distinction between church and state which was already embedded in our legal heritage from English common law.

Under our Constitution, property dedicated to religious use can be enjoyed and used by the religion to which it is dedicated and can be converted to any lawful use which the religion desires. No individual or entity, particularly the state, has the right to convert such property to any other use. If the power to tax is the power to destroy, intrusion by the state, through its authority to tax religious entities, arms the state with the ultimate weapon to dominate religion.

The church-state equilibrium established by centuries of political consensus could easily be damaged or destroyed if the corporeal activities of religious institutions and clerics may be scrutinized from a purely secular viewpoint in an attempt to apply a multitude of administrative rules and procedures, some of which cannot be explained even by those charged with that responsibility.[19] In the instant case, however, the trial court had no qualms with ratifying the government's purely subjective analysis of the Unification Church's activities to determine whether those activities were acceptable church activities according to the government's standards. By refusing to instruct the jury that it was required to accept the Unification Church's definition of what is sincerely considered to be its religious purposes, the jury was allowed to reach its own conclusions without any stated guidelines from the court in this regard.[20] In agreeing with the trial court that this

---

[19] *See, e.g.,* I.R.C. § 501 (c)(3). S. S. Weithorn, "Frontier Issues of Tax Exemption for Religious Organizations," *Government Intervention in Religious Affairs,* 64-65 (D. M. Kelley, ed. 1982).

[20] Although, under the principles of *United States v. Ballard,* 322 U.S. 78 (1944), the state need not respect religious "beliefs" which are fraudulently or insincerely proclaimed, no such claim was made in this case. Indeed, numerous appellate decisions have explicitly or implicitly recognized the sincerity and *bona fides* of the Unification Church as a religion. *See, e.g., Holy Spirit Association [Unification Church] v. Tax Commission, supra; Unification Church v. INS,* 547 F.Supp. 623 (D.D.C. 1982).

12

instruction was unnecessary, the court of appeals stated that *Holy Spirit Association* v. *Tax Commission, supra,* to the extent relied upon by the defendant, was "inapposite." *Id.* at 1227. That case, which held that the church's own definition of its religious beliefs was controlling, *is* directly relevant to the instant proceeding. The court in that case stated that:

> [I]t is for religious bodies themselves, rather than the courts or administrative agencies, to define, by their teachings and activities, what their religion is. The courts are obliged to accept such characterization of the activities of such bodies, including that of the Church in the case before us, unless it is found to be insincere or sham. 55 N.Y.2d at 527-28.

This principle should have been applied to this case as part of the American tradition of avoiding undue entanglement between the church and government. *See, Walz* v. *Tax Commission,* 397 U.S. 664 (1970); *Surinach* v. *Pesquera de Busquets,* 604 F.2d 73, 78 (1st Cir. 1978).

This prosecution must be viewed in the broad context of an increasing intrusion of the United States government into areas previously recognized as the sacred province of individual discretion and personal right. It is our belief that the government's actions in this case, as approved in the court of appeals decision, allowed the jury to impose its own lay standards as to whether the funds in question were properly treated as the Church's or as the personal property of Reverend Moon. The ultimate result of this intrusion is an overturn of church-state equilibrium by administrative fiat and an excessive government entanglement with religion in violation of the First Amendment.

13

II. INCOME ON FUNDS CONTRIBUTED BY CHURCH MEMBERS FOR THE BENEFIT OF THE CHURCH IS NOT TAXABLE AS INCOME TO A CHURCH OFFICIAL WHO HAD DOMINION AND CONTROL OVER SUCH FUNDS UNLESS THOSE FUNDS HAVE BEEN IMPROPERLY DIVERTED AND USED PRIMARILY FOR THE OFFICIAL'S OWN BENEFIT.

Amici agree with Petitioner Moon that the donors' intent should have been the critical factor in determining tax liability in this case. As pointed out by Petitioner, in considering the taxability of property placed in the hands of individuals for a charitable or similar purpose, federal courts have applied the following theory of tax liability:

> . . . while use of a portion of the property for the recipient's personal purposes may make *that portion* taxable as his income, the remainder—so long as held idle or used for the intended purpose—is not taxable to him. Nor is any of the interest earned on those idle funds taxable to him. (Petition for Certiorari at 23.)

Had this rule been applied in this case, interest earned on the funds donated for the benefit of the Unification Church would not have been taxable to Reverend Moon.

The court's instructions, which allowed the jury to ignore the crucial issue of donors' intent, constituted reversible error. But even if one assumes *arguendo* that the donors' intent was not the controlling factor in this case, the theory of tax liability applied by the lower court was incorrect. The trial judge's instructions to the jury and the court of appeals decision approving those instructions, ignore a basic principle of tax law which should have been applied if it is assumed that the reasoning adopted by the lower courts was applicable. This principle was enunciated by this Court more than forty years ago:

> The dominant purpose of the revenue laws is the taxation of income to those who earn or otherwise create the right to receive it *and enjoy the benefit of it when paid.* *Helvering* v. *Horst,* 311 U.S. 112 (1940). (Emphasis added.)

14

The Tax Court, applying the principle in the *Horst* case, has correctly recognized that the proper basis for taxation is not only the dominion and control of property *but the enjoyment of its economic benefit. Qualley* v. *Commissioner*, 35 T.C.M. 1976-208; *see also, Dawkins* v. *Commissioner*, 238 F.2d 1974 (8th Cir. 1956).[21] However, in this case, as Judge Oakes pointed out in his dissent, Reverend Moon was indicted and the case was tried on the theory simply that Reverend Moon had dominion and control of the assets, that he thus owned them and that he should have therefore reported *interest* income earned on the *corpus* of the funds. As noted in the majority opinion, Reverend Moon was not indicted, and the case was not tried, on the theory that he had diverted to his own use funds principally given to him for Church purposes, thereby incurring liability for failure to pay taxes on the *corpus* of the funds.

The government's theory that Reverend Moon "owned" the funds is clearly incompatible with the uncontradicted fact that the funds were given to Reverend Moon to be used for the benefit of the Church. Although the legal title to the assets was held by Reverend Moon, the equitable title remained with the Church as did the right to the beneficial use of the assets, a right which was legally enforceable. *Montana Catholic Missions* v. *Missoula County*, 200 U.S. 118 (1906). Consequently, the issue which should have been addressed by the court (again, that is, if one accepts the questionable proposition that the intent of the donors was not the controlling factor) was whether Reverend Moon used funds beneficially owned by the Church primarily for his own personal benefit, resulting in his "constructive" receipt of income. In order to treat the *interest* on the funds as income to Reverend Moon, the government should have been required to prove that the *funds* were "constructively" owned by Reverend Moon.

---

[21] This Court has also recognized that although the very essence of taxable income is the accrual of some gain, profit or benefit to the taxpayer, not every benefit received by a taxpayer is necessarily taxable nor is the mere dominion over money or property decisive in all cases. *Commissioner* v. *Wilcox*, 327 U.S. 404 (1946); *see also Buder* v. *United States* 354 F.2d 941, 944 (8th Cir. 1966); *Brittingham* v. *Commissioner*, 57 T.C. 91, 100, 101 (1971) acq. 1971-2 C.B.2.

15

The court's failure to properly address the concept of personal benefit as a prerequisite to imposition of tax liability stems in part from the manner in which this case was prosecuted. The government's original indictment alleged only that Reverend Moon had "dominion and control" over the Chase accounts, and that the Tong Il stock was "issued" to Reverend Moon. By relying on the theory of dominion and control, the government apparently intended to prove that Reverend Moon had received "constructive" income, or in the case of stock, a "constructive" dividend.[22] However, under a theory of "constructive receipt," the government would have had to prove that the Reverend Moon exercised dominion and control over the funds and assets primarily for his own personal benefit, rather than for the benefit of the Church.

The government's superseding indictment did not, in response to the defendant's objection, allege that Reverend Moon "owned the assets beneficially." The new indictment simply charged that Reverend Moon "owned" the funds. Under this theory, interest earned on the funds would be taxable to Reverend Moon, regardless of whether Reverend Moon or the Church benefited from the use of the funds. This indictment effectively allowed the government to avoid the burden of proving either that Reverend Moon used the funds primarily for his own personal benefit, thereby constructively receiving income, or that Reverend Moon impropery diverted Church funds to his own use—two theories which clearly could not be supported by the record in this case.

Under the reasoning relied upon by the court of appeals, if funds are given to a recognized leader of a church by members who intend those funds to be a charitable contribution to the church—to be used for the benefit of the church—those funds may be treated as "personally" owned by that representative,

---

[22] The government's reliance on the theory of "dominion and control" to impose tax liability, represented a tacit acknowledgement by the Government that it originally believed that the funds and assets were in fact legally and equitably the property of the Church. Thus, it was necessary to allege that the funds were "constructively" owned by the Reverend Moon in order to establish tax liability for interest income earned on those funds.

16

rather than "beneficially" owned by the church. The legal consequence of "personal" ownership, as that concept is applied by the court of appeals, is that criminal liablity may be imposed on the leader of a church for failure to report interest income earned on funds donated for the benefit of the Church. This would follow irrespective of the fact that: (a) the funds were used *primarily* for the benefit of the church; (b) there was no allegation that any funds were improperly diverted for the personal benefit of the church leader; (c) the leader of the church was *not* charged with failure to pay taxes on the *corpus* of the funds (under a theory of constructive receipt); and, (d) the church leader *did pay* taxes on those funds which were used for strictly personal purposes.

In the instant case, even if the court was correct in ignoring the primary factor of donors' intent—which it was not—the court's focus should have been directed to the issue of whether the funds and assets *admittedly* under the dominion and control of Revered Moon were used primarily for the benefit of the Church or primarily for the personal benefit of Reverend Moon. To impose criminal liability on Reverend Moon, the government should have been required to prove more than the fact that the funds and stock were "personally owned"[23] by, or "belonged to,"[24] Reverend Moon.

The court's failure to address the issue of personal benefit has resulted in a decision which is incorrect according to accepted principles of tax law. If allowed to stand, this decision will have far-reaching consequences when applied to traditionally accepted practices of many religious organizations in America today, or to any taxpayer in a position of custody or trust over funds.

---

[23] The government's theory, according to the court of appeals was that "the funds he [Reverend Moon] held were his own personal property." 718 F.2d at 1229-1230.

[24] The instructions to the jury presented the issue as whether or not the funds and stock "belonged" to the Reverend Moon.

17

III. THE TEST APPLIED BY THE COURT DISCRIMINATES AGAINST RELIGION AND IMPOSES A STRICTER STANDARD OF TAX LIABILITY ON REVEREND MOON THAN THAT WHICH WOULD BE APPLIED TO A CONTROLLING SHAREHOLDER OF A CORPORATION

The circumstances under which the government has imposed tax liability on Reverend Moon are analogous to cases in which the government has attempted to impose tax liability on a controlling shareholder or officer of a corporation for expenditure of corporate funds, which the government has contended should be treated as constructive income or dividends for tax purposes. In these cases, in order to determine whether there is constructive income, the courts have consistently used a two-pronged test. First, the corporation must have conferred an economic benefit on the shareholder without expectation of repayment, *Loftin and Woodward, Inc.* v. *United States*, 577 F.2d 1206, 1214 (5th Cir. 1978); *Rapid Electric Co.* v. *Commissioner of Internal Revenue*, 61 T.C. 232, 239 (1973); *Dean* v. *Commissioner of Internal Revenue*, 57 T.C. 32, 40 (1971).[25] A second test must be met, however, because not every corporate expenditure which incidentally confers an economic benefit upon a shareholder may be characterized as a taxable constructive dividend, *Crosby* v. *United States*, 496 F.2d 1384 (5th Cir. 1974). Under this second test, income may be attributed to a shareholder only where a distribution is made *primarily* for the shareholder's personal benefit, as

---

[25] In *Diedrich* v. *Commissioner of Internal Revenue*, 643 F.2d 499, 503-504 (8th Cir. 1981), *aff'd*, 102 S.Ct. 2414 (1982) the Court stated:

> It is a well-established principle of tax law that when a taxpayer constructively receives income, he is subject to income tax liability. It makes no difference whether he receives the benefit in the form of relief of encumbrance, or in the form of relief of tax liability; in either case, *the determinative factor is the receipt of the benefit.* (Emphasis added.)

See also, Sammons v. *Commissioner*, 472 F.2d 449, 453 (5th Cir. 1972) (". . . it is essential to the existence of a dividend, actual or constructive that the stockholder receives something from the corporation"); *Sachs* v. *Commissioner*, 277 F.2d 879, 883 (8th Cir. 1960) (". . . the courts, as arbiters of the true nature of corporate payments, have consistently used as a standard the measure of receipt of economic benefit as the proper occasion for taxation").

18

opposed to the advancement of the business interests of the corporation. *Ireland* v. *United States*, 621 F.2d 731, 735 (5th Cir. 1980); *United States* v. *Gotcher*, 401 F.2d 118 (5th Cir. 1968); *W. B. Rushing* v. *Commissioner of Internal Revenue*, 52 T.C. 888, 893 (1969). This requirement of personal benefit is not obviated by the fact that a corporation is controlled or dominated by one person. *Rapid Electric Co.* v. *Commissioner of Internal Revenue, supra; W. B. Rushing* v. *Commissioner of Internal Revenue, supra.*

The application of the theory of constructive receipt of income to the instant case can be most pointedly seen in the court's decision in *Nasser* v. *United States*, 257 F. Supp. 443 (N.D. Cal. 1966). There, the court addressed the issue of whether the transfer of corporate funds to the sole shareholder and president of a company constituted dividend income to him or whether the funds were transferred to him to be used on behalf of the corporation. The corporate funds in *Nasser* were transferred directly into the shareholder's personal savings and checking accounts. In deciding that the transferred funds were not constructive dividends, the court stated:

> ". . . although Nasser's dealings with the corporation were extremely informal and although at various times Nasser had apparent unrestricted control over the funds, . . . *at no point in all the transfers involved was the overriding corporate purpose aspect of the transactions sublimated to a personal or private usage.*"

Id. at 449. (Emphasis added.) In finding that the funds were not taxable to the shareholder, the court applied the economic benefit test and concluded that the transactions primarily benefited the corporation rather than the shareholder.[26]

In this case, to determine whether the Reverend Moon was criminally liable for failure to pay taxes, the trial judge instructed the jury that the key issue was ". . . whether or not the bank accounts at the Chase Manhattan Bank and the Tong Il stock issued in Reverend Moon's name *belonged* to Reverend

---

[26] *See also, Alisa* v. *Commissioner of Internal Revenue*, ¶ 76,255 P-H Memo T.C. (1976).

19

Moon." (Emphasis added.) Among eight factors which the jury was instructed to consider in determining ownership, the court made no reference to the concept of "personal benefit." This concept was addressed only incidentally at the end of the list, when the jury was instructed to consider the "manner in which the stock and funds were administered."

The court of appeals stated that evidence was introduced by the government that Reverend Moon ". . . used funds from the account for expenditures *which the jury could have concluded* were personal in nature" and that he ". . . used the accounts in a *seemingly personal* manner. . . ." (Emphasis added.) To prove constructive receipt of the funds in a corporate context, the government would have been required to prove not that a portion of the funds were on occasion used in a "seemingly personal" manner, but that the funds were, from the Church's point of view, used *primarily* for Reverend Moon's own personal benefit rather than for the benefit of the Church.

The distinction between a standard which requires a "primarily personal" benefit test and one which requires a "seemingly personal" benefit test is as critical in this case as it is in the corporate context. As pointed out in Judge Oakes' dissent, the religious context gives this case a special color:

> . . . the taxpayer here was the founder and leader of a worldwide movement which, regardless of what the observer may think of its views or even its motives, is nevertheless on its face a religious one, the members of which regard the taxpayer as the embodiment of their faith. Because Reverend Moon was the spiritual leader of the church, the issue whether he or the church beneficially owned funds in his name was not as crystal-clear as might seem at first glance to be the case. *United States* v. *Moon*, 718 F.2d at 1242.

Any suggestion of personal benefit becomes particularly attenuated, when, as acknowledged by the trial judge, a religious organization can properly pay the living expenses of its leaders to allow them to pursue religious purposes, or may

20

even make loans to its ministers on arm's length terms.[27] In such a context, it was essential that the jury be given clear guidelines to determine whether the primary purpose of the transactions was to benefit the Church or Reverend Moon. The trial judge, however, failed to instruct the jury specifically on this point and generally on the concept of personal benefit.

The instructions under which Reverend Moon was convicted treated him far more harshly than a controlling shareholder or officer of a secular corporation would have been treated. In this way the instructions inevitably discriminated against all of those religious bodies which, like the Unification Church and the Roman Catholic Church, have systems of property ownership conferring dominion and control upon church leaders. The resulting precedent is bound to be far-reaching and deleterious to churches everywhere in the United States. This is in clear violation of the anti-establishment tenets of the Constitution.

CONCLUSION

The violation of basic principles of tax law and even more fundamental considerations of constitutional law in this case are of the deepest concern to the *amici*. *Amici* urge that the Court grant certiorari in this matter and use this case to delineate clearly and sharply the principles which government may not violate, either to erode the integrity of *bona fide* religions or to subvert constitutional safeguards designed to protect both accepted and unorthodox faiths.

---

[27] *See Morey v. Riddell*, 205 F.Supp. 918, 921 (S.D. Cal. 1962). In dismissing the argument that contributions made by members of a Church were not deductible because they were used in part for the benefit of the ministers, who received the funds as agents of the Church, the court stated:

> The individuals benefitted were the church's recognized ministers, who employed a portion of the contributions given for the use of the church to pay their living expenses. Such use of the contributions does not constitute a departure from the statutory requirement that no part of the net profits of the organization shall inure to the benefit of any individual, for the sums expended to meet the living expenses of the ministers were no part of the net profits of the church. They were monies expended to meet legitimate expenses of the church in implementing its religious purposes.

21

Respectfully submitted,

EDWARD F. CANFIELD
Counsel of Record
JOSEPH D. CRUMLISH
ROBERT E. HEGGESTAD
MARK S. WEISS

CASEY, SCOTT & CANFIELD, P.C.
420 Washington Building
1435 G Street, N.W.
Washington, D.C. 20005
(202) 783-6490
Counsel for Amici Curiae

March 25, 1984

APPENDIX

1a

APPENDIX A

UNITED STATES SENATE
Washington, D.C. 20510

_____

January 9, 1976

Mr. Donald Alexander
Commissioner
Internal Revenue Service
1111 Constitution Avenue
Washington, D.C. 20224

Dear Mr. Alexander:

A large number of my constituents have contacted me about the Unification Church headed by Mr. Sun Myung Moon. Their questions and statements raise doubt in my mind about the tax exempt status of that organization.

A few constituents writing me have sons or daughters that have been or are members of the Unification Church. Their letters are enclosed for your information. Most of those contacting me have read articles by investigative reporters and copies of those articles are attached.

As I understand, the first test for a tax exemption on religious grounds is that the group must be organized and operated exclusively for religious purposes. The information provided suggests the Unification Church may not meet this test in three ways.

Most of those contacting me question whether the organization is based on a bona fide religion or on mind control techniques. Parents of members and former members state that while initial entry into the group is clearly voluntary, the subsequent actions of members suggest the loss of any ability to make any reasoned or unguided choice about continued participation in the group. This may indicate that the organization is maintained not by religious motivation, but by the calculated eradication or erosion of each member's ability to make an

2a

alternate choice. The well-documented process of training and initiation activities appears to substantiate that the organization is based more on mind control and indoctrination than on religious faith.

Many Kansans have advised me that a major purpose of the organization is the accumulation of wealth and power and not the practice or furtherance of a religion. Former members indicate that the primary emphasis of leadership within the organization is the collection of money through the sale of various items. Members of the organization are subjected to great pressure to obtain funds, suggesting that the exclusive purpose of the organization is not a religious one, but that in fact a major goal is the accumulation of wealth.

Some statements by Mr. Moon and activities by some of his followers indicate a substantial political purpose, contrary to the requirement that the group be organized and operated exclusively for religious purposes. As described by the enclosed materials, Mr. Moon has made several statements implying political and governmental objectives. Since many members of the group apparently perceive Mr. Moon to be the embodiment of the Church, the appearance is that his stated intentions are not simply the goals of a private individual but the stated purposes of the organization. The contacts of many followers with members of Congress suggest that the organization is being operated not exclusively for religious purposes but at least to some extent for political purposes.

A second test for a tax exempt religious organization, as I understand, is that no part of its net earnings inures to the benefit of any private individual. The attached articles by investigative reporters indicate that the head of the group, Mr. Moon, leads a far more affluent life than could reasonably be expected for any clergyman. This fact, if substantiated, suggests that a substantial portion of the group's net earnings, including the sizeable wealth collected by its members, may accrue to the private holdings and benefit of Mr. Moon. Based on the reports, Mr. Moon may hold properties in this country and others.

3a

Based on the facts reported by my constituents and by articles in the public media, it appears that the tax exempt status of the Unification Church is questionable. It is my feeling, on this basis, that an audit of the organization may be warranted.

Your response would be greatly appreciated.

Sincerely yours,

/s/

BOB DOLE
United States Senator

BD:cav
Enclosures

The Catholic League for Religious
and Civil Rights

i

INDEX

iii

TABLE OF AUTHORITIES

Cases

Other Authorities

1

No. 83-1242

IN THE

Supreme Court of the United States

OCTOBER TERM, 1983

SUN MYUNG MOON, *et al., Petitioners,*

v.

UNITED STATES OF AMERICA, *Respondent.*

BRIEF FOR THE CATHOLIC LEAGUE FOR
RELIGIOUS AND CIVIL RIGHTS AS AMICUS CURIAE

Pursuant to Rule 36.1 of the Rules of this Court, the Catholic
League for Religious and Civil Rights files this brief in support of
the petition for certiorari. Consent for filing of this brief has been
obtained in writing from the attorneys of record for the parties in
this case. Their original letters are filed together with this brief.

INTEREST OF AMICUS CURIAE

The Catholic League for Religious and Civil Rights is a non-
profit corporation, national in membership, organized to promote
good will and harmonious relations in the community, to combat
all forms of religious prejudice and discrimination and to defend
the rights and sanctity of each human life. In contrast to Church
officials or agencies who address social concerns largely in their
role as teachers standing outside the secular realm and to other
associations of Catholic citizens who undertake social action as a
purpose secondary to their primary fraternal, charitable or spiritual ends, the League is an organization of Catholic citizens whose
primary purpose is to protect the religious freedom rights and
advance the just interests of Catholics within secular society. In
furtherance of this primary purpose, the League has participated
in many judicial matters in which religious liberty interests have
been at stake. The League is concerned with the impact this case

2

has on the religious liberty of the petitioners and their followers and is very concerned with the impact this decision could have on other churches, most especially the Roman Catholic Church.

STATEMENT OF THE CASE

Amicus Curiae wishes to adopt, to the extent relevant, the Statement of the Case contained in the petition for certiorari.

Amicus Curiae further wishes to emphasize that the positions taken in this matter do not stem from any agreement with the theological premises of the religious movement led by petitioners. Indeed, our differences with Reverend Moon's theology are very significant. Rather, our concern is only with the unconstitutional treatment Reverend Moon has received and the potential deleterious effect the decision below could have on all churches, including the Roman Catholic Church.

SUMMARY OF ARGUMENT

The jury's decision below required the jury to determine whether certain property belonged to Reverend Moon or the Unification Church. In making this decision, the jury was permitted to render, at least impliedly, a determination that the property was not used for "religious purposes." This determination was made with few clear standards and was made neither in deference to the church's explanations concerning religious purpose nor clearly recognized neutral principles of law. Such an unguided jury determination on this issue runs afoul of the constitutional requirements that government avoid excessive entanglement with religion and respect religion's free exercise. The requirement that courts avoid doctrinal determinations, either through deference to the church's explanations or the use of neutral principles of law, is applicable whether the government determination involved resolves an internal property dispute, decides whether a church is entitled to a tax exemption, or determines whether property is held for religious purposes in a federal tax criminal prosecution.

The constitutional infirmity just elucidated is one which could have an impact on religions other than the one involved in this matter. A specific example of a church which could be adversely

3

affected by this precedent is the Roman Catholic Church. Like Unification Church leaders, Catholic leaders, such as bishops, often hold church property in their own name. To be sure, the Catholic Church has a highly developed body of canon law applicable to property questions. Were a court to defer to this body of canon law, a Catholic bishop would not find himself liable for taxes in factual situations similar to this case. However, the largely unlimited jury inquiry into religious purposes licensed by the decision below gives no assurance that courts would treat a Catholic bishop in such a deferential manner. The possibility of such adverse effect indicates that the issues involved in this matter have implications extending far beyond the involved parties and require resolution by this Court.

REASONS FOR GRANTING THE PETITION
I.

THE JURY'S *AD HOC* SUBSTITUTION OF ITS VIEWS OF "RELIGIOUS PURPOSES" FOR THOSE OF A CHURCH IMPERMISSIBLY ENTANGLED GOVERNMENT IN RELIGION AND IMPAIRED FREE EXERCISE OF RELIGION.

In its decision below, the jury determined that certain property was owned personally by Reverend Moon rather than by the church he heads. In making this determination the jury, at least implicitly, determined that these assets were used for personal rather than religious purposes.[1] This determination was made with few clear standards, certainly was not in deference to the church's position,[2] and was not an application of any clearly recognized neutral principles of law.

Amicus asserts that this type of jury determination has the constitutionally impermissible effect of substituting the jury's views of a religious organization's purposes for those of the organization and its adherents. While the applicable constitutional analysis is spelled out more fully in the *amicus curiae* brief filed on behalf

---

[1] *See* App. 25.

[2] *See id.*

4

of the Center for Judicial Studies by Prof. Charles E. Rice,[3] the basics of this analysis are outlined here.

Under *United States v. Ballard*, 322 U.S. 78, 86-87 (1944), a court is to avoid determinations considering the truth of a church's doctrinal positions, and may only inquire as to whether these doctrinal positions are adhered to in good faith by the church and its followers. The same constitutional policy of avoidance of judicial determination of questions of religious doctrine can be said to underlie this Court's resolution of internal disputes over church property such as *Jones v. Wolf*, 443 U.S. 595, 602-604 (1979), and *Serbian Orthodox Diocese v. Milivojevich*, 426 U.S. 696, 708-712 (1976), pursuant to the establishment clause's mandate that government avoid excessive entanglement with religion. These decisions require avoidance of the resolution of doctrinal issues either through deference to a church's internal decisions,[4] or the application of neutral principles of law capable of avoiding doctrinal issues.[5] In both of these decisions, it was not the fact of an internal property dispute which raised the specter of unconstitutional excessive entanglement, just as in the New York Court of Appeals' decision in *Holy Spirit Association [Unification Church] v. Tax Commission*, 55 N.Y.2d 512, 527-28 (1982), it was not the fact of a real property tax exemption issue which raised the question of contravention of the religion clauses. Rather, in all of these cases the preeminent danger sought to be avoided was constitutionally impermissible judicial resolution of questions of religious doctrine. Judicial determination of these doctrinal issues in a federal tax criminal prosecution is every bit as unconstitutional as determination of such doctrinal issues in internal property disputes or state real property tax exemption proceedings.

However, precisely such a constitutionally impermissible resolution of questions of religious doctrine was undertaken by the jury in this matter. This resolution was undertaken without any deference to the doctrinal views held in good faith by members

---

[3] *Amicus* Catholic League for Religious and Civil Rights supports fully the analysis made by Prof. Rice.

[4] See *Serbian Eastern Orthodox Diocese v. Milovojevich*, 426 U.S. at 724-725.

[5] See *Jones v. Wolf*, 443 U.S. at 604.

5

of this church. Indeed, this determination was made with little consideration of these views. Further, the jury's determination was made without any clearly explicit guidance from the court concerning "neutral principles" capable of avoiding the resolution of doctrinal issues. Thus, the court of appeals' approval of such a free-wheeling jury determination impairs the religion clauses' important purpose of avoiding judicial determinations of religious doctrine and is constitutionally impermissible.

II.

PERMISSION OF SUCH CONSTITUTIONALLY IMPERMISSIBLE JURY DETERMINATIONS COULD ADVERSELY AFFECT OTHER CHURCHES, INCLUDING THE ROMAN CATHOLIC CHURCH.

When an action violative of the religion clauses adversely affects even a single individual, such action should be corrected. However, when the application of a precedent created by such an action could penalize religious groups other than those immediately involved, its correction becomes even more urgent. The licensing of basically unguided jury determinations concerning funds' religious purposes, created by the decision below, presents exactly the kind of constitutional violation which must be corrected because of its detrimental impact on other religious movements.

Amicus curiae is both most familiar and most concerned with the adverse impact this decision might have on the Roman Catholic Church. As was the case in the Unification Church, Catholic religious leaders, such as bishops, often hold church property in their own names.[6] This is consistent with the canon law premise that, "In all juridical transactions of the diocese, the diocesan Bishop acts in the person of the diocese." Canon 393, The Code of Canon Law (1983).

---

[6] In these situations the bishop is often considered a "corporation sole." See Cauper and Ellis, "Religious Corporations and the Law," 71 Mich. L. Rev. 1499, 1523-24, 1536, 1540-41 (1973); P. Dignan, A History of the Legal Incorporation of Catholic Church Property in the United States (1784-1932) 267 (1935).

6

A Catholic bishop holding church property in his name potentially faces the same type of federal tax prosecution as befell
Reverend Moon. However, a Catholic bishop could point to a
highly developed body of canon law applicable to his situation.
Specifically, the bishop could point to Canon 1267, section 1 of
The Code of Canon Law (1983), which provides: "Unless the
contrary is clear, offerings made to Superiors or administrators of
any ecclesiastical juridical person, even a private one, are presumed to have been made to the juridical person itself." Further,
he could point to Canon 1254 of *The Code of Canon Law* (1983),
which provides:

§ 1. The Catholic Church has the inherent right independently of any secular power, to acquire, retain, administer and alienate temporal goods, in pursuit of its
proper objectives.

§ 2. These proper objectives are principally the regulation of divine worship, the provision of fitting support for
the clergy and other ministers, and the carrying out of
works of the sacred apostolate and of charity, especially
for the needy.

These canon law provisions make clear that the maintenance
of priests, such as a bishop, is a religious purpose, and ought to
place a Catholic bishop outside the scope of the type of federal
tax prosecution involved in this case. But, under the decision below, what deference would a jury be required to give canon law?
Would canon law be deferred to, or would the jury be permitted
to make its own determination as to religious purpose without
even giving consideration to canon law? Under the decision below, these questions could not be answered with any certainty.
Thus, the constitutional infirmity involved in the jury's decision
could adversely affect the Catholic Church, despite its highly
developed canon law, in much the same way as it would even
more certainly affect other churches which lack a developed
canon law. The far-reaching potential effects of the jury's unconstitutional determination should, thus, lead this Court to grant the
petition for certiorari.

7

CONCLUSION

For the foregoing reasons, the writ of certiorari should issue and the convictions of the petitioners should be reversed.

Respectfully submitted,

STEVEN FREDERICK MCDOWELL
Catholic League for Religious
    and Civil Rights
1100 West Wells Street
Milwaukee, Wisconsin   53233
(414) 289-0170

*Counsel of Record for
Amicus Curiae*

THOMAS PATRICK MONAGHAN
Catholic League for Religious
    and Civil Rights
1100 West Wells Street
Milwaukee, Wisconsin   53233
(414) 289-0170

Attorney for Amicus Curiae

FEBRUARY, 1984

The Center for Judicial Studies

i

TABLE OF CONTENTS

ii

TABLE OF AUTHORITIES

iii

Table of Authorities Continued

iv

Table of Authorities Continued

IN THE

Supreme Court of the United States

OCTOBER TERM, 1983

———

No. 83-1242

———

SUN MYUNG MOON *and* TAKERU KAMIYAMA,

Petitioners,

v.

UNITED STATES OF AMERICA,

Respondent.

———

On Petition For Certiorari To Thé United States
Court Of Appeals For The Second Circuit

———

BRIEF AMICUS CURIAE OF THE CENTER FOR JUDICIAL STUDIES IN SUPPORT OF PETITION FOR CERTIORARI

———

1

INTEREST OF THE *AMICUS CURIAE*

The Center for Judicial Studies, 632 Constitution Ave., N.E., Washington, D.C. 20002, is a tax-exempt, public policy institution founded in 1982 for the purpose of promoting judicial and legal reform. The Director of the Center is Dr. James McClellan. The Center is the only educational and public policy organization in the United States which focuses exclusively on the problem of judicial activism and seeks to confine the power of the federal judiciary within the bounds envisioned for it by the framers of the Constitution and of the Fourteenth Amendment.

The decision of the Court of Appeals in this case would confer on the courts a dangerous power to define the content of religious belief even contrary to the good faith profession of the believers as to what they themselves believe. The Center for Judicial Studies maintains that the religious liberty protected by the First Amendment will be seriously diminished if the principle is established that courts can tell sincere believers what they believe and can define authentically religious activities as secular so as to deprive them of the protections of the Religion Clauses of the First Amendment. The Center, therefore, is interested in this petition for certiorari because it presents an opportunity for a clarification of the extent of judicial power in an important and sensitive area.

In filing this brief, the Center for Judicial Studies does not imply that it agrees with the beliefs of the Unification Church. Nor does it offer any endorsement of Reverend Sun Myung Moon as a religious leader or an individual. Rather, the concern of the Center is exclusively with the constitutional issues involved in this case. In the view of the Center, they involve an unjustified expansion of judicial power and present a significant threat to the liberty of all religious groups.

SUMMARY OF ARGUMENT

In *United States* v. *Ballard*, 322 U.S. 78 (1944), it was established that, although courts may inquire into the good faith with which religious beliefs are held, the First Amend-

2

ment forbids a judicial inquiry into the truth or falsity of those beliefs. If the theory adopted by the Court of Appeals in this case were to be confirmed as the law, it would obliterate the *Ballard* principle and would invite an oppressive entanglement of government with religion. The taxability of the income to Reverend Moon depended on the ownership of the assets. Did they belong to him or to the Unification Church? But the answer to that question depended on whether they were given to him for religious purposes and whether his use of those assets was in accord with those purposes. The jury, however, was allowed to decide that issue without regard to the Church's own view of its purposes. Moreover, the question of what constitutes the religious purposes and activities of the Church is itself a religious question. If the jury decided that those purposes and activities were not believed by the Church to be religious, then the jury was telling the believers what they believed, despite their own good faith belief to the contrary. Such a result would violate the *Ballard* principle. If, on the other hand, the jury acknowledged that the Church believed those purposes and activities to be part of its religion, but then found instead that they were secular, then the result would involve the sort of excessive entanglement of government with religion that is forbidden by the First Amendment. Indeed, it is fair to construe the Court of Appeals' ruling as authorizing a regulation of religious belief rather than merely of conduct, contrary to the settled principle that the freedom of religious belief is an absolute right.

The trial court should have instructed the jury either to accept the decision of the Church leadership as to the content of its beliefs and purposes or to decide that question according to neutral principles of law. The power conferred upon the jury in this case is not justified by the precedents which allow the courts to distinguish religious from secular activities in some situations.

The assumption by courts of an unguided power to define what is secular and religious, contrary to the good faith belief of the Church in question, will result in a reduction of the religious sphere protected by the First Amendment, through the

3

progressive definition of more and more activities as secular. This prospect is especially real in light of the now established status of the income tax exemption under Section 501(c)(3) of the Internal Revenue Code as a subsidy.

Review by the Supreme Court of the decision of the Court of Appeals in this case is essential to clarify the legitimacy of judicial inquiry into the content of religious belief and judicial definition of what is secular and what is religious.

ARGUMENT

I. **The Jury Was Permitted To Make A Doctrinal Judgment As To The Purposes Of The Unification Church Without Even Taking Into Account The Sincere Beliefs Of The Adherents Of That Church, And The Jury Was Given A Blank Check To Decide Which Purposes And Activities Of That Church Were Religious And Which Were Secular.**

The decision of the Court of Appeals in this case permits the government to tell the adherents of a religious belief what they believe. It also permits the government to decide, without effective limitation, which beliefs and activities are religious and which are secular, thus opening the door to arbitrary official determinations excluding authentically religious activities from the protections afforded by the preferred status of religious freedom under the First Amendment.

To appreciate the implications of this case for religious freedom, it is important to understand what it does *not* involve. It does not involve any claim of exemption on religious grounds from the generally applicable rules of civil and criminal law. It therefore does not involve the principles established in such cases as *Sherbert* v. *Verner* 374 U.S. 398 (1963), *Wisconsin* v. *Yoder*, 406 U.S. 205 (1972), and *Thomas* v. *Review Board*, 450 U.S. 707 (1981). Nor does this case present any claim of religious exemption from generally applicable tax laws. *See United States* v. *Lee*, 455 U.S. 252 (1982). Nor does it involve the issue of whether and under what conditions religious organizations may qualify for exemption from federal taxation. *See*

4

Christian Echoes National Ministry v. *United States*, 470 F.2d 849 (10th Cir.), *cert. denied*, 414 U.S. 864 (1973); *Bob Jones University* v. *United States*, 103 S.Ct. 2017 (1983).

"The central issue for the jury to decide," said the Court of Appeals, "was whether the Tong Il stock and Chase Manhattan Bank accounts belonged to the Church or to Moon personally." *United States* v. *Moon*, 718 F.2d 1210, 1233 (2d Cir. 1983). Or, as Judge Oakes pointed out in his dissent, "the key issue was whether the funds were given to Moon for his own use or for that of his international church movement, and whether, even though some of the funds were utilized for his own living purposes, the donors intended to permit such use." *Id.* at 1243. The issue, therefore, was whether money was given to Moon for a religious purpose and whether his use of that money was within that religious purpose. The central importance of the determination of religious purpose can be seen from the trial court's charge to the jury:

> If you find that the funds in the Chase accounts were the property of International Unification Church Movement or were held in trust by Moon for the International Unification Church Movement and used *for church purposes* and that the interest on those funds also belonged to the International Unification Church Movement and were used for it, then that interest would not be taxable income to Moon." T6583-84[1] (emphasis added).

By what criteria could the jury properly determine what those "church purposes" were and whether Moon's use of the funds was in accord with those purposes, except in light of the Unification Church's own profession of those purposes? The jury was told that "[y]ou should consider all the evidence in making your determination." T6585. But the charge did not instruct the jury as to how it was to determine the "purposes" of the Church. The prosecution, moreover, objected when defense counsel attempted to elicit testimony as to Reverend Moon's state of mind to show the belief of the Unification

---

[1] Citations to the trial transcript will be denoted "T____".

5

Church's members as to the "relationship between church and business." T5255. The objection was sustained on the ground that Reverend Moon's state of mind on the relation between the Church and business was not "a direct issue in the case at all." T5256-57. The trial court also commented that if defense counsel were to introduce evidence on the subject, "you [would be] opening a door to something you wouldn't care to open the door to." T5257. The prosecutor indicated his desire to counter the introduction of religious defenses by exploring, in front of the jurors, "negative things about the church." T5760. Thus, defense counsel was repeatedly warned by the trial court that efforts to offer religious explanations of various church relationships and practices would "inadvertently open some doors" to the introduction of damaging evidence by the government. T3044; see T3042-45, 4818-20, 5257, 5735, 5759-60. The defense was thus deterred from offering more evidence than it did on the beliefs and purposes of the Unification Church due to the prospect that the prosecution would respond by introducing "negative things about the church" in a possibly inflammatory way that would fatally prejudice the defendant's case before the jury. As defense counsel was forced to conclude, "if your Honor's feeling is that my asking [a religion-oriented] question opens the door to the kind of thing they are talking about, then I feel precluded from asking the question." T4820.

The trial court did note that one fundamental issue raised by the case was "whether Moon can simultaneously be a business and a religion", T5520, and the court acknowledged that the Church members who gave the funds, in their own view, "thought they were working for a higher cause. They thought they were advancing the Unification Church's movement internationally. But when [the government] say[s] in effect it doesn't matter what they thought they were accomplishing, if he took these monies and spent them on his own businesses and on his own goals he was not doing so as a religious leader and you come back to the same question, can he simultaneously be a businessman and a religion." T5521. The trial court, however, refused defendant's request to charge the jury that, according to the Church's theology, Moon is the embodiment of the faith.

6

T6119. This belief would not make Reverend Moon's every act religious. Nor would it have dictated the jury's conclusion. But there is no way that the jury could have properly decided whether the assets were given to Moon for religious purposes and whether his use of them was within those purposes, except in light of the Church's own definition of its creed and of Moon's central status therein.

The trial court not only failed to instruct the jury that it was bound to accept the Church's own definition of the content of its beliefs and purposes; it also left the jury entirely free to follow its own unguided judgment in this regard. The jury was permitted "to find that if [Moon] used the Chase funds for his own business investments or personal ends—that is for other than religious purposes—such use would indicate the lack of a trust relationship." 718 F.2d at 1226. The Court of Appeals declared that "in this criminal proceeding the jury was not bound to accept the Unification Church's definition of what constitutes a religious use or purpose." Id. at 1227. But what criteria was the jury supposed to use in making this determination? In a secular light, certain purposes and activities might appear to be merely of a personal or business nature. But in light of the sincerely held tenets of the Church, those purposes and activities could be seen to be religious. The jury was not only not bound by those tenets, it was not required even to take them into account.

The problem is compounded by the charge to the jury that, "It is also your duty to appraise the evidence calmly and objectively and to reach your verdict in this case *without* prejudice or sympathy or *any consideration of* race, *religion* or ethnic origin. I have told you before and I repeat it again, that *the* race, *religion* and ethic origin *of the defendants is of no consequence whatever.* They are on trial in an American court before American jurors under the Constitution of the United States and *considerations of* race or *religion must have no part in your deliberations.*" T6538 (emphasis added). While this statement was evidently intended to warn the jurors to be "fair and impartial," T6538, and to avoid religious prejudice, the unqualified command to the jurors to avoid "any consideration

7

of . . . religion", *id.*, reinforces the conclusion that the jury's decision could have been made, for all we know, according to wholly secular standards of the jury's own devising without even any consideration of the sincerely held position of the Church as to what its own religious beliefs, purposes and activities were.

There are two possibilities: First, and despite the absence of any evidence of insincerity on the part of the Church or its members, the jury could have decided that the Church did not even believe that the purposes and activities in question were religious. If so, the jury was telling the members of the Church *what* they believe, despite their good faith protestations to the contrary. Second, the jury could have decided that, even though the Church did believe that those purposes and activities were religious, they were in fact merely secular. But the question of whether a belief or activity is part of a particular religion is itself a religious question. In either alternative, whether the jury found that the members of the Church did not really believe what they claimed to believe or that what they believed to be religious was not so, the verdict is contrary to the seminal principle of *United States* v. *Ballard*, 322 U.S. 78, 87 (1944). Under that principle, the courts may determine in an appropriate case whether a religious belief is held in good faith, but the First Amendment forbids a judicial inquiry into the truth or falsity of religious beliefs. Moreover, "[t]he articulation of the Supreme Court in foreclosing judicial inquiry into the truth or falsity of religious beliefs is equally applicable to judicial inquiry as to the content of religious beliefs." *Holy Spirit Association* v. *Tax Commission*, 55 N.Y.2d 512, 522, 435 N.E. 2d 662, 450 N.Y.S.2d 292 (1982).

II. **The Unguided Decision By The Jury As To The Content Of The Church's Beliefs And As To Whether Its Activities Were Religious Or Secular Results In An Unconstitutional "Excessive Government Entanglement With Religion."**

The determination by the jury that the purposes and activities at issue were secular rather than religious is a clear in-

8

stance of the "excessive government entanglement with religion," *Walz* v. *Tax Commission*, 397 U.S. 664, 674 (1970), forbidden by the First Amendment. "[T]he Supreme Court has been especially sensitive to an entanglement which requires the state to distinguish between and thus determine what is religious and what is secular." *Surinach* v. *Pesquera de Busquets*, 604 F.2d 73, 78 (1st Cir. 1979) In *Lemon* v. *Kurtzman*, 403 U.S. 602 (1971), the Court found such an entanglement in the Rhode Island school aid program because it could require "the government to examine the school's records in order to determine how much of the total expenditures is attributable to secular education and how much to religious activity. This kind of state inspection and evaluation of the religious content of a religious organization is fraught with the sort of entanglement that the Constitution forbids. It is a relationship pregnant with dangers of excessive government direction of church schools and hence of churches." *Id.* at 620.

The Court in *Widmar* v. *Vincent*, 454 U.S. 263, 265 (1981), held that a University of Missouri regulation barring the use of facilities by student groups "for purposes of religious worship or religious teaching" violated the Free Speech and Free Exercise clauses. The Court noted that a contrary result "would require the university — and ultimately the courts — to inquire into the significance of words and practices to different religious faiths, and in varying circumstances of the same faith. Such inquiries would tend inevitably to entangle the State with religion in a manner forbidden by our cases. *E.g.*, *Walz* v. *Tax Comm'n* . . ." *Id.* at 269 n.6. The *Widmar* Court further noted that "the University would risk greater 'entanglement' by attempting to enforce its exclusion of 'religious worship' and 'religious speech.' *See Chess* v. *Widmar*, 635 F.2d 1310, 1318 (8th Cir. 1980). Initially, the University would need to determine which words and activities fall within 'religious worship and religious teaching.' This alone could prove 'an impossible task in an age where many and various beliefs meet the constitutional definition of religion.' *O'Hair* v. *Andrus*, 613 F.2d 931, 936 (D.C. Cir. 1979) (footnote omitted). . . ." *Id.* at 272 n.11. The Supreme Court exhibited a similar concern in *NLRB*

9

v. *Catholic Bishop of Chicago*, 440 U.S. 490 (1979), where the Court observed that a construction of the governing statute so as to authorize the National Labor Relations Board's "exercise of jurisdiction over teachers in church-supported schools would implicate the guarantees of the Religion Clauses," *id.* at 507, because, among other reasons, "the schools had responded that their [alleged unfair labor practices] were mandated by their religious creeds. The resolution of such charges by the Board, in many instances, will necessarily involve inquiry into the good faith of the position asserted by the clergy-administrators *and its relationship to the school's religious mission. It is not only the conclusions that may be reached by the Board which may impinge on rights guaranteed by the Religion Clauses, but also the very process of inquiry leading to findings and conclusions.*" *Id.* at 502 (emphasis added); *see also,. Heritage Village Church* v. *State*, 299 N.C. 399, 263 S.E.2d 726, 735-36 (1980).

The principle that should have been applied by the Court of Appeals in the instant case was spelled out by the New York Court of Appeals in its 1982 ruling in *Holy Spirit Association* v. *Tax Commission*, 55 N.Y.2d 512, 435 N.E. 2d 662, 450 N.Y.S.2d 662 (1982). The court held that, in determining the eligibility of the Holy Spirit Association for the Unification of World Christianity [otherwise known as the Unification Church] for real property tax exemption, the taxing authorities were bound to accept the Association's own definition of the content of its religious beliefs. The court spelled out the limited role of the courts in matters of belief:

> When, as here, particular purposes and activities of a religious organization are claimed to be other than religious, the civil authorities may engage in but two inquiries: Does the religious organization assert that the challenged purposes and activities are religious, and is that assertion bona fide? Neither the courts nor the administrative agencies of the State or its subdivisions may go behind the declared content of religious beliefs any more than they may examine into their validity. This principle was firmly established in *Watson* v. *Jones* (13 Wall [80 U.S.] 679, 728) when the Supreme Court declared

10

that "[t]he law knows no heresy, and is committed to the support of no dogma, the establishment of no sect."

The *Holy Spirit* court criticized the tax authorities and the lower court because "each asserted the right of civil authorities to examine the creed and theology of the [Unification] Church and to factor out what in its or his considered judgment are the peripheral political and economic aspects, in contradistinction to what was acknowledged to be the essentially religious component. Each then took the view that beliefs and activities which could be objectively [sic] accurately described by knowledgeable outsiders as 'political' and 'economic' were by that fact precluded from being classified as 'religious.' As stated, it is not the province of civil authorities to indulge in such distillation as to what is to be denominated religious and what political or economic. *It is for religious bodies themselves, rather than the courts or administrative agencies, to define, by their teachings and activities, what their religion is. The courts are obliged to accept such characterization of the activities of such bodies, including that of the Church in the case before us, unless it is found to be insincere or sham."* 55 N.Y.2d at 527-28 (emphasis added).

The Court of Appeals in this case repudiated the approach taken by the *Holy Spirit* court and concluded that "in this criminal proceeding the jury was not bound to accept the Unification Church's definition of what constitutes a religious use or purpose. *Holy Spirit Association* v. *Tax Commission,* 55 N.Y.2d 512, 518 . . . (1982), is inapposite. That case dealt with the inquiry that a court may conduct when determining whether a religious organization is entitled to a real property tax exemption under New York law. The principles there enunciated upon which appellant relies are relevant in that context and do not serve as precedent in a federal criminal tax prosecution." 718 F.2d at 1227.

On the contrary, the "principles . . . enunciated" in the *Holy Spirit* case are basic ones of universal application. They forbid the government to prescribe, whether directly by positive command or indirectly by a process of exclusion, the content of religious belief. It is a special cause for concern that the Court

11

of Appeals in this case appears to be carving out for federal tax prosecutions a special status liberated from the restrictions of the Religion Clauses.

III. The Entanglement With Religion In This Case Is Not Justified By The Precedents Allowing Courts To Distinguish Religious From Secular Activities In Some Situations.

This case is not governed by the precedents sanctioning in some situations a threshold or otherwise limited inquiry as to whether certain beliefs or activities are religious or secular. Such an inquiry is inescapable in certain cases, for example, where the issue is the eligibility of a group for a subsidy. "In *Board of Education* v. *Allen*, 392 U.S. 236 (1968), . . . the Court upheld the loan of secular textbooks to parents or children attending nonpublic schools; though state officials were required to determine whether particular books were or were not secular, the system was held not to violate the Establishment Clause." *Mueller* v. *Allen*, 103 S. Ct. 3062, 3071 (1983). And the Court has sustained a program of aid to church-related colleges where "[s]uch inspection as may be necessary to ascertain that the facilities are devoted to secular education is minimal. . . ." *Tilton* v. *Richardson*, 403 U.S. 672, 687 (1971).

"There is no exact science in gauging the entanglement of church and state. The wording of the test, which speaks of 'excessive entanglement,' itself makes that clear." *Roemer* v. *Board of Public Works of Md.*, 426 U.S. 736, 766 (1976) (emphasis in original). The cases sanctioning a threshold or otherwise limited inquiry as to whether the purposes or activities of a group or its personnel are religious, in deciding, for example, whether a creed is entitled to recognition by prison authorities as a religion (*see Africa* v. *Pennsylvania*, 662 F.2d 1025 (3d Cir. 1982); *see also, Malnak* v. *Yogi*, 592 F.2d 197 (3d Cir. 1979), holding that Transcendental Meditation is a "religion" and therefore cannot be taught in public schools) or whether a group is entitled to religious tax exemption (*see, e.g., Christian Echoes National Ministry* v. *United States*, 470 F.2d 849 (10th Cir. 1973)), do not seriously threaten religious freedom.

12

Such inquiries are inescapable and tolerable in the limited areas where they are allowed. For example, tax exemptions are a legislative subsidy provided as "a matter of grace [that] Congress can, of course, disallow . . . as it chooses"; and the burden is on the taxpayer to establish that it is entitled to the exemption. *Regan* v. *Taxation with Representation*, 103 S.Ct. 1997, 2003 (1983); *Bob Jones University* v. *United States*, 103 S.Ct. 2017 (1983). "Both tax exemptions and tax-deductibility are a form of subsidy that is administered through the tax system. A tax exemption has much the same effect as a cash grant to the organization of the amount of tax it would have to pay on its income." *Regan* v. *Taxation with Representation*, 103 S.Ct. 1997, 2000 (1983). Under the terms of Section 501(c)(3) of the Internal Revenue Code, the courts are mandated, in determining eligibilty for exemption, to distinguish between religious purposes or activities and those which do not qualify, including those which are political or inure to the benefit of any private individual.

Abuse is prevented in such cases by the use of a broad concept of religion and of religious purpose. See *Church of the Chosen People* v. *United States*, 548 F. Supp. 1247, 1252-53 (D. Minn., 1982). The term "religion" must be broadly construed for purposes of the Establishment and Free Exercise clauses. *Torcaso* v. *Watkins*, 367 U.S. 488, 495 (1961); *Abington School District* v. *Schempp*, 374 U.S. 203, 220 (1963). In *United States* v. *Seeger*, 380 U.S. 163, 176 (1965), the Court held that the statutory term, "religious training and belief," includes "all sincere religious beliefs which are based upon a power or being, or upon a faith, to which all else is subordinate or upon which all else is ultimately dependent. The test might be stated in these words: A sincere and meaningful belief which occupies in the life of the possessor a place parallel to that filled by the God of those admittedly qualifying for the exemption. . . ." The task of the courts, in the view of the *Seeger* Court, "is to decide whether the beliefs proposed by a registrant are sincerely held and whether they are, *in his own scheme of things*, religious." 380 U.S. *Id.* at 185 (emphasis added). And in *Welsh* v. *United States*, 398 U.S. 333, 339 (1970), the Court

13

declared that "the central consideration in determining whether the registrant's beliefs are religious is whether these beliefs play the role of a religion and function as a religion in the registrant's life." The Court said that this definition would include purely moral or ethical beliefs "held with the strength of traditional religious convictions," *id.* at 340, but it would not include beliefs which do "not rest at all upon moral, ethical, or religious principle but instead [rest] solely upon considerations of policy, pragmatism, or expediency." *Id.* at 342-43. While the Court has not laid down a firm definition of "religion," these cases establish that the term is broadly construed. Of course, in this case there is no dispute about the fact that the International Unification Church Movement is a religion. Nor is there any doubt that the purposes and activities at issue are, in the church's "own scheme of things, religious." *See United States v. Seeger*, 380 U.S. at, 185. They include investments and other financial transactions, but they are no less religious on that account. "The appellants' ability to make decisions concerning the recruitment, allocation and expenditure of their funds is intimately bound up in their mission of religious education and thus is protected by the free exercise clause of the First Amendment." *Surinach v. Pesquera de Busquets*, 604 F.2d 73, 78 (1st Cir. 1979).

As long as a very broad concept of "religion" is employed, the precedents allowing threshold or otherwise limited inquiries, where inescapably necessary, into the religious or secular character of a belief or activity, involve only a minimal intrusion of government into religion. Indeed, the satisfaction of the very broad criterion of "religion" adopted in such cases as *Seeger* and *Welsh* is an indirect measure of assessing the good faith of a claim that a belief or activity is religious. However, once the minimum requirement for what constitutes a religion is met, the *Ballard* prohibition against judicial inquiry into the truth or falsity of religious belief must apply in all its rigor. *United States v. Ballard*, 322 U.S. 78 (1944). The *Ballard* principle works if we accept a minimal threshold criterion for "religion" and thereafter avoid all official determinations as to the content of sincerely held beliefs. Unfortunately, in this

14

case, the jury was permitted to roam at large with no instructions as to how they were to decide these questions of religious belief and purpose.

IV. The Trial Court Should Have Accepted The Decision Of The Leadership Of The Unification Church As To The Beliefs And Purposes Of That Church Or Should Have Applied Neutral Principles Of Law To Resolve The Question Of The Ownership Of The Assets In Accord With The Desires Of The Members Of The Church, So As To Avoid A Judicial Decision As To The Content Of Religious Belief.

The importance of keeping courts out of the business of deciding doctrinal issues has been repeatedly recognized by the Supreme Court:

> But First Amendment values are plainly jeopardized when church property litigation is made to turn on the resolution by civil courts of controversies over religious doctrine and practice. If civil courts undertake to resolve such controversies in order to adjudicate the property dispute, the hazards are ever present of inhibiting the free development of religious doctrine and of implicating secular interests in matters of purely ecclesiastical concern. Because of these hazards, the First Amendment enjoins the employment of organs of government for essentially religious purposes, *Abington School District* v. *Schempp*, 374 U.S. 203 (1963); the Amendment therefore commands civil courts to decide church property disputes without resolving underlying controversies over religious doctrine. . . . Thus, the departure-from-doctrine element of the Georgia implied trust theory requires the civil court to determine matters at the very core of a religion—the interpretation of particular church doctrines and the importance of those doctrines to the religion. Plainly, the First Amendment forbids civil courts from playing such a role. *Presbyterian Church* v. *Hull Church*, 393 U.S. 440, 449-50 (1969).

This case is, in a sense, an intra-church property dispute, involving the issue of who owns the Chase accounts and the Tong Il stock: Reverend Moon or the Church? That issue in turn depends upon whether the property was given and used

15

for religious purposes of the Unification Church. In determining those religious purposes, the court should have deferred to the decision of the Church leadership, *Watson* v. *Jones*, 80 U.S. (13 Wall.) 679 (1871), or should have applied neutral principles of law to "ensure that a dispute over the ownership of church property will be resolved in accord with the desires of the members." *Jones* v. *Wolf*, 443 U.S. 595, 604 (1979). In any event, both the *Watson* approach and the neutral principles approach of *Jones* v. *Wolf* are subject to the limitation that the courts must avoid the decision of doctrinal questions:

> In other words, the use of the *Watson* approach is consonant with the prohibitions of the First Amendment only if the appropriate church governing body can be determined without the resolution of doctrinal questions and without extensive inquiry into religious policy. *Maryland and Virginia Eldership* v. *Church of God*, 396 U.S. 367, 370 (1970) (per curiam) (concurring opinion of Justices Brennan, Douglas and Marshall).

> The neutral-principles method, at least as it has evolved in Georgia, requires a civil court to examine certain religious documents, such as a church constitution, for language of trust in favor of the general church. In undertaking such an examination, a civil court must take special care to scrutinize the document in purely secular terms, and not to rely on religious precepts in determining whether the document indicates that the parties have intended to create a trust. In addition, there may be cases where the deed, the corporate charter, or the constitution of the general church incorporates religious concepts in the provisions relating to the ownership of property. If in such a case the interpretation of the instruments of ownership would require the civil court to resolve a religious controversy, then the court must defer to the resolution of the doctrinal issue by the authoritative ecclesiastical body. *Serbian Orthodox Diocese*, 426 U.S. at 709. (*Jones* v. *Wolf*, 443 U.S. 595, 604 (1979); *see also*, *Korn* v. *Rabbinical Council of California*, — Cal. App. 3d —, 195 Cal. Rptr. 910, 913, 914-15 (1983), holding that "the court lacks jurisdiction" to decide "controversies concerning religious practice and doctrine.")

16

"*Kedroff* v. *St. Nicholas Cathedral*, 344 U.S. 94, 116 (1952), stated that religious freedom encompasses the 'power [of religious bodies] to decide for themselves, free from state interference, matters of church government *as well as those of faith and doctrine.'* " *Serbian Orthodox Diocese* v. *Milivojevich*, 426 U.S. at, 721-22 (emphasis added). Unfortunately, instead of deferring to the Unification Church's leadership as to the content of the Church's religious beliefs and purposes, and instead of formulating a neutral principles approach that would avoid the determination of doctrinal questions, the Court of Appeals in this case dismissed the "neutral principles" doctrine as having "no application to the facts of this case," 718 F.2d at 1228, and allowed the jury to make its own determination, pursuant to criteria unknown, as to the content of the Church's beliefs and purposes. If the jury decided as it did on the strength of its own determination of the content of the Unification Church's beliefs, the jury was sitting as an ecclesiastical rather than a civil tribunal in making a doctrinal judgment contrary to the belief of the Church itself. Even if the jury agreed that the Church believed that these purposes and activities were religious and then found that they were not religious but secular, that finding would still create an unconstitutional entanglement of government with religion. In either case, the jury was deciding that the good faith belief of the Church was false, contrary to the prohibition of the *Ballard* case. We have no way of knowing whether and to what extent the jury acted as a doctrinal tribunal, and for that reason, the instructions to the jury, as upheld by the Court of Appeals, were fatally defective. *See Stromberg* v. *California*, 283 U.S. 359, 367-68 (1931); *Williams* v. *North Carolina*, 317 U.S. 287, 292 (1942); *Terminiello* v. *Chicago*, 337 U.S. 1, 5-6 (1949); *Yates* v. *United States*, 354 U.S. 298, 311 (1957); *Street* v. *New York*, 394 U.S. 576, 585-86 (1969).

17

V. The Power Given To The Jury To Define The Content Of Religious Beliefs And Purposes Threatens The Destruction Of Religious Liberty Through The Progressive Definition Of More And More Religious Beliefs And Activities As Secular.

The jury in this case was given an open commission to determine the content of the creed of a religious group contrary to the sincerely held convictions of that group. The danger of excessive government entanglement with religion is no less when a court is making the substantive doctrinal judgments that are involved in defining the content of a particular religious faith than when the court is explicitly declaring that a religious tenet is false. In either case, the court is sitting as an ecclesiastical tribunal rather than as a court of civil law. Indeed, the intrusion of government through a determination of the content of a group's religious belief is, in one respect at least, worse than the entanglement from an explicit denial of the truth of a religious belief. A governmental denial of the truth of a religious tenet would not of itself deprive the group of its protected status as a religion. However, a governmental decision that what the group sincerely maintains as part of its creed is actually not even religious but rather secular, could deprive that group, as to the affected activity, of the special protections afforded by the First Amendment to religion. Religious freedom is a fundamental right. It may be limited by government only upon proof of a "compelling state interest." *Sherbert* v. *Verner*, 374 U.S. 398, 406 (1963). While "[t]he state may justify an inroad on religious liberty by showing that it is the least restrictive means of achieving some compelling state interest," *Thomas* v. *Review Board*, 450 U.S. 707, 718 (1981), "only those interests of the highest order and those not otherwise served can overbalance legitimate claims to the free exercise of religion." *Wisconsin* v. *Yoder*, 406 U.S. 205, 215 (1972); *see also Cantwell* v. *Connecticut*, 310 U.S. 296, 307-08 (1940). "The state may justify a limitation on religious liberty by showing that it is essential to accomplish an overriding governmental interest." *United States* v. *Lee*, 455 U.S. 252, 257-58 (1982); *see also Bob Jones University* v. *United States*, 103 S.Ct. at 2035. But if an activity is defined as secular, it can

18

be subjected to the much less demanding standard applicable to non-fundamental rights and activities, that they can be regulated merely if the regulation is "shown to bear some rational relationship to legitimate state purposes." *San Antonio School District v. Rodriguez*, 411 U.S. 1, 40 (1973).

Through the progressive definition of more and more religious activities as secular and therefore subject to regulation on the same basis as commercial activities, protected religious freedom will be restricted to the closet and the sanctuary. This prospect is especially ominous in light of the recent ruling that tax exemption is a "subsidy" provided by Congress as "a matter of grace" which Congress may grant or withhold as it chooses. *Regan v. Taxation with Representation*, 103 S.Ct. at 2000, 2003. "It is hardly lack of due process for the Government to regulate that which it subsidizes." *Wickard v. Filburn*, 317 U.S. 111, 131 (1942). Strict scrutiny does not apply to the classifications involved in granting and withholding such tax exemptions, since "[l]egislatures have especially broad latitude in creating classifications and distinctions in tax statutes." *Regan v. Taxation with Representation*, 103 S.Ct. at 2002. If a tax exemption is conditioned on the religious character of an organization's beliefs and activities; if the courts are vested with the sort of unlimited power to judge what is religious and what is secular, which was given to the jury in this case; and if a determination that such belief or activity is secular is not itself subject to strict judicial scrutiny, then churches will be vulnerable to a progressive and arbitrary denial of tax exemption which will force them out of the public dialogue and into the closet. This danger of progressive curtailment of eligibility for exemption complements the danger of progressive regulation from the definition of activities as secular so that they will be deprived of the preferred protection afforded to religion by the First Amendment. So if the power given to the jury in this case is upheld, the churches will be in trouble on both counts. They will be subject to both taxation and regulation without effective limitation. The result will be the privatization of religion. "It seems trite but necesary to say that the First Amendment to our Constitution was designed to

19

avoid these ends by avoiding these beginnings." *Board of Education* v. *Barnette*, 319 U.S. 624, 641 (1943).

It is fair, indeed, to describe the unlimited power conferred on the jury by the Court of Appeals decision in this case as a regulation of religious belief rather than of action. This is so because the jury verdict, in effect, told the members of the Unification Church what they believe. It defined the content of the religious purposes and activities of that church contrary to the good faith understanding of the members themselves. The jury made a doctrinal judgment. Its intrusion into the privileged area of religious belief cannot even be justified by a compelling state interest, since the freedom to believe, as distinguished from the freedom to act, is absolute:

> The door of the Free Exercise Clause stands tightly closed against any governmental regulation of religious *beliefs* as such, *Cantwell* v. *Connecticut*, 310 U.S. 296. . . . Government may neither compel affirmation of a repugnant belief . . .; nor penalize or discriminate against individuals or groups because they hold religious views abhorrent to the authorities. . . ; nor employ the taxing power to inhibit the dissemination of particular religious views. . . *Sherbert* v. *Verner*, 374 U.S. 398, 402 (1963) (emphasis in original).

It is fair to recall here the warning by the Supreme Court in *United States* v. *Ballard*, 322 U.S. at 87 that, "[i]f one could be sent to jail because a jury in a hostile environment found those [religious] teachings false, little indeed would be left of religious freedom." There is serious reason for concern, therefore, about the principles declared by the Court of Appeals in this case. That concern, however, is not at all dependent on one's view of the Unification Church or of Reverend Sun Myung Moon. The significance of this case, rather, is that the courts convicted Reverend Moon and affirmed that conviction by disregarding one of the most important protections afforded by the First Amendment against governmental domination of religious groups. It is essential that this case be heard by the Supreme Court and that the erroneous principles employed by the Court of Appeals be rejected.

20

VI. Conclusion

For the foregoing reasons, *Amicus Curiae* submits that the Petition for Certiorari should be granted in this case.

Respectfully submitted,

CHARLES E. RICE
NOTRE DAME LAW SCHOOL
Notre Dame, IN 46556
(219) 239-5667
Counsel for
The Center for Judicial Studies

The Church of Jesus Christ of Latter-Day Saints

i

QUESTIONS PRESENTED

Did the lower court correctly safeguard religious liberty in:

a) upholding the trial court's instruction to the jury concerning the structure of the defendant's church; and

b) permitting a jury to determine what is a religious activity under a religion's doctrines, rather than considering whether the religion's asserted doctrine was genuine?

iii

TABLE OF CONTENTS

*   *   *

Written consent to file this brief has been obtained from counsel for the parties. The original letters have been sent to the Clerk of this Court for filing.

v

TABLE OF CASES

CONSTITUTIONAL PROVISIONS INVOLVED

Amendment I

Congress shall make no law respecting an establishment of religion, or prohibiting the free exercise thereof . . . .

STATEMENT OF INTEREST AND INTRODUCTION

The Church of Jesus Christ of Latter-day Saints (the "L.D.S. Church") is an unincorporated association with headquarters in Salt Lake City, Utah. It is a Christian religion with membership exceeding five million world-wide.

The L.D.S. Church expresses no opinion about the teachings or beliefs of the Unification Church or its leader Reverend Sun Myung Moon ("Rev. Moon"). It takes no position on the matter of the guilt or innocence of the defendants and has no view as to the motivation behind or the reasonableness of the investigations that led to the indictments or the conduct of the prosecution. The defendants have raised a number of issues besides those concerning religion which they believe to be of Constitutional dimension. The L.D.S. Church takes no position on any of those other issues.

However, the instant case raises serious questions as to whether there was faithful attention paid to constitutional guarantees of religious freedom. A number of lawyers and commentators interpret the case as introducing harmful modifications to applicable standards for dealing with religions in courts of law. The L.D.S. Church is thus forced to ask whether the case can or will be construed as an unwarranted restriction upon religious freedom in this country.

SUMMARY OF ARGUMENT

The L.D.S. Church respectfully submits that this case should be reviewed by the Supreme Court because of the difficulties it presents in interpretation and the wide disparity of interpretation to which it has already been subjected. Given the nature of the case, there must be certainty that religious liberty has been properly protected, that any conviction be attained upon scrupulous attention to Con-

2

stitutional guarantees of religious freedom and that religions, not courts or jurors, be permitted to determine their own structure and beliefs and act accordingly without penalty, limitation or impingement, absent compelling state interests.

In their concern that the trial not be an inquisition of a religion or of an alien religious leader, the lower courts erred in jury instructions about a religion's ownership of property and its choice of structure and organization and also opened a door to government regulation, by court or jury, of religious doctrine. That door should not have been opened.

I. THE JURY WAS IMPROPERLY INSTRUCTED IN ITS CONSIDERATION OF THE RELIGION'S STRUCTURE.

It has been held that the Unification Church falls within the accepted parameters of religious entities, even though reported doctrines differ greatly from those of older or more traditional religions. *See, Unification Church* v. *INS,* 547 F.Supp. 623 (D.D.C. 1982) ; *Holy Spirit Association* v. *Tax Commission,* 55 N.Y. 2d 512 (1982).

Religious entities in this country and world-wide have various structures. Decisions about religious structure are, and always have been, made by the religion. It has long been recognized that religions make different arrangements regarding the administration of their temporal affairs. Courts in the past have refused jurisdiction to review such matters. *See, Kedroff* v. *St. Nicholas Cathedral,* 344 U.S. 94 (1952). Internal disputes are resolved by the rules adopted and the doctrine professed by the religion itself or upon neutral principles. *See, Serbian Orthodox Diocese* v. *Milivojevich,* 426 U.S. 696 (1976) . These are salutary principles: they give maximum freedom to religious belief, and they permit individuals to adhere to groups which express their own religious preferences.

3

In this case, the central question was whether the church or Rev. Moon owned specified funds. Despite testimony proffered on behalf of the church as to its ownership, the trial court permitted the jury to make its own, independent determination of ownership. The jury was also permitted to exercise its own, virtually unfettered discretion in determining what the Unification Church's structure and organization should have been in order to prove the church's claim of ownership. The trial court refused to charge the jury as to the special relationship of Rev. Moon to his church; it offered only the inadequate direction that the lack of a formal corporate structure would not prevent a religious entity from having beneficial ownership of property held in the name of another. *See, United States* v. *Moon,* 718 F.2d 1210, 1244, *n. 3* (2d Cir. 1983) (Oakes, J., dissenting) .

Because it is a religious entity, it must be assumed that the Unification Church is organized in accord with its doctrines. The manner of a church's organization, if at all relevant to a case, is something for the church to describe as a threshold issue to the court; the jury should be told that a particular structure is involved, and that their only concern is whether that structure is sham rather than a genuinely established activity of the church.

II. THE DETERMINATION OF WHAT CONSTITUTES A RELIGIOUS ACTIVITY SHOULD BE MADE BY THE CHURCH, NOT THE STATE, AND A CHURCH'S POSITION MAY NOT BE IGNORED IN LITIGATION ABSENT A CAREFULLY DEFINED COMPELLING STATE INTEREST.

The very statement of the second religious issue is difficult upon the record of this case. When the majority and dissenting opinions from the lower court are compared, they are more like two ships passing in the night than a

4

collision of opposing views. The decisions filed by the lower court highlight a major reason for review: the issue of religious freedom lurks but does not leap, and its harm there lies.

There are few pages in the lower court decision which relate to this problem. *See, United States* v. *Moon, supra,* 718 F.2d at 1226-28. These pages do not state the issue with clarity. Careful reading of the opinions and portions of the record in the case show that the issue is real; regardless of how it was handled at trial, a jury did in fact determine the question of what was or was not a religious belief or activity of Rev. Moon's church. The jury, not the religion, decided what the religion could believe about its purposes and its activities. The court charged the jury to decide religious purpose:

> If you find that the funds in the Chase [bank] accounts were the property of International Unification Church Movement or were held in trust by Moon for the International Unification Church Movement and used for church purposes and that the interest on those funds also belong to the International Unification Church Movement and were used for it, then that interest would not be taxable income to Moon.

United States v. *Moon, supra,* 718 F.2d at 1244 *n. 3.*

In the circumstances of this case, religious belief was directly probative on the question of ownership of the funds. Like a church's structure, the nature of its activities must be inherent in and proprietary to the religion itself. Such questions should not be given unguided to a jury. The First Amendment does not permit governments or jurors to pronounce or establish religion.

The problem arises to a large extent from the conscientiousness of the trial court to exclude religion from the case, even though the doctrines and purposes of the religion

5

were central to a determination of (1) the ownership of the funds, (2) any wrongful use of the funds and (3) possible diversion of the funds from religious to private purposes. The result of the non-religion approach to the case was that no one was bound to consider, let alone accept, the religious teachings of the religion.

The lower court justified the approach upon the rationale that the free exercise of religion is subordinate to the criminal law. That is a general statement, but it is one too broad and unsophisticated for the crime charged because ownership and purpose could have nullified criminal conduct. The consequence here was that the jury decided what did not constitute a religious purpose, and thus decided whether there had been a crime on that predicate basis. As the New York Court of Appeals correctly stated:

> It is for religious bodies themselves, rather than the courts or administrative agencies, to define, by their teachings and activities, what their religion is. The courts are obliged to accept such characterization of the activities of such bodies, including that of the Church in the case before us, unless it is found to be insincere or sham.

Holy Spirit Association v. *Tax Commission, supra,* 55 N.Y. 2d at 527-28.

Threshold descriptions of doctrine, usage and belief given by a religion must be accorded a weighty presumption of correctness. At this point it is not necessary to argue whether the presumption should be an irrebuttable one. It is clear, however, that a court and jury should not be able to decide what is or is not doctrine as believed by a particular religion. The finder of fact cannot, unguided, substitute its views of religious purpose for those of the religion itself. This principle was demonstrated in a recent example in which the trial court, on a motion for summary judgment, accepted the statement by church leadership that the church's newspaper, even though circulated beyond its membership, was a religious activity of the church because the church's doctrine required its membership to be informed and to read the paper. *Feldstein* v. *The Christian Science Monitor*, 555 F.Supp. 974 (D. Mass. 1983). In the instant case, the religion's description of its own purposes, activities and ownership of property were not given the benefit of any presumption whatsoever.

The flaw in the present case arises from an inversion in the appropriate analysis. The general rule is that a religious purpose cannot justify action which is prevented by a compelling state interest. The compelling state interest has defined the crime, but that test cannot be turned upon itself or used to place an unfair burden upon a religion. The logic endorsed by the Circuit was: there is a crime if there is no religious purpose, the jury says there is no religious purpose, therefore there is a crime. The syllogism should have been: There is a crime if there is no genuinely held religious purpose; the jury says the religion's stated purpose is (or is not) genuinely held, therefore there is (or is not) a crime. The jury may consider only whether the religious purpose asserted is a sincerely held religious belief. No one gave any real analysis or credence to the religion's own statements; hence the jury (and thus the government) made a prohibited determination on a religious question.

The concepts necessary to the proper treatment of religion flow from settled law, notably *United States* v. *Ballard*, 322 U.S. 78 (1944) in which this Court determined that courts (and consequently jurors) cannot inquire into the truth or falsity of religious beliefs, but may examine only the sincerity with which those beliefs are held. To hold otherwise or to permit other inquiry subjects religion and religious beliefs to the whims and prejudices of a jury, and hence would impinge improperly upon religion.

7

It is in this context that the lower courts have erred in their consistent and persistent efforts to keep religion outside the trial. In a normal case, the court and the jury should not consider whether the defendant is Mormon or Moslem, Adventist or atheist. Matters of conscience and religion do not ordinarily pertain. But in this case, religion was an essential element and had to be considered, but only on strict and appropriate standards set forth in the *Ballard* case. The religious dogma of the defendants and their church was crucial in determining whether there were funds which could be taxed or which could be the subject of fraud.

Under the lower court's decision, religions are left unprotected from both exercise and establishment invasions. In this case the jury adjudged both the nature and the propriety of a religion's beliefs and activities, not just sincerity. The invasions against religion were not blunt or highly visible in the instant case; they were subtle, making the precedent more pernicious and so imprecise as to multiply the case's impact. The inversion of burden upon religion, however, now has the approval of two lower courts, and that justifies a petition for review.

While religious leaders should not be permitted to manipulate the law, they should not be denied its protection. It is the role of this Court to provide the guidance and the tests and to oversee their application in cases such as this.

8

CONCLUSION

In order to uphold the constitutional guarantees of religious liberty assured by the First Amendment, in order to verify that proper principles have been applied, in order to prevent impingement on religion to grow from a well-intentioned but confused and improperly grounded decision and in order to provide guidance to prosecutors in situations involving possible wrongdoing by religious leaders, the L.D.S. Church respectfully requests that this Court grant certiorari to review the religious issues here raised.

Respectfully submitted,
WILFORD W. KIRTON, JR.
OSCAR W. McCONKIE
M. KARLYNN HINMAN
DAVID P. FARNSWORTH
Kirton, McConkie & Bushnell
330 South 300 East
Salt Lake City, Utah 84111
(801) 521-3680

*Attorneys for the Church of
Jesus Christ of Latter-day Saints*

Salt Lake City, Utah
February 24, 1984

The Coalition for Religious Freedom
and Christian Voice, Inc.

TABLE OF CONTENTS

ii

TABLE OF AUTHORITIES

iii

TABLE OF AUTHORITIES—Continued

iv

TABLE OF AUTHORITIES—Continued

Page

In The

Supreme Court of the United States

OCTOBER TERM, 1983

No. 83-1242

SUN MYUNG MOON and TAKERU KAMIYAMA,
Petitioners

v.

UNITED STATES OF AMERICA,
Respondent

On Petition for Certiorari to the United States
Court of Appeals for the Second Circuit

BRIEF AMICUS CURIAE
FOR THE COALITION FOR RELIGIOUS FREEDOM
AND CHRISTIAN VOICE, INC.
IN SUPPORT OF PETITION FOR CERTIORARI

STATEMENT OF INTEREST OF AMICI

Amicus Coalition for Religious Freedom is an association of ministers, rabbis and priests, whose aim is to emphasize the need to protect the nation's churches, and the constitutional right to speak, assemble and worship free from government interference.

The founders and active members of the Coalition for Religious Freedom are Reverend Jerry Falwell, of the Thomas Road Baptist Church; Dr. D. James Kennedy, of the Coral Ridge Presbyterian Church; Dr. Edward V. Hill, of the Missionary Baptist Church; Dr. James T. Draper, of the First Baptist Church, Eulers, Texas; Reverend Jimmy Swaggert, of the Jimmy Swaggert Min-

2

istries; Dr. William R. Bright, Chancellor of the International Christian Graduate University; Dr. Joshua O. Haberman, of the Washington Hebrew Congregation; Bishop Thomas J. Welsh, of Allentown, Pennsylvania; and, Dr. Charles Stanley, of Atlanta, Georgia. The Coalition and its founders have an active interest in the implications of this case: the intrusion of government into the freedom of religion; and, they support a full venting of the issues raised by Petitioner.

Amicus Christian Voice, Inc. is a nonprofit, tax-exempt corporation, organized and existing under the laws of California. It represents over forty-five (45) denominations of the Christian faith and has 350,000 members, of whom 40,000 are ministers. Christian Voice, Inc. is committed to advancing fundamental Christian morality and the preservation of religious freedom in the promulgation of federal and state legislation. The members of Christian Voice, Inc. have a deep interest in the issues presented by Petitioner and it thus desires to voice the concerns of its members on these issues.

Accordingly, Amici respectfully submit their brief in support of the Petition for a Writ of Certiorari to the United States Court of Appeals for the Second Circuit.

STATEMENT OF THE CASE

Amici adopt by reference the Statement of the Case as set forth in the petition for certiorari, insofar as the facts are relevant to the arguments set forth below.

SUMMARY OF ARGUMENT

This case turned on a question of church property ownership: were the assets in question beneficially owned by the International Unification Church Movement [1] or

---

[1] References to the "Church," "Unification Church," "Movement," "International Movement," and the like, generally, are intended to refer to the International Unification Church Movement, founded

3

by that Church's leader. This question should have been controlled by the well articulated law of the cases dealing with such questions.

In an unbroken line of decisions, this Court has held that when civil courts are called upon to resolve questions of property ownership involving churches, they must either defer to the definitive determinations of appropriate internal church bodies on the subject, *Watson v. Jones*, 80 U.S. 679 (1871), *Presbyterian Church v. Hull Church*, 393 U.S. 440 (1969), or resolve the issue by applying "neutral principles" of law in a manner so as to insure its resolution in accord with the desire of the members. *Jones v. Wolf*, 443 U.S. 595, 603-04 (1979).

The decision below, however, contravened constitutional and case teaching and rejected both these approaches. It disregarded the desire and intention of the members and refused to apply the "neutral principles" approach mandated as an alternative.

Instead the court adopted a new and highly debatable theory of ownership and consequent tax liability. Having placed the greatest determinative weight on (i) the uses of the funds, (ii) the fact that Unification Church members sometimes refer to the funds as "Father's" and (iii) that the International Movement was not incorporated, the Court obstructed and frustrated defense efforts to show that these factors actually evidenced and comported with Church, rather than individual, ownership. The court rejected clearly relevant evidence of Unification belief and doctrine which the defense offered to show were church-related and that the nomenclature adopted was also indicative of Church ownership.

The court permitted an unconstitutional inquest by the jury into questions of Church belief, doctrine, teaching,

---

and led by Reverend Moon and the religion which it embodied. Where reference to specific Unification Church branches, organizations or affiliated entities is intended, this will be indicated.

4

mission and ministry, with no guidance or limitation whatever, allowing the jury to find such doctrine true or false, religious or nonreligious as it wished and on whatever basis, or to reject it altogether. On the other hand, the court allowed the prosecution to use this religious context where it became convenient as an aid to conviction. In so doing, it denied due process and transgressed Religion Clauses protection.

ARGUMENT

I. **By Refusing to Apply Settled "Neutral Principles" of Law to Resolve a Question of Church Property Ownership, the Second Circuit Rejected the Uniform Holdings of this Court and Violated the First Amendment's Religion Clauses.**

As noted, the central question was one of property ownership: were the assets beneficially owned by the Church or by its leader? Usually these questions come before the courts when a dispute arises within a church, as to where ownership lies.

Here, however, there was complete unity within the Church on the issue; the only disputant was a stranger to the congregation; namely, the government. This does not, however, alter the plain fact that the core of the case was a classic dispute over the ownership of church property.

To resolve such disputes, this court has laid down clear and unmistakable ground rules. In a seminal holding, *Watson v. Jones*, 80 U.S. (13 Wall.) 679 (1871), this language is found:

> In this class of cases we think the rule of action which should govern the civil courts . . . is, that, whenever the questions of discipline or of faith, or eccelesiastical rule, custom or law have been decided

5

by the highest of these Church judicatories to which the matter has been carried, the legal tribunals *must accept* such decisions as final, and as binding on them, in their application of the case before them. *Id.* at 727. (Emphasis added.)

See also, Presbyterian Church v. Hull Church, 393 U.S. 440, 665 (1969). (Civil courts resolving such controversies inhibit the free development of religious doctrine.)

In other words, if it can be clearly determined, without internal dispute, that competent Church authorities or bodies have decided the question at issue, then that determination must be deferred to and accepted. To do otherwise would be to permit the courts to probe into and adjudicate matters of religious practice and doctrine, something prohibited by the First Amendment. The courts are not even permitted to inquire into the question of which authority within a church has the power to decide, for to permit the courts to judge such matters would violate the First Amendment in the same manner as civil determination of· religious doctrine. *Maryland and Virginia Churches v. Sharpsburg Church*, 396 U.S. 367 (1970). *See also, Kedroff v. St. Nicholas Cathedral*, 344 U.S. 94, 121 (1952) (when property right follows, as incident from decisions of church custom or law on ecclesiastical issues, church rule controls). *Accord, Jones v. Wolf*, 443 U.S. 595, 602 (1979).

In those situations where authoritative internal church determination may not be evident or ascertainable, resort may be had by civil courts to "neutral principles" of law, so long as these are applied in a manner best calculated to "ensure that a dispute over the ownership of church property will be resolved in accord with the desire of the members." *Jones v. Wolf*, 443 U.S. at 603-04.

There was no dispute within the Unification Church, and it was clear, looking to manifest Church desire and teach-

6

ing, where beneficial ownership lay. The uncontradicted evidence on the point showed that the assets came from fund raising efforts carried out by Church members on behalf of the Church, that they were entrusted to the Church's leader as a charitable gift with the intention that they be used for the benefit of the Church. "Neutral principles" of law, well settled, would require a holding that this established the existence of a trust, or at the very least, a fiduciary holding of these assets by Reverend Moon for the benefit of the Church, a result clearly consonant with the intentions and wishes of the Church and its members. This is pointed out and documented exhaustively by Judge Oakes in his dissenting opinion, 718 F.2d at 1242-43.

For centuries the law has favored charitable and religious trusts and has bent over backward in order to resolve ambiguities in favor of upholding them. *See* 4A A.W. Scott, The Law on Trusts, §§ 371.3 at 2885, 351 at 2797-98 (3rd ed. 1967) [hereinafter cited as *Scott*]; *In re Price's Will*, 264 A.D. 29, 35 N.Y.S.2d 111, 114-15, *aff'd*, 289 N.Y. 751, 46 N.E.2d 354 (1942); *In re Estate of Nurse*, 35 N.Y.2d 381, 389, 362 N.Y.S.2d 441, 446, 321 N.E.2d 537 (1974); N.Y. Est. Powers & Trust Law § 8-1.1 (McKinney 1967).

In numerous cases trusts have been found where there was no formal language and even where the gift was absolute in form, this being frequently inferred merely from the fact that the property came from a church source and was transferred to a church leader. *In re Durbrow's Estate*, 245 N.Y. 469, 477, 157 N.E. 747, 749 (1927); *New York City Mission Society v. Board of Pensions*, 261 A.D. 823, 24 N.Y.S.2d 395, 396 (1941); *Sears v. Parker*, 193 Mass. 551, 79 N.E. 772 (1907); *Jones v. Habersham*, 107 U.S. 174, 182 (1882); *Scott, supra*; *Fink v. Umscheid*, 40 Kan. 271, 19 P. 623 (1888); *Archbishop v. Shipman*, 79 Cal. 288, 21 P. 830 (1889).

7

Indeed, many cases have found implied trusts simply from the lone fact that the donee or legatee held a religious office or an office in a charitable institution, despite language or circumstances indicative of absolute gift. *See Scott,* § 371.3 at 2885 and cases there cited; *Id.* at § 351 at 2797-98. *See also In re Fitzgerald's Estate,* 62 Cal. App. 744, 217 P. 773 (1923); *Gibbons Estate,* 40 P.A. D. & C.2d 84, 86-87 (1966); *Williams v. Williams,* 215 N.C. 739, 743 (1939). This view is also reflected in several statutory enactments. *See, e.g.,* N.Y. Relig. Corp. § 91 (Consol.), which provides:

> The archbishop or bishop and the vicar-general of the Diocese to which any incorporated Roman Catholic Church belongs, the rector of such church, and their successors in office, shall, by *virtue of their offices,* be trustees of such church. . . . (Emphasis added).[2]

This line of holdings is entirely consistent with what appears to have been settled Internal Revenue Service (hereinafter "IRS") policy in this same regard, at least until the decision in this case. *See, e.g., Winn v. Commissioner,* 595 F.2d 1060 (5th Cir. 1979); *Morey v. Riddell,* 205 F.Supp. 918 (S.D. Cal. 1962); *Brittingham v. Commissioner,* 57 T.C. 91 (1971). The situation is by no means confined to religious situations but applies equally to those involving political campaigns or other causes. *C.F. O'Dwyer v. Commissioner,* 266 F.2d 575, 585-586 (4th Cir.), *cert. denied,* 361 U.S. 8621 (1959); *7-Up Co. v. Commissioner,* 14 T.C. 965 (1950); *Stratton v. Commissioner,* 54 T.C. 255, 282 (1970). *See, e.g.,* Rev. Rul. 74-23, 1974-1 CB 17; Rev. Proc. 68-19, 1968-1 CB 810, 811.

Indeed, the holding of church property in the personal name of a church leader has long been an accepted method

---

[2] *Town of Hardenburgh v. State,* 52 N.Y.2d 536, 421 N.E.2d 795, 796 (1981). "Real property held in trust by a clergyman . . . for the benefit of the members of his incorporated or unincorporated church shall be entitled to the same exemption from taxation . . . ." Quoting from § 436 N.Y. Property Tax Law.

8

of church property tenure. *See, e.g.,* Kauper and Ellis, "Religious Corporations and the Law," 71 Mich. L.R. 1499, 1506-09 (1973). Under the common law, title to real property of the parish in the Angelican church was taken in the name of the minister, and title to personalty in the name of the church wardens.[3] *Terrett v. Taylor,* 13 U.S. 43, 46-47 (1815). There are many cases holding that where church officials held title to property in their personal names, they did so as trustees for their Churches. *See, e.g., Sears v. Parker,* 193 Mass. 551, 79 N.E. 772 (1907); *Jones v. Habersham,* 107 U.S. 174, 182 (1882), *Fink v. Umscheid,* 40 Kan. 271, 19 P.623 (1888); *Morey v. Riddell,* 205 F.Supp. 918 (S.D. Cal. 1962); *Winn v. Commissioner,* 595 F.2d 1060 (5th Cir. 1979); *Scott* §§ 351, 371.3 at 2797-98, 2885.

Furthermore, this result would obtain regardless of the actual use to which the custodian might put the funds, since use or application inconsistent with trust purposes, under settled, "neutral principles" establishes, at most, a diversion (*not* charged in this case). It does not, by any previous holding, operate to convert the entire trust corpus into the custodian's personal property. 718 F.2d at 1246; (Oakes, J., dissenting); *United States v. Scott,* 660 F.2d 1145, 1151 (7th Cir. 1981), *cert. denied,* 445 U.S. 907 (1982); *Herbert v. Commissioner,* 377 F.2d 65, 70 (9th Cir. 1967).

---

[3] The holding of diocesan property in the personal name of Catholic prelates, whether as a corporation sole or otherwise, is equally well known. *See, e.g., Reid v. Barry,* 93 Fla. 849, 112 So. 846 (1927); *Mannix v. Purcell,* 46 Ohio St. 102, 19 N.E. 572 (1888); *St. Peters Roman Catholic Parish v. Urban Redevelopment Authority,* 394 Pa. 194, 146 A.2d 724 (1959), *cert. denied* and *appeal dismissed,* 359 U.S. 435 (1959); *Gospel Tab. Body of Christ Church v. Peace Publ. & Co.,* 211 Kan. 420, 506 P.2d 1135 (1973), *adhered to,* 211 Kan. 927, 508 P.2d 849; *Scott,* § 371.3 at 2884-85; 50 N.Y. Jur. Religious Societies § 111 at 11.

9

The Second Circuit majority, however, declined to follow the overwhelming weight of the foregoing authorities. Far from deferring to the manifest internal determination of the Church, as evidenced by the members' wishes and intentions, it brusquely swept these aside, holding specifically that these constituted *no* evidence of intent to create a trust,[4] and further stating, remarkably, that there is "no rule" equating a charitable gift with intent to create a trust. 718 F.2d 1224-25.[5]

The courts below thus confirmed the prosecution's theory that all it had to do to establish taxability was to show legal title in the defendant plus a use of some part of the assets in ways which could be characterized as personal. And this, in fact, is all the government really attempted to show.

---

[4] The court's specific holding that a donor's intent to create a trust must be "clear and unequivocal," laying emphasis on the importance of using the specific word "trust," is likewise counter to the tide of authority generally, *see, Scott*, § 371.3 at 2885; *Winn v. Commissioner, supra; Morey v. Riddell, supra*; and also to the trust law of New York State, governing in this case. *See, e.g., In re Pattberg's Will*, 282 A.D. 770, 123 N.Y.S.2d 564 (1953), *aff'd*, 306 N.Y. 835, 118 N.E.2d 903 (1954); *Mee v. Gordon*, 187 N.Y. 400, 80 N.E. 353 (1907); *Pierce Estates Inc. v. Commissioner*, 3 T.C. 875 (1944); *Manley v. Fiske*, 139 A.D. 665, 124 N.Y.S. 149, 150-151 (1910); *aff'd*, 201 N.Y. 546, N. 95 N.E. 1133 (1911).

[5] *Cf. Manley v. Fiske*, 139 A.D. 665, 124 N.Y.S. 149, 150-151 (1910), *aff'd*, 201 N.Y. 546, 95 N.E. 1133 (1911). (Trust can be established by will without express words of trust or gift, since "[a] trust is almost inseparably involved with a gift for charitable uses.") *See also, In re Price's Will*, 264 A.D. 29, 35 N.Y.S.2d 111, 114-15, *aff'd*, 289 N.Y. 751, 46 N.E.2d 354 (1942); *In re Durbow's Estate*, 245 N.Y. 469, 477, 157 N.E. 747, 749 (1927). Even if the Second Circuit majority's astonishing assertion were taken as a correct statement of the law, a charitable gift, which this concededly was, was in any event a gift *to the Church* and was thus flatly incompatible with a personal gift to Moon as an individual, which the government nevertheless contended and the court affirmed.

10

II. By Adopting, *Ad Hoc* and Contrary to Settled Principles, a New and Questionable Theory of Ownership Which Permitted Court and Jury to Weigh and Adjudicate the Content, Validity and Truth of *Bona Fide* Religious Doctrine, The Decision Violated The First Amendment's Religion Clauses and The Fifth Amendment's Due Process Guaranty.

Turning to the factors on which the Second Circuit majority did rely, we assert that the court opened the door to the very invasion of protected belief which the rejected authorities sought to prevent. These factors were: *first,* the fact that Reverend Moon held legal title to the assets and controlled them; *second,* the fact that the Church was unincorporated, while other Church branches and organizations were formally incorporated and had corporate bank accounts; *third,* that in his handling of the assets, Reverend Moon seemingly regarded them as his own, that is to say, "he used funds from the accounts for expenditures which the jury could have concluded were personal in nature"; and *fourth,* that high ranking members of the Church were told that the funds belonged to "Father," an indication which might, without explanation, be taken to mean that the assets were beneficially owned by Moon personally rather than his Church. 718 F.2d at 1220, 1222. These factors, which were adopted *ad hoc* by the court in substitution for the rejected "neutral principles" of law, are examined in greater detail below.[6]

Let us begin by considering the third factor, namely, how the funds were used. The government attempted to

---

[6] We omit discussion of element one, legal title, since, as indicated by the authorities cited above, this fact is not very helpful as an indicator of where beneficial ownership lies, particularly in a situation such as this. As the dissenting opinion points out, 718 F.2d at 1242, this issue was really conceded from the beginning, but is an equivocal indication at best, since every trustee must hold legal title and must exercise dominion and control, even though he does *not* hold beneficial ownership, in order to carry out the obligations of his trust.

11

show: that a portion of the funds was invested in two business enterprises, repeatedly characterized, *a priori*, as "personal" investments; that some were transferred to other church branches; that other funds were lent to the U.S. branch of the Church, an incorporated entity, to assist its acquisition of residence properties and other Church facilities; and, that the assets were referred to, on occasion, within the Church, as "Father's" money. Lastly, the government urged, a small portion of the funds was used for Reverend Moon's living expenses and for the education of his children.[7]

Whether the use of this property was personal as claimed by the government or was, instead, church-related thus became a critical issue.[8] It was not only rele-

---

[7] In 1973, these were paid directly from the principal Chase account, and the amounts were reported by Reverend Moon as taxable income to him on his return for 1973. GX 590, 591, 597, 800; T 3729-3730, through 3735, 3812-3813, 4094, 4982-4998; as from May 1974, these personal disbursements were made from a separate "household account." GX 597; T 3581-3582, 3630-3631. These kinds of personal disbursements, particularly with clerical personnel, have long been regarded as consistent with religious trust use and purpose, and well within the range of a trustee's discretion. *See, e.g., Morey v. Riddell, supra, Winn v. Commissioner, supra.* Citations to the record as reprinted in the appendix submitted to the court of appeals will be denoted as follows: citations to pleadings and rulings, "A——"; to pretrial transcripts, "P——"; to trial transcript "T——"; to post-trial transcripts, "S——"; to government exhibits, "GX——"; and to defense exhibits "DX——."

[8] Since the major portion of the funds was used for purposes which were patently church related, i.e., to fund or assist in the acquisition of residence, headquarters and other properties by the U.S. branch, to purchase furnishings and equipment for these and other properties owned by the U.S. branch and affiliated organizations, to provide funds for maintenance and operational expenses for these properties, together with outright transfers of funds to other church branches, the government's claims of even seemingly "personal" uses are properly attributable only to a portion of the total expenditures during the period in question.

12

vant and material, but vital to the defense to counter the suggestion of personal use by showing that these expenditures benefited various church ministries, advanced the Church's mission and were therefore, church-related. It sought to introduce evidence to establish that in the context of Unification Church doctrine, these expenditures advanced the Church's purpose.

For example, the defense proved it was a central tenet of Unification Church doctrine that the Church establish a strong financial base with which to support and further its mission, and that an important ministry was the investment of Church funds in sound business enterprises and the actual formation and operation of businesses, on a proprietary basis, by other Church entities and members—such as Tong Il Enterprises, the issuer of the stock in question.[9]

It was also undisputed that Reverend Moon, as founder and leader of the International Unification Church Movement, was regarded by his followers as the very embodiment of their faith. This fact, the defense showed, was central to an understanding of why, in Unification belief, a reference to Reverend Moon, who is frequently called by the affectionate term "Father," was the equivalent of a reference to the office he held—and the Movement he led—rather than to the individual himself.[10] Thus, as

---

[9] An obvious parallel is the example of the Christian Brothers Winery, owned and operated by a Catholic Order. The reason for this, of course, is that the fruits of this operation furnish valuable financial support to a recognized religious order, and it is clearly "church related" in this sense. It is important to bear in mind that this characterization was not being made for the purpose of claiming a tax exemption or investing an otherwise secular operation with an ecclesiastical gloss, but, rather, to say that its *use*, in this context, served a legitimate religious purpose, i.e., furnishing financial support, and was thus clearly church-related.

[10] To say that the Reverend Moon was the embodiment of the faith was *not* to say, as the court implies, that his person was indis-

13

the embodiment of the faith, he was at the same time the custodian of the assets marshaled for the furtherance of its mission.

As the majority opinion notes, Reverend Moon was the spiritual leader of his Church, just as the Pope is the spiritual leader of the Roman Catholic Church. 718 F.2d at 1227. Pope John Paul II is frequently referred to by the term "Holy Father," and in that context, a reference to the Holy Father's money or property would certainly be equated with ownership of the property by the Holy See, rather than by "John Paul" as an individual, for the term Holy Father bespeaks the office itself, *not* the individual who holds it at a given moment. The same point was asserted with respect to Reverend Moon by the defense in this case, but completely misconstrued by the Second Circuit.

The government met these explanations with insistent claims that the Church's theology had nothing to do with Reverend Moon's "personal" business ventures and by repeated objections to the introduction of such evidence. These objections were, in major part, sustained by the trial court.

The court also refused requested defense instructions which would have given effect to the members/donors' intent. It refused to instruct that the International Unification Church Movement was personified by Reverend Moon, as its founder and spiritual leader. Nor did the court caution the jury that it could not question or probe into matters of Unification belief or teaching, but must accept these things at face-value, particularly such evidence as there was concerning the religious uses or purposes of the expenditures, the relationship of the Reverend Moon to the Church and the like. Instead, the

---

tinguishable from his office. This is clear from the fact that a portion of the funds used by Reverend Moon for personal living expenses and his children's education were reported on his 1973 tax return as being personal to him, as an individual, and on which he paid taxes.

14

court specifically invited the jury to delve into, examine and decide these matters for themselves, on whatever basis they wished, or to reject them altogether.

The Second Circuit approved this open-ended, blank check authority which was thus handed to the jury, specifically holding that "the jury was not bound to accept the Unification Church's definition of what constitutes a religious use or purpose. . . ." It also approved the charge which enabled the jury to draw its own conclusions regarding the significance of Reverend's Moon's position in the Church, regardless of Church theology. 718 F.2d at 1227-28.

The jury was thus given a free hand to do just what the teaching of the cases tells us the Religion Clauses specifically forbid. It was empowered to look into the beliefs and theology of Reverend Moon's Church, evaluate their validity, their truth and their religious character. It was left perfectly free to judge the character of the expenditures by deciding what the Church's mission was or was not, what its purposes were or weren't. It was turned loose to rewrite church theology and assign whatever significance it chose to Reverend Moon's position in the Church, regardless of what he or his followers felt or thought about it. And, of course, it was also free to treat these percepts as rubbish and reject or ignore them altogether. Thus, under the Religious Clauses, no jury, or court or government agency, for that matter, should have been permitted to do.

Amici assert that while freedom of religious action may be subject to limitation in response to a compelling state interest, the freedom to believe is absolute. "The door of the Free Exercise Clause stands tightly closed against any governmental regulation of religious beliefs as such," *Sherbert v. Verner*, 374 U.S. 398, 402 (1963), *citing Cantwell v. Connecticut, supra*, 310 U.S. 296, 303 (1939).

15

Furthermore, the freedom to believe encompasses the freedom to determine, on the basis of one's own criteria, the shape and content of one's religious beliefs. The government enters upon a sensitive and perilous undertaking when it attempts to define the scope of religious belief, even within broad limits. *See, United States v. Seeger*, 380 U.S. 163, 184 (1965); *Welsh v. United States*, 398 U.S. 333, 339-40 (1970).

Thus, the truth or falsity of religious beliefs, sincerely held, may not be examined or questioned. *United States v. Ballard*, 322 U.S. 78 (1944). "If one could be sent to jail because a jury in a hostile environment found . . . [one's religious] teachings false, little indeed would be left of religious freedom." 322 U.S. at 87 (Douglas, J.). As held in that case, a jury may *not* determine the truth or falsity of the religious belief or doctrine of any sect. "When the triers of fact undertake that task, *they enter a forbidden domain.*" 322 U.S. at 87 (emphasis added). In matters involving religious belief, the only permitted inquiry is whether the belief is sincerely held—an issue not raised in this case. 322 U.S. at 81.

In similar fashion, a court must accept a religion's own good faith determination of what is religious, in accordance with its teaching, and what is not, at least when the only issue is whether various uses of the funds were religious and that the funds were held for the religion. When purposes and activities of a religious organization are claimed to be other than religious, the civil authorities may engage in but two inquiries: "Does the religious organization assert that the challenged purposes and activities are religious, and is that assertion *bona fide?" Holy Spirit Association v. Tax Commission*, 55 N.Y.2d at 521. Courts may not "go behind the declared content of religious beliefs any more than they may examine into their validity." *Heritage Village*

16

Church v. State, 299 N.C. 399, 263 S.E.2d 726, 735-36 (1980).[11]

The religious character of ancillary activities undertaken by churches of religious organizations in support or furtherance of their mission must likewise be respected. *Murdock v. Pennsylvania*, 319 U.S. 105, 108-09 (1943). The fact that such activities may be business enterprises—as in the case of the Christian Brothers Winery, or import companies, as in the instant case— which are not religious in themselves, does not mean that in the context of support and furtherance of a church's mission they may not, in that church's view, serve or fulfill a religious use or purpose. 319 U.S. at 111.[12]

In the instant case, no question was raised by the government regarding the *bona fides* of the Unification faith or of the precepts and teachings evidenced at the trial. The rules of the foregoing cases thus clearly applied. The court was bound to accept them at face-value and to instruct the jury that it was similarly bound. If, under Unification Church teaching, the expenditures were Church-related and in furtherance of the Church's re-

---

[11] *See, also, Serbian Orthodox Diocese v. Milivojevich*, 426 U.S. 696, 713 (1976). (The question of proper purposes is an ecclesiastical one.) *Lemon v. Kurtzman*, 403 U.S. 602, 620 (1971). (The Supreme Court has been especially sensitive to state entanglement in what is religious and what is secular.) *Accord, Korn v. Rabbinical Council*, —— Cal.App.3d ——, 195 Cal. Rptr. 910 (1983), holding that civil courts are *without jurisdiction* to determine ecclesiastical questions and dismissing a case where the determination of such a question was unavoidably central to the case.

[12] The issue in *Murdock v. Pennsylvania, supra*, was one of tax exemption. No real question was raised concerning the church related character of the activity in question, only whether it should be exempt from a license tax. As we emphasize above, *no* such consideration is present here, where the question is one of church property ownership. In this context, the only issue is whether, in the sincerely held belief of the competent church authorities, the uses and expenditures in question advanced and supported the Church's mission, a clearly protected determination.

17

ligious mission, the relevance of that fact is patent and undeniable, since Reverend Moon, in directing these uses of the funds was acting consistent with the fiduciary role alleged by the defense. All such evidence should have been admitted and accepted by the court.

The fourth factor upon which the Second Circuit majority relied was the fact that the funds were referred to as "Father's." If, under the teaching of Unification theology, a reference to Reverend Moon, or "Father," the founder and leader of the International Church Movement, was tantamount to a reference to the Movement itself, that fact, too, was clearly relevant as tending to show why references which might, in ordinary circumstances be taken as personal were, in this context, in fact, just the opposite. This, too, should have been admitted and accepted, and the jury so instructed in clear and unambiguous terms.[13]

Instead, the Second Circuit, in violation of the principles above expressed, approved a trial court approach and a jury charge which, to the extent that it did not exclude consideration of Reverend Moon's religion altogether, directed the jury to sit in judgment upon it, without any guidance or limitation whatever. In effect, the court authorized the jury, if it wished, to redraw, redefine or otherwise cancel or reshape the Church's doctrine, its missions and ministries, contrary to the determinations of the Church and the membership itself. A more thoroughgoing repudiation of the First Amend-

---

[13] On the continuum of constitutional religious protection running from belief, which is absolutely protected, on the one hand, *Cantwell v. Connecticut, supra,* to religious action, which by its nature is not absolutely protected, but may be circumscribed in response to a compelling governmental interest, *Sherbert v. Verner, supra,* the use of terms and nomenclature within a church, in accordance with sincerely held belief and doctrine, is certainly most proximate to belief and thus merits absolute protection. The decision in this case, however, does not simply impair or damage that protection; it strips it away altogether.

18

ment's promise of free exercise and violation of its prohibition against establishments of religion can scarcely be imagined.

Looking to the second factor relied upon by the Second Circuit, the government was permitted to develop and argue that the International Church's unincorporated status and lack of formalized structure meant that it did not exist at all, T.5516-17, 6227, 6229, 6488-92. Moreover, the trial court went further and dignified the argument by precise and detailed instructions which gave it prominent emphasis.[14] How could the court deny that this particular choice of structure, form of holding and deployment of resources were matters of decision internal to the Church and inseparably bound up with considerations of its purpose and mission.

Such matters of church organization, internal structure, polity and resource management are no less religious or ecclesiastical in character than other matters of doctrine and belief. *Serbian Orthodox Diocese v. Milovojevich*, 426 U.S. 696, 708-09, 721-23 (1976); *Kedroff v. St. Nicholas Cathedral*, 34 U.S. 94, 120-21 (1954). If such matters may not be questioned, consistent with the Religion Clauses, how much more clear must it be that such protected determinations as choice of structure, governance and the like, may not be made the subject of a penalty, whether visited upon the organization itself or one of its members? *Speiser v. Randall*, 358 U.S. 24 (1965); *Mt. Healthy City Bd. of Education v. Doyle*, 429

---

[14] As the very first element in the instruction dealing with the factors to be considered in determining whether a trust existed, the following language appears: "in determining whether in 1973, 1974 and 1975, the International Unification Church Movement existed and whether the Movement owned the funds in the Chase accounts and Tong Il, or whether Reverend Moon owned them, you should consider all the evidence, including such factors whether the Movement had a specific organizational structure, written charter or constitution, the existence of other Unification Church corporate entities during the relevant time period. . . ." 718 F.2d at 1244, n.3.

19

U.S. 274 (1977). *See also, Larson v. Valente*, 456 U.S. 228 (1982).

Despite the clear teaching of the above cases, however, the jury was empowered to declare that the International Unification Church was legally non-existent. The First Amendment clearly and explicitly forecloses such matters from any such inquiry or consideration.

CONCLUSION

In his eloquent "Memorial and Remonstrance Against Religious Assessments," *Everson v. Board of Education*, 330 U.S. 1 (1947), James Madison observed that, "it is proper to take alarm at the first experiment on our liberties . . . [rather than waiting until] . . . usurped power had strengthened itself by exercise, and entangled the question in precedents." One of the major evils in the bill, which was the subject of this document, was the fact that "the bill implies . . . that the Civil Magistrate is a competent Judge of Religious truth . . . an arrogant pretention falsified by the contradictory opinions of Rulers in all ages. . . ." *Id.* at 65, 67. Madison's prescient observations make it clear that neither the methods of religious tyranny nor their consequences change over the centuries.

The Second Circuit has sanctioned the government's use of religious faith and teaching as a weapon against a church official, while excluding and denying it as a shield in his defense.

By piercing and sundering constitutional barriers erected to protect religious belief and matters of internal, ecclesiastical jurisdiction, the court opens the way for outright persecution. This latter odor hangs about the case, admittedly containing "troubling issues of religious persecution and abridgement of free speech," 718 F.2d at 1216, for the court approved the criminal prosecution of a church leader, even while acknowledging that he was singled out for investigation because of his highly visible

20

position as the founder and prophet of a new and widely disliked religion.

Unless this court accepts and reviews the Second Circuit's decision, *amici* believe that they may yet live to realize the gloomy consequence foreseen by Justice Douglas in the seminal decision of *United States v. Ballard, supra,* for here, indeed, a jury, in a hostile environment, was empowered to sit in judgment upon the defendant's religious beliefs and decide whether they were true or false. If the decision is allowed to stand, "little indeed [will] be left of religious freedom."

For the foregoing reasons, the petition for a Writ of Certiorari should be granted.

Respectfully submitted,

J. CURTIS HERGE *
ROBERT R. SPARKS, JR.
PHILIP H. BANE
  SEDAM & HERGE, P.C.
  Suite 1100
  8300 Greensboro Drive
  McLean, Virginia 22102
  (703) 821-1000
*Counsel of Record for
  Amici Curiae
  Coalition for Religious Freedom
  Christian Voice, Inc.

The Freemen Institute

(i)

QUESTION PRESENTED

Is it constitutionally permissible for the courts to penalize or ignore a centuries-old practice of holding church property in the individual name of a church leader, particularly when that leader is seen by his followers as the very embodiment of their faith?

(iii)

TABLE OF CONTENTS

(iv)

TABLE OF AUTHORITIES

(v)

IN THE

Supreme Court of the United States

October Term, 1983

No. 83-1242

SUN MYUNG MOON and TAKERU KAMIYAMA,
Petitioners,

v.

UNITED STATES OF AMERICA,
Respondent.

**On Petition For Certiorari To The United States
Court Of Appeals For The Second Circuit**

BRIEF AMICUS CURIAE
OF THE FREEMEN INSTITUTE
IN SUPPORT OF PETITION FOR CERTIORARI

BRIEF OF THE FREEMEN INSTITUTE
AS AMICUS CURIAE

Pursuant to Rule 36.1 of the Rules of this Court, the Freemen Institute files this brief in support of the instant petition for certiorari, having obtained consent from the attorneys of record for the parties in this case. Their original letters have been filed with the Clerk of this Court.

INTEREST OF THE AMICUS CURIAE

The Freemen Institute is described by its very name. It is an organization devoted to the goals of individual freedom — not the least of which is religious freedom. The erosion of important

2

rights and freedoms rarely begins with a direct attack on the established, the respected and the powerful. Basic freedoms, in particular religious freedom, are most frequently destroyed when the more comfortable majority fails to defend the rights of an unpopular minority.

The Freemen Institute, founded in 1971, is a membership organization with more than 250,000 members and contributors. It publishes a wide variety of books, periodicals and journals dedicated to the understanding and realization of constitutional principles and freedoms.

The Institute is deeply concerned that the Court of Appeals for the Second Circuit has permitted and even encouraged judges and juries to disregard the Religion Clauses of the Constitution in penalizing churches and church leaders for their choices concerning the way assets used for religious purposes are to be held and maintained. It is especially concerned that the court's ruling in *United States v. Moon* has essentially outlawed the common and historically respected practice of religious leaders holding church assets in their own names to be used for religious purposes.

STATEMENT OF THE CASE

Amicus curiae adopt the Statement of the Case as set forth in the petition for certiorari, insofar as the facts set forth therein are relevant to this brief.

SUMMARY OF ARGUMENT

For more than a thousand years, church property has routinely and uneventfully been taken and held in the personal names of church leaders. This is true whether the property was devised, transferred from their predecessors in office, or received in the form of gifts or donations from communicants and followers. This ancient and still widespread practice is amply confirmed by both textual authorities and a host of reported decisions.

3

The instant case provides a classic example of this practice. But the evidence which demonstrated this practice within the Unification Church was, with the approval of the Court of Appeals, either (1) ignored by the trial court; (2) excluded by the trial court pursuant to government objection when offered by the defense; or (3) rendered virtually meaningless by the instructions given to the jury.

This brief documents the practice. It also demonstrates that the factual predicate was irrefutably presented below for a finding that the property at issue in this case belonged to petitioners' church, rather than to Reverend Moon as an individual. Nevertheless, the courts below failed to resolve these issues consistent with the clear line of historic and judicial authority. In so doing, the courts violated Reverend Moon's rights to equal protection and the free exercise of religion.

ARGUMENT

I. HOLDING CHURCH PROPERTY IN THE INDIVIDUAL NAMES OF CHURCH LEADERS HAS BEEN, AND REMAINS, AN ACCEPTED AND WIDESPREAD PRACTICE. THIS IS PARTICULARLY TRUE WHEN THE LEADER IS SEEN BY HIS FOLLOWERS AS THE VERY EMBODIMENT OF THEIR FAITH

A. The Unification Church and Reverend Moon

The status of the Unification Church as a *bona fide* church is no longer subject to serious question. It is settled law. "[B]y any historical analogy, philosophical analysis, or judicial precedent . . . [the Unification Church] must be regarded as a bona fide religion." *Unification Church v. Immigration and Naturalization Service,* 547 F. Supp. 623, 628 (D.D.C. 1982). Wrote the New York Court of Appeals: "[W]e conclude that on the record before us, as a matter of law, the primary purpose of the [Unification] Church (much of whose doctrine, dogmas and

4

teachings and a significant part of whose activities are recognized as religious) is religious. . ." *Holy Spirit Association v. Tax Commisison,* 55 N.Y. 2d 512, 528, 450 N.Y.S. 2d 292, 435 N.E. 2d 662 (1982).

Regarding the relationship between Reverend Moon and the Unification Church, the unanimous New York Court of Appeals stated: "The Holy Spirit Association for the Unification of World Christianity (the Church) is one of more than 120 national Unification Churches throughout the world propagating a common religious message under the spiritual guidance of the Reverend Sun Myung Moon, the Unification movement's *founder and prophet"* (emphasis added). *Id.* at 519.

Indeed, Reverend Moon's central position in the theology of the Unification Church, not just as its founder, prophet and worldwide leader, but also as the instrument for the accomplishment of its divine mission, *see id.* at 542, is so widely known as to be a matter of common knowledge. Why else would members of the Church be called "Moonies"? This key fact was not disputed by the government or the trial court. It had crucial relevance to the core issue in the case — the beneficial ownership of the assets in question. Nevertheless, it was excluded from consideration by the trial court in acquiescence to the government's contention that Reverend Moon's religion and his relation to it had nothing to do with the case.

As the prosecutor explained in post-trial proceedings: ". . .[W]e undertook to try Reverend Moon. . . like any ordinary person charged with tax fraud" S65;[1] "we have dealt with [him]. . .just as the government deals with any high ranking business executive." S125. The government in its closing argument stated: "This case is not about tax exemption of churches. It is about personal income tax to an individual who happens to be related to a church." T6174.

---

[1]References to pre-trial hearings will be cited as "P____"; references to the trial transcript will be "T____"; references to post-trial hearings will be "S____"; and references to the pleadings will be "A____".

5

Any high ranking business executive indeed! HAPPENS to be *related* to a church indeed! Just as Luther, in administering the religious affairs of his congregants, was like ANY high ranking business executive who HAPPENED to be *related* to the Lutheran Church. Like Baha'u'llah *happened* to be a Baha'i; like Mary Baker Eddy *happened* to be a Christian Scientist; like Brigham Young happened to be a Mormon; like Menachem Schneerson happens to be a Lubavitcher.

The error permeating the government's case was compounded by the refusal of the trial judge to instruct the jury on Reverend Moon's unique role as a religious leader who is viewed by his followers as the embodiment of the faith — an instruction that was amply supported by the only evidence on point. A1509-12, T5516, 5524, 6367-68.

Presiding Circuit Judge Oakes recognized this point in his dissent: "[T]he taxpayer here was the founder and leader of a worldwide movement which, regardless of what the observer may think of its views or even its motives, is nevertheless on its face a religious one, the members of which regard the taxpayer as the *embodiment of their faith*" (emphasis added). *United States v. Moon*, 718 F.2d 1210, 1242 (2d Cir. 1983).

And how does this "embodiment of their faith" consider and treat the money? How do *members* of the church regard money which he receives? To both Reverend Moon *and* Unification Church members, the money is church money to be used for church purposes. This does not make Reverend Moon "a walking unincorporated association." T6119. Nor does it create a "loophole" for religious leaders to hide behind the First Amendment and escape liability for violations of criminal or tax laws. It does not mean that the individual religious leader has no separate and distinguishable legal identity apart from the religion itself, nor that he is freed from an independent responsibility for taxes on personal income. Nevertheless, the court below apparently misconstrued Reverend Moon's defense entirely when it said: "We do not accept this defense. . .Moon's spiritual identity as a leader of the Unification Church move-

6

ment and his legal identity as a taxpayer are not the same." 718 F.2d at 1227. This has *never* been Reverend Moon's claim.[2]

To say that Reverend Moon or any other religious leader holds funds in his own name in this context simply means that the church entrusts its leader — be he a founder, prophet, or bishop — with the authority to administer the funds in a manner consistent with their religious intentions and purposes.

B. The Record

With an ordinary lay person, the mention of his name evokes primarily the image of the individual and only secondarily such key relationships as his profession or religion. In the case of a religious leader, particularly the founder and prophet of a religion, just the reverse is true. As with the Pope, *see* 718 F.2d 1227-28, the mention of the name evokes not the image of the individual but the image of the church and the office. As with both the Pope and the Reverend Moon, a reference to the individual is the equivalent of a reference to the institution he symbolizes.

The "oneness" of Reverend Moon and the Unification Church — and the "oneness" of the bank accounts here — is revealed in the record.

Testified Eugene Galbraith, the bank officer responsible for the Chase accounts in Reverend Moon's name: "I must say that the name of the church and of Reverend Moon became synonymous in the minds of everyone in the bank at or about that time." T3670. And Mr. Galbraith "really never in [his] own mind was able to separate the two." T3662.

Michael Runyon, the church member who served as Reverend Moon's representative in dealing with the accountants and

---

[2]It should be noted that Reverend Moon did in fact file tax returns for the periods in question and did pay income taxes on amounts used for his family's own needs.

7

lawyers regarding his 1974 and 1975 tax returns, also testified that the Chase account was representative of the holdings of the international movement, even though the monies were made out to the order of the Reverend Moon. T4651-52, 4784-85, 4817.

Douglas J. Green, the C.P.A. who prepared Reverend Moon's tax returns for the years 1974 and 1975, on direct:

Q. "Tell us as best as you recall what Mr. Runyon told you about that."
A. "Okay. In 1973, there was a personal checking account established that Reverend Moon had signatory power over to write checks on and so on and so forth and that they were church funds." T4183

Again, Mr. Green:

"They presented us with one Form 1099 in Reverend Moon's name and told us it was a time deposit, a church account and he was only the nominee for it." T4185.

Now from two of the affidavits submitted on point: First, David S.C. Kim, one of the church elders:

"It was further agreed that such a large scale international effort, the first ever undertaken by our Church as a worldwide movement, would be centered upon the Rev. Moon, the natural focus of unity and cooperation among us all. As to financial matters, our international church leaders expected to receive the most donations from Japan. At the meeting, Mr. Ishii made a suggestion that opening a bank account in Rev. Moon's name would help in asking for donations. The reason for doing so. . .was that Japanese members knew little about the American Church, since there were few Japanese members in America at the time. Rev. Moon willingly approved of the proposal and as a result a bank account was opened in Rev. Moon's name on behalf of the Church to receive funds from around the world." A194.

The presidents of the three national churches of America, Korea and Japan, in an affidavit submitted in support of Reverend Moon's motion for a new trial:

8

"In the eye of the devoted, Reverend Moon is thus one with the faith he founded — not with any of its individual and particular corporate extensions, each of which is self-governing under his spiritual guidance, but with the incorporeal faith itself. . . This is why Reverend Moon's followers are often known as "Moonies", just as the followers of Mohammed are called Mohammedans or of Buddha, Buddhists. Even while outsiders may use the term as a derisive description of the members of our faith, we regard it proudly as a symbol of our unity with the God-centered faith that Reverend Moon embodies. . .[W]hen monies and assets are entrusted to him by the faithful, they are considered to be placed in his hands as the instrument and personification of the religious movement as a whole — not just as one aspect of that movement, but of the movement in all of its complexities, diversities, and goals." A1510, 1512. *See also* A1486.

What was excluded from the record is also relevant. At trial the defense sought to argue that, given the defendant's special role within his religion, the meaning of the defendant's control and use of assets was that they belonged to the church as a whole, and were merely held *for* it by the defendant as the church's embodiment.

But defense efforts to present such evidence brought forth objections from the government which the trial court repeatedly sustained. On one occasion, a principal defense witness endeavored to explain, in response to questioning, that Reverend Moon's signature upon an investment agreement (characterized by the government as "personal") in fact signified an investment and an obligation undertaken by and on behalf of the church. The court summarily sustained the government's objection. T5681.

In the case of a knowledgeable government witness, the defense was prevented from eliciting testimony regarding Reverend Moon's and the Church's views on the relationship between the Church and business. T5254. The same pattern was repeated with other witnesses from whom the defense sought to

9

elicit similar testimony regarding the religious basis for the investments.

The efforts of the defense to develop this evidence were also opposed by a darker, more menacing tactic. For example, in one instance defense counsel attempted to show that various commercial enterprises were in fact entered into on behalf of the Church — in order to enable it to develop a financial base to support and advance its work. T4819. The government continually threatened that any such attempt to bring such "religious" evidence into the case would result in the government's disclosure to the jury of "negative things abut the Church," T5760, which would no doubt have inflamed the jury's bias against Reverend Moon and his religion.

This chilling of the defense argument was evidently approved by the trial court itself. More than once it warned the defense that any efforts to offer religious explanations would "inadvertently open some doors" to the introduction of prejudicial evidence by the government. T3044; *see* T3042-45, 4818-20, 5257, 5759-60. As defense counsel was forced to conclude: "if your Honor's feeling is that my asking [a religion-oriented] question opens the door to the kind of thing they are talking about, then I feel precluded from asking the question." T4820. *See also* A1486-87.

The prosecution apparently realized that the only way Reverend Moon could be found guilty was if he could be pried apart from the Unification Church. Only by so separating him and ignoring his religious status could his activities be considered secular, the practices of a private businessman. Even with ordinary clergy there can be an implied trust or agency whereby it is perfectly valid for a church leader to hold funds in his own name on behalf of his church. In the case of Reverend Moon, there is still more involved because his followers see him as the very embodiment of their church.

10

C. History

The "oneness" of church leaders and their churches has a long history. And that history records that it has been a common practice for church leaders to hold property in their own names in trust for their churches. That history is reflected in American case law which recognizes this fact and presumes this relationship. But, as explained above, to his followers Reverend Moon is no *ordinary* church leader.

Explaining the exact relationship between Reverend Moon and the Unification Church goes beyond the scope of this brief. However, in summary: It is well established that Reverend Moon is both the founder and leader of his church. He is a prophet. His adherents look to him to establish the True Family serving as the foundation for eradicating evil in the world and accomplishing humankind's salvation. A1107. The Unification Church is the manifestation of his theological teachings.

In explaining the relationship between founder-prophet Reverend Moon and the Unification Church, analogies are useful but difficult to make. Certainly he is more the embodiment of his church than, for example, the annually elected president of the Council of Bishops of the United Methodist Church.

Reference to the Baha'i Faith, an off-shoot of Islam, is instructive. The mainspring of the hostility to the Baha'i minority has been the Islamic clergy's rejection of the idea that there could be divine revelation after Muhammad, who they regard as the last of the Prophets. This faith had its beginnings in 1844 with the announcement by one of its two founders, "The Bab", that his mission was to prepare the way for the Messenger of God for that age. Baha'is believe that Baha'u'llah was that Messenger. It was Baha'u'llah who founded the Baha'i community and brought the teachings of the Faith in 1863. This is not unlike the position Reverend Moon holds in the Unification faith. *See* A621-22.

Could one doubt that monies entrusted to the Bab or

11

Baha'u'llah by their followers over a century ago, were for their church?

Brigham Young provides another instructive analogy. For it was not until the controversy over his estate that the world learned that the Mormon leader was not *individually* and personally a millionaire. And it was learned how property held in Brigham Young's name was in fact held for the Mormon Church. President Young's estate generally had been estimated at between two and two and a half million dollars. Some estimates ran as high as eight million. But when final settlement was made, the actual amount found to be held by Brigham Young in his personal capacity was under $225,000.[3]

How Brigham Young had come to hold title in so much property is described by Professor Arrington in these words:

> [Mormon] Church leaders adopted the studied and deliberate policy of placing properties acquired by the church in the hands of the church president and other trustworthy individuals, to be administered by them on behalf of the church, but in a private capacity. This consolidation of the functions of the trustee-in-trust under the names of Brigham Young and others resulted from a general agreement that the church, through its leading men, must continue to function as an instrument for the attainment of the economic objectives of the group. The policy led to a confusion between Brigham Young, trustee-in-trust, and Brigham Young, private businessman. . .The choice made by church leaders explains why, in all his

---

[3]*See* Arrington, *The Settlement of the Brigham Young Estate, 1877-1879,* Pacific Historical Review (Feb. 1952) at 9-10. *See also Young v. Cannon,* 2 Utah 560 (1879). In the instant case the trial court made an inference that the funds in question could not have been held in trust because the amount was somehow unprecedented in its size. P99. The analogy to such figures as Brigham Young and Cardinal Cody demonstrates the fallacy of this inference.

12

business dealings representing the church, President Young almost invariably signed for properties in his own name. . .It accounts for the wide-spread tendency among newspapermen, writers, and historians to give Brigham Young credit for many enterprises which were in reality enterprises of the church. [Footnotes] *Id.* at 4.

Another case in point is the Church of Christ Scientist. So much was Mary Baker Eddy the embodiment of the Christian Science religion that her great publication, *Science and Health with Key to the Scriptures,* is studied by her followers as the Koran is studied by Muslims and the Talmud is studied by Orthodox Jews. And this identification achieved Congressional recognition through a special law extending the copyright protection of her 1875 work. The Congressional enactment was Pub.L. No. 92-604:

Those who are students or adherents of the Christian Science religion and worship in the Church of Christ, Scientist, founded by Mrs. Eddy, also look to the Bible and *"Science and Health with Key to the Scriptures"* as the only Pastor of this Church. . .The purpose of seeking copyright for this book is. . .to preserve and maintain the purity and integrity of the statement of the religious teachings of this denomination, and thereby to protect members of the public against the possibility that. . .they might receive a distorted version of the teachings of Christian Science instead of the true and correct version thereof. . .*Id.* at 2-3.

Menachem M. Schneerson provides another useful analogy. Born in 1902, heir to the ultra-Orthodox mystic teachings of the Chassidim and heir of the great leaders of the Lubavitcher sect, he ascended to leadership as the 7th Lubavitcher Rebbe in 1950, a position he holds to date. Dedicated to the spreading of Chassidic teachings throughout the world, it was he who

13

established Lubavitch Centers and Chabad-Lubavitch Houses in many cities in both the United States and abroad. He is revered by his followers as Reverend Moon is revered by the Unification Church members. He is the fountainhead, the wellspring. His is the final word on theological matters. In this context he is more than a mere individual.

Rebbe Schneerson is the recipient of large sums of money from his followers — sums which he is supposed to devote (and does devote) to his religion. That religion, like that of the Unification Church, requires large sums for its teaching and missionary activities.

Rebbe Schneerson also provides an example of the church-man who holds cash on behalf of the congregation. He regularly gives "audiences" at which his congregants line up for short question-answer-advice sessions. It is during such "audiences" that envelopes filled with money are handed to the Rebbe for religious purposes. And often the next man in line is given monies just received by the Rebbe to assist him as a needy parishioner or as one who is to carry out the work of the religious organization.

Roman Catholicism provides yet another example. The bishop (or cardinal) is the principal repository of all ec-clesiastical power. Bishops are "the ordinary and immediate pastors of their respective dioceses, and as such have the right (and duty) to govern in spiritual and temporal matters, in accordance with the canons, employing legislative, judicial and coercive power." *Corpus Juris Canonici,* Canon 339.

Reviewing the investigation of the finances of the late John Cardinal Cody, head of the nation's largest Roman Catholic Diocese, the following appears in *Notes on Church-State Affairs,* 24 J. Church & St. 175, 196-97 (1982):

> The issue of most importance concerns the proper role of the U.S. government in the financial affairs of the Chicago archdiocese and John Cardinal Cody

14

. . . . "[C]ontingency funds not subject to audit and under the complete control of the Church leaders is common to the United States. Perhaps the most difficult issue focuses upon the federal government's subpoena of archdiocese corporate records. Under Illinois law, the archiocese of Chicago is a 'corporate sole,' a legal designation that gives incorporation status to the cardinal and his successors in perpetuity."

All of the foregoing analogies clarify that Reverend Moon's holding church property in his own name is consistent with the tradition followed by other major religious figures.

D. Case Law

(1) *History*

Case law analysis — that is, American case law analysis — begins with an excursion into history, early common law history. The tour guide is Austin Wakeman Scott.

The centuries-old common law practice of vesting title to church property in the name of individuals is a custom which can be observed in the case of the Franciscan friars as early as the Thirteenth Century. Here is how this came about: In feudal times, church property in England was held in Frankalmoign tenure by "religious corporations." As the wealth and influence of the churches grew, they began to be perceived as threats to the king and his feudal lords. Thus the practice of holding title to church property in the name of individuals was used as a form of protection against punitive measures taken by aggressive monarchs, jealous not only of the church's spiritual power but of its temporal possessions.[4]

---

[4]This history is instructive for it illuminates the fact that the practice was more than a mere convenience. It provided a substantive defense against aggressive government, a consideration as pertinent to U.S. Catholics in the 19th and 20th centuries as it was to those in 13th century England.

15

To avoid confiscatory laws directed against property held by "religious corporations," it became the custom of those desiring to benefit the church to convey property to an individual, but for the "use"[5] or benefit of the church. Since the land was held in the name of an individual person, it was not subject to confiscation. And since these individuals were usually clerics, they would be exempt from military fealty and service which normally attached to the land.

This practice gradually achieved official recognition and blessing, first by the Court of Chancery, which began to uphold such trusts in the sixteenth century. The trend culminated in the Statute of Charitable Uses in 1601 which specifically authorized them and provided for their enforcement by special commissioners. *See generally* IV A.W. Scott, The Law of Trusts (3d ed. 1967).

This legal heritage was carried to the American colonies. Authority (and an example) is provided by Justice Story in *Terrett v. Taylor,* 13 U.S. (9 Cranch) 43 (1815). In the Episcopal Church in the Colony of Virginia, title to real property was vested in the pastor and title to personalty was vested in lay officers known as church wardens:

> . . . the minister of the parish was, during his incumbency, seized of the freehold of its inheritable property, as emphatically *persona ecclesiae,* and capable, as a sole corporation, of transmitting that inheritance to his successors. The church wardens, also, were a corporate body, clothed with authority and guardianship over the repairs of the church and its personal property . . . *Id.* at 46.

And, as Circuit Judge Oakes pointed out in his dissent below ". . . there are numerous cases holding that a minister or other

---

[5]The term "use" may be taken as synonymous with the word trust. Indeed, for hundreds of years, the term use was commonly used to denominate a holding in trust.

16

church official who held title to property in his own name did so as trustee for the church." *United States v. Moon,* 718 F.2d at 1243.

(2) *The Trust Relationship*

The most recent case exploring this title-trust relationship in depth is *Winn v. Commissioner,* 595 F.2d 1060 (5th Cir. 1979). The discussion of this case is introduced in the dissenting opinion below in these words:

> It appears that the assets in question came to Moon largely from members of his faith, and there was some evidence that the donors intended their contributions to be used by him for religious purposes. The religious context involved gives the case a special color. As noted in cases such as *Winn v. Commissioner,* 595 F.2d 1060, 1065 (5th Cir. 1979), funds donated for the use of an individual involved in religious work may be considered gifts to the religious organization with which the individual is affiliated. 718 F.2d at 1242.

Winn was also a tax case. The taxpayers sought (and succeeded in obtaining) a deduction for a $10,000 check paid to the "Sara Barry Fund" to support Presbyterian mission work in Korea. Contributions were channeled by Sara Barry's father, an elder in one of the sponsoring churches, into her personal bank account for use in her mission work. The Fifth Circuit held that, although the tax-exempt churches never received or had possession of the Winns' contribution, the Winns were entitled to a deduction.

> Proof that the church . . . sponsored 'Sara Barry Days' for the express purpose of collecting funds for this part of its work, that an officer of that church took the funds donated and dealt with them as the church wished, and that the funds went to the support of the work the church intended is sufficient to establish that the funds were donated for the use of the . . . Presbyterian church. *Id.* at 1065.

17

Additional authority is found in two Kansas cases involving the same church: *Dawkins v. Dawkins,* 183 Kan. 323, 328 P.2d 346 (1958) and *Gospel Tab. Body of Christ Church v. Peace Pub. & Co.,* 211 Kan. 420, 506 P.2d 1135 (1973). Interestingly, both cases bear the identical Syllabus by the Court:

> The established fact that a minister of an unincorporated church acted as the sole trustee of the church in handling its property and affairs, and later, acted as the dominant member of the board of trustees of the church, did not support the legal conclusion that the minister held title to the church property for his personal benefit. . . .

The Reverend Moon-Unification Church analogy is readily apparent.

(3) *The Agency Relationship*

Some courts have reached the same conclusion based on an agency theory rather than a trust theory. The leading case for this position is *Morey v. Riddell,* 205 F. Supp. 918 (S.D. Cal. 1962). It was cited with approval by Judge Oakes in these words: "Similarly in *Morey v. Riddell* . . . it was held that where money contributed to a totally unorganized religious association by way of checks to individual 'ministers' was used to meet expenses of the church, including the ministers' living expenses, [tax] deductions for religious contributions would be permitted." *United States v. Moon,* 718 F.2d at 1243.

The I.R.S. disputed the deductibility because the donations had been in the form of checks payable to the order of four of the church's ministers, claiming that these were gifts to the ministers. In upholding the deductions the court said: "[I]t is clear from the evidence that plaintiffs did not intend to make contributions to the ministers, individually, but placed the funds in their hands, as agents, for the use of the church." *Morey v. Riddell,* 205 F. Supp. at 921. The evidence showed that the members had refused to adopt a denominational name or any written organizational guide because "to do so would be

18

to add an arbitrary gloss to biblical precepts, thus obscuring the word of God." *Id.* at 919. Having disavowed formal organization, their only recourse was to make donations which would be held in the name of their ministers.

(4) *Catholic Church Property*

The "oneness" between church leader and church in the handling of finances perhaps is best known in connection with the assets of the Roman Catholic Church.[6] The four principal cases illustrating this relationship (the numbers are legion) are:

1. *Mannix v. Purcell,* 46 Ohio St. 102, 19 N.E. 572 (1888);

2. *Reid v. Barry,* 93 Fla. 849, 112 So. 846 (1927);

3. *Fink v. Umscheid,* 40 Kan. 271, 19 p. 623 (1888);

4. *Archbishop v. Shipman,* 79 Cal. 288, 21 P. 830 (1889).

Here is the sentence from *Mannix v. Purcell,* 19 N.E. at 584, which ties up history and American practice: "The parties have gone back fifteen centuries into the laws and canons of the [Roman Catholic] church, for proof of the nature of the tenure by which the archbishop held the legal title to the ecclesiastical property, and the proof is overwhelming that he was not invested with an absolute title to it as his own." The fact "that from time to time during the archbishop's service he exercises acts of apparent private ownership over property held for ecclesiastical uses" was held irrelevant. *Id.* at 585.

In the course of the lawsuit, the court allowed testimony as to the canons of the Catholic Church in order to show that by these Church precepts, the property was church property. In other words, it permitted evidence which would give a *religious and theological* explanation to show that the property held nominally by Archbishop Purcell was beneficially owned by the

---

[6]*See* G. Myers, *History of Bigotry in the United States* (1960). The leading work on the subject is Rev. Patrick J. Dignan's dissertation *A History of the Legal Incorporation of Catholic Church Property in the United States (1784-1932)* (1933). *See also amicus curiae* brief filed by the Catholic League for Religious and Civil Rights in support of certiorari in the instant case.

19

Church. Had the court excluded such evidence, deeming it irrelevant as in the *Moon* case, the only evidence on the record would have been that record title to the real estate stood in John Purcell's name in fee simple.

Reid v. Barry, 93 Fla. 849, 112 So. 846 (1927), involved the validity of a deed of land made to the Bishop of St. Augustine. It was a suit to quiet title to property taken under a deed transferring it to the "Right Rev. John Moore, Bishop of St. Augustine, Florida . . . and his successors in office and assigns forever." *Id.* at 858, 112 So. at 850. As pointed out in the bill filed by the Bishop, "[I]t is and has been the custom of the said church since long before the year 1881, and up to the present time, to take title to property it acquires, in Diocese of St. Augustine, in the name of the Bishop of St. Augustine for the time being, and his successors in office." *Id.* at 856, 112 So. at 849.

After discussing both the nature of the agency relationship and the legal history of the corporation sole, the court concluded in these words:

> [W]hether we recognize the appellee, complainant in the court below, in his capacity as bishop, as a corporation sole or not, the analogy to the common-law corporation sole is so complete as to bring him within the spirit and reason of the doctrine relating thereto, and vindicate our conclusion on the other grounds mentioned. *Id.* at 887, 112 So. at 860.

Accord: Fink v. Umsheid, 40 Kan. 271, 19 P. 623 (1888). There a Catholic bishop had used money supplied by his congregation to purchase land, in his own name, to be used for maintaining a church and school. When the bishop later attempted to sell the property, representatives of the local unincorporated congregation successfuly overturned the conveyance on the ground that the bishop held the land in trust for the congregation and did not have absolute discretion in disposing of it.

Archbishop v. Shipman, 79 Cal. 288, 21 P. 830 (1889), was yet another case in which a Roman Catholic archbishop "pur-

20

chased the property for and with the money of the church, but took the deed in his individual name." *Id.* at 293, 21 P. at 831. Although the Archbishop "exercised exclusive control over said property as fully as if he were the sole and individual owner thereof," *id.*, the court in *Shipman* ruled that the property was held in trust for the church. Here again the facts run parallel to the instant case.

CONCLUSION

When the Second Circuit decision is considered in light of the history and law which have been documented in the foregoing pages, it seems clear that the majority misconstrued the context in which this case should have been viewed. As a consequence the court grieviously misread the applicable law, violating Reverend Moon's rights to equal protection and the free exercise of religion.

Such error merits review by this Court in order to avert a miscarriage of justice in a case which could send the founder and leader of a worldwide religious movement to jail for following the centuries-old practice of holding church property in his individual name. When the major constitutional issues ably presented in the petition and briefs of other *amici* are added to this consideration, the need for review by this Court becomes paramount.

Respectfully submitted,

Albert P. Blaustein
Rutgers University School of Law
Camden, NJ 08102
(609) 757-6373

Counsel for Amicus Curiae

The Freemen Institute
3740 West 1987 South
Salt Lake City, UT 84104

The Institute for the Study of
American Religion

i

Question Presented

Where a defendant in a criminal trial is the leader of a new or unpopular religion, and his trial inescapably entails judgments about his religious stewardship, does the Free Exercise Clause limit a trial court's authority to deny the defendant's request that he be granted a non-jury trial to minimize the influence of religious bias against him?

iii

TABLE OF CONTENTS

iv

TABLE OF AUTHORITIES

v

vi

In the

Supreme Court of the United States

OCTOBER TERM, 1983

No. 83-1242

SUN MYUNG MOON and TAKERU KAMIYAMA,

Petitioners,

v.

UNITED STATES OF AMERICA,

Respondent.

ON PETITION FOR CERTIORARI TO THE UNITED STATES
COURT OF APPEALS FOR THE SECOND CIRCUIT

BRIEF *AMICUS CURIAE* FOR THE INSTITUTE FOR THE STUDY OF AMERICAN RELIGION IN SUPPORT OF PETITION FOR CERTIORARI

Pursuant to Rule 36.1 of the Rules of this Court, this brief is filed with the written consent of counsel for the parties. Their original letters are filed with the Clerk of this Court.

Interest of *Amicus Curiae*

The Institute for the Study of American Religion (ISAR) is a scholarly research facility devoted to the study of American religious groups, particularly the smaller and minority religions, those which have most frequently been subjected to religious prejudice and intolerance.

Established in 1969, ISAR is a non-membership organization. Out of its research has come the *Encyclopedia of American Religion* (1978), the standard reference on American religious groups, as well as its companion volume, the *Directory of Religious Bodies in the United States* (1977).

2

The ISAR submits this brief out of its deep concern over the upsurge of religious prejudice against what are seen as unconventional religions in America. In particular, ISAR believes that the prosecution and conviction of Reverend Moon must be understood in the context of the long history of religious intolerance in this country.

Statement of the Case

Amicus curiae adopts, to the extent relevant, the Statement of the Case as set forth in the petition for certiorari.

Summary of Argument

The government's refusal to accede to petitioner's election of a non-jury trial in a prosecution for criminal tax fraud and conspiracy is but the most recent manifestation of a tragic history of unfair and unconstitutional efforts in America directed against new and unpopular religions, currently called "cults." History shows that such religions are frequently the subject of fear and hatred on the part of the general public from which a jury is drawn, as well as on the part of the nation's executive, legislative, and prosecutorial agencies.

These feelings of antipathy are too often manifested in efforts to destroy or at least to punish such religions, through whichever efforts, legal or non-legal, may prove effective. *Amicus curiae* submit that, irrespective of other guarantees contained in the Constitution and Bill of Rights, imposition of a jury trial upon the leader of a church in a criminal case directly involving his religious stewardship violates his Free Exercise rights—at least where, as here, the religious leader and his followers are demonstrably the targets of widespread fear and hatred. In insisting upon a jury trial in a criminal case against the leader of the international Unification Church, the government practically assured itself of a conviction. Thus obtained, the conviction is a violation of the petitioner's constitutionally protected rights.

3

I.

An Historical Background of Religious Persecution in America.

A. *The Historical Background.*

In order to grasp the magnitude of error in the Second Circuit's affirmance of the trial court's refusal to accede to the petitioner's request for a non-jury trial, a brief survey of the historical setting is in order. For we do not think that the trial judge was correct, at least in respect to the application of the Religion Clauses, in implying that the present case is *sui generis.*[1]

The history of the struggle for religious freedom and church-state separation is in large measure one against persecution and for equality of treatment on behalf of religions which in their formation days were hated and feared by the general community. It was the purpose of the Religion Clauses in the First Amendment (as well as the ban in Article VI on religious tests for public office) to bring an end to discrimination against these religious groups.

Many, if not most of those who settled in what is now the United States, did so to escape religious persecution and discrimination in England. Unfortunately, the majority of them manifested little reluctance to impose upon religious non-conformists on these shores what they themselves had suffered in England. Nor did they hesitate to use the instrumentalities of law to effectuate their purposes.

---

[1] The judge said: "Let me say that I think Reverend Moon is *sui generis.* I don't think there is anyone is this country similar to him . . . I am not so naive as to believe that if Reverend Moon was a non-controversial person whose religion was Pollyannish, who nobody took exception to, that the government would not have had as much interest in looking at his taxes as they did . . ." S36-37. References to the trial transcript will be designated as "T—"; to post-trial transcripts "S—"; to pre-trial transcripts "P—"; and to pleadings "A—".

4

What follows in this section is a brief survey of how our forefathers dealt with religious dissidents such as those who would be today called "cultists." Among these were Baptists, Unitarians, Friends, Catholics, Jews, Mormons, Adventists, Amish, Jehovah's Witnesses, and many others. What members of these faiths share is a history of discrimination through a variety of legal and extra-legal devices all having the purpose of destroying those who were viewed as the particular social enemy at a given time in our history. Reflecting in their actions the prejudice of the communities which empowered them to act, governmental authorities visited upon such despised groups penalties ranging from banishment, fines, and imprisonment, to the use of stocks for public derision and scorn. Indeed on occasion other, more severe penalties—including death—were imposed.[2]

In significant ways the present hysterical reaction to "cults", the consequent trials and the inevitable guilty verdicts are reminiscent of the anti-witchcraft trials evoked by Cotton Mather in Salem, Massachusetts, and spread elsewhere in the colonies in the 17th century. In one Salem case, all twelve of the jurors later signed a statement admitting their error in handing down guilty verdicts. Of the defendants in other widespread jury trials (involving several hundred young women and "afflicted children"), nineteen were hanged.[3]

In the same period, Anne Hutchinson and her brother-in-law Reverend John Wainwright were banished for heresy in preaching the covenant of grace rather than of works. So, too, was Roger Williams, a founder of the Baptist Church in North America.[4]

---

[2] L. Pfeffer, *Church, State and Freedom* 76 (rev. 1967).

[3] I A. Stokes, *Church and State in the United States* 169-70 (1960).

[4] In the present case insofar as they opposed his motion for a recommendation against deportation, the government sought the

5

Roger Williams' experiences of prejudice because of his religion were shared by other Baptists, who, however, suffered imprisonment rather than exile. During the "period of the Great Persecution" (1768 to 1774), they were whipped, beaten, arrested, fined and imprisoned, sometimes living only on bread and water.[5] In 1774 James Madison wrote to a friend:

> That diabolical, hell-conceived principle of persecution rages among some. . . . This vexes me the worst of anything whatever. There are at this time in the adjacent county not less than five or six well-meaning men in close jail for publishing their religious sentiments, which in the main are very orthodox. I have neither patience to hear, talk, or think of anything relative to this matter; for I have squabbled and scolded, abused and ridiculed, so long about it to little purpose, that I am without common patience. So I must beg you to pity me, and pray for liberty of conscience to all.[6]

Members of a religious "cult", formally called the Society of Friends, but popularly and derisively known as "Quakers" (just as adherents to the Unification Church are called "Moonies"), were another religious sect who suffered persecution (in a few cases even through a death sentence) because their beliefs were unacceptable to the people. So, too, were the Catholics, popularly and derogatorily called "Papists". Except in Maryland, where Catholics constituted a majority, they were widely subjected to religious

---

banishment of Reverend Moon through deportation, but the trial judge refused to concur. S190-91. In addition, the government returned the indictment while Reverend Moon was out of the country and might perhaps have been tempted to not return. S.162.

[5] E. Humphrey, *Nationalism and Religion in America 1774-1789* at 368-69 (1924).

[6] I *Writings of James Madison* 18-21 (G. Hunt ed. 1900-1909).

6

discrimination and group defamation. The General Court of Massachusetts, for example, decreed in 1647 that

> [n]o Jesuit or ecclesiastical person ordained by the pope or the see of Rome shall henceforth come into Massachusetts. Any person not freeing himself of suspicion shall be jailed, then banished. If taken a second time, he shall be put to death.[7]

In 1689, a new charter was granted decreeing that "forever thereafter there shall be liberty of conscience allowed in the worship of God to all Christians (except papists)."[8]

This fear and hatred of Catholics endured well into the 20th century. Although a Catholic (Roger Taney) could be appointed Chief Justice of the Supreme Court in 1837 with the consent of the Senate, it was more than a century later before one could be elected President. Incorporation statutes, with the Catholic Church in mind, often required lay representation on the boards of directors in respect even to properties used exclusively for religious purposes.[9] In the mid-19th century, the Nativist or "Know-Nothing" Party stated its comprehensive purpose as "Anti-Romanism, Anti-Bedinism, Anti-Pope's Toeism, Anti-Nunnerism, Anti-Winking Virginism, Anti-Jesuitism, and Anti-the-Whole-Sacredotal-Hierarchism with all its humbugging mummeries."[10]

That this Party was in tune with popular prejudice is evidenced by the fact that, for a time, it was able to capture the legislatures in quite a number of states. In Con-

---

[7] S. Cobb, *The Rise of Religious Liberty in America* 177 (1902).

[8] *Id.* at 233.

[9] A. Stokes and L. Pfeffer, *Church and State in the United States* (1964).

[10] *Id.* at 236.

7

necticut, for example, it was able to enact a law requiring corporate rather than individual holding of property.[11] In Massachusetts the Know-Nothing legislature appointed a "Nunnery Committee" to report on "such theological seminaries, boarding schools, academies, nunneries, convents, and other institutions of like character as they may deem necessary."[12] The appointment of such a committee reflects a widespread belief that young women did not voluntarily commit themselves to serving their religion as nuns but were the victims of physical duress or "mind-control" (a belief reflected today in a practically universal assumption respecting "cults"). There was, indeed, strong condemnation of convents on the ground that unlawful means were supposedly used to force young women into them.[13]

Perhaps the faith which in recent years has been, more than any other, the victim of prejudice, hatred and fear—incorporated in legislation, and manifested in criminal prosecutions and guilty verdicts—is that of the Jehovah's Witnesses. But the Witnesses are now an accepted member of the family of American faiths. They reached that enviable station only after a period of trials and tribulations instigated by government officials hostile to their beliefs and practice. New laws were enacted and old laws resurrected to supply weapons to curb their activities and, if possible, to completely destroy them. All kinds of laws were used or were attempted to be used for that purpose—anti-peddling ordinances, traffic regulations, revenue laws, laws forbidding the use of sound trucks, and many others were invoked against them.[14]

---

[11] *Id.* at 237.

[12] *Id.*

[13] III A. Stokes, *Church and State in the United States* 818-22 (1950).

[14] H. W. Barber, *Religious Liberty* v. *Police Power: Jehovah's Witnesses*, 41 American Political Science Review 226 (1947). *See also* R. Manwaring, *Render Unto Caesar* (1966).

8

America owes a great debt of gratitude to the Witnesses insofar as much of the current law relating to religious freedom resulted from the Witnesses' persistence in asserting their constitutional rights and appealing adverse verdicts to the Supreme Court. The hostility vented against the Witnesses was in large measure motivated by what was generally considered to be their non-Americanism in refusing to salute or pledge allegiance to the flag[15]—just as prejudice against Reverend Moon's Korean origins may in part account for his own plight in this case. Another and no less substantial a factor in the persecution of the Witnesses was their criticism of recognized and respected religions, particularly Catholicism, itself a formerly reviled faith.[16]

It is difficult to believe, until the Witnesses survived persecution and prejudice and were generally considered to be a legitimate faith, that they could receive a fair and impartial verdict from juries anywhere in the United States; and this is so no matter how emphatically prospective jurors asserted in voir dire that they would not allow their own religious biases to influence their verdict. Nevertheless, automatic exclusion of Catholics as a group from juries in criminal trials against Jehovah's Witnesses would obviously have violated the Constitution.[17] Indeed, it is by no means certain that the Constitution would even have permitted questioning veniremen as to the content of their religious beliefs and practices. Thus the only practical remedy available to Jehovah's Witnesses in most cases would have been to do what the defendant in the present case sought

---

[15] *See Minersville School District* v. *Gobitis*, 310 U.S. 586 (1940); *West Virginia State Board of Education* v. *Barnette*, 319 U.S. 624 (1943). *See also Murdock* v. *Pennsylvania*, 319 U.S. 105 (1943); *Follett* v. *Town of McCormick*, 321 U.S. 573 (1944).

[16] *See Cantwell* v. *Connecticut*, 310 U.S. 296 (1940).

[17] *Torcaso* v. *Watkins*, 367 U.S. 488 (1961).

9

to do, that is, to waive a jury trial to protect himself from religious prejudice. *We are aware of no other case in which the government has ever vetoed a defendant's exercise of this right in such circumstances.*

B. *The Relevance of History.*

The foregoing account we suggest, indicates quite clearly that, throughout our history, persons who, in the arena of religion, have at various times been called heretics, atheists, nonconformists, sectarians, and other such sobriquets, have been the subjects of persecution at the hands of secular governmental authorities—including lawmakers, prosecuting attorneys, and jurors. What was true in the past in respect to these faiths is at least equally true today in respect to new religious groups now commonly called "cults."

It should be noted that the term "cults," though originally neutral,[18] has now become an intensely derogatory appellation; and of various "cults" today, the "Moonies" undoubtedly comprise the most despised of all. Indeed, the very term "Moonie," like the term "cult," is an expression of derision. It is simply impossible to believe that the jurors were not aware that the defendant was the head of the "Moonies", the most notorious of all "cults." Indeed, Reverend Moon himself is the focal point of the group's notoriety. The fact that the jurors themselves were aware of this notoriety was fully borne out by the voir dire. T. 473, 847-48, 857, 1391, 1394, 1514-15, 2052, 2106.

There was simply no practicable means to isolate the jurors from what was known or assumed throughout the United States and its Territories, as distant from New York as Guam. This was verified by the random survey of 1,000 persons in the Southern District conducted under

---

[18] "Sociologically, a cult is the starting point of every. religion . . . .Jesus and his twelve disciples offer a classic example of a cult." D. Bromley & A. Shupe, Jr., *Strange Gods* 23 (1981).

10

the direction of Stephen Roth, which showed that more than 40% of the respondents indicated that they were ready to "throw the Reverend Sun Myung Moon in jail without hearing any evidence or even knowing the charges against him, if any." A822-23.

While the terms "brainwashing" and "cults" frequently mentioned in Roth's survey may not have originated in respect to Reverend Moon, their widespread use, always in a derogatory sense, is a fact which, we suggest, is judicially noticeable. So, too, is the term "Moonies."

"Cultists," generally, and "Moonies," specifically, have been verbally pummeled and degraded in all media of mass communication—radio, television, newspapers, magazines, and cinema. At least three commercially presented motion pictures, depicting "cultist" leaders as villains, and the people flocking to them as dupes—"Ticket to Heaven", "Moon Child" and "Split Images"—have been exhibited in recent years.

Historically the transition from "cultism" to the status of an accepted faith or religion varies in respect to time. It was two centuries after the deaths of Jesus and his eleven disciples (Judas having hanged himself), by the grace of the emperors Constantine and Licinius, that Christianity was promoted from "culthood" to this coveted status. In the United States, of course, such an elevation cannot be formalized by government action because of the First Amendment's ban on laws respecting an establishing of religion. The nearest we can come to such formal approval is the grant of tax exempt status and income tax deductibility for contributions, benefits made available to the Unification Church, T4273, see *Holy Spirit Association for the Unification of World Christianity* v. *Tax Commission*, 55 N.Y.2d 512 (1982) and not challenged by the government in this case. As this case attests, however, even the conferral of such benefits on a church does not assure freedom from persecution for the church's leaders.

11

Government recognition of the Unification Church's tax exempt status cannot mitigate the hatred, fear and animosity visited upon Reverend Moon or upon his Church. Nor can it be expected that these intense feelings will or can be set aside when the public acts through its jury system against any "cult." Thus, in October, 1979, a jury in Portland, Oregon, after 18 hours deliberation following four weeks of testimony, handed down a verdict for $2,067,000.20 against the Church of Scientology, another "cult", which allegedly defrauded the plaintiff by inducing her to pay tuition in the sum of $3,000.20 for courses at the church school. The gravamen of her complaint was that the church had falsely represented that she would receive superior psychological understanding and additional capabilities in her civil engineering field. Of the $2,067,000.20 verdict, wholly $2,000,000 represented punitive damages.[19] It hardly seems likely that a bench trial would have resulted in the same verdict or anything near it.

II.

In the Circumstances of This Case, the Free Exercise Clause Required the Trial Court to Grant the Defendant's Request for a Non-Jury Trial.

As the historical record demonstrates, religious liberty in this country has been repeatedly put at risk—despite the fact that the Europeans who first settled the land were themselves victims of religious persecution. Nevertheless, because of our unique historical commitment as a people to religious freedom—a commitment to which we have, tragically, not always been true—our Bill of Rights accords even greater latitude for religious liberty than for other protected rights. Thus, although in some contexts

---

[19] On appeal to the Oregon Court of Appeals, the judgment was reversed and remanded. *Christofferson* v. *Church of Scientology of California*, 57 Or. App. 203, 644 P.2d 2877 (1982).

12

"freedom of conscience [may not claim] a broader protection than freedom of mind," *Prince* v. *Massachusetts*, 321 U.S. 158, 164 (1944), religious liberty under the Free Exercise Clause generally is accorded leeway not afforded other rights that also occupy "a preferred position in our basic scheme." *Id.*[20] We submit that, irrespective of other clauses in the Constitution and Bill of Rights, imposition of a jury trial upon the leader of a church in a criminal case directly involving his church leadership violates the Free Exercise Clause in respect to him and the church, at least where there is, among the general population, a universal fear and hatred of both.

The Supreme Court's precedents make clear that such special deference must be accorded to rights protected by the Free Exercise Clause. For example, the Supreme Court has invalidated under the Free Exercise Clause a state statute which denied unemployment compensation to a Sabbatarian whose religious conviction impelled refusal to accept a job offer that required working on Saturdays. *Sherbert* v. *Verner*, 374 U.S. 398 (1963). It is fair to assume that the decision would not have been the same if the plaintiff had pleaded the right not to be penalized for missing work to attend Saturday meetings of his political party.

Similarly, in *Thomas* v. *Review Board*, 450 U.S. 707 (1981), the Supreme Court ruled unconstitutional under the Free Exercise Clause the denial of unemployment compensation to a claimant whose religious commitments forbade working in a plant manufacturing war materials. It may be assumed that the result would not have been the same if the refusal had been based on a general intellectual conviction as to the futility of all wars.

And in *Wisconsin* v. *Yoder*, 406 U.S. 205 (1972), the Supreme Court held violative of the Free Exercise Clause

---

[20] *See also* L. Pfeffer, "The Supremacy of Free Exercise," 61 Geo. L. Rev. 1115 (1973).

13

a statute requiring school attendance until the age of 16, as the law was applied to children of the Amish faith which forbids attendance beyond the age of 14. Such indulgence would presumably not be extended to a parent who wished to keep his child at home after age 14 on nonreligious grounds.

Finally, in *NLRB* v. *Catholic Bishop of Chicago,* 440 U.S. 490 (1979), the Supreme Court noted that there would be a significant risk of infringement of the Religion Clauses if the National Labor Relations Act were construed to confer NLRB jurisdiction over church-operated schools. Accordingly, the Court construed the act as exempting such schools. This it did notwithstanding the fact that in *Associated Press* v. *NLRB,* 301 U.S. 103 (1937), the Court upheld application of the law to news organizations over First Amendment objections that freedom of the press would be endangered thereby.

The import of these cases is clear. Whatever might be the situation in the case of a criminal defendant requesting a non-jury trial to minimize the risk of political oppression or even racial prejudice, the Free Exercise Clause mandates special deference to such a request in the case of a criminal defendant seeking to minimize *religious* prejudice at his trial—especially a defendant who leads a new and unpopular religion, whose trial inescapably entails judgments about whether assets he claims to hold for that religion instead belong to him personally. *United States* v. *Moon,* 718 F.2d at 1217. Such judgments go to the heart of his religious stewardship, and thus present an unusually sharp risk of bias.[21]

---

[21] *Cf.* H. Kalven, Jr. & H. Zeisel, *The American Jury* 24 (1966): "In rare instances . . . the court will insist that the public requires jury trial; and at least in a few cases the prosecution has refused to consent to jury waiver possibly as a tactical move to disadvantage the defendant . . . However even in the Federal courts such refusal by the prosecutor is an extremely rare event."

14

III.

The Trial Court's Denial of the Defendant's Request for a Non-Jury Trial Threatens the Religious Liberty of All Communities of Believers.

Ever since Madison's Memorial and Remonstrance and Jefferson's Virginia Statute for Establishing Religious Freedom, it has been recognized that taxation has the potential for impairing religious freedom. It is clear that a tax law expressly aimed at disfavored religions, or the discriminatory application of a facially neutral tax law against them, would violate the Free Exercise Clause. *See also Larson v. Valente,* 456 U.S. 228 (1982).

What we argue here is that the government's attorneys in the present case sought to accomplish through the jury what the Supreme Court has made clear in the cases described above may not be constitutionally done—that is, to penalize the exercise of religious rights. We believe that the government here prosecuted a controversial religion's leader for not paying a religiously neutral tax for the purpose of destroying or seriously injuring his religion. Indeed, we need not go that far, but need only urge that the risk that the jury would misuse a neutral tax law to injure the defendant and his religion entitled him to choose a bench trial, and thus to rely upon the fairness of the trial judge.

We do not maintain that the result in this case would necessarily have been different had the case been tried to a judge without a jury. What is contended here is that the petitioner's conviction would not have been virtually preordained in a bench trial. Thus the petitioner at least should have been allowed to place his trust in the court rather than in a jury. We submit that it was reversible error for the trial court not to allow him that option.

15

We suggest that, if juries are allowed to translate their fear and hatred of "cults" into guilty verdicts in criminal trials, or into exorbitant damage awards in civil cases, such groups may well find that, in order to survive, they have no choice but to radically alter their sincerely and deeply held religious beliefs and practices—lest they and their leaders "[be] persecuted for righteousness sake." *Matthew* 5:10 (King James). This result, we respectfully submit, would constitute the very antithesis of religious liberty.

CONCLUSION

Our brief has been limited to the Free Exercise Clause; we do not intend thereby to suggest that no other constitutionally protected rights are implicated. To the contrary, several clearly are. The government's intent to punish Reverend Moon for what he said in front of the courthouse, A811-12, and for his advertisement in the *New York Times*[22]—manifested by its demanding a jury trial in which conviction was practically inevitable—clearly violated the Free Speech and Free Press Clauses.[23] The guarantee of a fair trial inherent in the Due Process Clause was also undermined in a myriad of ways—for example, the defendant, forced to try the case to a jury, had to play down any "religious defense" that might have inflamed juror prejudice.

However, limiting ourselves to the Free Exercise claim, we submit that the evidence in this case and the facts judicially noticeable lead to but one conclusion: there was no realistically feasible means of constituting a jury untainted by the prejudicial influences of a society extremely

---

[22] Reverend Moon stated: "I would not be standing here today, if my skin were white and my religion were Presbyterian." A815.

[23] *See Craig* v. *Harney*, 311 U.S. 367 (1977); *Wood* v. *Georgia*, 370 U.S. 375 (1962).

16

hostile to the "Moonies," and particularly to Reverend Moon himself, the petitioner herein.

Many recent, serious sociological studies treat the "Moonies" and other "cults" scientifically and objectively.[24] Members of this or any other jury, however, generally do not read such scientific books.[25] Rather, they are continually lambasted by hostile accounts and lurid descriptions of "cults" in newspapers, magazines, radio and television broadcasts, and motion pictures.

Even if sequestered, juries cannot be insulated from these prior influences, and when, as in the present case, they are not sequestered, the added possibility of prejudicial influence from their families, friends and neighbors —practically all of whom share their feelings of hostility and fear—unavoidably aggravates the situation.[26]

In a case such as the present one, the Constitution's guarantee of the free exercise of religion, as well as basic concepts of justice and fair play, mandate that the trial court honor a defendant's request for a bench trial not-

---

[24] *See, e.g.,* I. Zaretsy & M. Leone, *Religious Movements in Contemporary America* (1974); D. Bromley & A. Shupe, Jr., *Strange Gods: The Great American Scare* (1981); D. Bromley & A. Shupe, Jr., *"Moonies" in America: Cult, Church and Crusade* (1979); C. Glock & R. Bellah, *The New Religious Consciousness* (1976); *Alternatives to American Mainline Churches* (J. Fichter ed. 1983); *The Coming Kingdom* (M.D. Bryant & D. Dayton ed. 1983); J.G. Melton & R. Moore, *The Cult Experience* (1982); *The Social Impact of New Religious Movements* (B. Wilson ed. 1981). All of these works have extensive bibliographies.

[25] In fact the trial judge recognized that "in attempting to get an unbiased jury, the leaning has been heavily towards people who won't read much, don't talk much and don't know much . . ." T1759-60.

[26] Admonitions by the trial judge not to discuss the case while it is pending, when directed at "a jury in a hostile environment," *United States* v. *Ballard*, 322 U.S. 78, 87 (1944), are not only unenforceable but are, realistically speaking, futile.

17

withstanding the prosecutor's refusal to consent. We submit that for all the foregoing reasons, the petition for certiorari should be granted.

Respectfully submitted,

LEO PFEFFER
Counsel of Record
29 Ridge Terrace
P. O. Box 261
Central Valley, N. Y. 10917
(914) 928-6409

March, 1984

The National Council of the
Churches of Christ in the U.S.A.,
The Presbyterian Church (U.S.A.),
The American Baptist Churches in
the U.S.A., The African Methodist
Episcopal Church, The National
Association of Evangelicals and the
Christian Legal Society

QUESTIONS PRESENTED

1. Did the court below err when it permitted the government to penalize a religious organization for its choice of organizational structure or form when:

(a) that structure developed in response to theological determinations and beliefs, and

(b) members of that organization were aware of and accepted that structure as a part of their sincerely held religious beliefs?

2. Did the court below err in allowing a jury:

(a) to impose its notion about the ownership of funds of a religious organization when its notion runs contrary to the religious beliefs and practices of the ministers of and donors to that religious organization, or

(b) to decide when funds of a religious organization have been properly spent for "religious" purposes or for the carrying out of the religious mission of the organization?

3. Did the court below err in concluding that, when someone's religious beliefs and practices are relevant to his defense to charges against him in proceedings before governmental authorities, those beliefs and practices may be disregarded in assessing that person's challenged conduct?

iii

INDEX

iv

v

TABLE OF CASES AND AUTHORITIES

vi

No. 83-1242

IN THE

𝔖upreme Court of the United 𝔖tates

OCTOBER TERM, 1983

SUN MYUNG MOON, *et al.*, *Petitioners*

v.

UNITED STATES OF AMERICA, *Respondent*

BRIEF OF THE NATIONAL COUNCIL OF CHURCHES OF
CHRIST IN THE U.S.A., THE PRESBYTERIAN CHURCH
(U.S.A.), THE AMERICAN BAPTIST CHURCHES IN THE
U.S.A., THE AFRICAN METHODIST EPISCOPAL CHURCH,
THE NATIONAL ASSOCIATION OF EVANGELICALS, AND THE
CHRISTIAN LEGAL SOCIETY AS AMICI CURIAE

Pursuant to Rule 36.1 of the Rules of this Court, the organizations named above file this brief in support of the instant petition for certiorari. Consent for filing of this brief
has been obtained in writing from the attorneys of record
for the parties in this case. Their original letters have been
filed with the Clerk of this Court.

INTEREST OF AMICI

1. The National Council of the Churches of Christ in the
U.S.A. is the cooperative agency of 32 national Protestant
and Eastern Orthodox religious bodies in·the U.S., having
an aggregate membership of over 40,000,000. This brief
does not purport to represent the views of all of those persons, but is based on policy determined by their representatives sitting as the Governing Board of the National Council of Churches, a deliberative body of about 250 persons,
chosen by the member denominations in proportion to their
size and support of the Council. The policy which underlies
this action was expressed by the Board in 1955: "The National Council of Churches defends the rights and liberties

2

of cultural, racial and religious minorities." *Policy Statement: Religious and Civil Liberties in the U.S.A.* Three of the national denominations which are members of the National Council of Churches have been particularly concerned about this case and, from their own respective policy bases, have joined this brief as *amici* in their own right in addition to being represented by the Council.

2. The Presbyterian Church (U.S.A.) is a national, Christian denomination with churches in all 50 States. It has approximately 3,150,000 active members and approximately 11,750 congregations organized into 195 Presbyteries and 20 Synods. The General Assembly is the highest governing body of the Church, meets annually, and is composed of approximately 600 delegates elected by the Presbyteries, known as commissioners, one-half of whom are ordained ministers, the other half ordained lay officers known as ruling elders. This brief does not purport to reflect the views of all members of the Church, but is based upon policies decided by the General Assembly or incorporated into the Constitution of the Church by vote of the Presbyteries. Chapter I of the Form of Government, a part of the Church's present Constitution, was first published in 1788 by an antecedent body, the Synod of New York and Philadelphia, where the founders of the Presbyterian Church asserted (and the Church still affirms in its basic documents) that "they consider the rights of private judgment, in all matters that respect religion, as universal and inalienable: they do not even wish to see any religious constitution aided by the civil power, further than may be necessary for protection and security, and, at the same time, be equal and common to all others." Consistent with this "principle of common rights," they recognize that every church is entitled to declare "the whole system of its internal government."

3. The American Baptist Churches in the U.S.A. is a national Baptist denomination of some 6,000 congregations with some 1.5 million members, with national offices in Valley Forge, Pennsylvania. The American Baptist Churches in the U.S.A. has a mandate from its General Board to speak whenever Baptist principles are involved. The pres-

3

ervation of religious liberty is a tenet of the Baptist religious belief. The issues present in this case are basic to the Baptist principles of religious liberty and separation of church and state.

4. The African Methodist Episcopal ("AME") Church was founded in Philadelphia in 1787. It arose because of the racial discrimination within the existing Methodist Episcopal Church. Today, the AME Church includes 6,000 churches with 2,050,000 members operating 5,500 Sunday or Sabbath schools with enrollments of 156,000. The Church includes 6,170 ordained clergy with 18 Bishops for 18 Districts, plus a Bishop in charge of Ecumenical Relations and AME Chaplaincy Relations, in addition to six retired Bishops in the AME Church. The Church joins the instant brief out of deep concern for the issues of religious freedom involved— issues which seem especially compelling when, as here, the defendants on trial are men of color.

5. The National Association of Evangelicals, located in Wheaton, Illinois, is a nonprofit association of evangelical Christian organizations, colleges and universities, as well as some 36,000 churches from 74 denominations. It serves a constituency of 10 to 15 million people through its commissions and affiliates. These affiliates include the National Religious Broadcasters, the World Relief Corporation, and the Evangelical Foreign Missions Association. The Association has participated in many religious liberty cases as *amicus curiae.*

6. The Christian Legal Society is a non-profit Illinois Corporation founded in 1961 as a professional association of Christian attorneys, judges, law professors, and law students. Today it includes over 3,500 members throughout the United States. The Center for Law and Religious Freedom is a division of the Christian Legal Society founded in 1975 to protect and promote the freedom of Christians and others to exercise their religious beliefs. Since its founding, the Center for Law and Religious Freedom has filed *amicus curiae* briefs in cases where religious liberty issues are at stake.

4

STATEMENT OF THE CASE

Amici adopt the statement of the case set forth in the petition for certiorari, insofar as the facts set forth therein are relevant to the arguments below.[1] We accept for purposes of this brief the conclusion of the New York Court of Appeals and the United States District Court for the District of Columbia that the Unification Church is a religious organization entitled to the protection of the First Amendment, a characterization not disputed in the court below. *See, Holy Spirit Association* v. *Tax Commission*, 55 N.Y. 2d 512, 528 (1982); *Unification Church* v. *INS*, 547 F. Supp. 623, 628 (D.D.C. 1982). The Second Circuit itself acknowledged that the Unification movement's traditions are akin to those of "centuries-old" religious orders. 718 F.2d at 1233 n.7.[2]

We stress that our filing of this brief is motivated not by any particular sympathy for Reverend Moon, or by any agreement with his faith. Those of us who are members of the National Council of the Churches of Christ accept the finding of its Faith and Order Commission that the doctrine of the Unification Church is not consistent with that of traditional Christian theology as believed through twenty centuries. All of us are motivated, nevertheless, by deep alarm at the means by which defendant Moon's conviction below was secured, the basis upon which it was upheld by the Circuit Court, and the consequences for religious liberty should the decision below be allowed to stand.

SUMMARY OF ARGUMENT

No claim is made here that religious officials or indeed entire churches enjoy absolute immunity from the law sim-

---

[1] We urge that this Court review the Second Circuit's affirmance of both Reverend Moon's and Takeru Kamiyama's convictions inasmuch as the convictions of both petitioners were secured and upheld on a basis that violates fundamental precepts of religious liberty and due process.

[2] See also *Ward* v. *Connor*, 657 F.2d 45 (4th Cir. 1981), *cert. denied*, 102 S.Ct. 1253 (1982); *Troyer* v. *Town of Babylon*, 483 F.Supp. 1135, 1137 (E.D.N.Y.), *aff'd*, 628 F.2d 1346 (2d Cir.), *aff'd mem.*, 449 U.S. 988 (1980).

5

ply by virtue of their religious status; many legal principles apply in the same way to church officials as they do to others. Nothing in the First Amendment, properly construed, sets any religion or religious leader "above the law." We do not accept the view that any act or practice of a religious body or its officials is *ipso facto* "religious" and therefore automatically beyond scrutiny by civil authorities.

We support review, instead, because we firmly believe that, when a defendant's religious belief and practices become *relevant* to refuting the charges against him, treating him *as though* religion had nothing to do with the matter is the very essence of unfairness and discrimination. Equally intolerable, we submit, is the exploitation of religious *prejudice* to secure a defendant's conviction. Either to disregard religion when it is relevant to that person's defense, or to use antipathy toward a defendant's religion as a means of establishing his "guilt," violates the Religion Clauses of the First Amendment and the Due Process Clause of the Fifth Amendment.

We submit that the decision below affirmatively upholds, or effectively places beyond redress, a grave subversion of religious liberty and due process—one that is cause for deep alarm and manifestly warrants this Court's review. For as the court below chillingly prophesied, Reverend Moon's case "plainly . . . will not be the last" of its type, 718 F.2d at 1230; the principles upon which the Second Circuit sustained his conviction are principles of potentially unlimited reach, applicable in *any* criminal *or* civil proceeding in which the acts or practices of a religious body or its leaders are drawn into question. On the narrower issue of church property use and ownership, we believe that the judgment below represents a uniquely grave threat to church autonomy; the recognition of this threat, indeed, forms the basis of Judge Oakes's powerful dissent from the decision below. For these and the other reasons stated below, *amici* urge that the instant petition be granted and the far-reaching questions presented by the decision below resolved.

6

REASONS FOR GRANTING THE WRIT

The decision below established a number of precedents which *amici* believe seriously threaten religious liberty protected by the First Amendment. We urge this Court to review that decision for the reasons which follow.

I.

THE DECISION BELOW STANDS FOR THE PROPOSITION THAT JUDGES AND JURIES MAY OVERRIDE A RELIGIOUS ORGANIZATION'S DECISIONS ON ITS OWN ORGANIZATION, HOW IT WILL ALLOCATE RESPONSIBILITY OVER CHURCH MATTERS, AND HOW IT WILL SPEND ITS RELIGIOUS RESOURCES.

An assertion such as this requires detailed substantiation. The following is offered at this time in support:

A. The decision below affirms the government's authority to disregard and override a church's own views on issues of organization, responsibility, and resources.

To prove its position that the assets held in Reverend Moon's name belonged to him personally rather than to his international religious movement, the government relied heavily on two premises: (1) that this international religious movement did not really exist because it had no formal corporate status; and (2) that the assets held by Reverend Moon were his own because they were treated in ways that the jury could consider, on any basis it wished, not to be "religious."

1. Choice of structure

In order to discredit Reverend Moon's claim that he held the assets at issue in trust for his international religious movement, the government tried to show that the movement *did not exist* by pointing to the fact that Reverend Moon and his followers "avoid[ed] the structures that exist in the United States where ... funds [contributed to a religious entity] should rightly go." That Reverend Moon's international religious movement had no "corporate structure" during the period in question was, indeed, the central element of the government's contention that Reverend Moon was lying when he claimed to hold the money in trust

7

for the movement. Moreover, the government took the position that the international movement's unincorporated status was especially suspicious in light of the fact that some movement entities here and abroad were in fact incorporated. However, it is logical to assume that an international movement might not want to be limited by the strictures which would be placed on it by incorporating in one country.

Only if it is assumed that a religion must incorporate *all* of its entities or *none* of them in order to prove its legitimacy may a religion's choice to incorporate only *some* of its entities support any adverse inference as to its bona fides.

The trial court *instructed* the jury to take this religious movement's organizational characteristics into account in determining whether the assets in question belonged to it or to the defendant, lecturing defense counsel that "the nonexistence of [some organizational characteristics] would be proof the other way"—*i.e.*, proof that the religious movement did not exist.

The court below upheld the offending instruction. In the name of eschewing "word-by-word parsing of a jury charge," 718 F.2d at 1225 [citing *Cupp* v. *Naughten*, 414 U.S. 141, 146-47 (1973)], the circuit court sustained the trial court's instruction that the Unification movement's corporate structure could be taken into account in determining whether or not a trust had been created.

2. Choice of Expenditures

The government itself conceded that the sources of the funds in question were "evangelical activities, fund raising, things like that." And the trial court recognized during the argument on Reverend Moon's mid-trial motion for a judgment of acquittal that the assets he held had been given to him "for a higher cause," by church members who "thought they were advancing [their common religious movement] internationally." As Judge Oakes in his dissent noted, "the assets in question came to Moon largely from members of his faith, and there was some evidence that the donors intended their contributions for religious purposes." 718 F.2d at 1242. Ordinarily these facts would be enough to establish

8

that the donors had intended to create a religious trust in turning over to Reverend Moon monies they had raised.[3]

But the government here was permitted to deny the existence of such a trust by relying heavily on how Reverend Moon used the assets he had received from his followers. Simply, the government argued that Reverend Moon's use of the monies in question "for . . . business ventures primarily and real estate investments" was itself *proof* that no religious trust existed—despite the fact that churches routinely and necessarily invest their funds in "business ventures" as part of the effort to sustain and spread their spiritual mission.[4]

No relief from such prejudicial and profoundly misguided argument was afforded by the trial court. Thus, the trial court, in a misstatement of trust law, *directed* the jury to find that the funds at issue all belonged to Reverend Moon personally—rather than to the international church—if the jury concluded that he was free to use any part of the funds as "personal" compensation, or if the jury concluded that any of the ways in which he expended or invested the funds did not serve what the jury, applying its own standards, deemed to be "church purposes." As noted above, the circuit court accepted the jury's conclusion in this regard.

B. In affirming such governmental authority over a church's choices of structure and spending practices, the decision below threatens religious freedom and church autonomy.

Religious liberty encompasses not only the freedom to believe in and worship one's God in solitude and peace,

---

[3] Inexplicably, the circuit court decided that the evidence established nothing more than that "a charitable *gift* had been made to the *church*." 718 F.2d at 1225. This is inexplicable both because of the trial court's recognition that the funds had been given "for a higher cause" (implying a trust) and because the circuit court's assessment of the evidence, even if correct, is itself inconsistent with the conclusion that the funds were given to Reverend Moon *personally*.

[4] For example, the Presbyterian Church (U.S.A.) has invested more than $357.9 million in securities of more than 175 corporations, and the four National Boards of the American Baptist Churches in the U.S.A. have combined investments of some $370 million in securities of more than 100 corporations.

9

but also the power of those of shared faith "to decide for themselves, free from state interference, matters of church government as well as those of faith and doctrine." *Kedroff* v. *St. Nicholas Cathedral*, 344 U.S. 94, 116 (1952); *Serbian Eastern Orthodox Diocese* v. *Milivojevich*, 426 U.S. 696 (1976) (state cannot reorganize church even for supposedly violating its own by-laws). Solicitude for a religious movement's choice of structure is especially warranted where the movement is still in its infancy, and its structure and practices therefore somewhat fluid.

Yet the government asked the jury to draw adverse inferences from this international religious movement's failure to incorporate itself, and from the particular mix of structures chosen by this religious movement for its subordinate national or other entities. For a jury to be allowed to draw adverse inferences from any religious movement's choice of structure obviously penalizes that choice in violation of the Free Exercise Clause.[5]

Similarly, the Constitution forbids the government to defeat a religious trust, or otherwise to transform church assets into personal assets, by characterizing the uses to which parts of such assets are put as "business" or "personal" rather than "religious." There is no doubt, after all, that most churches feel that they must make "business" investments and that they must pay many of their religious officials' "personal" living expenses—all as part of their use of church assets to support the religion's spiritual activities.

At stake is who shall decide which such investments and payments advance a given religion's aims, and which do not. The First Amendment tolerates only one answer to this question: *Each church must decide for itself.* It is surely impermissible under the First Amendment for the gov-

---

[5] It should not be forgotten that some noted long-established religious bodies in this country have never been incorporated, and probably never will be. The Episcopal Church in the United States is not incorporated as such; all of its national property is held for it by a corporation known as "The Domestic and Foreign Missionary Society of the Protestant Episcopal Church in the U.S.A." Nor is the United Methodist Church incorporated as such in the United States; but its major agencies, such as the General Council on Finance and Administration, are continuing and corporate bodies.

10

ernment, including any civil or criminal court or jury, "to determine which expenditures are religious and which are secular." *Lemon* v. *Kurtzman*, 403 U.S. 602, 621-22 (1971). *Cf. Widmar* v. *Vincent*, 102 S.Ct. 269, 274 n.6 (1981). The principle asserted by the government to obtain the result in this case, first sanctioned by the trial court and then ratified by the court below, would interpose the supervision and control of civil authorities over spending decisions by church leaders—despite the settled precept that "allocation and expenditure of [church] funds is intimately bound up in [the church's religious] mission . . . and thus is protected by the free exercise clause." *Surinach* v. *Pesquera de Busquets*, 604 F.2d 73, 78 (1st Cir. 1979).

Allowing the conviction in this case to stand would thus create a precedent even more susceptible of abuse than *Jones* v. *Wolf*, 443 U.S. 595 (1979).[6] For the trial court's approach, aproved by the Second Circuit, in effect overrode the intention of the donors in violation of *Wolf*, 443 U.S. at 603-04, and alienated assets the church faithful had entrusted to Reverend Moon for religious purposes, awarding the corpus of such assets to Reverend Moon and his heirs *as their personal property*—a gift he undoubtedly found most unwelcome in his capacity as leader of his flock. Such an alienation of assets given in trust could readily befall any religious body if the approach of this trial court, approved on appeal, should escape this Court's review. The upshot is a forbidden taking and governmental redistribution of religious property in contravention not only of the First Amendment but of the Fifth Amendment as well. *See, Terrett* v. *Taylor*, 13 U.S. 43 (1815). *Cf. United States* v. *564.54 Acres of Land*, 441 U.S. 506, 515-16 (1979).

---

[6] See Dallin H. Oaks, "Trust Doctrines in Church Controversies," 1981 B.Y.U.L. Rev. 805, 907 (criticizing Jones for "secularizat.on of the resolution of church property disputes," and for applying a neutral principles approach that may mean "inhibiting the freedom of hierarchical churches to govern their internal affairs").

11

II.

THE DECISION BELOW STANDS FOR THE PROPOSITION THAT JURIES MAY DISREGARD THE RELIGIOUS REASONS FOR, AND THE RELIGIOUS MEANING OF, A DEFENDANT'S CONDUCT HOWEVER RELEVANT TO THE DETERMINATION OF INNOCENCE OR GUILT.

In stating that "defendants are only entitled to 'a fair trial but not a perfect one,'" 718 F.2d at 1216 [quoting *Lutwak* v. *United States*, 344 U.S. 604, 619 (1953)], the Second Circuit rejected Reverend Moon's contention that the trial court had impermissibly hampered his ability to establish the religious significance of the various acts and practices for which the government sought to condemn him. The court below thus countenanced an extraordinary breach of the protections guaranteed by the First Amendment.

A. The government denied critical religious explanations of this religious leader's actions and relationships.

Because the Second Circuit's opinion manages to ignore so many of the aspects of Reverend Moon's trial that cause us such serious concern, a brief review of certain aspects of the trial record is appropriate.

1. The Government's Approach

At trial, the government's argument in chief was that certain assets placed in Reverend Moon's hands by his followers and held by him in his own name were *personal* assets, the receipt of which or the interest on which Reverend Moon should have reported as personal income. The focal point of Reverend Moon's trial, therefore, was the question of what was *meant* by the entrusting of assets to him by followers of his faith and by the holding and investment of such assets in his name. The government sought to prove Reverend Moon's personal ownership of those assets substantially on the basis of the *uses* to which they were put, arguing that he used them "for business for the economics of his empire." Accordingly, the government repeatedly urged the jury to accept *its* label of each investment made with the assets entrusted to Reverend Moon as

12

being a "strictly business deal." The defense sought to argue that, given Reverend Moon's special role within his religion, the meaning of his control and use of those assets was that they belonged to the church as a whole, and were merely held *for* it by Reverend Moon as the church's embodiment. There was no dispute at trial, or in the court below, over the defendant's central place within the Unification Church.

The government's strategy was to proceed against the defendant "as if . . . [he had been] an ordinary high-ranking businessman." Reverend Moon was stymied in two respects—each of which is discussed below—in his effort to show that, with respect to the use of the assets in question, he could *not* be treated simply as a businessman, without regard for either his role in his church or his religion's commitment to establishing a firm financial base for itself through religious investments in commercial enterprises.

2. Evidentiary Rulings

On key occasions the defense was prevented from placing before the jury explanations that would have translated Reverend Moon's position in his religion into a convincing account for the jury of *why* various supposedly "business investments" indeed had to be viewed as investments of the Church, by the Church, and for the Church—albeit in the name of Reverend Moon as the Church's embodiment.

The practice of making religious contributions directly to a religious leader for his discretionary use did not originate with nor is it uniquely related to the defendant in this case. In England as well as in this country religious contributions have been solicited by and made to religious leaders in their own name. That is the clearest and most direct way in which an adherent can make a gift to the movement.

The developmental stage of Methodism is illustrative. John Wesley, in his *Journal* of May 9, 1739 discussed the building of a meeting house. He noted that the contributors insisted that the funds go directly to him rather than to the trustees, or "feoffees," on the grounds that "such feoffees always would have it in their power to control [him]; and if [he] preached not as they liked, to turn [him] out of the

13

room [he] had built." The significance of this entry is that religious leaders, particularly in relatively new movements, must exercise a high degree of control over the movement and its assets lest the movement be subverted or destroyed. That many present day religious leaders have substantial funds which belong to their church and which may be used at the discretion of those leaders is a truism which has been rather fully documented.

Also, defense counsel was prevented from eliciting from a church witness on cross-examination testimony "that the purpose [of various commercial enterprises with which Reverend Moon was involved] is to allow the church to develop a financial base so that it can be self-supporting and go on and do [its] work." The defense was also prevented from asking a knowledgeable government witness to testify as to Reverend Moon's stated views with respect to the "relationship between church and business," and was prevented from eliciting testimony from other witnesses that would establish their belief—or Reverend Moon's—that investments made with the funds held by him in his own name were for religious purposes.[7]

Corporate executives are not denied the opportunity to explain the *business* meaning of their activities, signatures, or statements. Here, religious explanations of the uses to which Reverend Moon put the assets entrusted to him were undoubtedly critical to convincing the jury that the assets in fact belonged not to the defendant but rather to the movement. Yet Reverend Moon was refused the opportunity to offer such explanations, prevented from doing so in key instances both by the trial court's evidentiary rulings and by prosecution threats that introduction of such explanations would be met with disclosures by the government to the jurors of all manner of supposedly "negative things about the church."[8]

---

[7] Such testimony was hindered even though the defendant's "state of mind concerning ... religious matters," as the trial court acknowledged, "may explain why certain things were done or not done."

[8] It was the fact that the defendant was forced to be tried before a jury he suspected of bias that rendered potent the prosecution's threats—and the trial court's warnings—that questions by the defense

14

Amici respectfully submit that denying to religious officials the same opportunity that would be afforded to business executives in like circumstances not only reduces religion from the high status assigned it by the First Amendment, but also assigns it a rank distinctly *lower* than that of its secular counterparts. Religion is *sui generis* and, under the First Amendment, must not be treated as a business is treated. *No* religion is safe when *any* religious group may be so dismissively treated. The Second Circuit's conclusion that the evidence was sufficient to support a conviction, resting as it did on the premise that Reverend Moon was not entitled to establish his version of that evidence's religious significance, and hence his innocence, is a serious rejection of settled norms of even-handed treatment of religion.

3. Jury Instructions

The fact that religion was inescapably involved in Reverend Moon's tax trial is clear both from the nature of the charges and from the trial court's own comments. Thus, the trial judge recognized that he had to

> get before the jury the notion that if the jury believes that the people who gave the money intended it to be for the International Unification Church Movement, and if Moon believed he was holding it for that purpose, and if he believed he was using [it] for that purpose, even though he may have in a few instances made bad investments or used some of it for himself, ... the monies could still be viewed as not being his but being the Movement's.

As Judge Oakes put it in his dissent from the decision below, "it was essential that the court's instructions precisely state the law on the creation of a trust relationship and the implications of the jury's finding that such a relationship existed in this case." 718 F.2d at 1242.

---

as to religious motive would "open the door" to the introduction of damaging evidence by the government. As the court itself recognized, a defense based on expounding such matters "would have been disastrous to try before a jury."

15

Nevertheless, the trial court *refused* Reverend Moon's request to instruct the jury that, in determining whether the assets held in Reverend Moon's own name were those of the religious movement, simply being held for it by him, the jury should take into account Reverend Moon's ample evidence that the assets in fact "came from ... church sources"; that they were given with *intent* that they be used "for ... church purposes"; and that they were not "primarily" used for *personal* purposes. In refusing to instruct the jury to take such uncontradicted evidence into account, the court failed to apply the settled *presumption* that a religious trust exists in such circumstances.[9]

The trial court also refused Reverend Moon's request to instruct the jury that, according to the Unification Church's theology, he is the embodiment of the faith—an instruction that was also amply supported by the only evidence on the point—even though, as Judge Oakes observed in dissent, the issue of beneficial ownership that lay at the heart of the case was critically affected by the fact that Reverend Moon "was the spiritual leader of the church." 718 F.2d at 1242. For not only was there no dispute at trial over Reverend Moon's central place within his religion; in fact, the identification of Reverend Moon with his religion was acknowledged even by nonchurch witnesses called by the government, and the government in fact *relied* on Reverend Moon's role as founder and prophet of his religious movement to *discredit* him and church witnesses generally. The trial court itself recognized that, even "[l]ooking at the evidence from a favorable standpoint to the government[,] ... [the defendant] conceived ... himself, the embodiment of the International Church."

Reverend Moon's requested instruction as to his place within his religion was obviously crucial if the jurors were to understand his explanation of why he signed certain documents in his own name, why others of his faith referred to the assets as "his," and why intra-church loans involving

---

[9] Judge Oakes in his dissent lucidly explained why the trial court's trust instructions were nevertheless fatally defective on this, "the crucial issue in the case." 718 F.2d at 1245.

16

funds held in his name were often described as loans to or from him. But the trial court summarily dismissed his request for such an instruction, commenting that treating Reverend Moon as the embodiment of the faith would render him "a walking unincorporated association." But Reverend Moon was not asking for an instruction that would have placed him above the law, as the trial court seemed to imply, but only for an instruction that would enable the jury to understand what it signified for him to hold and use assets entrusted to him by others of his faith.

As a result of the trial court's failure to give such critical instructions, the government was allowed to rely precisely upon certain evidence that the assets held by Reverend Moon had been collected through religious donations and fund raising, thereby painting a highly prejudicial picture of the defendant as running, in the court's words, a "Fagin-like operation" with "hundreds of people collecting money and turning it over to him." As defense counsel observed, such an approach violates the First Amendment because "it ignores the existence of the church. It ignores the fact [of] the church's right to treat Reverend Moon as they choose to treat him." Surely the right of the church's members to treat Reverend Moon as trustee of assets they have placed in his control for religious purposes cannot be denied.

The court below, like the trial court, proved entirely inhospitable to Reverend Moon's claim that he be allowed jury instructions on the religious *meaning* of the acts and practices upon which the government proposed to secure his conviction. Not only did the Second Circuit refuse to concede the *need* for an instruction on the trust issue, denying that any evidence had been introduced of an intent on the part of Reverend Moon's followers to place their funds with him in trust, 718 F.2d at 1225, but also it specifically affirmed the trial court's refusal to instruct the jury as to the place Reverend Moon occupies in Unification religion. Because, in the Second Circuit's view, the funds at issue had been "held individually and used personally," *id.* at 1228, it was unnecessary, the court below concluded, to require the jury to consider Reverend Moon's religious status, *id.* at 1227-28. This obviously put the cart before the

17

horse, for Reverend Moon's status is highly relevant to *whether* the funds were "held individually and used personally."[10]

Given (1) the resistance with which Reverend Moon was met in seeking to explain the religious purposes for which the assets were used, and (2) the trial court's refusal to instruct the jury, as requested, on the significance of the source of the assets and the intent with which they were donated, Reverend Moon was put in a "no win" situation. He was portrayed as having huge sums of money and other property placed at his disposal by zealous followers, and then spending those sums as just a "businessman," engaged in "strictly personal" business deals. Thus the government was able to draw from the jury a negative answer to the question regarded by the court as central to the case—that is, "the question of whether [the defendant] can *simultaneously* be a business and a religion."

A refusal to instruct the jury on such relevant matters as Reverend Moon's role as leader of this religious movement and the objectives of the religious movement's economic activities and fund raising, in a case involving alleged financial misconduct by the religion or by its leader, constitutes a refusal to expose the jury to *the relevant religious view of what was actually going on in the case, and what the underlying facts signified.* If the Second Circuit's affirmance of the district court's rulings in this respect is allowed to stand as a precedent in other prosecutions, much tax-exempt activity by even the most traditional religious groups may well become taxable, and much innocent behavior by religious groups today could be made to appear suspect or even criminal tomorrow.

---

[10] In an injurious aside, the Second Circuit dismissed as "inapposite" the New York Court of Appeals' conclusion that the Unification movement is a *bona fide* religion on the ground that the principles announced there "do not serve as precedent in a federal tax prosecution." 718 F.2d at 1227.

18

B. The government's approach, as approved by the Circuit Court, would destroy many of the protections guaranteed by the free exercise clause of the First Amendment.

As we have argued, it is settled principle of this nation's legal heritage that only an illusory and inadequate evenhandedness is achieved when the law, in a supposed exercise of "neutrality," chooses to disregard religious explanations for an individual's or group's actions—for example, a couple's decision as to the education of their children, *Wisconsin* v. *Yoder*, 406 U.S. 205 (1972), or an individual's explanations for his decisions as to employment, *Thomas* v. *Review Board*, 450 U.S. 707, 714-19 (1981); *Sherbert* v. Verner, 374 U.S. 398 (1963). *Cf. Welsh* v. *United States*, 398 U.S. 333, 338-39 (1970); *United States* v. *Seeger*, 380 U.S. 163 (1975). If the decision below were allowed to stand, the law would take a major step backward from this tradition of respect for religion and the religious.

Moreover, as is clear from a review of the cases cited above, the principle that religious notions and explanations must be least be fully taken into account when offered by a defendant to explain or justify his actions is critical to followers of *all* faiths, not simply those faiths that are new or small or in disfavor; and the principle is applicable not simply in criminal contexts but in civil contexts as well. From the tax-exempt status of a church parking lot, to the validity of an unincorporated church association's assertion of power to direct the actions of a church corporation, little of what even modern-day *mainstream* churches routinely do would survive intact if squeezed through a religion-extracting filter. The decision below applies such a filter in flat disregard of the First Amendment.

III.
A RULE OF "DEFERENCE" TO A DISTRICT COURT'S DISCRETION CANNOT STAND IF IT PERMITS GRAVE BREACHES OF FIRST AMENDMENT PRINCIPLES.

In denying defendant's post-trial motions for relief, the trial court said it had "played the case" as though "the the-

19

ology of the church had nothing to do with the tax charges." The violation of fundamental principles of religious freedom would have been severe even if the court's only error had been to permit the government to try this religious leader, as the government put it, "just as [it would have tried] any high ranking business executive." But the violation of First Amendment rights here was rendered even more egregious by the trial court's rulings allowing the government to use Reverend Moon's religion *against* him, while forbidding Reverend Moon at critical junctures to use his religion in his defense.

In the name of appellate restraint, the court of appeals for all practical purposes has held beyond review the grave breaches of First Amendment principles permitted by the trial court in allowing such "evidence." As worrisome as we find the abuses the circuit court affirmatively upheld, we also find deeply disquieting the lesson of the decision below that many of the abuses tolerated by the trial court may simply be without hope of redress. This stark abdication of the judicial function is an ominous portent for all religious groups, plainly presenting questions worthy of this Court's review.

20

CONCLUSION

Our alarm at the injustice in this case arises from the complete disregard of Reverend Moon's First and Fifth Amendment Rights, first by the trial court and then, on appeal, by the court below. No particular sympathy for the defendant in this case, and no agreement with his faith, is required to feel grave distress at the resulting breach of religious liberty. The government's use below of Reverend Moon's religion—exploiting its unpopularity, and precluding him at key junctures from asserting defenses based on the practices and teachings of his religion—severely threatens rights of all religious groups. Accordingly, for this and for all of the foregoing reasons, we urge this Court to grant the petition for certiorari, and decide the important questions presented by this case.

EARL W. TRENT, JR.
Board of National Ministries
American Baptist Churches in the U.S.A.
Valley Forge, Pennsylvania 19481
(215) 768-2487
Attorney of record for amici curiae

FEBRUARY, 1984

The National Emergency Civil
Liberties Committee

- i -

QUESTION PRESENTED

Did the denial of petitioners'
application for a bench trial violate
their Fifth and Sixth Amendment right to
fair trial and their First Amendment
right of free speech where: (i) the trial
judge ruled that a bench trial would be
"fairer" and, (ii) the government
withheld its consent because petitioner
had publicly accused it of religious
prejudice?

- iii -

TABLE OF CONTENTS

- iv -

TABLE OF AUTHORITIES

- v -

No. 83-1242

IN THE

·SUPREME COURT OF THE UNITED STATES
OCTOBER TERM, 1983

SUN MYUNG MOON, et al.,

Petitioners,

v.

UNITED STATES OF AMERICA,

Respondent.

**ON PETITION FOR A WRIT OF CERTIORARI TO
THE UNITED STATES COURT OF APPEALS FOR
THE SECOND CIRCUIT**

**BRIEF OF THE NATIONAL EMERGENCY CIVIL
LIBERTIES COMMITTEE AS AMICUS CURIAE**

Pursuant to Rule 36.1 of the Rules

of this Court, the National Emergency

Civil Liberties Committee files this

brief in support of the pending petition for certiorari. The attorneys of record for the parties have consented in writing to the filing of this brief. Their letters are on file with the Clerk of this Court.

INTEREST OF THE AMICUS

The National Emergency Civil Liberties Committee is a non-profit organization created in 1951 for the purpose of protecting the constitutional rights of American citizens. It has done so through its counsel, in litigation in this Court, including Kent v. Dulles, 357 U.S. 116 (1958); Lamont v. Postmaster General, 381 U.S. 301 (1965); and Uphaus v. Wyman, 360 U.S. 72 (1959). Its Legal Committee has authorized the filing of this brief because it believes that the

denial of a bench trial in this case
presents a serious violation of the Fifth
and Sixth Amendment rights to a fair
trial and the First Amendment right of
freedom of speech. It does not address
the other important issues raised by the
petition for certiorari.[1]/

STATEMENT OF THE CASE

Amicus will not seek to repeat all
the facts of this case since they are
fully set out in the petition for
certiorari. Three facts are particularly
relevant to the single question presented
by the amicus: an extraordinary
community hostility toward defendants and
their Church, defendants' awareness of

----

[1]/We advise the Court that the writer of
this brief and his firm have represented
the Unification Church in litigation
unrelated to this case.

it, and their consequent attempt to avoid
its effect by waiving trial by jury. The
trial judge, also aware of the community's hostility, expressly stated that a
bench trial would be "fairer". (T.1760-
1761).2/ Nonetheless, the judge denied
the motion for a bench trial under Rule
23(a) of the Federal Rules of Criminal
Procedure when it became clear that the
government would refuse to give its
consent to the waiver. The government
had insisted upon a jury trial, its
stated purpose being to "defuse the
public criticism that had been leveled"
by the petitioner against his prosecution. (App. 7). The government asserted
that a jury trial would give a better

2/ "T" refers to the transcript of the
record filed in the court below; "App."
to the Second Circuit's opinion appended
to the petition for certiorari; "A" to
the pleadings in the court below.

"appearance...of a fair trial" than a
bench trial and would protect the judge
from public criticism. Id.

SUMMARY OF ARGUMENT

Extraordinary community hostility
towards defendants and their religious
group entitles them, under the due
process clause of the Constitution, to a
bench trial, particularly where the trial
judge agrees that such a trial would be
fairer. Such are the "compelling
circumstances" contemplated by this Court
in Singer v. United States, 380 U.S. 24,
37 (1965).

The special responsibility of
federal prosecutors under this Court's
decision in Berger v. United States, 295
U.S. 78 (1935) requires them to consent
to a bench trial where it concededly

would be fairer to the defendants in view of the community's hostility. The government's refusal to consent was admittedly based upon the petitioner Moon's public assertion that the criminal prosecution was religiously and racially motivated. This is in effect a punishment, in violation of the First Amendment, for the public expression of one's views. The government had other less restrictive means to meet this public statement. Its argument that the public would have more confidence in a jury trial than in a bench trial has no basis in fact.

ARGUMENT

A JURY TRIAL IS NOT THE PREFERRED
TRIBUNAL UNDER THE CONSTITUTION OR THE
SINGER RULE WHEN A DEFENDANT WHO IS THE
SUBJECT OF PASSION, PREJUDICE, AND
ADVERSE PUBLIC FEELING SEEKS A
A BENCH TRIAL INSTEAD.

Introduction

"If one could be sent to jail
because a jury in a hostile environment
found [his religious] teachings false,
little indeed would be left of religious
freedom." United States v. Ballard, 322
U.S. 78, 87 (1944).

These words were perhaps never more
relevant in the trial of a religious
figure than in the trial of Reverend Sun
Myung Moon. This case, however complex
factually and legally on other issues, is
rather simple on the issue of whether,
under the precise circumstances
surrounding him and his unpopular

- 7 -

religious movement, Reverend Moon received the fair trial to which he was entitled. The issue comes down to whether or not the trial court should have granted Reverend Moon's waiver of a jury trial in favor of a bench trial.

It appears to this <u>amicus</u> that the state's interest in the mode of trial should be to provide the greatest possibility of a fair tribunal to such a defendant. A defendant is therefore entitled to a bench trial when a bench trial would be "fairer". It goes without saying that the motivation behind the creation of the jury method in the first place was out of concern for fairness.

A.   <u>The Singer Exception Applies Here</u>

     The difficulty with the position the government has taken is that this Court anticipated this type of case and situation twenty years ago in <u>Singer v. United States</u>, 380 U.S. 24 (1965). In words which precisely describe defendants' circumstances, the Court noted that there may be "situations where 'passion, prejudice,...public feeling' or some other factors may render impossible or unlikely an impartial trial by jury." <u>Id.</u> at 37-38.

     There is more to the background of the Court's opinion in <u>Singer</u> than Singer's own argument. The Court had before it an <u>amicus</u> brief of a young woman student who had sought a bench trial because of the pervasive prejudice then existing in the venue of trials

- 9 -

against white persons, in the South,

particularly women, active in the civil

rights movement.3/ That brief argued the

need for a bench trial where there was

community prejudice. The government

accepted the validity of that position

by:

> "Assuming arguendo that a
> denial of a non-jury trial
> under some circumstances
> might be so unfair as to
> present constitutional
> questions under the due
> process clause of the First
> Amendment * * *". Brief for
> the United States in

3/ Rabinowitz v. United States, 366 F.2d
34 (5th Cir. 1966). The Rabinowitz case,
presenting a factual situation comparable
to the Moon case, was ultimately decided
on a related issue -- the unfairness of
the jury selection method then prevalent
in many parts of the United States. The
Court's holding led to the new jury
selection statute, Jury Selection and
Service Act of 1968, P.L. 90-274, 82
Stat. 54 (codified at 28 U.S.C. 1861, et
seq.). The House Report on the bill
referred several times to the Rabinowitz
case.   H.R. Rep. No. 1076, 90th Cong.,
2d Sess., reprinted in [1968] U.S. Code
Cong. & Ad. News 1792, 1794, 1795.

> Opposition at 6, <u>Singer</u> v.
> <u>United States</u>, 380 U.S. 24
> (1965).

This Court foresaw that circumstan-

ces may exist -- although they did not

reach that height in <u>Singer</u>[4] -- where

due process requires acceptance of a

defendant's waiver of jury trial over the

government's objections. Those

circumstances do exist here, where the

community's prejudice against petitioners

was not denied by the government nor by

the courts below; indeed, the trial judge

made a finding unquestioned by the Court

----
[4] Singer "gave no reason for wanting to
forego jury trial other than to save
time." 380 U.S. at 38. Because Singer's
reason for seeking a bench trial was
merely one of convenience, the Court
ruled that it need not reach the issue of
whether Singer was denied an impartial
trial when the government refused to
consent to his waiver.

of Appeals that a bench trial would have
been "fairer" because of community
hostility.5/

The Court of Appeals' response to
the petitioners' Singer argument was that
"compelling circumstances are not
demonstrated simply by claims of an
atmosphere poisoned by a negative press."
(App. 9-10). The Court simply missed the
point. The petitioners' claim, as we
understand it, was not limited to a
"negative press", which often can be

5/   Mr. Justice Holmes believed that
"there is a growing disbelief in the jury
as an instrument for the discovery of
truth. The use of it is to let a little
popular prejudice into the administration
of law -- (in violation of their oath)."
I Holmes-Pollack Letters 74 (M. Howe ed.
1941). While one may not agree with the
Justice on the general proposition, a
bench trial is clearly mandated in a case
where there was far more than "a little
popular prejudice."

sifted out and cured on <u>voir</u> <u>dire</u>.<u>6</u>/
Petitioners' claim was much more far-
reaching: that of pervasive community
hostility in the sensitive and specially
protected area of religion. Again
neither the prosecution nor the courts
below doubted this hostility. It seems
to us that where, as here, such hostility
has gone beyond an acceptable level, a
defendant <u>willing</u> to waive his right to a
jury trial in favor of a bench trial is
entitled to do so as a matter of due
process.

Even the trial judge recognized at
the conclusion of the voir dire that "to
the extent people know [Reverend] Moon

<u>6</u>/ The Roth Survey, introduced in advance
of voir dire, showed the extent of this
hostility. The overwhelming majority of
the 1,000 persons surveyed knew of and
were negatively predisposed toward
Reverend Moon. (A.818, 822).

and his religion it is true that their
attitudes are negative." (T.1758}.
Nevertheless, the trial judge proceeded
with the jury because he thought that the
jury that was impanelled was

> "if not totally free from
> bias, by and large capable of
> putting aside the bias...
> [But] in attempting to get an
> unbiased jury, the leaning
> has been heavily towards
> people who don't read much,
> don't talk much and don't
> know much because they are
> obviously the persons who
> start off with the least
> bias...I would have thought
> it fairer to have this case
> tried without a jury...having
> the jury make the determina-
> tion of guilty or innocen[ce]
> is just fine by me. But I do
> think I would feel better
> about the fairness from the
> position of the defendants
> had they been granted a non-
> jury trial." (T.1759-61).

It seems obvious that a judge who is
free from bias -- or at least more
capable of putting that bias aside -- a

reasonable premise of our argument, is a
more appropriate trier of the facts than
a jury which has <u>some</u> bias, even though
it is predicted that they will <u>by and
large</u> be capable of putting that bias
aside. "By and large" is hardly an
acceptable standard for an unbiased trier
of the facts in our constitutional scheme
where the defendant wants to waive a jury
trial and where the option of a bench
trial is otherwise available.[7]/ Nor,
incidentally, do we believe that the
government's veto of a jury trial can
properly require petitioners to be tried,
in the district court's words, before

----

[7]/ See also Note, <u>Government Consent to
Waiver of Jury Trial Under Rule 23(a) of
the Federal Rules of Criminal Procedure</u>,
65 Yale L.J. 1032, 1039 (1956)
(indicating that, in the case of a highly
unpopular defendant, when the alternative
of trial by the court is available, trial
by a jury with <u>any</u> amount of bias will
not suffice).

"people who don't read much, don't talk
much and don't know much." See p. 13
supra. This is hardly the jury of one's
peers in a complicated tax case.

In any event, amicus does not ask
that this Court go any further than the
exception already carved out in Singer
which recognized the possibility of
"compelling circumstances" requiring a
bench trial. We submit that if this
Singer exception is to have any value or
meaning for defendants who justifiably
fear public hostility, this is one case
where it must be applied.

B. <u>Due Process Requires the Use of the</u>

<u>Concededly Fairer Available Tribunal</u>

The Court of Appeals began its
opinion in this case by saying that the
"defendants are only entitled to a 'fair
trial but not a perfect one'", <u>quoting</u>
<u>Lutwak v. United States</u>, 344 U.S. 604,
619 (1953). Admittedly no one can insist
on the perfect trial, but due process
requires that a defendant who is willing
to waive a jury trial be given the fairer
available tribunal. As Chief Justice
Burger stated in <u>Press - Enterprise</u>
<u>Company v. Superior Court of California,</u>
<u>Riverside County</u>, 52 U.S.L.W. 4113, 4115
(1984), "No right ranks higher than the
right of the accused to a fair trial."
In light of the trial court's repeated
assertions that a bench trial would have
been "fairer", it is consistent with this

high esteem given to fairness that the
trial court should have granted
petitioners' motion for bench trial,
regardless of the government's veto. We
do not dispute that, in normal circumstances, the jury is preferred as the
"tribunal which the Constitution regards
as most likely to produce a fair
result."[8]/ Singer v. United States, 380
U.S. at 36. However, in circumstances
where the defendant is the subject of
"passion, prejudice", id. at 37, and
undisputed public hostility, rendering a
jury trial less likely to be fair, the
constitutionally preferred mode of trial
is, a fortiori, a bench trial.

----
[8]/ The rule should not be jury trial for
the sake of jury trial. Rather the
emphasis must be on "fairness."

C. The Government's Veto of Bench Trial
    was Unjustified, Improper, And In
    Violation of Petitioners' First
    Amendment Rights.

This Court's decision in Singer had

one other relevant component: a

recognition of "the prosecutor's special

responsibility as a servant of the law." .

Id. at 37, quoting Berger v. United

States, 295 U.S. at 88. The Court had

"confidence that it is in this light that

[the prosecutor's veto power under Rule

23(a)] will continue to be evoked by

government attorneys." 380 U.S. at 37

(emphasis supplied). Said the Court:

> Because of this confidence in
> the integrity of the federal
> prosecutor, Rule 23(a) does
> not require that the
> Government articulate its
> reasons for demanding a jury
> trial at the time it refuses
> to consent to a defendant's
> proffered waiver. Nor should
> we assume that federal

> prosecutors would demand a
> jury trial for an ignoble
> purpose. Id.

We do not presume to characterize
the motive of the prosecution in this
case for withholding its consent to a
jury waiver in the face of a judicial
willingness to accept that waiver. Nor
are we faced, as was the defendant in
Singer, with the need to conjecture or
speculate on what these motives were,
since in the instant case they were
candidly expressed by the prosecution.

First, the prosecution asserted the
need for a jury verdict to meet the
petitioners' claim of government
prejudice. This seems a most questionable reason for trying a defendant before
a concededly more prejudiced tribunal.
The petitioners had a constitutional
right to express their belief that they

were being prosecuted because of their
race or religious affiliation. This
Court is aware of the religious and
political trials throughout history in
which similar claims have been made by
those facing inquisitional or political
heresy trials. It seems strange, even
aberrant, for the government to impose
what in this context is a penalty because
of the petitioners' adherence to a
traditional defense to a government
indictment, that is, to speak out in the
forum of public opinion. The courts
below expressed doubt that "the
government's reason for refusing to
consent to a bench trial was impermissibly to punish Moon for exercising First
Amendment rights." (App. 8). But this is
exactly what the government did. Its
expressed rationale -- to give the public

confidence through a jury -- does not
obfuscate its equally expressed purpose
of protecting itself from Reverend Moon's
exercise of free speech. Nor does it
obfuscate its effect -- that is, a
tribunal less likely to give petitioners
the fairer mode of trial which they would
have received had Reverend Moon not
criticized the government. If petitioner
Moon had not made his statement, there is
nothing whatever to indicate that the
prosecution -- whose statement here we
accept at face value -- would have denied
him the bench trial he sought.

There are less drastic means than
denying a "fairer" trial to meet a
petitioner's public claims of religious
persecution. The government was entitled
to make an equally forceful denial of
religious persecution. It could have

stated that a grand jury, free from government control, had handed down the indictment. It could have specified other criminal proceedings brought in the past against churches and church leaders in order to show its non-discriminatory approach to the petitioners. These and other alternative means would have been less drastic than depriving the petitioners of a trial concededly fairer than the one insisted upon by the government.

This brings us to the government's second point: that the public would have more confidence in a jury trial than in a bench trial. (App. 7). This is a most doubtful speculation and one which denigrates the respect which the public quite properly has for our federal judges. The government may have greater

confidence in a jury verdict in a case
such as this, but that is certainly not
true of the public. Indeed, the public
is often even in awe of judges in
contrast to its view of its fellow
citizens.

We are even more puzzled by the
government's expressed desire to spare
the trial judge from being placed in an
"untenable" position. (App. 7). This,
too, denigrates both the character and
the high responsibilities of our judges
and unjustifiably questions their
ability, even their courage, to carry out
their sworn duty. The trial judge was
quite capable of protecting himself.
Indeed his reason for yielding to the
government's veto was not on the ground

of self-protection, but rather in the erroneous belief that he lacked the power to override that veto.

CONCLUSION

The petition for certiorari should be granted so that the Court can address the petitioners' due process and First Amendment rights.

LEONARD B. BOUDIN
Counsel of record for
Amicus Curiae

National Emergency Civil
Liberties Committee
30 East 42nd Street
New York, N.Y. 10017
(212) 697-8640

March 1984

The Southern Christian Leadership
Conference, The National
Conference of Black Mayors, The
National Bar Association, and the
Honorable Mervyn Dymally

i

QUESTIONS PRESENTED

1. Did the court below err in ruling that the Government may force an unpopular religious leader to be tried by jury because he has exercised his First Amendment rights to criticize the Government's motives for prosecuting him?

2. Did the court below err in ruling that a jury may be permitted to examine the internal structure of a church or the uses to which church assets are put in order to determine whether the leader of that church holds the assets personally or in trust for the church?

ii

TABLE OF CONTENTS

iii

TABLE OF AUTHORITIES

IN THE

𝔖upreme 𝔔ourt of the 𝔘nited 𝔖tates

OCTOBER TERM 1983

———

SUN MYUNG MOON, et al.,

Petitioners,

v.

UNITED STATES OF AMERICA,

Respondent.

———

ON PETITION FOR A WRIT OF CERTIORARI
TO THE UNITED STATES COURT OF APPEALS
FOR THE SECOND CIRCUIT

———

BRIEF OF THE SOUTHERN CHRISTIAN LEADERSHIP CONFERENCE, THE NATIONAL CONFERENCE OF BLACK MAYORS, THE NATIONAL BAR ASSOCIATION AND THE HONORABLE MERVYN DYMALLY AS AMICI CURIAE IN SUPPORT OF PETITIONERS

———

By consent of the Petitioners and the Respondent as evidenced by the letters of consent filed herewith, the Southern Christian Leadership Conference, The National Conference of Black Mayors, The National Bar Association and the Honorable Mervyn Dymally respectfully submit this joint brief *amici curiae* in support of the Petition for a Writ of Certiorari.

2

INTEREST OF AMICI

The Southern Christian Leadership Conference ("SCLC"), the National Conference of Black Mayors ("NCBM") and the National Bar Association ("NBA") Are predominently Black organizations which have a special interest in this case because of the threat which it poses to the rights of minority group members both with respect to the right to a fair trial and the right to freedom of worship. The Honorable Mervyn Dymally is the United States Representative from the Thirty-first Congressional District in California.

The Southern Christian Leadership Conference ("SCLC") was founded in 1957 by the Reverend Martin Luther King and other religious leaders to provide Christian guidance and leadership in the struggle for interracial unity, human rights and equality of opportunity. Committed to nonviolent direct action as the means to achieve social justice, the SCLC has over 300 chapters and affiliates nationwide. Its membership consists of churches, labor unions, student groups and other organizations as well as individuals.

The National Conference of Black Mayors was founded in 1974 and currently is composed of 252 Black mayors who serve municipalities ranging in population from 100 to well over 5,000,000. The NCBM's purpose is to provide its members with information and assistance as they work to improve the quality of urban life for all.

The National Bar Association (NBA) is a professional organization for lawyers. Currently, it has over 7,000 members most of whom are Black. Founded in 1925, the NBA has had special concern from its inception for the constitutional and civil rights of all Americans.

The Honorable Mervyn Dymally is the United States Representative from the Thirty-first Congressional District in California and the former Lieutenant Governor of that State. Congressman Dymally represents approximately 525,000 constituents from a wide variety of racial and ethnic backgrounds.

3

He joins in this brief as an expression of his concern that the right of freedom of worship and to a fair trial be preserved for all citizens.

The dedication of these *Amici* to the principles of equal justice and freedom of worship and their grave concern that the decision of the Appellate Court in this case poses a threat to those principles has prompted them to file this brief *amici curiae* in support of Reverend Moon's Petition for a Writ of Certiorari.[1]

The SCLC, NCBM, NBA and the Honorable Mervyn Dymally file this brief not out of sympathy for Reverend Moon and his movement, but rather out of deep concern that Reverend Moon was denied equal justice because of his status as the controversial leader of an unpopular religious movement. The *Amici* believe that Reverend Moon's trial and conviction for tax fraud and conspiracy raise grave constitutional questions which were inadequately considered by the Appellate Court which affirmed Reverend Moon's conviction. The *Amici Curiae* fear that the opinion of the United States Court of Appeals for the Second Circuit, if allowed to stand, will constitute dangerous precedent whenever the Government prosecutes unpopular religious or political leaders.

Two issues are of most urgent concern to the *Amici Curiae:* first, whether the Government may force an unpopular religious leader to be tried by a jury because he has exercised his First Amendment rights to criticize the Government's motives for prosecuting him; and second, whether a jury may be permitted to examine the internal structure of a church or the uses to which church assets are put in order to determine whether the leader of that church holds the assets personally or in trust for the church.

---

[1] Although the limited resources of the several *Amici* represented herein required the Unification Church to defray certain printing and travel costs and attorneys' fees incurred in the preparation of this brief, the brief was written and is being filed by Jewel Lafontant solely at the direction and in the interest of the *Amici* themselves.

4

The first issue is of particular concern to the SCLC, NCBM, NBA and Congressman Dymally because minority group members must rely upon the courts if they are to enjoy the full rights of citizenship and, conversely, are especially vulnerable to oppression and unfairness if the courts cease to safeguard the rights of unpopular defendants.

The *Amici* are gravely concerned by the second issue because of the devastating impact which it may have on unsophisticated unstructured ministries which serve the poor community. Many ministers lack the resources and legal sophistication to incorporate their churches. Few poor parishioners are sophisticated enough to utter the magic words "to be held in trust" when they make contributions to their churches. Under the Appellate Court's opinion, such ministers would be vulnerable to criminal conviction for tax evasion at the whim of a jury.

SUMMARY OF ARGUMENT

Given the clear evidence showing that it was unlikely or impossible for Reverend Moon to receive a fair trial by jury, it was violative of his constitutional rights for the Government to withhold its consent to a waiver of the right to trial by jury and for the trial court to fail to order a bench trial notwithstanding the Government's failure to consent.

The jury instructions trammeled the religious liberty of Reverend Moon and his followers in that: (1) the jury was not instructed with respect to Reverend Moon's position and role within the Unification Church; (2) the jury was impermissibly permitted to consider the structure of the Unification Church in considering whether Reverend Moon held certain assets personally or in trust for the church; (3) the jury was impermissibly permitted to decide for itself, on any basis it chose, whether various expenditures made by Moon were made for "personal" or "business" purposes as opposed to "religious" purposes.

5

ARGUMENT

A.

Forcing Reverend Moon to Submit to Trial by Jury Was Manifestly Unfair

Under the circumstances of this case, it was a violation of Reverend Moon's rights to force him to stand trial by jury.

It is a matter of common knowledge that Reverend Moon is the leader and prophet of a novel religious movement, one which many view as incompatible with traditional Christian beliefs. History clearly demonstrates that no one is so vulnerable to popular hatred and persecution as the leaders of novel religious or political movements. In this case, Reverend Moon documented through use of a careful public opinion survey that he is the object of widespread public hostility (A. 801-03; 818-20; 916-1002). This evidence strongly indicated that it was most unlikely, and perhaps impossible, for Reverend Moon to receive a fair trial by jury. Rather than eliminating the possibility of unfairness in this case, the jury selection process simply confirmed that Reverend Moon could not receive a fair trial by jury. Although allowed far more than the usual number of challenges, Reverend Moon's defense was unable to eliminate from the jury all who held negative views about Reverend Moon and his church. Of the jury which was ultimately selected, ten of the twelve held negative preconceptions about Reverend Moon or his movement.[2] Under these circumstances, the *Amici* believe that it was a clear violation of Reverend Moon's rights to force him to stand trial by a jury.

---

[2] As summarized by the Petitioners (App. Br. p. 23) the negative preconceptions articulated by the jurors were as follows:

—Mary K. Nimmo, forelady, had heard that the Unification Church was a "cult," "making money on young people," and "wouldn't have wanted [her] children to have been a part of it." T473; see also 449, 477-80.

—Esperanza Torres knew of a "deprogramming" controversy involving a Unification Church member and concluded "that the

(Footnote continued on following page)

6

The Sixth Amendment guarantees criminal defendants the right to an *impartial* trial by jury. This right exists "primarily for the protection of the accused," *Patton* v. *United States,* 281 U. S. 276 (1930) overruled on other grounds, *Williams* v. *Florida,* 339 U. S. 78 (1970). The purpose of trial by jury is to provide, through community participation in the determination of guilt or innocence, a bulwark against Government oppression. *Williams* v. *Florida,* 339 U. S. 78, 100 (1970); *Duncan* v. *Louisiana,* 391 U. S. 145, 156-57 (1968).

Where a defendant is the object of popular hostility as well as government prosecution, a jury can become a frightening

---

(Footnote continued from preceding page)

parents [of the member] are right . . .," doubted Reverend Moon was a genuine spiritual leader (T847-48), and considered the Unification Church a "cult" involving "mostly young people" (T857). See T849, 852, 862-63, 871, 873-75.

—Rose Spencer did not "think" that it was proper for religious groups to invest in businesses, and felt that it was improper for religious groups to solicit funds publicly. T1349-50; see also 1358.

—Doris Torres had heard that "some people think [Moon] is a god" (T1391) and that the Unification Church "brainwashes" people. T1394.

—Claudette Ange had heard that Moon "was brainwashing some teenagers" and "has children selling . . . things . . . to get the money to buy property." T1514-15.

—Maria Abramson had not heard of Moon, but thought that religious cults brainwash young people (T1588), and believed religious groups "should collect their money in the church," not in public (T1587-88).

—Paul Stanley had heard about deprogramming and young people being "brainwashed" and "used for selling things." T1650; see T1631-32, 1636.

—Freddie Bryant thought that churches should raise funds by donations from their own members and not by "go[ing] into a complete business." T1683-85.

—Amerria Vasquez had heard that the "Moonies" "indoctrinate the young people in the church," and "are taking over New York City." T2052.

—Ernest Fetchko had heard that the "Moonies" get members "by brainwashing them." T2106.

7

weapon of oppression rather than a bulwark of liberty. As John Stuart Mill stated:

> "When society itself is the tyrant . . . its means of tyrannizing are not limited to the acts which it may do by the hands of its political functionaries . . . . Protection against tyranny of the magistrate is not enough: there needs protection also against the tyranny of the prevailing opinion and feeling . . ." Mill, *On Liberty,* Crofts Classics Ed. (1947) p. 4.

When defendants are hated or feared because of their political or religious beliefs, bench trials rather than jury trials may be the surest safeguard of civil liberties since the jury may be little more than an enthusiastic accessory to governmental oppression.

That defendants may need protection from juries was recognized in *Singer* v. *United States,* 380 U.S. 24 (1965). There, this Court, while holding that the Constitution does not give criminal defendants an absolute right to waive a jury trial, affirmed that government prosecutors are not ordinary parties to a proceeding, but " 'servant[s] of the law' with a 'twofold aim . . . that guilt shall not escape or innocence suffer.' " 380 U.S. at 37. The Government's duty to consider the rights of the accused necessarily includes the obligation to agree to a bench trial in cases where popular hostility toward a defendant makes it unlikely that a defendant will receive a fair trial before a jury." Thus, in *Singer,* the Court stated that there:

> "might be some circumstances where a defendant's reasons for wanting to be tried by a judge alone are so compelling that the Government's insistence on trial by jury would result in the denial to a defendant of a fair trial." 380 U.S. at 37.

Surely, this is precisely such a case. Reverend Moon's evidence of public hostility toward him and the negative opinions about Reverend Moon elicited from the veniremen during *voir dire* made it manifestly unfair for the Government to withhold consent to a bench trial.

8

Standing alone, the Government's refusal to consent to a bench trial would have been a violation of Reverend Moon's constitutional rights, but the Government compounded its wrong by withholding its consent for an impermissible reason. Although not required to give any reason for its refusal to consent to a waiver of jury trial, the Government did volunteer a reason—namely, that Reverend Moon's criticism of the prosecution, in a public speech which was later published in the *New York Times,* made a jury trial necessary lest he "blame any adverse result in this case on religious or racial bigotry." A. 1028. Thus, by the Government's own admission, the sole reason for its refusal to consent to Reverend Moon's request was the public criticism which he had leveled against it and its fear that he would similarly criticize the decision if the Government won. The Government's insistence on a jury trial specifically because of Reverend Moon's exercise of his First Amendment rights is a clear violation of the Constitution. *Perry* v. *Sindermann,* 408 U.S. 593, 597 (1972).

The *Amici* are deeply concerned that the Second Circuit failed adequately to consider this issue. Its decision affirming denial of a bench trial is tantamount to authorizing the Government to use the threat of a jury trial as a weapon to silence unpopular defendants and the jury trial itself as punishment for the recalcitrant. This is precedent which cannot be allowed to stand and which must be reviewed and reversed by this Court.

Further, this Court should clearly establish that the trial judge had authority to overrride the Government's objection to waiver of the jury trial and that he erred by failing to use that authority. The trial judge expressly recognized that a nonjury trial would have been fairer (Tr. 1760; 1752; 1759; 1761) but denied Reverend Moon's motion for a bench trial in the belief that the law "seem[s] to put no restrictions upon the prosecution being able to insist upon a jury." (Tr. 1752). Based on what proved to be an erroneous assumption that the case would

9

involve only "pretty dry and pretty dull" (Tr. 1739) tax issues rather than issues concerning the beliefs of the Unification Church (Tr. 1758-59), the judge gave no consideration to the compelling circumstances exception set forth in *Singer.* This was error. In cases involving far less public hostility toward defendants, other trial courts have recognized the need to grant requests for nonjury trials over Government objections. Thus, in *United States* v. *Braunstein,* 474 F. Supp. 1 (D. N. J.), the court granted the defendant's motion for a bench trial over the Government's objection where:

> "the government puts nothing in the balance other than good reputation and motive to weigh against the overwhelming showing of sound reasons presented by the defendants." 474 F. Supp. at 14.

Accord: United States v. *Panteleakis,* 422 F. Supp. 247 (D. R. I. 1976) (request for bench trial granted over government objection where government's refusal to consent is "unreasonable and arbitrary." 422 F. Supp. at 250); *United States* v. *Schipani,* 44 FRD 461 (E. D. N. Y. 1968) (request for nonjury trial granted over Government's objections where substantial danger that defendant's association with organized crime would prejudice a jury.)

The *Amici* firmly believe that all criminal defendants are entitled to receive as fair a trial as possible. There can be no doubt in this case that it would have been fairer, as the trial judge found both before *voir dire* and after, to give Reverend Moon a bench trial than to force him to stand trial in front of a jury which was bound to be negatively predisposed toward him and his religion. That the Government withheld its consent to a bench trial because of Reverend Moon's public criticism compounds its wrong. It is urgently important for this Court to affirm the duty of the Government to agree to bench trials, and the power and duty of trial courts to authorize bench trials over the Government's objection, where, as here, public hostility toward a defendant makes a fair trial by jury unlikely or impossible.

10

B.

The Jury Instructions Infringed Upon the Religious Liberty of Reverend Moon and His Followers

A second issue of deep concern to the *Amici* is that the jury instructions in this case permitted the jury to ride roughshod over the religious beliefs of Reverend Moon and his followers. The critical issue in this case was whether certain assets held by Reverend Moon in his own name were his property or whether, on the contrary, he held those assets in trust for the Unification Church. This was an issue which was inextricably linked to Reverend Moon's role in the Unification Church and to his religious views and those of his followers. As Judge Oakes wrote in his dissenting opinion:

> "this case did not involve a claim that an ordinary lay taxpayer held certain assets in a private trust for the benefit of another. On the contrary, the taxpayer here was the founder and leader of a world-wide movement which, regardless of what the observer may think of its views or even its motives, is, nevertheless on its face, a religious one, the members of which regard the taxpayer as the embodiment of their faith." (Oakes, J., dissenting opinion, p. 3)

No one disputes that the most important consideration in determining whether Reverend Moon owned the disputed assets personally or in trust for the Unification Church is the intent of the donors. If the donors intended Reverend Moon to use their gifts on behalf of the church, the assets would be held by Reverend Moon in trust for the church regardless of whether the donors had actually used the correct legal terminology. (See, Oakes, J., dissenting opinion, pp. 5-6). Obviously, the intent of the donors could be understood in this case only if the jurors understood Reverend Moon's position and role within his church. Yet, the trial court refused to instruct the jurors that Reverend Moon's followers view him as the embodiment of their faith, commenting that such an instruction "makes him a walking unincorporated association." (Tr. 6119). The refusal

11

to give this instruction demonstrates the disregard with which the beliefs of Reverend Moon's followers were treated and the license which the jurors were given to impose their own views of appropriate organization on the Unification Church.

Consistent with the short shrift given to the views of Reverend Moon's followers with respect to his role within the church is the fact that the trial court's instructions permitted the jury to determine for itself, on any basis it wished, whether the structure of the Unification Church supported the Government's contention that Reverend Moon owned the assets personally and whether the uses to which he put the assets were religious.

The organization of a church is a matter of transcendent theological importance. A church's organization or lack thereof directly reflects its theology with respect to man's relationship with God. *See, e.g., Morey* v. *Riddell,* 205 F. Supp. 918 (S. D. Cal. 1962) (lack of formal organization "stem[s] from the very doctrinal ties that bind its members together." 205 F. Supp., at 919). An essential element of religious liberty is the liberty of the church to choose its own structure. *Maryland and Virginia Eldership* v. *Church of God,* 396 U. S. 367, 369 (1970); *Serbian Eastern Orthodox Diocese* v. *Milovojevich,* 426 U. S. 696, 721 (1976). Yet, in this case, the jury was expressly permitted and even urged to consider the fact that Reverend Moon's international religious movement had no "corporate structure" (Tr. 5521) as evidence that Reverend Moon was lying when he stated that he held the assets in trust for his church. Indeed, the very first factor listed by the trial judge for the jury to consider in his instructions on the law of trusts was the organization of the Unification Church. This instruction permitted the jury to intrude upon the religious prerogatives of the Unification Church to an extent wholly inconsistent with the Constitution's protection of religious liberty.

The Appellate Court's opinion sanctioning this instruction poses a special threat to ministers who serve the poor. Many

12

such ministers lack the legal sophistication and resources to incorporate their churches even if such a formal structure were consistent with their theology. The Appellate Court's opinion which demands formal structure if a church is to be considered legitimate poses a real and intolerable risk of criminal tax liability for ministers who are unable or unwilling to achieve the type of formal organization demanded by the Appellate Court.

Equally troubling is the fact that the trial court's instructions permitted the jury to decide for itself, on any basis it chose, whether various expenditures made by Moon were made for "personal" or "business" purposes as opposed to "religious" purposes. This again is an area into which the jury had no right to intrude. A religious movement has the right to define for itself "which expenditures are religious and which are secular" *Lemon* v. *Kurtzman,* 403 U. S. 602, 621-22 (1971). If juries may arbitrarily label certain expenditures as "secular" rather than religious, every church which invests funds in secular enterprises in order to finance church activities would be subject to a jury determination that its investments were not religious. This would be an impermissible intrusion of civil government into the right of the churches to organize their affairs as they see fit.

Again, the Appellate Court's opinion poses a particular threat to poorer churches and congregations who lack the sophistication necessary to structure their affairs in the highly formal manner demanded by the Appellate Court. Frequently, inner city and rural congregations entrust funds to their ministers intending such funds to be used for the support of the church as well as for the minister's necessary living expenses. These congregants lack the legal sophistication to utter the words "to be held in trust." The Appellate Court's opinion makes it possible for the ministers who accept these funds in good faith to become subject to prosecution on the theory that the funds were their own personal income. The Appellate Court's decision would rarely burden wealthier churches whose

13

lawyers and sophisticated congregants have the knowledge to insure that their intentions are clear; rather, by elevating legalistic formalities over true intention, the decision poses an intolerable threat of tax prosecution to poor, unsophisticated religious groups.

In sum, the jury instructions approved by the Circuit Court which upheld Reverend Moon's convictions (by a 2-1 vote) were, in effect, a roving commission for the jury to impose its own views about appropriate organization and expenditures on Reverend Moon and the Unification Church. The result is a precedent which threatens all religious groups and especially poor religious groups by openly authorizing public intrusion upon their internal affairs. It is urgently important that this Court grant certiorari to remove this threat to religious liberty.

14

CONCLUSION

For all of the reasons stated above, the Southern Christian Leadership Conference, the National Conference of Black Mayors, the National Bar Association and the Honorable Mervyn Dymally as *amici curiae* urge the Court to grant certiorari.

Respectfully submitted,

JEWEL S. LAFONTANT
(counsel of record)

ANDREA R. WAINTROOB
VEDDER, PRICE, KAUFMAN &
KAMMHOLZ
    115 South LaSalle Street
    Chicago, Illinois 60603
    (312) 781-2200

Dated: February 1984

The Spartacist League

QUESTIONS PRESENTED

1. Did the court below deny First Amendment protection to a religious organization when it affirmed a method of prosecution which abrogated the internal integrity of the organization's decisions of the core concerns of structure, contributions and expenditures?

2. Did the court below deny an unpopular religious organization the legal protections afforded other organizations in violation of the First Amendment and due process?

INDEX

SUMMARY OF ARGUMENT

The court of appeals affirmed a prosecutorial method which sanctions the denial of First Amendment protection to the acknowledged spiritual and organizational leader of a religious organization. The court licensed the abrogation of organizational integrity concerning the core questions of structure, expenditures and contributions. In so doing, legal precedent, practice and constitutional protections were ignored.

The method of the prosecution treated the despised Moon organization and its leader differently than other organizations and violated established constitutional protections for those religious, political and other organizations viewed as unpopular and

expressing minority opinions. The method
and process of this ₁ conviction has
dangerous consequences for any
organization which the government choses
to single out for harassment and
victimization.

BRIEF OF THE SPARTACIST LEAGUE AS AMICUS CURIAE

Pursuant to Rule 36.1 of the Rules of this Court, the organization named above files this brief in support of the instant petition for certiorari. Consent for filing of this brief has been obtained in writing from the attorneys of record for the parties in this case. Their original letters have been filed with the Clerk of this Court.

INTEREST OF AMICUS CURIAE

The Spartacist League is a Marxist political organization with a history of twenty years of activity in the United States, including running candidates for public office. The Spartacist League is an unincorporated association which receives financial support from members and other political supporters.

The Spartacist League does not hold the Unification Church to be a religious entity. It is the position of the Spartacist League that this question belongs to the domain of public debate and is in no way a matter for governmental or juridical determination. However neither the trial court nor the court of appeals disputed the characterization of the Unification Church as a religious organization nor Sun Myung Moon's asserted position with the Unification Church as its spiritual and organizational leader. Rather, the posture of this case is that the First Amendment implications of this prosecution were acknowledged - and then denied application.

It is the withholding of First

Amendment protection from Moon in denying

him the right to explain the religious

reasons for and the religious meaning of

his conduct, thereby abrogating a

religious organization's determination of

its structure, contributions and

expenditures which compels the filing of

this brief amicus curiae.

The Spartacist League has no

agreement with or support for the

policies or activities of the Unification

Church. But the method by which Moon's

prosecution was conducted and the

principles upholding his conviction have

broad First Amendment consequences

extending from the right to religious

worship to political advocacy. The

autonomy of religious organizations is

linked historically to the development of

the legal status of all associations.

And First Amendment protection of

religious organizations is analagous to
and impacts heavily on other
organizations protected by the
constitution. Thus the method and
principles underlying Moon's conviction,
if left unchallenged, have potentially
unlimited reach, jeopardizing the
associational rights of those engaged in
religious, social or political advocacy.

STATEMENT OF CASE

Amicus adopts the statement of the
case as set forth in the petition for
certiorari to the extent relevant to the
argument below.

The undisputed central question of
this criminal prosecution was whether the
ownership of funds in a Chase bank
account and certain stock rested with Sun
Myung Moon or the Unification Church. The

man accused by the government of ownership of those assets, and therefore of having concealed taxable income, was acknowledged as the spiritual and organizational leader of the Unification Church, the status of which as a religious organization was not challenged. Nor was it disputed that the funds Moon received were from Unification Church followers, intending their contributions to be donations for church purposes.

Yet, court of appeals sanctioned a prosecution which denied a religious organization and its leader the protections of the First Amendment. The organizational decisions of the church were abrogated by denying Moon the right to explain the religious reasons and purposes of his actions. And the much despised Unification Church was denied

he benefits of established law, practice
nd precedent accorded other, more
stablished religions.

REASONS FOR GRANTING THE WRIT

I.THE METHOD OF THIS PROSECUTION
BROGATED **THE INTERNAL INTEGRITY OF A**
ELIGIOUS ORGANIZATION IN VIOLATION OF
HE FIRST AMENDMENT

The critical and central issue of
his criminal prosecution was whether
oon owned the assets in question and
herefore was required to pay income tax
n the bank interest and the value of the
tock, or Moon held these assets merely
eneficially or as a trustee for the
nification Church.

This prosecution clearly invoked
irst Amendment considerations. The

_ourt of appeals noted the "myriad of constitutional problems presented" and the "troubling issues of religious persecution and abridgement of free speech." Moreover, this case did not present new issues, but was prosecuted in the context of established constitutional principles and legal precedents regarding religious autonomy, government intervention, control of religious groups and taxation.

But in affirming the method which secured Moon's conviction, the court of appeals denied First Amendment protection as irrelevant and inapplicable, specifically because this case was a federal criminal tax prosecution. A process which denies the applicability of the First Amendment Religion Clauses in a criminal prosecution and vitiates the undisputed internal decisions of an organization, when those decisions concern the <u>core</u> of organizational existence, is a violation of both the First Amendment and due process.

The fundamental concern of the Religious Clauses of the First Amendment is the relationship between religious expression and the state. The underlying historical perception is that a union between church and state leads to persecution and civil strife, <u>Everson v. Board of Education</u>, 330 U.S. 1 (1947), and "tends to destoy government and degrade religion," <u>Engel v. Vitale</u>, 370 U.S. 421, 431 (1962). The power of the state is no greater than in a criminal prosecution wherein religious practices can be rendered unlawful, its adherents can be jailed. Contrary to the opinion of the court of appeals, in criminal matters, no less than civil, the First

Amendment prohibits either the courts or government from trying the truth or falsity of religious beliefs. <u>United States</u> <u>v.</u> <u>Ballard</u>, 322 U.S. 78 (1944). It was not constitutionally permissible for the jury to be given license by the courts below to substitute themselves for the Unification Church regarding religious determinations of structure, contributions and expenditures of the church. "When the triers of fact undertake that task, they enter a forbidden domain." <u>Id</u>. at 87.

If the issues posed had been in the context of an intra-church dispute, there would have been no quarrel from the courts below that religious autonomy and court abstention from the Unification Church's internal decision making process was constitutionally mandated. See, <u>Watson</u> <u>v.</u> <u>Jones</u>, 80 U.S. (13 Wall.) 679

(1871), Serbian Eastern Orthodox Diocese v. Milivojevich, 426 U.S. 696 (1976); Presbyterian Church v. Mary Elizabeth Blue Hull Memorial Presbyterian Church, 393 U.S. 440 (1969). Where there are disputes over religious doctrine, administration, or organization, the courts have no authority but must accept the decisions of church bodies "as it finds them," Serbian Orthodox Diocese, 426 U.S. at 713. There is no constitutionally permissible authority for government intrusion into "questions. . . at the core of ecclesiastical concern," defined as including matters of religious doctrine, organization and discipline. Id. at 717. The undisputed decisions of a church and its membership should be entitled to more, not less, protection from government intervention than those marked with internal dissention.

The First Amendment right of
political association, considered "one of
the foundations of our society,"
N.A.A.C.P. v. Claiborne Hardware Co.,
102 S.Ct 3409 (1982), provides additional
authority for protecting organizational
integrity from government intervention.
This Court has repeatedly recognized the
close nexus between freedom of
association and freedom of speech.
N.A.A.C.P. v. Claiborne, supra.,
Democratic Party of U.S. v. Wisconsin,
450 U.S. 107 (1981). And "any
interference with the freedom of a party
is simultaneously an interference with
the freedom of its adherents." Sweezy
v. New Hampshire, 354 U.S. 234, 250
(1957)]. "A state may not
constitutionally substitute its own
judgment for that of a party," even where
the government or court "view a

particular expression as unwise or irrational." Democratic Party v. Wisconsin, supra. at 124.

Thus the powerful authority of constitutional principles regarding religious organizations required the court of appeals to reject the abrogation of church policy and assault on organizational integrity which formed the basis of Moon prosecution. Instead, the court of appeals sanctioned a process which attacked the core of organizational existence, violating both the First Amendment and due process. Moon's relationship to the Unification Church was denied legal import, religious reasons for his actions were deemed irrelevant, the validity of an unincorporated organizational status was challenged, and an unprecedented theory of taxation was applied to funds placed in trust in Moon's name.

Organizational form and finances, both contributions and expenditures, are the core of an organization's ability to exist and give expression to its beliefs and policy. By not accepting the religious explanations and internally undisputed determinations of the Unification Church in matters of structure, expenditures and finances, principles of neutrality and non-intervention into decisions of a church body were violated, <u>Jones</u> <u>v.</u> <u>Wolf</u>, 443 U.S. 595 (1979); and constituted an impermissible "governmental evaluation" of religious practices and entanglement of government in "classifications of what is or is not religious," <u>Walz</u> <u>v.</u> <u>Tax</u> <u>Commission</u>, 397 U.S. 664, 674 (1970).

The unincorporated status of the

international Unification Church was
claimed by the government, with
subsequent approval by the court of
appeals, as proof of <u>non-existence</u>. This
impugns the legality of centuries of
unincorporated associational gathering
for religious, social, educational and
political purposes and vitiates the
constitutional principle that religious
bodies have the "power to decide for
themselves, free from state interference,
matters of church government." <u>Kedroff</u>
<u>v. St. Nicholas Cathedral</u>, 344 U.S. 94,
116 (1952).

Nor can a religious organization be
denied the ability to expend its assets
to secure additional financial support
nor precluded from determining which
expenditures have a religious purpose and
which do not. "This is exactly the
inquiry that the First Amendment

prohibits. . ." <u>Serbian</u> <u>Eastern</u> <u>Orthodox</u> <u>Diocese</u> <u>v.</u> <u>Milivojevich</u>, <u>supra</u>. at 713.

The court of appeals not only found no error in the trial court's jury instructions on the issue of whether Moon held the assets as a religious trust, but denied that the trust instruction was even necessary. It was conceded by the government and substantiated by the evidence that the source of the funds was "evangelical activities" by Unification Church members, donated and intended for religious purposes. Yet the trial court denied instructions which would provide the jury with the religious meaning and purposes of the acts and practices upon which the government premised its prosecution. Thus Moon, the acknowledged international spiritual and organizational leader of the Unification Church, was convicted of tax fraud

because funds were held in his own name,
some assets applied to uses determined by
the court to be "business" or "personal"
uses, and monies received without
specific "in trust" declarations. The
jury was given license, if not a court
mandate, to impose its own standards of
legtimate religious conduct and policy on
Moon and the Unification Church.

The denial of religious trust status
to Moon's holdings is contrary to legal
precedent, including IRS regulations. A
contribution for religious purposes
occurs whenever it is "for the use of"
that charitable purpose regardless of the
actual identity of the recipient. <u>Winn</u>
<u>v.</u> <u>Commissioner</u>, 595 F.2d 1060, 1065
(5th Cir. 1979); <u>Brittingham</u> <u>v.</u>
<u>Commissioner</u>, 57 T.C.91, 100-01 (1971),
acq. 1971-2 C.B.2. Moreover, the process
and determination that the entirety of

the assets held in Moon's name belonged
to him personally constitutes a seizure
of assets from the organizational members
who placed them with Moon for application
to the purposes and policies of their
church as decided by that church. Cf.
Jones v. Wolf, supra. at 606.

II. DENYING UNPOPULAR ORGANIZATIONS
THE LEGAL PROTECTIONS AFFORDED OTHER
ORGANIZATIONS VIOLATES THE FIRST
AMENDMENT AND DUE PROCESS

The method of this prosecution was a
backdoor assault on a virulently disliked
organization rendering various norms of
organizational existence and functioning
illegal or suspect. The prosecution did
not directly challenge the principles and
legal precedents which apply in general
to government control of, intervention
into, or taxation of religious
organizations. Instead, Terrett v.

Taylor, 13 U.S. (9 Cranch) 43 (1815),
(holding church property legally free
from government interference); Walz v.
Tax Commission, supra., (holding tax
exemptions for religious groups not
violative of First Amendment); and Jones
v. Wolf, supra. (prohibiting the
resolution of intra-church disputes by
civil courts interpreting religious
doctrine) were denied legal relevance.
Moon, the acknowledged church leader, was
denied the ability to place his actions
in that context.

Having acknowledged the Unification
Church as a religious organization, and
Moon as its leader, First Amendment
protection under either the Religion
Clauses or freedom of speech and
association could not then be denied.

The First Amendment right of freedom
of association establishes that an

organization cannot be "outlawed" or
rendered illegal, whether on a conspiracy
theory or otherwise, in absence of a
clear showing that the group is actively
engaged in illegal conduct. See, Yates
v. United States, 354 U.S. 298 (1957).
Criminal prosecution of an individual
associated with a protected organization
can be based on violation of a valid law,
but the state cannot seize upon protected
acts as the basis for a criminal charge.
See, N.A.A.C.P. v. Claiborne, supra.; De
Jonge v. Oregon, 299 U.S. 353 (1937).

This prosecution rests on denying
the Moon organization the First Amendment
protections and legal precedents accorded
other, albeit more established,
respectable, and less despised religious
organizations. The historical lawful
unincorporated structure of religious
societies, social groups, and political

organizations was used as proof of organizational non-existence. A trust was denied where the assets were held and expended in a manner comparable to that used by religious and other organizations. Lawful, constitutionally protected conduct was transformed into criminal activity by denying Moon the ability to give religious reasons for his actions and abrogating the integrity of the internal decision making process of an organization engaged in First Amendment activity.

Where the government is condoned for a criminal prosecution based on a method which treats one religious organization differently from another, First Amendment freedom for any organization is at risk. Unpopular, minority political organizations are endangered by the method of this prosecution. After almost thirteen years of persecution of the Communist Party, U.S.A. on questions of taxable income the Court of Appeals for the D.C. Circuit remanded the matter to the Tax Court for findings of fact consistent with the principle that the Communist Party could not be treated differently from other political parties. <u>Communist Party v. Commissioner</u>, 373 F.2d 682 (D.C.Cir. 1967). This Court has recognized that membership or support of unpopular, minority political organizations has resulted in government harassment and persecution requiring strict protection of associational rights. <u>Brown v. Socialist Workers '74 Campaign Committee</u>, __U.S.__, 103 S.Ct. 416 (1982); <u>Buckley v. Valeo</u>, 424 U.S. 1 (1976). The political organizations in those cases were unincorporated entities, and this Court recognized not only the need to protect contributors of "disfavored minority parties", but also the necessary expenditures made by these organizations, including those for commercial transactions. Brown v. Socialist Workers, supra. at 423.

The injury which could be inflicted on political and other associations, particularly unpopular, minority political groups by sanctioning the method of the Moon prosecution is not a matter of speculation. It could have powerful negative ramifications on the integrity of an organization regarding its structure, administration and financial operations. This prosecution provides the framework for harassment and victimization for targeted religious, social and political organizations and serves to criminalize heretofore established and lawful practices.

CONCLUSION

For the above-stated reasons, <u>amicus</u> urges that a writ of certiorari be granted and this Court decide the important and urgent questions presented by this case.

RACHEL H. WOLKENSTEIN
General Counsel, Spartacist League
299 Broadway
New York, New York 10007
(212) 233-1886

JONATHAN W. LUBELL
Cohn, Glickstein, Ostrin, Lurie, Lubell
    and Lubell
1370 Avenue of the Americas
New York, New York
(212) 757-4000

APRIL 1984

The States of Hawaii, Oregon and Rhode Island

i

QUESTION PRESENTED

Whether, in the course of resolving the principles of tax law and constitutional law put at issue by the petitioners in the courts below, the decision of the Second Circuit herein fundamentally skews heretofore unquestioned principles of trust law in a manner that, if adopted in other jurisdictions, would handicap states in their efforts to enforce accountability upon those to whom funds are entrusted for the benefit of others.

ii

TABLE OF CONTENTS

iii

TABLE OF AUTHORITIES

iv

Other

No. 83-1242

In the

Supreme Court of the United States

October Term, 1983

———————◆———————

Sun Myung Moon *and* Takeru Kamiyama,

Petitioners,

—v.—

United States of America

Respondent.

———————

ON PETITION FOR CERTIORARI TO THE UNITED STATES
COURT OF APPEALS FOR THE SECOND CIRCUIT

BRIEF FOR THE STATES OF HAWAII, OREGON AND RHODE ISLAND SUPPORTING A GRANT OF CERTIORARI

STATEMENT OF INTEREST

The *amici* states urge that certiorari be granted in this case because of the serious implications of the Second Circuit's decision with respect to the enforcement of charitable trusts. The states are charged with assuring the probity of officials and individuals entrusted with the possession of funds belonging to others, the preservation of the funds themselves and the faithful discharge of the trusts upon which they are given. Chief among the states' responsibilities in this area is the oversight and enforcement of charitable trusts. It is essential that the states be able to

2

enforce accountability upon trustees, both civilly and, in the case of defaults and defalcations, criminally. The trust concept is vital to a significant segment of social and legal intercourse, and the integrity of that concept is equally vital to the enforcement tools which the states have provided to preserve and maintain it.

The decision of the Second Circuit in *United States v. Moon* casts doubt upon the integrity of the trust concept itself. The decision alters the rules for determining whether a relationship of trust exists in the first instance. By focusing decisive attenton on the use to which funds are put rather than on the intent with which they are conveyed, the court in effect puts the fox in charge of the hen house, since it is the custodian's application of funds to his own use—whether or not the donors contemplated some freedom to use funds in just this way—which "proves" that the funds are personal in character, thus negating trust existence. This is a shocking concept and one whose dismaying implications are not difficult to project.

The law of trusts, of course, varies from state to state. The decision of the Second Circuit, applying New York law, has no direct effect on the trust laws of the *amici* states. Nevertheless, the majority's analysis in this case so fundamentally skews heretofore unquestioned principles of trust law that its potential ramifications cannot responsibly be ignored. If the Second Circuit decision is allowed to stand, it may inform and thereby distort the law of other jurisdictions. At best, the decision of a leading federal circuit court will provide a basis for inventive litigants to reopen previously settled questions of trust law in the *amici* states. If this Court were to endorse, tolerate or ignore the treatment of trust law issues in this case, the potential mischief of the Second Circuit decision would be abetted.

Amici therefore urge that the Petition for Writ of Certiorari in this case be granted and that the Court take this opportunity to disapprove the Second Circuit's trust analysis—an analysis that manifestly pervades and underpins the circuit court's rulings with respect to the federal tax and constitutional law issues addressed by the petition of defendant Moon. *Amici* take no position on those other issues raised in that petition. We believe, however, that the trust issue itself warrants review by this Court.

3

ARGUMENT

UNDER THE RULES ESTABLISHED BY THE COURT BELOW, A DEFAULTING TRUSTEE MAY TURN TO ADVANTAGE THE VERY ACTS CONSTITUTING HIS EMBEZZLEMENT BY USING THEM TO FASHION A FORMIDABLE DEFENSE.

(a) **Introduction**

In this case, funds raised by Church members were entrusted to their spiritual leader, the Church's founder, and placed in bank accounts standing in his name. Unrebutted testimony of certain members indicated that the funds were intended as gifts for the Church. *United States v. Moon,* 718 F.2d 1210, 1224 (2d Cir. 1983). Some of the funds were invested in business enterprises; other portions were made available to Church entities for the acquisition and furnishing of properties and facilites. *Id.* at 1219-21; Trial Transcript, *United States v. Moon,* [hereinafter cited as Tr.] 2863-64, 2991, 3017, 5694-95, 4547, 5766-68, 5770-71, 5818-19, 3422-92, 4083-84, 5613-19. Still others were used by the defendant leader for personal living expenses and the education of his children. 718 F.2d at 1220. These latter items were reported on his personal returns as income to him. Tr. 3729-30, 3735, 3812-13, 4094, 4982-98.

In opposition to the claim that the funds were held by the defendant as trustee for the benefit of the International Unification Movement, an unincorporated body, the government contended, successfully, that the defendant was the *beneficial* as well as the legal owner of the corpus and was therefore taxable on the income it earned.[1] 718 F.2d at 1224-25.

The Court below agreed that the government had proved this

---

1   The issue of beneficial ownership was concededly "central to the determination of guilt or innocence" in the case. *United States v. Moon,* 718 F.2d 1210, 1242 (2d Cir. 1983) (Oakes, J., dissenting); *id.* at 1217. If the assets were beneficially owned by the International Unification Movement, then Moon held them as trustee and vice versa. Beneficial ownership and trust existence, *vel non,* are simply two ways of describing the same question.

4

contention beyond a reasonable doubt on the basis of evidence indicating that:

(a) Defendant held title to the funds and control over them;

(b) Certain Church entities (other than the claimed beneficiary) were formally incorporated and maintained corporate bank accounts;

(c) The funds were put to uses which, in the jury's secular view, appeared personal rather than religious in character, and the defendant thus "seemingly regarded . . . [the funds] as his own. . . ."[2]

(d) Elders in the Church were told that the funds belonged to "Father" (a reference to the defendant as the Church's spiritual leader), rather than to other Church entities. *Id.* at 1220.

The majority of the Second Circuit panel excluded from its consideration of this issue all evidence regarding the source of the funds, the purpose for which they were raised, or the intent of the Church members who contributed them. *Id.* at 1245 (Oakes, J., dissenting); *id.* at 1220-22. Nor did the panel majority reply to Judge Oakes' dissenting observation that the jury's charge left it free to find against Moon on the issue of beneficial ownership without even considering the crucial issue of donor's intent. *Id.* at 12-45-46 (Oakes, J., dissenting).

(b) Trust Creation

We first discuss what have hitherto been regarded generally as settled principles of trust law before addressing the changes wrought by the decision below.

---

2 Evidence showing that the uses to which the funds were put were, under the doctrine and teaching of the Unification Church, actually religious in character rather than personal to the defendant, was either disregarded by the appellate court or excluded by the trial court which emphasized several times to the jury that the defendant's religion had *nothing* to do with the case. Tr. 6538; *see also* 718 F.2d at 1227-28.

5

All that is necessary for the creation of a voluntary trust[3] is a gift or transfer coupled with an intent on the part of the trustor or donor that a trust or use be attached to it. Restatement (Second) of Trusts §2 (1959) [hereinafter cited as Restatement]; I A.W. Scott, The Law of Trusts §17 at 174 & n.1 (3d ed. 1967) [hereinafter cited as Scott]. This intent is the critical factor. Restatement §23; I Scott §§2.8, 23 at 44, 190. With it a trust can come into being; without it, there is merely a conveyance of a gift absolute. The donor's intent to qualify a gift or limit its purpose and usage separates the legal and beneficial ownership of the corpus, placing legal title in the trustee and beneficial ownership in the individual or entity which is the object or beneficiary of the trust. Restatement §2; I Scott §2.3 at 37-38.

Often, intent is expressly stated.[4] This is the purpose of a written declaration of trust, the usual means by which express trusts are created. I Scott §17 at 174. Intent can as well be orally expressed. Restatement §24(1). Even where no specific statement is made, however, the circumstances surrounding a gift may themselves supply the requisite evidence of intent, in which case an implied trust will be raised. *Id.* §24(2); I Scott §24 at 192.

Evidence that a trustee misused trust property or diverted it to personal applications may establish a breach of trust in the civil context or theft such as embezzlement in a criminal context. Such evidence, in itself, is not ordinarily even relevant to the issue of beneficial ownership—i.e., whether, in the first instance, a trust exists or not. *See Herbert v. Commissioner,* 377 F.2d 65 (9th Cir. 1967); *accord, United States v. Scott,* 660 F.2d 1145 (7th Cir. 1981), *cert. denied,* 455 U.S. 907 (1982);

---

3   As distinguished from resulting trusts, constructive trusts and other "involuntary" trusts which arise by operation of law. V Scott §§404, 404.1, 440.1, 461, 462 at 3211-13, 3315-17, 3410-13.

4   This is less frequently the case with church donations in small amounts, e.g., to the collection plate in the course of a church service.

6

Rev. Rul. 71-499, 1971-2 C.B. 77; *see also People v. Swanson,* 174 Cal. App. 2d 453, 457-58, 344 P.2d 832 (1959).

(c) **Charitable Trusts**

The law traditionally has looked with favor upon charitable and religious trusts.[5] It has consistently construed both instruments and circumstances liberally to resolve ambiguities and to assist in the raising and preservation of such trusts. IV Scott §§371.2, 371.3 at 2883-84, 2885; 718 F.2d at 1243 (Oakes, J., dissenting); *In re Price's Will,* 264 A.D. 29, 35 N.Y.S. 2d 111, 114-15, *aff'd,* 289 N.Y. 751, 46 N.E.2d 354 (1942); *Estate of Connolly,* 48 Cal.App.3d 129, 133, 121 Cal. Rptr. 325 (1975). A religious or charitable trust, in contrast to the private express trust, will not fail for lack of a definitely named, identifiable beneficiary. In fact, *no beneficiary at all* need be named so long as it is clear that the use or purpose is religious or charitable in nature. Restatement §§364, 351, 348; IV Scott §§ 348, 351 at 2769, 2794; *see also In re Faulkner's Estate,* 128 Cal.App.2d 575, 578, 275 P.2d 818 (1954).

Courts consistently have construed gifts from church members to church leaders as being gifts in trust for the benefit of the church rather than as personal gifts to the individual church officers, where the evidence establishes nothing more than the fact of a gift from a *congregant* to a *church official. Winn v. Commissioner,* 595 F.2d 1060, 1065 (5th Cir. 1979); *Morey v. Riddell,* 205 F.Supp. 918, 921 (S.D. Cal. 1962); *Archbishop v. Shipman,* 79 Cal. 288, 21 P. 830 (1889); *Fink v. Umscheid,* 340 Kan. 271, 19 P. 623 (1888); IV Scott §§351, 371.3 at 2797-98, 2885 & n.4. Even where the gifts were seemingly absolute in form, the same result has in the past obtained. 718

---

5   While it is quite possible for a "religious" trust to be wholly private in character—e.g., a gift to Archbishop X in trust for the saying of masses for the soul of Y—the terms "religious" and "ecclesiastical" are used herein in their general sense as being interchangeable with the word "charitable," it being universally held that religious or ecclesiastical purposes are indeed charitable purposes. Restatement §368; IV Scott §§368, 371 at 2853-56, 2879-80.

7

F.2d at 1243 (Oakes, J., dissenting); IV Scott §§351, 371.3 at 2797-98, 2884-85; *Monaghan v. Joyce,* 12 Del. Ch. 28, 103 A. 582, 583-84 (1918); *In re Flinn,* [1948] Ch. 241; *In re Garrard,* [1907] 1 Ch. 382; *In re Delany,* [1902] 2 Ch. 642; *In re Barclay,* [1929] 2 Ch. 173; *In re Durbrow's Estate,* 245 N.Y. 469, 477, 157 N.E. 747, 749 (1927); *see also New York City Mission Society v. Board of Pensions,* 261 A.D. 823, 24 N.Y.S.2d 395, 396 (1941). It is sensible and desirable as a matter of policy for courts to treat religiously inspired gifts as donations in trust. Each gift must be considered on its own facts for the purpose of determining the donor's intent. In a vast majority of cases, however, it is likely that a gift made by a follower to a spiritual leader is intended to be used by the leader for the furtherance of the faith. This is true despite the fact that the individual who contributes in response to a solicitation, whether it be on a street corner or in church, seldom attaches a formal declaration of trust to his or her donation. From a policy standpoint, the vulnerability of adherents to solicitations from their religious leaders favors a strong presumption that gifts made to such leaders by their congregants are made for the benefit of the religion rather than for the private benefit of the individual.

(d) **The Rule of United States v. Moon**

The court below approaches the determination of trust existence (and beneficial ownership) from a radically different perspective—one which runs counter to the settled weight of authority. If adopted in other jurisdictions, the potential adverse consequences of this rule for the enforcement of trusts generally and for the maintenance of the integrity of charitable trusts specifically are alarming.

To begin with, the court severely downgraded the significance of donors' intent as a determinative factor in deciding whether a trust exists. It did this in two ways. First, it created an unrealistically exacting standard for proof of intent by holding that to establish the existence of *any* voluntary trust, there must be evidence of "clear and unequivocal" intent to create a trust

8

and also by laying emphasis on the need for the specific word "trust" in this expression.[6] 718 F.2d at 1224. *Inter alia,* the decision thus specifically extends this requirement, as a matter of first impression, to charitable and religious trusts.

Aside from the fact that all this runs flatly contrary to the settled weight of trust law, in New York and elsewhere, it virtually eliminates, by definition, the creation of an implied trust. It also specifically rules out, in the court's own words, a trust where "only . . . charitable intent of the contributors" is demonstrated. Thus, in the instant case, where Church members specifically testified that they intended the money as a donation to their church, the court excluded consideration of the testimony stating that it was not only insufficient to create a trust but that upon such evidence, the trial court *was not even obliged to instruct on the law of trusts. Id.* at 1224, 1225.

As Judge Oakes emphasized in his dissent, citing the abundant New York and other authority, the very thing which gives rise to most charitable trusts *is* a charitable gift or charitable intent; *no* specific words, let alone the word "trust" itself, are necessary. Indeed, many trusts have been confirmed and upheld where there were *no words at all,* only circumstances from which intent could fairly be inferred. *Id.* at 1245-46, 1245 n.4 (Oakes, J., dissenting).

The lower court's holding is all the more troubling because, although the majority expressly concedes "that a charitable *gift* has been made to the Church", it nevertheless asserts that "there is no rule of law that presumes simply from a charitable gift the donors' intent to create a trust." *Id.* at 1225 (emphasis in original). A charitable gift to a church is *incompatible* with a personal gift to an individual and his heirs. As a matter of sound public policy, there *ought* to be a presumption of trust in such

---

6   In so doing, it raised by several notches the already rigorous and demanding requirement stated in the trial court's instructions . . . "that intent must be clear and unambigous." 718 F.2d at 1244 n.3 (Oakes, J., dissenting).

9

circumstances to prevent the conversion of a charitable gift into a personal windfall.

The other way in which the element of intent is either debased or discarded is found in the trial court's instructions, approved on appeal, which listed intent as merely one factor among several which the jury might consider. *Id.* at 1244-45 (Oakes, J., dissenting). The appellate court specifically rejected the suggestion that intent, as an element, was deserving of special emphasis, holding that all of the factors articulated were of *equal* relevance. *Id.* at 1225. As the dissent pointed out, this had the effect of permitting the jury to determine the admittedly crucial issue of trust existence or nonexistence "*without even considering* the crucial issue of donors' intent." *Id.* at 1245 (Oakes, J., dissenting) (emphasis added).

The lower court further departs from generally settled principles of trust law with respect to the elements or circumstances to which it *does* accord weight in determining whether there is an implied trust. Having depreciated donors' intent and relegated it to an obscurity amounting to impotence, the court focuses, rather, on the other facts, which would hitherto have been regarded as peripheral to the establishment of trust existence *vel non,* such as:

(a) Title and control of the funds and property;

(b) Form of organization of claimed beneficiary, e.g., whether formally incorporated or not;

(c) Character of the use to which the funds or property were subsequently applied or put;

(d) Whether the putative trustee seemingly regarded or treated the funds or property as his own;

(e) Whether other persons regarded the funds as being his.

These elements are delineated and discussed in the portion of the court's opinion which finds that the government's evidence was sufficient to establish, beyond a reasonable doubt, that no

10

trust existed, because the funds "belonged" to, i.e., were beneficially owned by, the defendant.[7] *Id.* at 1220, 1222.

We note at the outset that the very first element is a group of
factors—title, dominion and control—which are, under the circumstances, wholly uninformative in terms of evidentiary value on

---

7　These elements track fairly closely the factors outlined by the trial
court to the jury in its so-called "laundry list" instruction, admittedly not
exhaustive. These were:

  1) whether the Unification Church movement had a specific or-
     ganizational structure;
  2) whether other Unification Church incorporated entities existed;
  3) whether title to the accounts in question was held in the de-
     fendant's name;
  4) the source of the funds;
  5) the intent of the parties who caused the stock and funds to be
     transferred to Reverend Moon's name;
  6) evidence of any agreements as to how the funds would be used;
  7) the manner in which the assets were actually used;
  8) whether defendant accounted to anyone for the use of the funds.

It will be noted that the instruction directs attention *not* to the intent of the parties who actually *donated* or gave the funds (the source),
but rather to the intent of the *parties who caused title to the funds to be
placed in defendant Moon's name.* These, as the evidence unequivocally
showed, were a handful of key advisors, one of whom was Moon's co-defendant, Kamiyama. Since the intent of the *donors*—i.e., the Church members who actually collected and contributed the funds—was *not even
mentioned,* it could hardly have been considered or even taken into account
by the jury.

Shortly after enumerating the list of factors the court stated as
follows: "There is no trust if the person who receives the money is free
to use it for his own benefit." 718 F.2d at 1244 n.3 (Oakes, J., dissenting).
To a lay jury which was wholly uninstructed regarding the nice distinction
between what one is "free" to do—i.e., is legally *empowered* to do, whether
rightly or wrongly—and what one *ought* to do—i.e., is legally *obliged* to do
as a trustee—this statement could only have conveyed the idea that in determining where beneficial ownership lies, decisive importance attaches
to the personal use of funds or property by the individual who holds legal
title. Moreover, it surely left the jury with the view that the money could
not be held in trust for the Church so long as the trustee had the discretion
to use *any portion* of it for his own living expenses and to pay income taxes
on the portion so used, a view that would literally destroy scores of charitable trusts, including those which many churches have purposely chosen
as vehicles for placing discretionary funds in the hands of their clergy.

11

this issue. These factors merely establish the location of legal title and the degree of control that naturally accompanies such title. But *every* trustee holds legal title and must possess dominion and control in order to function as a trustee.[8] The dissent points out, *id.* at 1242 (Oakes, J., dissenting), that this element is one which was virtually conceded from the outset, but which the government, nevertheless, went to great lengths to "prove". This first element thus points neither one way or the other with respect to the critical determination, which is the location of *beneficial,* not legal, ownership.

The second element, form of organization, is simply irrelevant to the existence of the type of trust which was here under consideration. While it is true that a private trust may fail for lack of a definite beneficiary, form of organization is at most an equivocal indication even so, but it has no significance whatever

---

8   As the dissent also observes, *id.* at 1243 (Oakes, J., dissenting), the holding of title to property is even less reliable as an indication of beneficial ownership in the case of a minister or other church official, since this is a time honored method of church property tenure. Under the common law, title to real property of the parish in the Anglican Church was taken in the name of the minister and title to personalty in the name of the church wardens. *Terrett v. Taylor,* 13 U.S. (9 Cranch) 43, 46-47 (1815). The holding of diocesan property in the personal name of Catholic prelates, whether as a corporation sole or otherwise, is equally well known and still widespread. *Reid v. Barry,* 93 Fla. 849, 112 So. 846 (1927); *Mannix v. Purcell,* 46 Ohio St. 102, 19 N.E. 572 (1888); *Biscoe v. Thweatt,* 74 Ark. 545, 86 S.W. 432 (1905); *In re Fitzgerald's Estate,* 62 Cal. App. 744, 217 P. 773 (1923); *In re Geppert's Estate,* 75 S.D. 96, 59 N.W.2d 727 (1953); *St. Peter's Roman Catholic Parish v. Urban Redevelopment Authority,* 394 Pa. 194, 146 A.2d 724 (1958), *cert. denied* and *appeal dismissed,* 359 U.S. 435 (1959); *Gospel Tabernacle Body of Christ Church v. Peace Publishers & Co.,* 211 Kan. 420, 506 P.2d 1135 (1973), *adhered to,* 211 Kan. 927, 508 P.2d 849 (1973); *Winn v. Commissioner,* 595 F.2d 1060 (5th Cir. 1979); IV Scott §371.3 at 2884-85; 50 N.Y. Jur.2d *Religious Societies* §111 at 11. There are literally hundreds of cases holding that where church officials held title to property in their personal names, they did so as trustees for their churches. *See, e.g., Sears v. Parker,* 193 Mass. 551, 79 N.E. 772 (1907); *Jones v. Habersham,* 107 U.S. 174, 182 (1882); *Mannix v. Purcell,* 46 Ohio St. 102, 19 N.E. 572 (1888); *Morey v. Riddell,* 205 F.Supp. 918 (S.D. Cal. 1962); *Winn v. Commissioner,* 595 F.2d 1060 (5th Cir. 1979); IV Scott §§351, 371.3 at 2797-98, 2885.

12

in the case of a religious or charitable trust, where *no beneficiary at all* need be designated.

The third element, perhaps the most startling and potentially harmful of all, is the use to which the funds or assets were put. The prosecution urged, and the court agreed, that if some of the funds were applied or put to personal use, rather than to claimed trust use (here, religious use), this fact disproved trust *existence* and established beneficial ownership in the defendant. In other words, the rule of the case is that beneficial ownership follows use. Hitherto the rule has been that evidence of personal use, if inconsistent with donors' intent, establishes nothing more than a diversion or breach. Under the rule enunciated by the court below, the fact of such use transforms the entire corpus and awards it to the individual rather than to the institution intended by the donors, thus advancing private gain at the expense of public or charitable benefit.[9]

The fourth element simply bootstraps the preceding one and is corollary to it: if an individual uses funds for personal purposes and seemingly treats some of them as his own, he will be held to be the beneficial owner.

Lastly, a further bootstrap: if others' opinions reinforce the preceding indications, conclusive weight will be given to the determination.

It will be observed that every one of these elements save the second—which is demonstrably irrelevant—is under the control of the individual in possession of the funds or assets, i.e., the putative trustee, and that he is thus placed by the Second Circuit in a position to orchestrate or manipulate the very elements relied upon to determine beneficial ownership. On the other hand, the one element *not* subject to such control or manipulation, donors' intent, is hedged about and sharply diminished in importance.

---

9   The decision also contradicts other federal cases holding that "personal" use of some part of trust funds by trustees—e.g., for salaries or living expenses—is by no means necessarily inconsistent with trust existence or purpose. *See, e.g., Morey v. Riddell,* 205 F.Supp. 918, 921 (S.D. Cal. 1962); *Winn v. Commissioner,* 595 F.2d 1060, 1065 (5th Cir. 1979).

13

(e) Enforcement Implications

Although the lower court's decision in this case ostensibly only articulates a rule applicable to federal criminal proceedings, it may, if followed by other courts, have planted the seeds for emasculation of effective charitable trust enforcement. If carried to its logical conclusion, it may, in fact, mark the elimination of criminal charges such as embezzlement as a remedy for extreme abuses. This consequence, of course, shocks the conscience, but if the rule of this decision is properly understood, it is not difficult to see how this conclusion might follow.

In order to prove civil or criminal charges against a trustee relating to misappropriation of trust assets, it is first necessary to establish the existence of a trust. Applying the rules enunciated by the court below, a defaulting trustee has only to take a few simple steps that make the offense obvious in order to negate trust existence and thus be clothed with a formidable defensive armor. One need only make certain that title to the property or funds is placed in his or her own name; that they are spent or applied to uses which appear conspicuously personal; and that, in using the funds, the trustee clearly and overtly regards the funds as his or her own. It will further be helpful to the cause if the trustee so states to friends in the hope that they will so opine to others. Lastly, the trustee might be well advised to report at least the interest from the funds as personal income on his or her tax returns.

Under the principles enunciated by the Second Circuit, the trustee would, in the absence of a specific written declaration of trust, be virtually invulnerable to enforcement of the trust or penalty for its abuse. The trustee could point to the very elements emphasized by the court as being conclusively determinative that no trust existed. An attorney general charged with enforcing and protecting the integrity of charitable trusts would be hard-pressed to establish the factual predicate of jurisdiction: the existence of a charitable trust. Even in cases in which the Second Circuit's factoral analysis of trust existence *might* permit a conclusion that a trust existed, an attorney general would be required to divert resources from trust enforcement in order to

14

meet the Second Circuit's enhanced burden to prove trust existence.

Under the lower court's analysis, even the clearest cases, where a trust is evidenced by written declaration, are complicated. The writing evidences at most an intent on the part of the trustor/donor to create a trust; and this, according to the court's teaching, is simply one of several elements, all of which are to be accorded *equal* weight. *Id.* at 1225. In other words, the putative trustee's personal use (or misuse) of the funds; his treating of them as his own; his title, dominion and control over those funds; and the opinions of his acquaintances are all elements which are to be considered each on an equal footing with the lone element of the trustor's intent, which, indeed, need not actually be considered at all. *Id.* at 1242, 1245 (Oakes, J., dissenting).

The Second Circuit's decision, if followed elsewhere, would not merely handicap the states in their efforts to enforce charitable trusts. Under this rule, the beneficiaries of all trusts would be faced with similar difficulties in attempting to enforce accountability against fiduciaries. The potential for mischief is virtually limitless, for the rule is akin to saying that a thief, by virtue of his conversion, acquires full and defensible title to the subject of his theft. Little imagination is needed to appreciate the chaos to which such a rule could lead.

This precedent demonstrably casts a cloud over an important role and responsibility of the attorney general offices of the *amici* states—namely, that of enforcing and protecting charitable trusts. To hold that the existence of certain uses triggers a federal conclusion that the assets belong in their entirety to the individuals who control them, as this case does, is to turn the guiding principles of trust law and enforcement upside down. It is no wonder that Judge James L. Oakes, formerly the Attorney General of Vermont, dissented so forcefully from the Second Circuit's ruling.

Even if a state attorney general would not be wholly disabled, vis-a-vis faithless trustees, by this federal precedent, and even if such an attorney general could continue to invoke principles of ordinary and charitable trust law in his own state, the attorney

15

general's office is, at the very least, placed in a position of antipathetic tension with federal tax and criminal justice authorities by the Second Circuit's holding.

CONCLUSION

Because of the strong, but limited, focus of their direct concern, which is the impact of the subject case upon a vital aspect of state trust law, *amici* do not address or take any position with respect to the "myriad of constitutional problems involved here" or the "troubling issues of religious persecution and abridgement of free speech" which, as noted in the majority opinion, *id.* at 1216, are presented by other aspects of the case. Even if these constitutional issues did not exist, however, the concern of these *amici* and the urgency of the issue they have argued herein would warrant this Court's attention. The rules enunciated by the Second Circuit threaten mischief at best and havoc at worst in a vital area of the law hitherto regarded as well settled.

Amici therefore strongly and respectfully urged that the Petition for Certiorari be granted.

TANY S. HONG
Attorney General of Hawaii
MICHAEL A. LILLY
First Deputy Attorney
General, Hawaii
State Capitol
Honolulu, Hawaii 96813
(808) 548-2427

DAVE FROHNMAYER
Attorney General of Oregon
WILLIAM F. GARY
Deputy Attorney General,
Oregon
Justice Building
Salem, Oregon 97310
(503) 378-4400

DENNIS J. ROBERTS II
Attorney General of
Rhode Island
72 Pine Street
Providence, R.I. 02903
(401) 274-4400

United States Senator Orrin G. Hatch, Chairman, Subcommittee on the Constitution, United States Senate Committee on the Judiciary

i

TABLE OF CONTENTS

ii

TABLE OF AUTHORITIES

Pursuant to Rule 36.1 of the Rules of the United States Supreme Court, this brief is filed with the written consent of the Petitioners and Respondent. Their original letters of consent have been filed with the clerk of this Court .

INTEREST OF THE AMICUS

United States Senator Orrin G. Hatch submits this brief as a member of the United States Senate and Chairman of the Subcommittee on the Constitution, Senate Committee on the Judiciary. The Subcommittee is vitally interested in all activities in which constitutional rights are defined and interpreted. Senator Hatch is particularly concerned about this case because it represents, in his view, a troubling and unwarranted exercise of judicial interference by the courts below with fundamental religious freedoms.

Contrary to the First Amendment and time-honored precedents of this Court, the majority opinion of the Second Circuit Court of Appeals unconstitutionally permits unfettered jury inquiry into the practices and procedures of a religious institution. It should, therefore, be reviewed and reversed by this Court.

This *amicus* brief is not submitted as an endorsement of Reverend Sun Myung Moon or of the Unification Church. It is submitted because the undersigned has a vital concern that all matters constitutional, especially those involving invaluable religious freedoms, are correctly entertained and treated in the United States Courts. As stated so eloquently by Thomas Jefferson: "It behooves every man who values liberty of conscience for himself to resist invasions of it in the case of others, or their cases may, by change of circumstances, become his own." Swancara, F., *Thomas Jefferson versus Religious Oppression*, 53 (*citing* letter) (1969).

SUMMARY OF ARGUMENT

Certiorari must be granted because the lower courts, in failing to follow guiding principles established in controlling

2

decisions of this Court, violated important constitutional religious rights.

From the outset of the government's case, the defense of both defendants, Reverend Moon and Mr. Kamiyama, was that the property in question belonged not to Reverend Moon but to the Unification Church. They consistently asserted that the property had been donated to the church and entrusted to Reverend Moon who was unquestionably the Unification Church's worldwide leader. Such a practice of placing church property in the name of the church's leader is no different from the practice followed in many other established religious denominations. The defendants' position was bolstered by undisputed evidence at trial that the Unification Church, through its members, unanimously and unquestionably agreed and claimed that the property belonged to the Church, not Reverend Moon.

The trial court was thus confronted with a dispute over property ownership in which one of the parties was a church. Accordingly, the Court was obligated to resolve the ownership question in accordance with specific principles of law enunciated by this Court to protect the religious freedoms guaranteed by the United States Constitution. These principles require the courts to scrupulously avoid any interference with the tenets or practices of the church involved in the ownership dispute and to resolve the dispute by giving full deference to the church's position on all matters religious and to thereafter apply purely neutral principles of law, if applicable.

The courts below failed to follow these binding legal guidelines and instead permitted the jury to use whatever method it desired in determining the critical issue of ownership. The Second Circuit's statement that such legal guidelines do not pertain to a federal criminal tax case is without precedent, contrary to controlling decisions of this Court and entirely lacking in merit. The required use of neutral principles of law and deference to the church's position in deciding property ownership questions will in no respect curtail the ability of

3

criminal courts to make full factual inquiries on the question of guilt or innocence of an accused. They will, however, prevent the unauthorized intrusion into constitutional freedoms as was permitted below.

The actions of the trial court, as affirmed by the Court of Appeals, represent a dangerous deviation from controlling decisions of this Court. If followed, the decision below significantly increases the possibility of further unconstitutional governmental intrusions into the affairs of all churches. Such cannot be condoned. In this case the church and its religious leader were unpopular. Perhaps because of that unpopularity, the government and courts below strained to uphold a conviction despite the clear trampling of constitutional rights. But the Constitution must be satisfied in all cases and if the religious rights of Reverend Moon and the other members of the Unification Church are permitted to be callously ignored as they were in the proceedings below, then the religious freedoms cherished by our founding fathers are lost for all churches, popular and unpopular alike. The decision, therefore, must be reviewed and reversed.

REASONS FOR GRANTING THE PETITION

I. Established Principles Of First Amendment Law Were Ignored When The Trial Court Gave The Jury Unrestricted Latitude In Deciding The Critical Issue Of Ownership.

The case below involved the criminal tax evasion trial of Reverend Sun Myung Moon, the undisputed leader and embodiment of a worldwide religious movement known as the Unification Church. Like many religious leaders before him, Reverend Moon is both loved by his followers and hated by his detractors. Not inconsequentially, his detractors at the time of his trial included the vast majority of the American public.[1]

---

[1] Jury selection was rendered most difficult because of Reverend Moon's widespread unpopularity. As the trial judge himself noted, it

4

Reverend Moon, a Korean native, came to the United States in the early 1970's primarily for the purpose of expanding his growing church. He took up residence in New York and during the next several years spread his religious views in America. Because Reverend Moon's views were unacceptable and distasteful to many Americans, he was frequently maligned by the media, publicly denounced and held in strong disfavor by the general populace. In 1976, after years of such treatment, the Internal Revenue Service began an investigation of the tax returns of Reverend Moon and the records of the Unification Church. The investigation culminated in 1981 in a criminal indictment charging Reverend Moon with wilfully concealing personal income derived from certain property (hereinafter "the property") for the years 1973, 1974 and 1975.

In defense, Reverend Moon contended the property was not his but rather the property of the Unification Church. The question of ownership of the property was thus introduced into the case. All parties and both courts below agree this was the central issue upon which the defendants' guilt or innocence depended. 718 F.2d at 1217.

Resolution of this primary issue depended in turn on answers to the key questions: 1) where did the property come from? and 2) for what purpose did Reverend Moon recieve the property? If the property came from Unification Church members as donations to their church, then the property was obviously the church's and not Reverend Moon's. If, on the other hand, the property came from Unification Church members or any other source to Reverend Moon as his own, then the property would be personal to Moon and subject to his personal taxation.[2]

---

became necessary to empanel jurors "who don't know much, because they are obviously the persons who start off with the least bias." T1759-60.

[2] An additional question—how was the property used?—was inserted by the government into the trial. Of course, this issue is relevant only to the extent it assists the fact finder in answering the key questions of where the property came from and why the property

5

With the issues so framed, the trial court was faced with a property dispute in which one of the contestants was an established religion.[3] The setting was therefore not, as the government and courts below suggest, simply the trial of a businessman for tax evasion. T6174, T6472, A1905, S125. Given the Unification Church's claim of ownership of the property, the case encompassed a larger field which included religious freedoms guaranteed to the church and its members by the United States Constitution, Amendment I: "Congress shall make no law respecting an establishment of religion, or prohibiting the free exercise thereof. . . ."

There is an abundance of authority from this Court describing the minimum safeguards the trial court should have employed to assure adequate protection of Reverend Moon's and the Unification Church's religious rights. Without question the role of courts in resolving church property disputes is "severely circumscribed" by the First Amendment. *Presbyterian Church* v. *Hull Church*, 393 U.S. 440, 449 (1969). The general and undisputed principle is enunciated in *Watson* v. *Jones*, 13 Wall. 679, 728 (1872): "the law knows no heresy, and is committed to the support of no dogma, the establishment of no sect." The judiciary is constitutionally precluded by the First

---

was given to Reverend Moon. If the property was not used to advance the purposes of the Unification Church, then it could be inferred the property came to Moon as his own. Conversely, a use of the property to advance purposes of the Unification Church, through investments or otherwise, would carry the inference that the money was given to Moon as a contribution to the church. If, however, the evidence is clear that the donors of the property intended their donations to be to the church and not to Reverend Moon, as was the case in the trial of the present case, the issue regarding use of the property becomes irrelevant.

[3] The question whether the Unification Church is a "religion" was decided fully in favor of the church in *Holy Spirit Association for the Unification of World Christianity* v. *Tax Commission*, 55 N.Y. 2d 512 (1982).

6

Amendment from inquiring into issues pertaining to a church's practices, customs, laws, or beliefs and in respect of any property issues decided by the church itself, the courts must "accept such decisions as final. . . ." *Id.* at 727.[4]

In *Gonzalez* v. *Archbishop*, 280 U.S. 1 (1929), this Court, following the guidelines established in *Watson*, held that "in the absence of fraud, collusion, or arbitrariness," on the part of the church itself, the decisions of a church as to matters pertaining to the church's practices or beliefs must be "accepted in litigation." *Id.* at 16. Similarly, in a case dealing with a church's internal organizational structure, *Kedroff* v. *St. Nicholas*, 344 U.S. 94 (1952), this Court recognized that churches have the constitutional right "to decide for themselves, free from state interference, matters of church government as well as those of faith and doctrine." *Id.* at 116.

Serbian Eastern Orthodox Diocese v. *Milivojevich*, 426 U.S. 696 (1976) followed the principles of *Watson*, *Gonzalez*, and *Kedroff* and clarified that the "arbitrariness" exception referred to in *Gonzalez* did not permit the Illinois Supreme Court to inquire whether the Serbian Orthodox Church had properly conducted defrockment proceedings against one of its bishops. Although the Illinois Supreme Court's decision was based on a finding that the church's defrockment decision was "arbitrary," the lower court's decision was nevertheless reversed as

---

[4] In a recent report examining the substance of the First Amendment, the Senate Committee on the Judiciary observed that "the original intent of the 'establishment clause' [requires] that Congress be neutral as between competing religious views." S. Rpt. 98-347, 35-36 Senate Committee on the Judiciary, 98th Cong., 2d session (1984). This principle of neutrality embodies the basic understanding that governmental institutions should not attempt to dictate, endorse or even comment upon religious practices or beliefs. To the extent the court in this case invited the jury to substitute its judgment for that of the Unification Church regarding the broad ecclesiastical authority of Reverend Moon to accept and dispose of funds donated to the church, it offended this First Amendment principle of neutrality.

7

unconstitutional because the court in reaching its decision engaged in the review and determination of internal church practices. *Id.* at 718.

In the present case, the government did not suggest or allege fraud, collusion or arbitrariness by the Unification Church with respect to the Unification Church's position that the property belonged to the church and had been used solely for church purposes. Despite the lack of such an allegation, the government and the trial court nevertheless entirely disregarded the constitutionally protected position of the Unification Church on this important aspect of the case.

Serbian Orthodox Diocese and *Jones* v. *Wolf*, 443 U.S. 595 (1979) typify and embody the standard of law to be applied in any property dispute involving religious institutions. Consistent with the First Amendment and *Watson*, these cases stand for the proposition that courts are constitutionally precluded from making any inquiry into religious practices and doctrines and must defer, where possible, to the resolution of the property dispute by the church itself. In those cases where the ownership question is susceptible to resolution without reference to church practices or doctrines, the courts are granted the limited latitude of applying neutral principles of law to decide the issue. But, even when thus authorized, the courts must scrupulously avoid even the slightest invasion of any religious matters. *Id.* at 602-604.

In this case, the facts differ from *Jones* v. *Wolf* and other intra-church property dispute cases because here the church itself is not divided in its position on the ownership of the property. At trial, the church's position that it was the sole owner of the property was clearly made. Instead, in this case, the dispute is between the United States Government and an undivided church with the government alone questioning the church's ownership of the property. This difference makes the principles of *Serbian Orthodox Diocese* and *Jones* even more important and applicable in the present case. Certainly, the government must be held to at least the same guidelines as a rival faction within the church itself.

8

The constitutional protections of *Watson, Gonzalez, Serbian Orthodox Diocese* and *Jones* are equally applicable in cases where the inquiry is whether a certain church activity, such as the use of funds, is religious or secular in nature. Citing and relying on *Watson*, the New York Court of Appeals in *Holy Spirit Association for the Unification of World Christianity v. Tax Commission*, 55 N.Y. 2d 512 (1982) (hereinafter referred to as "Holy Spirit Association") held that when confronted with such an inquiry, a trial court or other civil authority is constitutionally obligated to accept the church's position on the distinction between "religious" and "secular" unless and until it finds the church's position was not made in good faith. "Civil authorities may engage in but two inquiries: Does the religious organization assert that the challenged purposes and activities are religious, and is that assertion bona fide?" *Id.* at 521 (*citing Watson v. Jones*).

A comprehensive analysis of the above authorities inescapably establishes the governing standard of law which must be applied in any case, including the case below, where the property ownership claims of a religious institution are at issue. Courts must accept the church's position unless it can be shown that the position was "fraudulent, illegal or arbitrary" or not asserted in good faith. At a bare minimum, the standard requires the jury to be given instructions that it not in any way substitute its lay views for those of the church itself on any issue involving the church's practices, beliefs or procedures.

In the present case, there was no assertion of fraud against the church but the trial court failed to apply even the minimum proper standard of law and instead allowed the jury to decide the critical question of ownership in any manner it desired. Furthermore, the court took an even greater step away from the First Amendment by instructing the jury that religion was to play no part whatsoever in their deliberations.[5] This was

---

[5] The jury was instructed that "considerations of . . . religion must have no part in your deliberations." T6538 .

9

especially prejudicial in light of the Unification Church's clear claim that it owned the property. The only evidence at trial as to the source of the funds and the purpose for which they were given to Reverend Moon was that the funds were given to Reverend Moon by members of the Unification Church as donations to the church.[6] The government failed to show that any part of the money came from a non-church member or was advanced to Reverend Moon for any other purpose than to further the work of the church. Given this state of the evidence, the trial court, per *Watson, Jones* and *Holy Spirit Association*, should have instructed the jury to 1) ascertain, as a factual matter, the position of the Unification Church on ownership of the property, being restricted to the use of secular principles in doing so, 2) give full deference to the church's position unless they first find as a matter of fact (again using purely secular principles) that the church's position was not advanced in good faith, and 3) in all respects limit their deliberations to avoid a decision based in any degree on the jury's lay views as to the propriety, desirability or validity of the stated practices and procedures of the Unification Church.

Furthermore, on the tangential question whether the property was used for Moon's personal benefit or that of the church, the court should have instructed the jury to give full deference to the church's statement as to what constituted "religious" purposes.

In contrast to the constitutionally mandated standards discussed above, the trial court permitted the jury to use whatever standards it wished to decide the critical question of ownership. Listed as only fifth in a long line of factors which the jury was told it may, but was not limited or required to,

---

[6] In its majority opinion, the Court of Appeals acknowledged that "the *only* evidence even remotely touching on this issue [whether donors had intended to create a trust] was the testimony of church members . . . who simply stated that they gave the money to Moon, intending it as a donation to their church." 718 F.2d at 1224.

10

consider was "the intent of the parties who caused the stock and funds to be transferred to Reverend Moon's name." 718 F.2d at 1244 n.3. At no time was the jury told to give any deference whatsoever to the constitutionally protected good faith position of the church. In his dissenting opinion in the Second Circuit, Judge Oakes recognized this error by the trial court:

> Rather than simply including intent as one of the things for the jury to consider, the court in my view should have advised the jury to afford the greatest weight to this factor. The church source of the funds and Moon's role as church leader were likely to cast light on the issue of the donor's intent and accordingly the charge should have specifically directed the jury's attention to them.

Id. at 1245.

The Second Circuit upheld the trial court's refusal to properly instruct the jury and with the mere stroke of its pen brushed aside *Jones* and *Holy Spirit Association* by referring to the latter as "inapposite" and the former as having "no application" to a "federal criminal tax prosecution." *Id.* at 1227-1228. There was no justification for the Court of Appeals to create this new exception to constitutional protection. The majority opinion's fleeting references to broad pronouncements of this Court to the effect that religious freedoms cannot be used to protect criminals from prosecution [See 718 F.2d at 1227 *citing Davis* v. *Beason*, 133 U.S. 333 (1890)] are not applicable to the present case and only serve to confuse the issue. Appellants and this *Amicus* agree fully with *Davis* v. *Beason* and do not contend in any respect that a religious leader or any other person is above the law. It is fully conceded that the religion clauses cannot be abused to permit those who violate the criminal law to go unpunished. The First Amendment must yield, where necessary, to permit the laws of society to be invoked and enforced. But the standard urged in this appeal— proper instructions to the jury pursuant to the guidelines of *Watson, Jones* and *Holy Spirit Association*—would in no manner interfere with the criminal tax laws. Nor would it increase the government's burden of proof or place Reverend Moon

11

above the law. The proper standard would, however, assure protection of fundamental religious freedoms and to that end should have been given.

Furthermore, the Court of Appeals' holding that criminal tax cases are, in effect, immune from judicial rules otherwise governing church property disputes is in violation of the principle established by this Court in *United States* v. *Ballard*, 322 U.S. 488 (1961) that juries in criminal cases, as well as in civil cases, are required by the First Amendment to be instructed to avoid any decision based on the jury's lay opinions as to the validity, truthfulness or propriety of a church's practices and beliefs.

As in *Holy Spirit Association*, discussed above, *Ballard* recognized that given a sufficient factual basis, a jury may inquire into the good faith of a religion's beliefs, but may not, in a criminal trial, inquire into the truthfulness or propriety of such beliefs. Accordingly, the *Ballard* Court affirmed as constitutionally necessary the trial court's instructions to the jury to not engage in any discussion or analysis of the defendants' religious beliefs and in no respect to substitute their lay views for those of the church.

As in this case, the criminal defendants in *Ballard* belonged to a religion generally in disfavor with the public.[7] The Ballard court correctly observed that the defendants' constitutional religious rights were no less important for the unpopularity of their beliefs:

> The religious views espoused by respondents might seem incredible, if not preposterous, to most people. But if those doctrines are subject to trial before a jury charged with finding their truth or falsity, then the same can be done with the religious beliefs of any sect. When triers of fact undertake that task, they enter a forbidden domain.

Id. at 87.

---

[7] As noted in the Petition for Certiorari, "almost half of the 1,000 people polled prior to voir dire said that [i]f [they] had the chance, [they'd] throw Reverend Sun Myung Moon in jail." Appellants' Petition at page 22, n.36, *citing* A822-23.

12

The safeguards required in *Ballard* are equally necessary in the present case. The jury should have been charged to avoid any intervention into the beliefs and practices of the Unification Church while at the same time giving deference to the church's views on certain factual issues.

By not properly instructing the jury in accordance with *Ballard*, the court permitted the taking of church property against the wishes of the church itself without any showing or factual finding by the jury of bad faith, fraud or illegal collusion on the part of the church. The government may contend on this appeal that the trial court's failure to properly instruct the jury was harmless error because the same verdict would have been reached with proper instructions. Unfortunately, however, we do not know upon what factors the jury's verdict was based, but it very possibly rested on impermissible jury interference with the practices and procedures of an established church. The jury may well have concluded, for example, that the practices of the Unification Church regarding the donation and use of the property were not, according to the jurors' individual lay views, acceptable "religious" practices or activities. Because such conduct enters the constitutionally protected area of religious freedom, even the possibility of infringement, which most certainly exists in the present case, cannot be condoned.

II. The Opinion Below, If Followed, Establishes A Grave Danger Of Unconstitutional Governmental Intrusion Into The Affairs Of All Churches.

The decision below, if permitted to stand, seriously threatens the internal workings of every church in the country. The governmental intrusion into the activities of the Unification Church allowed below is repugnant to the very core of our democratic way of life.[8] By investigating the tax affairs of

---

[8] Noted Historian Sanford H. Cobb correctly observed: "[A]mong all the benefits to mankind to which this soil has given rise, this pure religious liberty may be justly rated as the great gift of America to

13

Reverend Moon and the Unification Church, the government chose perhaps the easiest available method, through the guise of legitimate governmental activity, to interject itself into the affairs of an unpopular church and leader. Whatever the merit of such an investigation, the government and courts below were nonetheless obligated at trial to fully respect and safeguard Reverend Moon's and the Unification Church's constitutional rights. As discussed above, they failed to protect such rights and instead allowed the jury to wander at will through the protected domain of the church, giving no legal heed whatsoever to the good faith position of the church itself.

The religious freedoms guaranteed by the Constitution were never intended to bend or depend on the relative popularity of the church involved. Indeed, the trials of unpopular persons, such as the trial below, demand more, not less, care to assure the unquestioned protection of religious rights. If religious freedoms can be so callously disregarded in the case of an unpopular person, as they were in the case below, the same can happen in any other trial involving the claims of churches. No church is safe if lay juries are permitted, as was the jury in this case, to substitute their views for those of a church regarding the church's practices, beliefs and procedures. The next case may involve another generally unpopular leader, such as Reverend Moon, or it may be someone from one of the more "established" religions. But whoever the leader and whatever the church, another case following or expanding on the so-called exception created by the Court of Appeals below is sure to follow. Once the door is open, the possibilities of governmental intrusion into the heretofore protected area of church related fundraising, accounting or other activities are many and dangerous. The government, over time, may be found dictating the manner in which churches handle internal funding, how

---

civilization and the world, having among principles of government policy no equal . . . ." Cobb, S., *The Rise of Religious Liberty in America* 2 (1970).

14

they must invest their funds and how their bookkeeping records must be established. These serious ramifications cannot be permitted to occur. The decision below is accordingly viewed with concern and alarm by a wide-ranging group of churches, political organizations and other institutions throughout America who join this *Amicus* in urging the United States Supreme Court to grant petitioner's petition and review and reverse the decision below.[9]

CONCLUSION

1.   Despite the widespread public hatred and persecution Reverend Moon and his church experienced in American society, Reverend Moon was nonetheless absolutely and constitutionally entitled to a trial in which his and his church's religious freedoms were fully respected and protected.

2.   In the case below, the courts permitted the government and the jury to run roughshod over Reverend Moon's and the Unification church's constitutional rights. The jury was allowed to decide the critical issue of ownership without regard to the unanimous position of the church and to substitute its lay views for the good faith views of the church.

3.   The unfettered fact finding allowed by the trial court below and affirmed by the Court of Appeals may not be permitted with respect to any church, popular or unpopular. The Court of Appeals' refusal to apply controlling constitutional guidelines and its bold declaration that "the jury was not bound to accept the Unification Church's definition of what constitutes a religious use or purpose" in a federal criminal tax case [718 F.2d at 1227] creates an unconstitutional exception completely unwarranted by the First Amendment.

---

[9] As of the date of the filing of this *amicus* brief, other *amici* filing briefs with this Court include The National Council of the Churches of Christ in the U.S.A., The African Methodist Episcopal Church, the National Association of Evangelicals, the Christian Legal Society, the Southern Unitarian Leadership Conference and the Center for Judicial Studies. Others are expected to follow.

15

4.   Had the jury been properly charged, the verdict as to the defendants' guilt or innocence may or may not have been different. Regardless of the effect on the ultimate verdict, however, the important judicial principles enunciated by this Court in *Watson, Jones*, and *Ballard* to assure the continued protection of First Amendment freedoms in criminal and civil proceedings alike should have been employed.

5.   The decision below, if allowed to stand, poses a serious threat of further governmental interference into the affairs of all churches.

Given the state of the case below and the considerable public outcry over the treatment Reverend Moon received in the courts below, this Court should review the decision of the Court of Appeals and reverse with proper guidance to assure the protection of religious freedom in all future cases.

The position taken by this *Amicus* is adopted solely for the purpose of urging that the religious rights of all persons and churches remain unequivocally protected. It is taken without any comment on the Unification Church as a religious organization, other than to recognize it as such, a factor that alone affords it the fullest protection of the First Amendment. The courts of this country owe it no less.

Respectfully Submitted,

UNITED STATES SENATOR ORRIN G. HATCH
Chairman,
Subcommittee on the Constitution, United
   States Senate Committee on the Judiciary